Aesthetics of Music

VOLUME 3

Books by David Whitwell

Philosophic Foundations of Education
Foundations of Music Education
Music Education of the Future
The Sousa Oral History Project
The Art of Musical Conducting
The Longy Club: 1900–1917
A Concise History of the Wind Band
Wagner on Bands
Berlioz on Bands
Aesthetics of Music in Ancient Civilizations
Aesthetics of Music in the Middle Ages

The History and Literature of the Wind Band and Wind Ensemble Series

Volume 1 The Wind Band and Wind Ensemble Before 1500
Volume 2 The Renaissance Wind Band and Wind Ensemble
Volume 3 The Baroque Wind Band and Wind Ensemble
Volume 4 The Classical Period Wind Band and Wind Ensemble
Volume 5 The Nineteenth-Century Wind Band and Wind Ensemble
Volume 6 A Catalog of Multi-Part Repertoire for Wind Instruments or for Undesignated Instrumentation before 1600
Volume 7 Baroque Wind Band and Wind Ensemble Repertoire
Volume 8 Classic Period Wind Band and Wind Ensemble Repertoire
Volume 9 Nineteenth-Century Wind Band and Wind Ensemble Repertoire
Volume 10 A Supplementary Catalog of Wind Band and Wind Ensemble Repertoire
Volume 11 A Catalog of Wind Repertoire before the Twentieth Century for One to Five Players
Volume 12 A Second Supplementary Catalog of Early Wind Band and Wind Ensemble Repertoire
Volume 13 Name Index, Volumes 1–12, The History and Literature of the Wind Band and Wind Ensemble

www.whitwellbooks.com

David Whitwell

Aesthetics of Music

VOLUME 3
AESTHETICS OF MUSIC IN THE
EARLY RENAISSANCE

Edited by Craig Dabelstein

Whitwell Publishing • Austin, Texas, USA

Whitwell Publishing, Austin 78701
www.whitwellbooks.com

© 1995, 2012 by David Whitwell
All rights reserved. First edition 1995.
Second edition 2012

Printed in the United States of America

Paperback
ISBN-13: 978-1-936512-37-9
ISBN-10: 1936512378

Composed in Minion Pro

CONTENTS

	Foreword	vii
	Acknowledgements	xi
1	*Fourteenth-Century Italy*	1
2	*Petrarch*	17
3	*Boccaccio*	45
4	*Fourteenth-Century France*	69
5	*Fourteenth-Century England*	105
6	*Chaucer*	137
7	*Fifteenth-Century Italy*	161
8	*Leonardo Da Vinci*	191
9	*Fifteenth-Century France*	211
10	*The Low Countries in the Fourteenth and Fifteenth Centuries*	227
11	*Johannes Tinctoris*	237
12	*The German-Speaking Countries in the Fourteenth and Fifteenth Centuries*	253
13	*Fourteenth- and Fifteenth-Century Spain*	287
14	*Fifteenth-Century England*	303
	Epilogue	323
	Bibliography	325
	Index	333
	About the Author	337

FOREWORD

We define Music to be that form of music performed live before listeners. We define Aesthetics in Music to be a study of the nature of the perception of music by the listener.

We believe the performance of music in actual practice falls naturally into four classes. These are Art Music, Educational Music, Functional Music and Entertainment Music.

I. Art Music

Art Music we believe is defined by four conditions, *all* of which *must always be present*. These are:

1. *Art music is inspired*. Art music is music in which it seems evident that the composer has made an honest attempt to communicate genuine feelings. Feelings, which may range from lofty and noble to superficial and vulgar, must be presumed to be generally recognizable in music, as they are in any other art form, including painting, sculpture, dance, and architecture. In Art Music, lofty and noble feelings are paramount.

    Due to the common genetically understood nature of emotions, it must also be understood that in music emotions or feelings cannot be 'faked.' They will always be recognized as such by any contemplative listener.

2. *Art Music has no purpose other than the communication of its own aesthetic content*. Art Music is free of any purpose or function, save the spiritual communication of pure beauty.

3. *Art Music is that which enjoys a performance faithful to the intent of the composer*.

4. *Art Music must have a listener capable of contemplation*.

If any of these conditions are missing, the performance must result in a lesser aesthetic experience. For example, the *Ninth Symphony* of Beethoven played in a stadium, during the half-time of a professional football game, would fail for the lack of the presence of Condition Number Four. The same Symphony heard in a concert hall, but in a poor performance, not faithful to the intent of the composer, would fail for the lack of the presence of Condition Number Three.

II. Educational Music

Educational Music may or may not have the same conditions as Art Music, excepting Condition Number Two; it may or may not occur within an educational institution. Educational Music is didactic music, music which has the specific and *additional* aim to educate. In the strictest sense, if the *primary purpose* of Music is to educate, it cannot be Art Music—for Art Music has no purpose.

III. Functional Music

Functional Music is music put at the service of something else. We include here, for example, all kinds of religious music, music for weddings, music for the military, and occupational music. Functional Music may share the same conditions as Art Music, excepting Condition Number Two.

One may ask, How can a Mozart Mass be called Functional Music, and not Art Music? If the observer were not contemplatively listening to the music, but were rather contemplating religious thoughts, then the Mozart Mass becomes merely a very high level of Functional Music. If, on the other hand, the observer is a contemplative listener of music, forgetting about religion, then the Mozart Mass is Art Music, but has failed in its purpose as church music.

Military and wedding music are examples of music in which the contemplative listener is missing entirely. How about airport, supermarket and elevator music where there is no listener at all? According to the definition we have given above, recorded music without listeners is not to be considered music at all.

IV. Entertainment Music

Entertainment Music is music with no object other than to please. It will always be missing Condition Four, the contemplative listener. For this reason, Entertainment Music may be inspired music, but the composer is unlikely to be inspired by lofty and noble emotions, knowing there will be no contemplative listener. Entertainment Music and Art Music can never be the same thing because of Condition Number Two: Art Music has no purpose other than the communication of its own aesthetic content. It is inconsistent with the nature of great art to have any extrinsic purpose, including the purpose to entertain.

The first philosopher to address the impact which Art has on an observer was Aristotle, in his *Poetics*, as part of a discussion of Tragedy, which like music has both a material, written form and a live performance form. In this treatise, Aristotle first considers the nature and contribution of each of the specific components of the written form of the Tragedy in his typically methodical style. His great contribution, however, comes when he has completed this discussion, for he then goes beyond the material form of the play itself to discuss the observer. He makes it clear that not only is the end purpose of the elements of the play to produce a specific experience in the observer, but that the nature of this experience is what distinguishes Tragedy from other dramatic forms, such as Spectacle. It was in this moment that he created a new branch of Philosophy which we call 'Aesthetics.'

Our purpose is to provide a source book of representative descriptions of actual performances, observations by philosophers, poets and other commentators which contribute insights to our understanding of what music meant to listeners during the early Renaissance. It is for this reason that when discussing contemporary treatises on music that we concentrate on those passages which offer insights relative to the aesthetics of music and musical performance rather than the usual technical subjects such as scales, modes and counterpoint which fill most books on Renaissance music.

Since traditional musicology has focused almost exclusively on sacred and secular vocal music of the Renaissance, we have also included numerous references which we hope will reveal a much wider world of music during this period.

We are also interested in contemporary views on the physiology of knowing, especially with regard to the relationship of the senses and Reason, and related psychological ideas, such as Pleasure and Pain and the Emotions, which might offer a frame of reference for their perspective on the perception of music.

This is the third volume in a series of eight, ranging from the music of the ancient civilizations through the Baroque Period.

David Whitwell
Austin, Texas

ACKNOWLEDGMENTS

This new edition would not have been possible without the encouragement and help of Craig Dabelstein of Brisbane, Australia. His experience as a musician and educator himself has contributed greatly to his expertise as editor of this volume.

David Whitwell
Austin, 2012

1 FOURTEENTH-CENTURY ITALY

The term 'Renaissance' was first coined in 1840, by Jules Michelet, to mean 'discovery of the world and man.'[1] Perhaps a better definition would be the '*re*discovery of the world of *man*,' for it is the rediscovery of the values of the human and his secular life, in contrast to a galaxy of Christian spirits, angels and the sacred dogma of the Church. With the new ability of man to think of himself apart from the Church came a great sense of self-confidence, which was a necessary prerequisite for many of the advances in science and the arts. There is no better symbol of this new self-confidence than an incident which occurred during the trial of Galileo. Though he was forced, prostrate on the floor before a commission of cardinals, to retract his view that the earth moves in an orbit and is not the center of the universe, when he rose from the floor he quietly whispered 'Nevertheless, it moves!'

Important societal developments also contributed to the new environment. In Italy, in particular, the growth of trade and industry produced the wealth by which more enlightened princes could imitate the fostering of the arts they had learned from the East through the crusades. The rediscovery of the ancient literature, again through the East, went hand in hand with the developing sophistication of the vernacular languages. Finally, all of these developments joined to provide the courage and freedom of thought necessary to break the long domination of thought by the Church. Man at long last could freely begin to think independently, and to ask questions—something the early Church had distinctly discouraged.

These new attitudes, which were all essential parts of humanism, rapidly repaid society with accomplishments which the Church had been unable to achieve in a thousand years. In a relatively short period of time come the achievements of da Vinci, Michelangelo, Isaac Newton, Galileo, Copernicus and Gutenberg.

In Italian literature, it was Petrarch and Boccaccio who carried this new banner of humanism at the dawn of the Renaissance.

1 John Addington Symonds, *Renaissance in Italy* (New York: Holt, 1881), 1:15n.

The nineteenth-century scholar, Francesco de Sanctis, writing in defense of Boccaccio's *The Decameron*, has written a passage which we believe goes right to the heart of the essential difference between the philosophy of life in the Middle Ages and the Renaissance.

> Many people blame Boccaccio, saying that he spoiled and corrupted the Italian spirit. He himself, in his old age, was overcome by remorse, became a religious clerk, and condemned his book. But his book would not have been possible if the Italian spirit had not been well on its way to being spoiled—if spoiled is the correct word for it. If the things Boccaccio laughed about had been venerated, his contemporaries would have felt indignation. But the opposite proved to be true. The book seemed to respond to something in people's souls which had been wanting to come out for a long time. It seemed to proclaim what everyone had been saying secretly, in the depths of their souls, and it was received with so much applause and success that the good Passavanti became frightened and set against it his *Specchio di penitenza* as an antidote. Boccaccio was, then, the literary voice of a world about which men, in their consciousness, were already confusedly aware. A secret existed: Boccaccio guessed it and everyone applauded him. This fact, instead of being damned, deserves to be studied.
>
> The essential quality of the Middle Ages was transcendence: a sort of ultrahuman and ultranatural 'beyond' outside of nature and man, the genus and the species outside the individual, matter and form outside their unity, the intellect outside the soul, perfection and virtue outside life, the law outside consciousness, the spirit outside the body, and the purpose of life outside the world …
>
> The natural product of this exaggerated, theocratic world was asceticism. Life here on earth was losing its seriousness and value, so that while man continued to dwell here, his spirit was in the next life …
>
> Feeling, as the product of human or natural propensity, was always considered a sin. Passions were banned and poetry was considered the mother of lies. The theater was the food of the Devil and stories and romances were regarded as profane types of literature. All these things were called by one name: 'the senses' …
>
> But a state of tension and imbalance like this cannot last. Art and culture, the knowledge and experience of life, work to modify it and transform it. Thus art, by seizing this world, had begun to humanize it, bring it closer to man and nature …[2]

2 Francesco de Sanctis, 'Boccaccio and the Human Comedy,' quoted in *The Decameron*, trans. Mark Musa and Peter Bondanella (New York: Norton, 1977), 216ff.

A modern writer writes of the same issue and of Petrarch's contribution to the new humanism.

To the centuries before Petrarch the world was a place in which to prepare for a life beyond; the noblest subject of thought was theology; the saving of the soul was the one important task. The centuries since have realized in some measure that the present life is precious in itself, and is not to be thus subordinated. This shifting of the view is of immense significance; and it is owing to Petrarch, more than to any other one man.[3]

3 James Robinson, *Petrarch, The First Modern Scholar and Man of Letters* (New York: Putnam, 1914), 227, 229.

From the perspective of the musician, the beginning of the Renaissance appears clearly, and almost suddenly, defined. The changes desired in Church music by the composers of the early fourteenth century were sufficiently different as to give birth to the terms *ars nova* and *ars antiqua* to distinguish these composers from their teachers. Outside the Church the explosion of thirteenth-century troubadour repertoire was no less dramatic in its new emphasis, indeed this music was the harbinger of humanism.

Our view of music performance in the Renaissance has been clouded in several ways as the result of directions taken by nineteenth-century musicology. The subsequent traditional view has been, basically, that to study music, you have to study extant music. The problem is that relative little music in the fourteenth century was notated, and that which has survived has been mostly the Church music of the Northern countries. No where in music history texts can one find extensive discussion of the broad early Renaissance musical practice which is documented in the literature of that period. Indeed, in reading some of the most revered music history texts you might get the impression that music somehow disappeared from Italy after 1350. But Pirrotta, one of the really knowledgeable persons in this field, knows better.

It is not surprising to me that no attempt to solve the case of the missing Quattrocento music has led to a satisfactory answer. It has been my contention that the secret, if there is one, is in the island, not in the gap that divides it from the continent. For the island is largely a mirage of our historical perspective, a tiny object magnified by our faith in the written tradition, at best a floating island, not only surrounded but also supported by the waves of a sea now opaque to our eye, once full of light, of life, and of sound—the sound of unwritten music.[4]

4 Nino Pirrotta, 'Ars Nova and Stil Novo,' in *Music and Culture in Italy from the Middle Ages to the Baroque* (Cambridge: Harvard University Press, 1984), 28, where he devotes a more lengthy argument to this contention.

What he means is that written music, namely Church music, was really just one kind of music performance. Pirrotta hastens to add that we must not assume that the 'unwritten' music of the fourteenth century was only monophonic.[5]

Palisca, another distinguished authority on fourteenth-century Italian music, addresses the same limited perspective found in general music history texts:

> The conditions that led to the reanimation of literature, the visual arts, and learning also deeply affected music in Italy throughout the period of the Renaissance. Music historians generally have overlooked many of these manifestations because their stated objective has been a history of musical style. But style is only the audible surface of a musical culture, the essence of which must be sought beneath. Style as a criterion is particularly misleading in the Italian Renaissance, because some of the most characteristic music of the period is not preserved in writing, and much of the written music exhibits style elements of undeniably transalpine origin. But this should not lead us to the conclusion that the Renaissance was a northern phenomenon.[6]

But, we would go further than Palisca here. He is correct to say that music historians have concentrated on style. A traditional textbook attempting to find the Renaissance in a church work of Machaut will generally describe the conceptual parts, the components of that work, things like the major chords passing unobtrusively by. But these things are not what makes Machaut sound different, they are only the *result* of what makes Machaut sound different. A new emphasis on the importance of expressing *feeling* is what prompted Machaut to make the choices he made. Most music texts which look for early humanists speak primarily of the renewed interest in ancient Greek writings. But for us *feeling* is the key, not scholarly retrospection. It was not their interest in Greek treatises, but what they found in them which distinguishes the humanistic point of view. In our view, it was the intellectual freedom to think about and value his own feelings which most distinguishes the Renaissance man from Medieval man.

The humanist was the man who discovered that music has to do with the communication of feelings, not numbers. There are theorists today who still don't 'get it,' who teach altered tones and altered chords without reference to the change in feeling which necessitate

[5] Nino Pirrotta and Elena Povoledo, *Music and Theatre from Poliziano to Monteverdi* (Cambridge: Cambridge University Press, 1982), 26.

[6] Claude V. Palisca, 'An Italian Renaissance in Music?,' in *Humanism in Italian Renaissance Musical Thought* (New Haven: Yale University Press, 1985), 4ff.

them in real music. And certainly not every fourteenth-century theorist understood either.

Marchetto of Padua[7] is a case in point. He seems almost pulled apart by Reason, on one hand, and by his instinct and the common experience around him on the other. His dilemma seems to go beyond what could simply be called the contrast of *musica speculativa* and *musica practica*. First, out of respect for the long tradition of philosophers before him, he is still talking about numbers. He says you do not judge music by hearing, for the senses can be deceived. Rather, the judgment of music must lie in 'the relation of numbers, which governs everything in it.'[8]

But then later, during his discussion of the voice, he touches on the real essence of music, which is diametrically opposed to his previous emphasis on numbers. In considering the etymology of the word 'voice' [*vox*] he notes that it comes from 'vows' [*vota*], 'because it expresses vows of the heart.' He then quotes Aristotle as saying, similarly of the spoken voice, 'Things spoken are symbols of the passions of the soul.'[9] He concludes it is appropriate, therefore, that we speak of 'notes' of music, which derives from *nota* ('symbol'), but since he passes so briefly by this, we have to wonder if he really understood the fundamental meaning of this, that music is feelings and not numbers.

Still later he seems to seek some compromise between the theoretical and the practical.

> Nothing concerning numbers and their proportions is relevant to the musician in his capacity as musician. Rather such matters pertain exclusively to arithmetic: to consider how three is related to five is the main concern of the arithmetician, not of the musician.
>
> But to study numbers and proportions as they apply to melody does pertain to music, for the study of music alone informs about melody.
>
> To consider from which numerical proportions—setting numbered notes and syllables in melody in proportion—consonance arises from which one's dissonance arises is, therefore, the consideration of the musician.
>
> Experience shows that this can be understood only in the realm of music itself—that is, in sounding bodies.[10]

7 Little is known of Marchetto, other than he was a singer and choirmaster at the cathedral of Padua during the first decade of the fourteenth century.

8 Marchetto of Padua, *Lucidarium*, trans. Jan W. Herlinger (Chicago: University of Chicago Press, 1985), I, 4, ii and v.

9 Ibid., I, 10, iiiff.

10 Ibid., treatise 2, I, 10, v.

Finally, at the very end of his treatise, Marchetto loses courage and retreats to a more traditional line of thought characteristic of previous centuries.

> The musician knows the power and nature of the musical proportions; he judges according to them, not according to sound alone.
>
> The singer is, as it were, the tool of that musician—who is an artisan in that he is occupied with a tool, but a musician inasmuch as he puts into practice what he has previously investigated through rational process.
>
> Thus the musician is to the singer as the judge is to the herald.[11]

This struggle on Marchetto's part to understand the essence of music should remind us, as we stand before a class and distinguish the Renaissance from the Middle Ages by a mere chalk line on a blackboard, how real and difficult the struggle must have been, to break free from centuries of accepted and official dogma.

A similar struggle occurred within the Church. Toward the end of the fourteenth century, those monks who had embraced humanism suddenly found themselves under attack by a conservative backlash. The old battle fought a thousand years before in the Church reemerged among some who said the reading of pagan [the ancient Greeks] authors was impious. A leading spokesman for the Church humanists, Coluccio Salutati (1331–1406), argued that Virgil should be read allegorically and that those who knew how to thus understand Virgil would find in his poetry the mysteries of the Christian faith. He also pointed out that the early Church fathers, such as Jerome and Augustine, had read these Greek classics.

> Is it possible that anyone can be considered so foolish and senile, so deceived by false opinion as to condemn the poets with whose words Jerome overflows, Augustine glistens, and Ambrose blossoms? Gregory and Bernard are not devoid of them.[12]

This philosophical dispute was enlivened in 1397 when Carlo Malatesa, a captain of the guard of the Florentine League, ordered a statue of Virgil in Mantua destroyed. At this time Salutati extended his defense of the humanists by noting that the Scriptures were themselves written with the figural and allegorical language of the poets. It is ironic, he said, that the Scholastic theologians who did not study classical literature must run to schoolboys to learn what they could not understand in the teachings of the Fathers.

11 Ibid., treatise 16, I, ivff.

12 Charles Stinger, *Humanism and the Church Fathers* (Albany: State University of New York Press, 1977), 8ff.

Thus he makes the argument made a thousand years earlier, that study of the Liberal Arts was fundamental to the understanding of the Scriptures.

We do not find among the humanists much discussion of the physiological and psychological problems of man, perhaps because such discussions had been so recently associated with Scholasticism. Franco Sacchetti (ca. 1335–1400), in his humorous *Tales*, touches on some of the ancient questions in a light-hearted way. Here, for example, he demonstrates how not only the emotions, but the senses as well can block the intellectual side of man.

> The blind are of much more subtle understanding than are other men. For most often doeth it happen that, whilst we gaze now at one thing and now at another, the light engrosseth completely the intelligence within, and of this many proofs can be made, of which I will relate one small one in particular. Suppose two men are talking together; when one is in the midst of his discourse there passeth by a woman, or other thing, and the man gazeth upon her, and his speech is arrested and he continueth it not; and when he wisheth to continue he saith unto his companion, 'What was I saying?' And this happened only because that gazing did occupy the whole of his intelligence, so that his speech, which was directed by his intelligence, was not able to continue its course. And it was for this reason that Demoncritus, the philosopher, destroyed his own eyes, that he might have a more subtle understanding.[13]

In another of his tales, Franco Sacchetti makes the point that pain is relative. He tells of an ambassador, so stricken with gout that he remained in bed and could not walk. But when the people rose up in arms, crying 'Death to the ambassador,' he quickly leaped out of bed and ran 'as fast as a greyhound' to a nearby monastery.[14]

Perhaps such ideas were expressed more frequently in popular song than by philosophers. In the troubadour tradition of the thirteenth century many poets commented on the unique mixture of joy and pain experienced in Love. We find this idea still prevalent in the fourteenth century, as in this particularly poignant example:

> Many there are who when they hear me sing,
> Cry: There goes one whose joy runs o'er in song!
> But I pray God to give me succoring;
> For when I sing, 'tis then I grieve full strong.[15]

---

13 Mary Steegmann, trans., *Tales from Sacchetti* (Westport: Hyperion Press, 1978), cxcviii, 250. Sacchetti was born into a wealthy family of merchants in Florence. He also followed in this profession, but actively wrote poetry and his famous *Tales* on the side. After 1383 he became active in politics and traveled as an ambassador on behalf of Florence.

14 Ibid., clxvi, 172.

15 Anonymous, *Villotta*, quoted in John Addington Symonds, *Renaissance in Italy* (New York: Capricorn Books, 1964), 1:230.

Aside from Petrarch and Boccaccio, there is also little discussion of the philosophical foundations of aesthetics. Marchetto of Padua in his chapter 'On the Beauty of Music,' argues that among the arts, music exceeds in beauty.

> The tree of music is more wonderful than the others: its branches are beautifully proportioned through numbers; its flowers are the species of consonances; its fruits are the sweet harmonies produced by these consonances.[16]

16 Marchetto of Padua, *Lucidarium*, I, 2, ii and iv.

We find a reference to the old question regarding Art imitating Nature in one of the tales of Franco Sacchetti. His story involves a group of artists debating whether all the great artists were dying out. One, a Maestro Alberto, says no, in fact the women of Florence are so gifted in the art of painting (cosmetics) that they even surpass nature.

> Florentine women are the greatest artists of painting and carving there have ever been, because as may clearly be seen, they supply what nature lacks.[17]

17 Steegmann, *Tales from Sacchetti*, cxxxvi, 116.

ON THE AESTHETICS OF MUSIC

Marchetto of Padua clearly defines music as having both an aesthetic and a physical nature. He uses the expression 'the art and science' of music, which one can find in numerous places during the Renaissance.

> Music is an art [*ars*] both admirable and delightful; it resounds in heaven and on earth.
> Moreover, music is that science [*scientia*] which consists in numbers, proportions, consonances, intervals, measures, and quantities.[18]

18 Marchetto of Padua, *Lucidarium*, I, 5, ii and iii.

The important distinction is that music is no longer described as a 'craft,' as it so often was during the preceding two thousand years. He returns to this distinction at the end of his treatise when he states,

> Every art or discipline has a nature more worthy of honor than a craft practiced by the hand and labor of an artisan.[19]

19 Ibid., treatise 16, I, iii.

He next categorizes music as being either 'harmonic, organic or rhythmic.'[20] Harmonic music is that which is produced by the voice. Organic music is that produced by breath, but not of the voice. Here he includes trumpets, shawms, pipes and organs.[21] Rhythmic music is that produced without breath, including the monochord, psaltery and bells.[22]

With regard to aesthetics, we find particularly interesting Marchetto's comments on altered tones. These he says are called 'chromatic,' from *chroma*, or 'color' in Greek, and have 'the color of beauty, because it is on account of the elegance and beauty of the dissonances that the whole tone is divided.'[23]

He also speaks of consonance and dissonance in aesthetic terms, calling the first 'amicable' and the second 'hateful.'[24] In commenting on the similitude of the consonance of the octave, he mentions the 'pyramid principle' known to all conductors, that a true combination tone occurs only when the lower voice is two-thirds the volume and the upper octave one-third.

> If one [the lower pitch] is sung by men, the other by boys, they present to the ear one and the same pitch, as it were.[25]

Regarding the purposes of music, Marchetto chooses to mention only the more utilitarian ones. He maintained that the uses of music could be witnessed by common experience: it makes warriors stronger in battle, physicians judge the pulse by the aid of music and even animals enjoy it.[26]

One anonymous author from the early fourteenth century disagrees and indeed finds music harmful to the character. Although he is relating tales from a much earlier period, we must assume that his choice of these anecdotes reflects to some degree his inclinations.

> Antigonus, the teacher of Alexander [the Great], when one day the latter was having a cythera played for his delight, took hold of the instrument and cast it into the mud, saying 'at your age it behooves you to reign and not to play the cythera. For it may be said that luxury debases the body and the country, as the sound of the cythera enfeebles the soul. Let him then be ashamed who should reign in virtue, and instead delights in luxury.'
>
> King Porrus who fought with Alexander ordered during a banquet that the strings of a player's cythera should be cut, saying, 'it is better to cut than to play, for virtue departs with sweet sounds.'[27]

20 Ibid., I, 8, 11ff.

21 Ibid., I, 12, ii.

22 Ibid., 14, ii.

23 Ibid., treatise 2, I, 8, vi.

24 Ibid., treatise 5, I, 1, xi.

25 Ibid., treatise 6, I, 4, xxv.

26 Ibid., I, 3, 5ff.

27 Anonymous, *Il Novellino*, trans. Edward Storer (London: Routledge, 1925), XIII.

ART MUSIC

Very little art music of the *Ars nova* in Italy is extant, indeed only six major manuscripts and a number of fragments. To those music historians who have concerned themselves only with extant representatives, this might suggest there was very little performance in Italy during the fourteenth century. But, as we know from hints in literature, there was a great deal of composition and a great deal more activity in the realm of unwritten music. Gustave Reese, for example, points to an early madrigal of Jacopo da Bologna in which the text mentions that 'everyone is writing ballades, madrigals, and motets.'[28] The early madrigal is a case in point. We know from literature that such works existed in the fourteenth century, and that Petrarch already calls it an art form,[29] yet how many examples survive to be studied?

Some writers mention everyone is writing music, as did Jacopo da Bologna above, but also complain that some of them are not so gifted. Franco Sacchetti notes,

> The world is full of people who want to make rhymes … so it is with songs too: without any skill.[30]

And, similarly, a madrigal by Landini complains,

> Everyone wants to arrange musical notes,
> To compose madrigals, *cacce*, *ballate*,
> Believing that his own are fine.[31]

But there must have been many distinguished musicians of the fourteenth century who are barely known to us today. We wish general music history texts told us more about such musicians as the blind composer, Francesco Landini (1335–1397). He was a well-rounded man, honored by King Peter I of Cyprus as a musician and poet. He was skilled in many instruments and even invented a sort of 'one-man band' called the 'Siren of Sirens.' Though employed in an ecclesiastical position, most of his *ballate* are concerned with love. He was remembered by Domenico da Prato, in his 'Paradiso degli Alberti,' as a leading humanist and as a performer on the *organetto* 'whose playing could attract the nightingale.'[32]

One form of art music which must have began to flourish in the fourteenth century was the non-functional performances by

---

[28] Gustave Reese, *Music in the Middle Ages* (New York: Norton, 1940), 371.

[29] Pirrotta, 'Ars Nova and Stil Novo,' 161ff.

[30] Quoted in John Larner, *Culture and Society in Italy, 1290–1420* (New York: Scribner's, 1971), 172.

[31] Quoted in ibid., 172.

[32] Quoted in ibid., 170.

civic musicians. A growing sense of civic pride, not unrelated to humanism, led to the construction in many towns of the city hall, the *Palazzo Comunale*, beginning in the late thirteenth century. The *palazzo* stood in competition with the cathedral, in pride if not in scope, representing the affairs of today rather than those of the next life. It was this civic pride which was the object of such compositions as Johannes Ciconia's (1335–1411) 'O Padua' and 'Venetia mundi splendor.'

It is in the fourteenth century, following the same sense of civic identity, that many Italian towns began to expand their corps of civic musicians. By the end of this century Florence maintained three separate ensembles in the service of the city, a shawm ensemble [*pifferi*] of three players on daily call to play in the *palazzo*, an ensemble of six trumpets and a third ensemble called *trombadori*. Siena had nine civic players by the beginning of the fourteenth century and they were held in such jealousy by the city fathers that they were not permitted to associate with former friends or to visit their families. They were, however, housed, fed and educated by the city. Several towns already had uniforms for their civic bands by the fourteenth century and the musicians of Pisa were subject to a fine if they forgot to wear their official red gowns.

Such civic records as are extant define numerous official duties, primarily of a functional nature (the Bologna *pifferi* had to perform each day at three o'clock in the morning!). We must assume that some of their performances were genuine concerts, and there are some hints to suggest this. A fourteenth-century contract for the Perugia civic band, for example, after listing various functional duties, says that they must also play in the civic square 'for the joy of the public.' A document of Florence, dated July 1333, mentions,

> Since in almost every noble city, whether in Lombardy or Tuscany, fine singers are retained for the delight and joy of the citizens.[33]

33 Quoted in ibid., 171.

And even in the relatively small town of Treviso, we read in a document of 1395 that money will be given to Pietro di Bartolomeo Boldrani to buy a trumpet, 'for the presence of artists increases the honor of the whole community.'[34]

34 Quoted in Don L. Smithers, *The Music and History of the Baroque Trumpet* (London: Dent, 1973), 75ff.

Another form of art music which flourished during the Renaissance, yet scarcely is mentioned in general music history texts, was the solo art song. This was in part, of course, an expression of the humanists' interest in the ancient Greek model and a fifteenth-century authority credits Petrarch himself for reviving this form.

> Those forms of poetry usually are numbered which consist of eight lines [*strambotti*] or three lines [*elegies*], which type Francesco Petrarch is said to have first established among us as he sang his exalted poems with a lute.[35]

There is no doubt that much poetry in the fourteenth century was still sung in performance. A note in Petrarch's hand in the margin of his copy of his *Canzoniere* reads,

> I must make these two verses over again, singing them and I must transpose them: 3 o'clock in the morning, October the 19th.[36]

That the ability to sing poetry was expected of young aristocrats, we have the evidence of the stories of *The Decameron*. Larner believes that the majority of middle-class men and women also sang and performed on instruments.[37]

Among the working class, the songs of Sacchetti enjoyed great popularity. He himself was a good musician and set many of his poems to music himself. Symonds suggests that these pastoral part-songs were a harbinger of the madrigal as we know it in the sixteenth century.[38]

Sacchetti mentions a working class singer in one of this tales. Dante is walking through Florence and hearing a blacksmith singing one of his poems, but with great inaccuracy. Dante throws the smith's tool out into the road and, upon the objection of the smith, responds,

> DANTE. If thou desirest that I should not spoil thy things, do not thou spoil mine.
> SMITH. What am I spoiling of yours?
> DANTE. Thou are singing out of my book, and art not singing it as I wrote it; I have no other trade but this, and thou are spoiling it for me.[39]

There are a few accounts of art music being used for a rather utilitarian purpose. In one famous instance, at a time in 1342 when the war against Pisa was not going well for the Florentines, a locally famous popular singer, Antonio Pucci, took up his lute and began singing under the windows of the palazzo a song of the Virgin Mary,

---

35 Cortesi, 'De Cardinalatu,' quoted in John D'Amico, *Renaissance Humanism in Papal Rome* (Baltimore: Johns Hopkins University Press, 1983), 106.

36 Quoted in Larner, *Culture and Society in Italy*, 163.

37 Quoted in ibid., 172.

38 Symonds, *Renaissance in Italy* (New York: Capricorn Books, 1964), 1:135.

39 Steegmann, *Tales from Sacchetti*, cxiv, 84ff. In another tale Dante criticizes a trash collector who is also incorrectly singing one of his poems. The latter sticks his tongue out at Dante, who observes 'I would not give thee one of mine for an hundred of thine.' [Ibid., cxv, 87].

intended to urge the civic leaders to sue for peace.[40] Similarly, in one of the tales of the anonymous 'Il Novellino,' we read of a rather utilitarian use of poetry and song by an unhappy knight whose lady had rejected him.

> Then he composed a very beautiful song; and in the morning early went up into the pulpit and began to sing his song as best he knew, and well he knew how to sing it …

The members of the church, upon hearing this song, 'cried out mercy, and the lady pardoned him.'[41]

[40] Quoted in Symonds, *Renaissance in Italy*, 1:222.

[41] Anonymous, *Il Novellino*, LXIV.

EDUCATIONAL MUSIC

The documents of the Arts Faculty of the University of Bologna no longer exist, but a letter of 1308 by Giovanni Bonandrea, a lecturer in rhetoric and poetry lists music as one of the subject taught.[42]

There is also evidence that music was a part of the curriculum at the University of Padua during the fourteenth century. The names of several important students or teachers who were active in music at this university are still known, including Antonio Lido, a professor of medicine, whose epitaph begins, 'Musicus Artista …'.[43] Pietro Vergerio, an important humanist and professor of logic at the university in 1391, wrote a treatise, 'De ingenuis moribus,' in which he recommends the study of both the theory and practice of music 'as an aid to the inner harmony of the soul.'[44]

Marchetto of Padua's interest in music education seems limited to the old late medieval goal of theorists to raise the unlearned singer to the level of the philosophical *musicus*.

[42] Nan Cooke Carpenter, *Music in the Medieval and Renaissance Universities* (Norman: University of Oklahoma Press, 1958), 33.

[43] Ibid., 39.

[44] Ibid., 40.

FUNCTIONAL MUSIC

There is little discussion of large-scale performances in the Church in fourteenth-century Italy, but some of the iconographic information is unusually interesting. In particular, the fourteenth-century fresco in the apse of the church of San Leonardo al Lago near Siena pictures an extraordinarily large ensemble accompanying angelic singers, including a large number of string and wind instruments (even an aulos) and a percussion section which includes not one, but two timpani players.[45]

A document of 1331, of the University of Padua, mentions that the graduating doctoral student was escorted through the city accompanied by trumpets and other instruments.[46]

ENTERTAINMENT MUSIC

Entertainers similar to the old medieval jongleurs were still to be found, now called *buffoni* (buffons), *uomini del corte* ('men about the court') or *giullari* (probably minstrels). The musical representatives of this broad class of entertainers must have been numerous, for in a knighting ceremony at Rimini in 1324 there were five hundred present. Some of the musicians were no doubt distinguished, as for example Dolcibene, who is mentioned in the *Tales* of Sacchetti, and who was knighted by Charles IV when he visited Rome.[47]

Others had long since fallen from musical activities to the lowest forms of popular entertainment. Sacchetti tells of one, for example, who fastened a cymbal to the saddle of his horse. By putting a thistle under the horse's tail, he caused the horse to continuously jump, causing the cymbal to sound for the purpose of attracting the public.[48]

There were also *cantastorie*, wandering singers of romances such as that of Roland. An early fourteenth century poem by Lovato de' Lovati describes these singers.

> I was going by chance through the town of the springs
> Which takes its name from its three streets [Treviso],
> Passing the time by strolling along,
> When I see on a platform in the piazza
> A singer declaiming the story of Charlemagne
> And the gestes of the French. The rabble hang round,
> Listening intently, charmed by their Orpheus.
> In silence I hear it. With a crude pronunciation
> He deforms the song written in French,
> Mixing it all up at his whim, without heed
> To art or the story. Still, the mob liked it.[49]

---

45   A discussion of the fresco, together with reproductions of the pictures, can be found in Federico Ghisi, 'An Angel Concert in a Trecento Sienese Fresco,' in Jan LaRue, ed., *Aspects of Medieval and Renaissance Music* (New York: Norton, 1966), 308ff.

46   Carpenter, *Music in the Medieval and Renaissance Universities*, 37ff.

47   Larner, *Culture and Society in Italy*, 175.

48   Steegmann, *Tales from Sacchetti*, ccxxv, 292.

49   Quoted in Larner, *Culture and Society in Italy*, 176ff.

Some musicians wandering through town were perhaps not so welcome. We read an account, in Florence in 1384, of three Germans, 'pipers and players of bagpipes and other instruments,' being thrown into jail for playing too early in the morning.[50]

All were welcome, on the other hand, when the daughter of a great duke was to be married. The entertainments accompanying the marriage of the daughter of Gian Galeazzo Visconti of Milan in 1368 lasted eight days and a contemporary account tells us that in addition to the usual *buffoni* there were four hundred instrumentalists [*quattrocento sonator*]. These musicians, in addition to their own performances, also accompanied singing and dancing and were richly rewarded in money and clothes.

When Prince d'Acaia visited Gian Galeazzo on another occasion 'menestrelli e trombettieri' played constantly from his arrival, throughout the day and at each meal.[51]

50 Quoted in ibid., 176.

51 Alessandro Vessella, *La Banda* (Milan: Istituto editoriale nazionale, 1935), 50. Vessella also mentions [page 49] three of the shawm players of this prince by name, as well as the fact that the prince sent them to a minstrel school in 1378.

2 PETRARCH

FRANCESCO PETRARCH (1304–1374) was one of the first of the important humanists. Born to the family of a very successful lawyer, he enjoyed the advantages of the best available education, including the study of law at the universities of Montpellier and Bologna. But he found he could not follow this profession, for he had concluded that to be successful one must 'practice dishonestly.'[1]

Petrarch's attention turned to reading the works of the ancient Roman writers and while still in his early twenties developed into an important classical scholar. He became a man obsessed with the past, begging friends to look for lost titles he had come across in his readings, discovering manuscript works of Cicero in a library in Verona and even writing letters addressed to Homer and Cicero. After 1330, when he joined the service of Cardinal Colonna, he was able to continue his studies with little other obligations.

Most of his hundreds of poems deal with Laura, a woman whom history cannot document. Other than his declaration that he met her in church on Easter Sunday, 1327, there is little proof she actually existed. But his poetry, much of it in some ways in the spirit of the previous troubadours, made him famous and he was rewarded by his coronation as poet laureate in Rome in 1341. This decade saw many of his friends, including his lover Laura and his son, killed by a great plague known as the Black Death. In 1350 he met Boccaccio, with whom he enjoyed a close personal and professional relationship for the rest of his life.

In 1337 he purchased a small house at Vaucluse, near Avignon, where like an early Rousseau he began to extol the virtues of Nature. But it was not Romanticism that he introduced to the fourteenth century, but Humanism and the Renaissance. We appreciate Durant's summary of his contribution in this regard.

> His revival of interest in antiquity fostered the Renaissance emphasis on man and the earth, on the legitimacy of sensory pleasure, and on

[1] Letter to Boccaccio, quoted in Robinson, *Petrarch, The First Modern Scholar and Man of Letters*, 67.

mortal glory as a substitute for personal immortality … Though Petrarch was already seventeen when Dante died, an abyss divided their moods. By common consent he was the first humanist, the first writer to express with clarity and force the right of man to concern himself with this life, to enjoy and augment its beauties, and to labor to deserve well of posterity. He was the Father of the Renaissance.[2]

2 Will Durant, *The Renaissance* (New York: Simon and Schuster, 1953), 9.

ON THE PHYSIOLOGY OF AESTHETICS

As we have noted, Petrarch was a man much absorbed by the ancient Greek and Roman writers. He collected every early work he could find, bemoaned works which appeared to be lost and had probably read as much early literature as any man of the fourteenth century. He found in these writers a wisdom which he believed should have a practical value for his contemporaries.

> Don't you learn from sailors about sailing, farmers about farming, warriors about warfare? But you reject the advice of philosophers on how to conduct your life. You call the doctor to heal your body, but you do not go to the philosopher to heal your mind, although philosophers are the physicians of the mind and teachers of the art of living.[3]

3 Francesco Petrarch, *Remedies for Fortune Fair and Foul*, trans. Conrad Rawski (Bloomington: Indiana University Press, 1991), II, cxvii, 286.

But, then as now, this material had little appeal to the average person.

> 'Philosophy, you go poor and naked!' says the mob, bent on low gain.[4]

4 'La gola e 'l sonno et l'oziose piume,' in Francesco Petrarch, *Petrarch's Lyric Poems*, trans. Robert Durling (Cambridge: Harvard University Press, 1976), 42.

No doubt this attitude contributed to Petrarch's tendency to disassociate himself from the general public, a characteristic which is found in much of his writing.

> But, far from desiring such popular recognition, I congratulate myself, on the contrary, that, along with Virgil and Homer, I am free from it, inasmuch as I fully realize how little the plaudits of the unschooled multitude weigh with scholars.[5]

5 Letter to Boccaccio, quoted in Robinson, *Petrarch, The First modern Scholar and Man of Letters*, 187.

Aside from this distance from the public which Petrarch felt, there was a certain pessimism which also runs through much of his writing. One can see an example of this in a general comment about the mind.

> Nature has provided for all other living creatures the wonderful remedy of a certain ignorance. Only man has memory, intellect and foresight ... which he turns to his ruin and suffering.[6]

6 *Remedies*, I, Preface, 1.

Petrarch compares man with the lower animals again in a reference to the relationship of the senses to intellect, a subject he rarely discussed in detail.

> Of all the pleasures reaching your mind through the senses of the body, those must be defined as most shameful which are caused by touch and taste. These are the senses most akin to those of animals.[7]

7 Ibid., I, xviii, 53.

He placed a high value on the contribution of personal experience to knowledge, although he does not discuss the obvious connection between personal experience and the senses. He quotes Marcus Brutus,

> For you cannot prevent a man from seeing things in that particular light in which they present themselves to him.

To which he adds that any judgment based on someone else's judgment merely reports that of another. It is one's personal experience which develops a personal judgment.[8]

8 Ibid., I, Preface, 5.

Whatever the contribution of the senses or personal experience, like all early philosophers Petrarch firmly believed that Reason must dominate. In his 'Remedies for Fortune Fair and Foul,' Reason speaks for itself.

> SORROW: My mind is rent into conflicting parts.
> REASON: The philosophers divide the mind into three parts, the first of which they place at the very top, as if in a citadel, that is, in the head. This is the ruler of human life, heavenly, serene, and always close to God, where tranquil, decent intentions dwell. The second part is located in the chest, where anger and malice boil; the third, in the lower parts which house lust and desire.[9]

9 Ibid., II, lxxv, 171.

In the Preface to this same book, he states this even more strongly.

> You should read the book *as if* those four most famous, twin-born passions of the mind, HOPE or DESIRE and JOY, FEAR and SORROW, brought forth at the same time by the two sisters Prosperity and Adversity, fiercely assaulted from all sides the mind of man, and

REASON, who governs this citadel, took on all of them at once. In her buckler and helmet, by stratagem and proper force, and, more so, with God's help, she fends off the weapons of the roaring enemies around her.[10]

And, once again, in one of his poems,

> My two usual sweet stars are hidden; dead among the waves are reason and skill; so that I begin to despair of the port.[11]

In only one place does Petrarch seem to attribute equality to something other than the rational side of man, and here almost as we would today speak of the left and right hemispheres of the brain.

> We had another master for poetry, since necessarily we had to follow one supreme guide in prose and another in Verse. We were moved to admire one who spoke and one who sang.[12]

Higher education meant, to Petrarch, the traditional seven Liberal Arts, which still included music. For the extent of these studies he had a clear respect.

> Life is too short for any of the [liberal] arts … To know completely but one art in all its respects has never been accomplished even by the most outstanding scholars.[13]

For the common man, such extensive development of the mind he probably felt was not possible, which led him to this definition of a good mind: 'If it serves liberal studies it is a precious instrument; if not, it is ponderous, perilous and laborious.'[14]

Thus, in his 'Remedies,' he makes it clear that he believed that attempts to educate the general public were largely a waste of time.

> SORROW: It was my lot to get an unteachable pupil.
> REASON: You are tilling barren soil! Unhitch your oxen—why torture yourself? Quit bothering him and yourself. There are so many needed and inevitable chores; it is sheer stupidity to look for useless ones!
> SORROW: I have a pupil who cannot be taught how to pursue the study of letters.
> REASON: If he can be taught to pursue virtue, urge him to do that: and you will have enriched him with the best of all the arts. But if he cannot do either, leave him alone, lest you try pouring into

---

10 Ibid., I, Preface, 10.

11 'Passa la nave mia colma d'oblio,' in *Petrarch's Lyric Poems*, 334.

12 Second letter to Cicero, in Francesco Petrarch, *Letters from Petrarch*, trans. Morris Bishop (Bloomington: Indiana University Press, 1966), 208.

13 *Remedies*, I, xlvi, 149–150.

14 Ibid., I, vii, 23.

a leaky jug water, which will not stay in it, and exhaust yourself in continual weariness.[15]

......

Teach those who can be taught, do not bother with those who cannot learn, and avoid tiring them as well as yourself. Art rarely overcomes nature.[16]

......

Sorrow: I have a weak body.
Reason: Cherish your mind and exercise it in its arts, and do not doubt that they are superior and longer lasting than brute strength—and leave manual labor to the peasants, the sailors, and the workmen.[17]

It follows that Petrarch seemed to have little respect for the teacher whose duty it was to attempt this futile public education. In this same passage he makes a surprising reference to the value of the liberal arts.

Let them teach who can do nothing better, whose qualities are laborious application, sluggishness of mind, muddiness of intellect, prosiness of imagination, chill of the blood, patience to bear the body's labors, contempt of glory, avidity for petty gains, indifference to boredom … What is more, neither grammar nor any of the seven liberal arts is worth a noble spirit's attention throughout life. They are means, not ends.[18]

Regarding his own teacher, Convenevole da Prato, he anticipates the phrase commonly heard today, 'Those who can, do; those who can't, teach!'

I had from boyhood a schoolmaster who taught me my first letters, and later grammar and rhetoric. He was an excellent teacher of both subjects; at least in theory, for in practice he was like Horace's whetstone, which can sharpen steel but cannot cut.[19]

Petrarch reflects on the extent of his own early education in his little biographical essay addressed to posterity,

I learned as much of grammar, logic, and rhetoric as my age permitted, or rather, as much as it is customary to teach in school: how little that is, dear reader, thou knowest.[20]

---

15 Ibid., II, xli, 103.

16 Ibid., I, lxxxi, 223.

17 Ibid., II, ii, 18.

18 Letter to Zanobi da Strada, in *Letters from Petrarch*, 108.

19 Letter to Luca da Penna, in ibid., 297.

20 Quoted in Robinson, *Petrarch, The First modern Scholar and Man of Letters*, 66.

ON THE PSYCHOLOGY OF AESTHETICS

For Petrarch the emotions were first and foremost an obstacle to the reign of Reason.

> There are three poisons to sound judgment—love, hate, and envy. Be careful lest, by excess of love, you make public what had better be concealed. Love may stand in your way; other passions will perhaps move other men.[21]

Of these emotions, it was his own experience that Love was the one which most interfered with his rational stability.

> Love, I transgress and I see my transgression, but I act like a man who burns with a fire in his breast; for the pain still grows, and my reason fails and is almost overcome by my sufferings.[22]
>
> ……
>
> If to love another more than oneself—if to be always sighing and weeping, feeding on sorrow and anger and trouble—
> If to burn from afar and freeze close by—if these are the causes that I untune [*distempre*] myself with love, yours will be the blame, Lady, mine the loss.[23]
>
> ……
>
> If my little intellect had been with me at need, and another hunger had not driven it elsewhere and made it stray …[24]

He observed that which we understand today regarding the separation of emotions from speech in the twin hemispheres of the brain. Words or speech cannot adequately describe emotions, especially those of Love and those expressed in music.

> We did not need many words, for these are mere indications of the spirits and emotions that dwell in them, while our spirits, though in silence, lie bare to one another.[25]
>
> ……
>
> O poor little song, how inelegant you are! I think you know it: stay here in these woods.[26]
>
> ……
>
> But my excessive delight, which is an obstacle to my tongue …[27]
>
> ……

---

21 Letter to 'Socrates,' in *Letters from Petrarch*, 18.

22 'Amor, io fallo et veggio il mio fallire,' in *Petrarch's Lyric Poems*, 394.

23 'S' una fede amorosa, un cor non finto,' in ibid., 380.

24 'Solea de la fontana di mia vita,' in ibid., 522.

25 Letter to Laelius, in *Letters from Petrarch*, 43.

26 'Se 'l pensier che mi strugge,' in *Petrarch's Lyric Poems*, 242.

27 'Quando io v'odo parlar sì dolcemente,' in ibid., 288.

> Many times already have I opened my lips to speak, but then my voice has remained within my breast.[28]

Sometimes his emotions caused the words to come out wrong,

> Sorrow, why do you lead me out of the way to say what I do not wish to say?[29]

Only in the passionate poetry addressed to his lover, Laura, could Petrarch attempt to find the words to express his feelings.

> So in my distress the fire in my heart burst forth through my lips; but as some say, it filled the air and the valleys with a sweet murmur. Here had their origin those songs in Italian of my youthful woes, which today fill me with shame and regret; but, as we are aware, they are very welcome to those afflicted by the same disease.[30]

Regarding Pleasure and Pain, Petrarch reflects traditional medieval thought, that one cannot comfortably enjoy pleasure for it so easily turns into pain. In one of his poems, he complains, 'thus my singing is converted to weeping.'[31] And again in his essay, 'To Posterity,'

> But alas! nothing mortal is enduring, and there is nothing sweet which does not presently end in bitterness.[32]

We find this same thought again in his 'Remedies.'

> JOY: I delight in song and the music of stringed instruments.
> REASON: Ah, how much better to delight in tears and sighs. For weeping that ends in joy is preferable to joy that ends in sorrow.[33]
> ……
> Sorrow is the closest neighbor to earthly delights.[34]

It is the common experience, Petrarch concludes, that life is a constant mixture of pleasure and pain.

> Anyone who has made life's journey with his eyes open knows how the world, the beguiler of the human race, showers us with bitter-sweet satisfactions amid snares and delusions.[35]

Much in the spirit of the thirteenth-century troubadours, Petrarch warns that Love is more often pain than pleasure.

---

28 'Vergognando talor ch' ancor si taccia,' in ibid., 54.

29 'Perché la vita è breve,' in ibid., 156.

30 Letter to Luca Cristiani, in *Letters from Petrarch*, 70.

31 'Mia benigna fortuna e 'l viver lieto,' in *Petrarch's Lyric Poems*, 526.

32 Quoted in Robinson, *Petrarch, The First modern Scholar and Man of Letters*, 75.

33 *Remedies*, I, xxiii, 70.

34 Ibid., I, liv, 168.

35 Letter to Giacomo Colonna, in *Letters from Petrarch*, 29.

> I remain in [Love's] power,
> as against my will he carries me off to death;
> only to come to the laurel, whence one gathers bitter fruit that, being tasted, afflicts one's wounds more than it comforts them.[36]
>
> ......
>
> I complain as much as of a veil that shades two lovely eyes and seems to say: 'Now suffer and weep.'[37]
>
> ......
>
> I never wish to sing again as I used to, for I was not understood, wherefore I was scorned, and one can be miserable in a pleasant place.[38]

But, distinctly unlike the lovers of the troubadour repertoire, Petrarch seemed to take a certain pleasure in the pain of love.

> Strange pleasure that in human minds is often found, to love whatever strange thing brings the thickest crowd of sighs! And I am one of those whom weeping pleases, and it seems that I exert myself that my eyes may always be pregnant with tears, as my heart is with sorrow.[39]
>
> ......
>
> Whether I live or die or languish, there is no nobler state than mine under the moon, so sweet is the root of the bitter![40]

Petrarch's conclusions on man's struggle with pleasure and pain suggest that he could not finally resolve this problem, philosophically. In one moment, perhaps in a moment of frustration, he declares, 'A noble intellect despises both pleasure and pain, and will not yield to either of them.'[41]

On another occasion he is more optimistic,

> To the wise man all of life is pleasant. He enjoys it freely when it is happy, endures it patiently when it is sad, and takes pleasure in being patient if the circumstances themselves are unpleasant—for nothing is more joyous, nothing sweeter than virtue.[42]

Yet, in another place he concludes man cannot find happiness in this life.

> No one is happy until he moves out of this vale of miseries.[43]

---

36 'Sì traviato è'l folle mi' desio,' in *Petrarch's Lyric Poems*, 40.

37 'Orso, e' non furon mai fiumi né stagni,' in ibid., 104.

38 'Mai non vo' più cantar,' in ibid., 208.

39 'Si è debile il filo a cui s'attene,' in ibid., 100.

40 'Cantai, or piango; et non men di dolcezza,' in ibid., 384.

41 *Remedies*, II, cxiv, 277.

42 Ibid., II, cxviii, 292.

43 Ibid., I, cviii, 293.

ON THE PHILOSOPHY OF AESTHETICS

Being a lyric poet at heart, even if he denied it later in life, we are not surprised that Petrarch's writing on Beauty is centered first in the beauty of woman. While his attraction to this form of beauty is documented in his poetry, there was a part of him which was reserved. It was another manifestation of the problem which concerned him with regard to the emotions distracting Reason. He seemed to distrust the idea that Beauty alone was a virtue, rather one must find an additional virtue. In his 'Remedies,' Petrarch quotes from a letter by the Roman prince, Domitian, 'Be assured that nothing is more pleasing than beauty, but nothing shorter-lived,' and then observes,

> I fail to see just what should be so desirable about this beauty, unstable as it is, glittering on the surface only, covering many filthy and abominable things, titillating the senses and deceiving them with a peachy complexion. Therefore, it is better to take delight in true goods that last, rather than in false and transitory ones …
>
> Nothing is more ardently coveted than an attractive appearance, nothing more apt to dazzle the mind, hence nothing more vehemently suspected.[44]

Later in this same work, Petrarch recasts Domitian's observation in his own words,

> There is nothing more fleeting than beauty, especially a woman's. Remember: He who loves his wife because of her beauty will soon hate her.[45]

Where then, does one find virtue in Beauty? Petrarch quotes Seneca as saying, 'worth is more pleasing in a form that's fair,' then objects that this is wrong because it suggests only the eye of the beholder makes the judgment. 'Worth,' instead should be a matter of the value inherent in the thing itself.[46] Subtle is better, adds Petrarch, for 'hidden beauty is sweetest.'[47]

Petrarch does not explore this question much further, preferring to evade the issue by declaring that the mind is more beautiful than the body.

44 Ibid., I, ii, 16ff.

45 Ibid., I, lxvi, 194.

46 Ibid., I, ii, 18.
47 'Mai non vo' più cantar,' in *Petrarch's Lyric Poems*, 210.

> For the beauty of the mind is much sweeter and longer lasting than that of the body, and it too has its laws regarding the beautiful and the ordering of parts.[48]

[48] *Remedies*, I, ii, 18.

Regarding the aesthetic purpose of Art, Petrarch provides the most familiar definition, that it is to delight.

> All earthly things have been made to be subordinate to man. Some to feed him, some to clothe him, some to carry him, others to protect him, others yet to train and teach him, and remind him of his place—some also to delight him and to revive his spirits when his affairs have tired him.[49]

[49] Ibid., II, xc, 211.

And for him, there was no delight which compared to reading.

> Gold, silver, gems, purple robes, a marble palace, broad lands, paintings … and all such things bring only a mute, a superficial pleasure. But books thrill you to the marrow.[50]

[50] Letter to Giovanni dell'Incisa, in *Letters from Petrarch*, 40.

Petrarch makes an interesting observation: it is possible for Art to delight the observer, even if the observer does not know why. In this regard he quotes from his favorite philosopher, Cicero.

> … it merely tickles their ears, without their knowing why, but cannot penetrate their thick heads, because the avenues of intelligence are obstructed.[51]

[51] Letter to Boccaccio, in Robinson, *Petrarch, The First modern Scholar and Man of Letters*, 184.

That this happens is part of what we call Universality in art. The artist understands what communicates universally, without the necessity of the observer knowing anything about the actual details of the craft of the art. Thus, Cicero's comment reminds us of an almost identical one by Mozart,

> … these passages are written in such a way that the less learned cannot fail to be pleased, though without knowing why.[52]

[52] Letter to his father, December 28, 1782.

This universality is related to what we call Truth in Art and Petrarch addresses this with respect to poetry.

> There is one labor more important yet—to seek the truth. But this involves these two: to seek and to set forth in a distinguished form. And to express something so that it delights the ear is a great thing, hard, troublesome, and, hence, most rare. True poets certainly devote

themselves to both these duties. Poets of the more common sort neglect the first and are content with the sonorous phrase.[53]

53   *Remedies*, I, xlvi, 149.

Finally, on the subject of delight in art, Petrarch pays tribute to an acquaintance, a goldsmith, whom he seems to have regarded as a model citizen in this regard.

He enjoys moreover the best gift that nature can bestow, for he is an admirer and lover of all that is good and beautiful.[54]

54   Letter to Neri Morando, in Robinson, *Petrarch, The First modern Scholar and Man of Letters*, 170.

An aesthetic question which Petrarch seems to have given some thought to, is the relative virtues of originality and imitation. Originality, he believed, comes not as an original artistic idea in itself, but from something which must be found in the artist himself.

Certainly each of us has naturally something individual and his own in his utterance and language as in his face and gesture. It is better and more rewarding for us to develop and train this quality than to change it.[55]

55   Letter to Boccaccio, in *Letters from Petrarch*, 183.

Thus, one discovers originality by looking inward, reflecting on one's own experience. Petrarch adds, 'Experience makes art, says Aristotle. All the arts prove his statement.'[56]

Petrarch qualifies this by recognizing that to some degree imitation is not only inevitable, but embraced by fine artists.

56   Letter to Francesco Bruni, in ibid., 228.

I won't say that [the young poet] will avoid all imitation, but he will conceal it, so that his work won't resemble any particular author but will appear to bring to Italy something new out of the work of the ancients. But now, as is the way of youth, he delights in imitations; and sometimes he is so enraptured by others' beauties that, contrary to good poetic practice he becomes, as Horace says, so entangled in the rules that he cannot extricate himself without revealing his originals …

A proper imitator should take care that what he writes resembles the original without reproducing it. The resemblance should not be that of a portrait to the sitter—in that case the closer the likeness is the better—but it should be the resemblance of a son to his father. Therein is often a great divergence in particular features, but there is a certain suggestion, what our painters call an 'air,' most noticeable in the face and eyes, which makes the resemblance.[57]

57   Letter to Boccaccio, in ibid., 198.

Petrarch also addresses the very important aesthetic question of the obligation of the artist to the public, or the audience. It was immediately clear to him that for an artist to have the goal of pleasing the audience was wrong.

> It's idiocy to regulate our lives not according to intelligent reason but to suit popular fads ... To follow the fashions of the vulgar mob, whose manners we laugh at and whose lives and opinions we despise, is to be more idiotic than the mob.[58]

> ......

> Experience, the great teacher, is on my side, though the silly, unteachable mob is against me.[59]

Probably Petrarch felt this was an impossible goal to begin with, for he wondered, 'How can I please all? I have always striven to please only the few.'[60] Further, 'audiences' consist of individuals and Petrarch believed, at least in the case of the writer, that it is to the individual that one must address his work.

> The varieties of men are infinite; there is no more similitude of minds than of faces. As the palate of one man—let alone those of many men—does not always relish the same food, so one mind is not always to be fed on the same literary style. So the writer has a double task: to envisage the person he is writing to, and then the state of mind in which the recipient will read what he proposes to write.[61]

He mentions this again in a letter to Boccaccio.

> It is important to know for whom we are writing, and a difference in the character of one's listeners justifies a difference in style.[62]

The artist who purposely desires to please the general audience usually does so for the purpose of money. Here, Petrarch exempts the highest artist.

> If anyone says that craftsmen are not seeking fame but money, I would probably have to agree as far as the common sort is concerned. But I deny it regarding the very best craftsmen. There are many indications of this—the way they persist in their efforts, regardless of the time they spend and the material losses they suffer. They even spurn cash lest they impair their fame.[63]

> ......

[58] Letter to his brother, Gherardo, in ibid., 92.

[59] Letter to Laelius, in ibid., 159.

[60] Letter to 'Socrates,' in ibid., 18.

[61] Letter to 'Socrates,' in ibid., 20.

[62] Letter to Boccaccio, quoted in Robinson, *Petrarch, The First modern Scholar and Man of Letters*, 192.

[63] *Remedies*, II, lxxxviii, 204.

> Money, certainly, does not appeal at least to noble minds as a worthy reward of study. It is for the mechanical trades to strive for lucre; the higher arts have a more generous end in view.[64]

In general, however, Petrarch sadly observes that his high ideals with respect to the relationship between artist and public were not followed during his lifetime.

> Not that I am deploring my own lot, or looking for personal gain; I am mourning the common fate of mankind, as I behold the reward of the nobler arts falling to the meaner.[65]

Petrarch also makes some interesting observations on several of the individual arts, which we might introduce with his belief that one should restrict oneself to only one discipline.

> No one intellect should ever strive for distinction in more than one pursuit. Those who boast of preeminence in many arts are either divinely endowed or utterly shameless or simply mad.[66]

Regarding painting, it would appear from Petrarch's comments that this art was widely treasured during the fourteenth century—but for the wrong reasons. Not only had paintings become a status symbol, but Petrarch was concerned that a man might like them *too* much, admiration turning to devotion.

> JOY: Paintings delight me.
> REASON: An inane delight ... A remarkable unsoundness of the human mind—to admire anything, save itself, although among all the works, not only of art, but also of nature, there is nothing more admirable ...
> JOY: Paintings delight me more than anything.
> REASON: You take delight in the pencil strokes and colors which please because of price and skillfulness—their variety and artistic composition. And you are fascinated by the lifelike gestures, the movement in these inanimate and immobile pictures, the faces jutting out of posts, and the portraits that seem about to breathe and make you think that they might utter words. The danger here lies in the fact that great minds, in particular, are captivated by these things—and what a peasant will pass off with brief enjoyment, a man of intellect may continue to venerate with sighs of admiration. This is a complicated matter, and our task here is not to inquire into the origins of art and its development, nor

64 Letter to Tomasso da Messina, quoted in Robinson, *Petrarch, The First modern Scholar and Man of Letters*, 221.

65 Letter to Boccaccio, quoted in ibid., 180.

66 Letter to Giovanni Andrea di Bologna, quoted in ibid., 286.

the wonders of its works, the dedication of the artists, the mad extravagance of princes, and the enormity of the prices which brought paintings from far across the oceans to Rome and hung them in the temples of the gods, the bedrooms of the emperors, on public avenues, and in galleries. Nor was this sufficient. The Romans themselves had to apply their right hands, as well as their minds, which should have been applied to greater tasks, to the pursuit of painting …

Thus, when these fictions and contours in feckless colors delight you too much, turn your eyes to Him, who painted feelings on the face of man, intellect on man's mind, the stars on the heavens, the flowers on the earth—and you will disdain the paintings you admired.[67]

Sculpture, because of its additional dimension, Petrarch found to be a higher art to the extent that it was closer to nature. Here again, however, he was disturbed that art had become 'popular.'

> JOY: But I enjoy statues.
> REASON: A different art, but the same madness—and there is but one origin and one purpose of all the arts, though there are various materials … Sculpture is nearer to nature than painting. Pictures appeal much to the eye, but sculptures can be touched, feel substantial and solid, and are of durable body. This is the reason why no paintings by the ancients survive today, but countless statues …
>
> There is one of those arts in which the human hand imitates nature, called *plasticen*—the plastic art. It works with plaster, wax, and retentive white clay and is, perhaps, the most attractive among all related arts—closer to virtue or, at least, less hostile to moderation and frugality, which suggest that images of gods and men be made of simple clay rather than gold …
>
> Once, statues were the hallmarks of virtue; now, they are attractions for the eyes. Once, they were erected in honor of great accomplishments … Today, priceless statues of foreign marble are erected unto rich merchants.
> JOY: Artistic statues give me pleasure.
> REASON: Nearly any kind of material admits artistic treatment. I understand that in all things your pleasure is brought about by noble skill joined with noble materials …
>
> The enjoyment of talent, engaged in with moderation, is acceptable—enjoyment, particularly of those who excel in it, because, if envy does not hinder you, it is easy to admire in another what one loves in oneself.[68]

---

67 *Remedies*, I, xl, 125ff. It is also interesting here that Petrarch correctly identifies that it is the entire face which expresses emotions. Most early writers mistakenly believed that it was only the eyes.

68 Ibid., I, xli, 130ff.

Petrarch's views on the theater are as hostile as those of the early Church fathers and for the same reasons, the bad influence on the character of the observer and for the inherent lack of Truth.

> Joy: I enjoy all kinds of spectacles.
> Reason: The circus or the theater, perhaps—two places notoriously inimical to decent conduct. Even a bad person who goes there returns worse. This path is unknown to good people, and if they follow it because of ignorance, they risk contagion …
>
> A performance which is neither rendered nor viewed with honesty; nor is it easy to say whether the actor is more infamous or the spectator, the stage more than the audience—unless we acknowledge the fact that men are drawn to the former often by poverty, but to the latter by ostentation.[69]

[69] Ibid., I, xxx, 90ff.

Although himself one of the great poets of the fourteenth century, Petrarch seems to have developed a disdain for his own art, again in part because it had become too popular. Too many common people had begun to write poetry and to think of themselves as poets.

> Poetry, a divine gift granted to few, has fallen into the hands of the mob; I shan't go so far as to say it is profaned and prostituted.[70]

[70] Letter to Francesco Nelli, in *Letters from Petrarch*, 115ff.

He goes on to mention such an amateur poet, observing, 'He has never really worked at the art; and without serious application not even easy tasks are well done.'

He attributes this popularity to poetry's superficial pleasure, whereas its great virtue, appealing to deep meditation, was possible only by a superior mind. In a letter to Pierre d'Auvergne, Petrarch again complains that so many common people are trying to write poetry, quoting Horace, 'Lettered and unlettered, we all write poems all the time.'

> Need I dwell on minor excesses? Carpenters, cloth-fullers, farmers abandon their plows and the tools of their trades to prate on the Muses and Apollo. One can't imagine how far has spread this plague, which used to afflict only a few. If you ask why, I should answer that poetry is very sweet to the taste, but it is to be appreciated by only a few superior minds possessing a lofty, incurious contempt for common concerns, given to high meditations, and with an appropriate natural gift. Thus, as we learn from experience and from the testi-

mony of the greatest scholars, there are none of the arts in which mere zeal is of less avail …

I live in distress, and I hardly dare to appear in public, for these cranks pop up from everywhere. They interrogate me, they snatch at me, they instruct me, they dispute, they quarrel …[71]

[71] Letter to Pierre d'Auvergne, in ibid., 120ff.

Petrarch's reaction was to once again separate himself from what he refers to as 'the mob,' and turn his attention to spiritual literature.

I think that the Muses and Apollo will not merely grant me permission, they will applaud, that after giving my youth to studies proper to that age, I should devote my riper years to more important matters.[72]

[72] Letter to Francesco Nelli, in ibid., 190.

In mentioning this change in his tastes in his biographical essay, 'Francesco Petrarca to Posterity,' he goes further and now denigrates poetry in general.

I possessed a well-balanced rather than a keen intellect, one prone to all kinds of good and wholesome study, but especially inclined to moral philosophy and the art of poetry. The latter, indeed, I neglected as time went on, and took delight in sacred literature. Finding in that a hidden sweetness which I had once esteemed but lightly, I came to regard the works of the poets as only amenities.[73]

[73] Quoted in Robinson, *Petrarch, The First Modern Scholar and Man of Letters*, 64.

ON THE AESTHETICS OF MUSIC

It is a particular disappointment in reading the works of this thoughtful man, to find that he speaks so rarely of music—even though he was a musician, as we know from a letter in which he mentions 'those sweet sounds I used to draw from my lute.'[74] Even in a letter to the great French composer, Philippe de Vitry, Petrarch extols the beauties of the Italian countryside, but says nothing of Italian music.[75]

It may be that his taste in music was for the 'old-fashioned' styles, for in a letter to Boccaccio, while no doubt thinking primarily of literature, Petrarch's words sound very much like the criticism which the members of the *ars antiqua* of this period were leveling at de Vitry and his *ars nova* colleagues.

[74] Letter to Giovanni Colonna, in *Letters from Petrarch*, 35. In his will Petrarch bequeathed his lute to the impresario Bombasi.
[75] Letter to Philippe de Vitry,' in ibid., 86ff.

O inglorious age! that scorns antiquity, its mother, to whom it owes every noble art,—that dares to declare itself not only equal but superior to the glorious past.[76]

Regarding the aesthetic purpose of music, Petrarch, as we see in his own poems, gives as its chief virtue the ability to soothe.

It is right and just that I sing and be joyful.
It is just that at some time I sing, since I have sighed for so long a time that I shall never begin soon enough to make my smiling equal to so many sorrows.[77]

......

Therefore if at any time I laugh or sing, I do it because I have no way except this one to hide my anguished weeping.[78]

Nevertheless, for the listener, Petrarch finds a hidden danger in this capacity of music.

Joy: I am charmed by songs and sounds.
Reason: Also wild animals and birds are tricked by song. More remarkable yet, even the fish are touched by the sweetness of music ... Not believed but known by experience is the fact that, daily, man deceives man with smooth words and, to be short, that there is nothing more suited to deceit than the voice.
Joy: I am soothed by pleasant music.
Reason: And so, they say, soothes the spider before it bites. And the physician anoints before he cuts. And the fouler, and a woman, both cajole whom they want to deceive. And the murderer embraces whom he will kill and the octopus whom he will drown. And some of the worst men are to be feared all the more when they are most gentle in manner and voice, which we read in particular of Prince Domitian. Hardly any kind of soothing is beyond suspicion.[79]

......

Joy: I shall not weep. I shall sing and cheer myself with poetry, as lovers do.
Reason: I must admit that this special folly of lovers is one of the most remarkable things—not only confined to the vulgar crowd, whose habit to find any madness excusable has become their second nature, but also affecting men of the highest culture among them the Greeks and Romans. Thus we know that the poets of Greece and your own country have written brilliantly, some about the loves of others, most about their own, and have earned fame

[76] Letter to Boccaccio, quoted in Robinson, *Petrarch, The First Modern Scholar and Man of Letters*, 208.

[77] 'Lasso me, ch' i' non so in qual parte pieghi,' in *Petrarch's Lyric Poems*, 150.

[78] 'Cesare, poi che 'l traditor d'Egitto,' in ibid., 204.

[79] *Remedies*, I, xxiii, 70.

for their eloquence although they deserved notoriety for their conduct …

Yet, when it comes to what you call 'cheering yourself' in this malady, which you imagine to be done by poetry, let Horace's little poem and its query serve as my answer:

> Do you suppose that with verses such as these,
> sorrow and passion and the burden of care can
> be lifted from your breast?

By talking and singing love is strengthened and inflamed, not extinguished or relieved; and the songs and poems which you utter do not heal, but irritate the wound.[80]

In his fourth pastoral *Eclogue*, however, Petrarch returns to the traditional praise of the ability of music to provide solace, as he patriotically comes to the defense of Italy in a debate between Gallus (France) and Tyrrhenus (Italy) as to whom the gift of poetic expression belongs. Petrarch declares the god Daedalus first makes a gift of music to Tyrrhenus and one of its primary purposes is to provide solace.

> TYRRHENUS: Bearing his lyre he drew near me. 'Take this, my lad,' so he bade me;
> 'Let it console your cares and beguile your long days of labor.'

Gallus desires to possess the virtues of music, represented by the lyre, and says,

> GALLUS: Fix yourself the price you would take for that little Object, and high though it be I'll pay—and add something to it.
> TYRRHENUS: So for this 'little' thing you'd pay a great price? Nay, you know not
> What it is worth or you'd call it a great thing. In troubles it soothes us,
> Raises our weary spirits, affords our friends consolation,
> Rids our heart of their sorrows, making them once more joyful,
> Dries up our tears and appeases all our complaints and even
> Banishes fear, brings hope to our hearts and calm to our faces.[81]

So effective is this capacity of music, that it provides him the courage to face the trials of the world.

80 Ibid., I, lxix, 202ff.

81 Francesco Petrarch, *Petrarch's Bucolicum Carmen*, trans. Thomas Bergin (New Haven: Yale University Press, 1974), IV, 22, 41ff.

> TYRRHENUS: Nay my wealth is my lyre. By its virtue alone I am free of
> Fortune's incessant onslaughts and poverty—all of the fetters
> Fastened on me by the world. With my music I traverse full often
> Wasteland and woods and ascend barren crags and fearlessly wander
> Through the dark silence of night, while the birds and the caverns
> applaud me.
> All of my cares, as I sing, fall away and are lost in the shadows.[82]

[82] Ibid., IV, 56ff.

Petrarch also acknowledges that one of the powerful attributes of music is its power to *move* the minds of men.

> JOY: Song moves me.
> REASON: But to what purpose? Without doubt music has great power over the noble hearts of men. But its effects are various beyond belief. And, to omit what is of no concern, it moves some to shallow mirth, others to pure and devout joy and, sometimes, even to pious tears. This variety has led many great minds to different conclusions. Athanasius, as everybody knows, forbade the use of singing in the churches to ward off vanity. Ambrose, eager to kindle active devotion, decreed that they should sing. Augustine states truthfully in his *Confessions* that he allowed both views and that it was difficult for him to settle his doubts in this manner.[83]

[83] *Remedies*, I, xxiii, 71.

This power of music he finds, in his third pastoral *Eclogue*, can even work its magic on the 'stern and tenacious mind.'

> And tell how their voices blending
> Sang one harmonious song as they danced, each one in her circle,
> Hymning the spirit of mankind in all of its various motions,
> Whence comes our love of sweet fame, our cultivation of music,
> Joy in the use of our minds, be it wit or the stern and tenacious
> Cult of the intellect; aye and thereto the sources of rapture,
> Righteous judgment, and art in discerning the will of the heavens,
> Power to charm our hearers.[84]

[84] *Petrarch's Bucolicum Carmen*, III, 112ff.

Petrarch finds that sometimes this characteristic of music can have a disturbing effect.

> Song, you do not quiet me, rather you inflame me to tell of what steals me away from myself …[85]

[85] 'Percheé la vita è breve,' in *Petrarch's Lyric Poems*, 160.

Observing this power of music no doubt made Petrarch take special notice of the fact that the ancient philosophers emphasized the influence of music on character development. He mentions this in a passage in which he has been praising the music of angels and of heaven.

> Right now you relegate the judgment of the sounds to a deaf sense, which so far some may still regard as a small matter, although it has troubled great men. Nor was it without cause that Plato, a man of divine intellect, considered music as pertaining to the state and the improvement of moral conduct in the commonwealth.[86]

In another place Petrarch mentions, almost with a sense of surprise, the esteem for music held by the ancients. Here, he concedes that appreciating music represents a measure of refinement, but, as in the case of painting and sculpture, he cautions once again against the listener being *too* involved.

> JOY: It is pleasant to sing.
> REASON: What gives you pleasure now once gave pleasure to the Greeks. Among them anyone who could not sing or play instruments was considered ignorant. This, Cicero writes, happened to Themistocles of Athens, the most illustrious of the Greeks, when he refused to play the lyre at banquets … It is amazing that Socrates should in his old age devote his efforts to the harp. But it should not surprise us that Alcibiades was made to study the [aulos] by his uncle Pericles, because this was regarded as most worthy by the ancients and, in fact, was even taught among the liberal arts …
>
> In the present age such an ardent zeal for music has as yet not come to possess the mind of every prince, but it has taken possession of the hearts of a few, particularly the worst ones. For Caligula was extremely fond of singing and dancing. As for Nero, it is unbelievable how much he was devoted to the study of the kithara and what pains he took with his voice. But it is stupid and utterly ridiculous when in the very night that was the last one of his life … he should grievously bewail again and again the downfall, not of such a great prince, but of such a great musician. I omit others. Even today, in your own age, we find here and there that pleasure of the ear which to enjoy honestly and soberly constitutes a measure of humane refinement. Yet to be overwhelmed and voluptuously possessed by it is nothing but sheer foolishness.[87]

---

86 *Remedies*, I, xxiii, 73.

87 Ibid., I, xxiii, 71ff.

In one curious passage, Petrarch, the important early Italian humanist, lapses back into the old medieval Scholastic concept of music being an expression of mathematics. As a musician himself, how could he make this statement?

> A deaf person can know the tones and numbers characterizing the intervals of fifth and octave, as well as the other proportions of the musical scale with which musicians work. Although one does not hear the sounds of the human voice, of strings or the organ, he nevertheless may understand in his mind their fundamental canon and, doubtless, will prefer the intellectual pleasure to a mere titillation of the ear.[88]

Petrarch makes a few interesting observations about performance. First, speaking of rhetoric, he emphasizes that content cannot be equated with eloquence. Today, thinking of music, we might say, you can't judge the music by the performance.

> Sweetness and elegance—I do not know how alluring or deceptive they are, but they do not imply anything noble or truthful. Before just judges the sweet and flowery pleading of a dishonest man matters no more than the makeup of a streetwalker.[89]

Regarding performance in general, he returns again to his belief that, above all, one must not have the audience foremost in mind.

> No way is more prone to error or leads more directly to the brink of disaster, than the steps of the multitude. Almost everything which the crowd praises deserves to be condemned.[90]

In conclusion, we should mention that Petrarch, in his tenth pastoral *Eclogue*, pays tribute to a long list of ancient authors with whom he was familiar. Among these, he says, are,

> Many I saw who scorned riches, the root and prize of our troubles,
> Lauding instead works of art …[91]

Among those to whom he joins an association with music, we find,

> Plato:
> There stood the painter and gymnast and, in adolescence, the singer,
> And in his age a traveler and a diviner …[92]
> ……

[88] Ibid., II, xcvii, 241.

[89] Ibid., I, ix, 27.

[90] Ibid., I, xi, 32.

[91] *Petrarch's Bucolicum Carmen*, X, 128.

[92] Ibid., X, 142.

Varro:
> Another told of the sea-gods and how they put into our music
> Strange, esoteric matters.[93]

......

Terence:
> I heard a foreign born slave, to whom a fair prison had given
> Freedom at last and moreover endowed with a marvelous talent,
> Sing of the manners of men and their tricks and their wiles, of the secret
> Fears of uneasy old age and of youth and its sport and the guileful
> Arts of procurers. He used an Italian [plectrum] for his verses,
> Having long since forgotten his native African patois.[94]

......

And, Virgil:
> Truly a kingly shepherd he governed he fields and the woodlands,
> Second in song to none, had he but the leisure for singing.[95]

From these earlier artists, Petrarch learned also that hard work and practice is necessary even for the modest results he attributed to his own music.

> Saw too a race of melodious singers, all of them masters,
> Content to stand under its shade and fashion the rarest of garlands.
> And on that greensward I too have learned—for much avails practice
> Long and laborious—how to vary my notes, singing many
> Albeit modest songs, and have dared to crown my own temples
> Finally with that same leafage.[96]

ART MUSIC

Once again, considering Petrarch himself played the lute, we are disappointed that he makes almost no specific reference to the performance of art music which he actually heard. Only in the most indirect references can one surmise that such activity existed. For example, in a letter scolding his son, Petrarch mentions in passing, 'at a harmonious concert who hates the lute?'[97] In another place, referring to finding comfort in the sounds of nature, Petrarch says even the nocturnal noises of frogs might be imagined as 'the sweet consort of viols.'[98]

[93] Ibid., X, 195. Not all modern scholars agree whom Petrarch is thinking of in this fascinating reference.

[94] Ibid., X, 232.

[95] Ibid., X, 289.

[96] Ibid., X, 366ff.

[97] Letter to his son, Giovanni, in *Letters from Petrarch*, 184.

[98] *Remedies*, II, xc, 213.

In a letter to an old university friend, Petrarch mentions that in Bologna music was experiencing the same decline he had mentioned regarding the arts in general. In speaking of the choral-dance performances, he mentions that songs have been replaced with laments and 'girls dancing in chorus' by gangs of bandits.[99]

In these volumes, one of the chief descriptors of art music which we have looked for is the appearance of the contemplative listener. In Petrarch it is in his pastoral settings which he describes such listeners. In the first of his *Eclogues*, for example, which deals with the relative virtues of the monastic life versus the literary life, a listener hears music which stirs and moves his soul.[100] And later, in the same *Eclogue*,

> Here, in the depths of night, you will see a shepherd tuning
> Notes of unrivaled sweetness, to make you in time forgetful,
> Heedless of all other matters. And surely you cannot call idle
> Music which now can arouse you, now hold you fixed
>   and enraptured.[101]

Similarly, in one of his poems, the listener is moved by the singing of birds.

> And from its shade came forth such sweet songs of divers birds
> and so much other delight that it had rapt me from the world.[102]

Because they are inspired, serious and have real listeners, we consider love songs in the style of the troubadours as also being Art Music. Much of Petrarch's poetry is in this style. As Durling points out, 'Petrarch's wide familiarity with troubadour poetry is evident on every page.'[103] We know from later writers that Petrarch not only intended his poetry to be sung, but was himself instrumental in reviving the ancient tradition of sung poetry in Italy. Additional clues that this poetry was sung are found in poems which begin such as 'Io canterei d'Amor' (I would sing of love).[104] Others associate verses and 'notes,'

> For the last need, O wretched soul,
> mobilize all your wit, all your power,
> while we still have the breath of life.
> There is nothing in the world that cannot be done by verses;
> they know how to enchant asps with their notes,
> not to speak of adorning the frost with new flowers.

99 Letter to Guido Sette, in *Letters from Petrarch*, 266.

100 'Ecologue I,' lines 20ff.

101 *Petrarch's Bucolicum Carmen*, I, 54ff.

102 'Standomi un giorno solo a la fenestra,' in *Petrarch's Lyric Poems*, 502.

103 Ibid., 9.

104 Also *And I go singing*, in 'Per mezz' i boschi inospiti et selvaggi'; *I sang, now I weep*, in 'Cantai, or piango; et non men di dolcezza'; *I wept, now I sing*, in 'I' piansi, or canto; ché 'l celeste lume'; *I went singng of you many years*, in 'Alma felice che sovente torni'; and *I dared, singing, to complain of Love*, in 'Mentre che 'l cor dagli amorosi vermi.' Also in the spirit of the lyric poets, Petrarch mentions the 'angelic singing' of his lover Laura, in 'Amor m´à posto come segno a strale.'

> Now the meadows are laughing with new grass and flowers:
> it cannot be that her angelic soul
> will be deaf to the sound of the amorous notes;
> if our cruel fortune has greater power,
> weeping and singing our verses …
>   [*cantando i nostri versi*][105]

We have referred to his rejection of this repertoire in his later years. But once again, in this regard, it is interesting that in a letter to his brother he refers to the poems as songs, as he recalls 'our silly songs, full of false and indecent praise of loose women.'[106]

Art Music must be inspired, a point which Petrarch also makes in his love poetry. Indeed, in the second of these, he maintains that if he fails, it will be for lack of inspiration, not craft.

> Song, one of your sisters has gone before, and I feel the other in the same dwelling making herself ready, wherefore I rule more paper.[107]
>
> ……
>
> Whence comes the ink, whence the pages that I fill with words of you (if in that I err, it is the fault of Love, not at all a lack of art).[108]

Petrarch also mentions the quality of the performance, with regard to this repertoire. In his third *Eclogue*, which is a pastoral allegorical tale of his pursuit of Laura, the shepherd turns to music as the means of gaining the love of the girl, only to discover his ability is not sufficient.

> Indeed I have bent every effort,
> Hoping my song would avail me; I knew that you were responsive
> Sooner to notes of the Muse than the jingle of gold. At first, though,
> Doubts began to assail me, concerning the road I had chosen:
> Only hoarse sounds emerged from my pipe.[109]

After practicing before goats and bees, and aided by the god Argus, he improves.

Finally, in his tenth pastoral Eclogue, Petrarch pays tribute to the ancient Greek singers, the original lyric poets. In this passage he is thinking of Simonides, Stesichorus, Alcaeus, Sappho, Philetas of Kos, Antimachus of Colophon, Callimachus and Anacreon.

---

[105] 'Là ver l'aurora, che sì dolce l'aura,' in ibid., 400.

[106] Letter to his brother, Gherardo, in *Letters from Petrarch*, 94.

[107] 'Gentil mia Donna, i' veggio,' in *Petrarch's Lyric Poems*, 166.

[108] 'Io son già stanco di pensar sì come,' in ibid., 174.

[109] *Petrarch's Bucolicum Carmen*, III, 60ff.

There too stood a singer of sacred things and their priesthood, beside him
One who glorified arms and the trumpets of war; the former
Dear to the gods and the latter to men. And another was singing,
Armed with a bow and lyre, of the captured wolf and the sheepfolds
Spared in the Lesbian plains; so his song and his deeds won him honor.
Among these great doctors of art stood a girl no less skilled than they are;
Sweetly she sang of love and its snares and its burning anguish.
Touching her rosy lips with a cinnamon flute she could often
Move the bright stars above with her gentle and soft lamentations.
Many admirers she has; one from Kos, widely known of his verses
Praising his Bittis, and one, from Klaros, whose song was of Lyde,
And the Cyrenian bard who was Africa's gift to the Nile and
Likewise the shepherd of Teos consumed by a Samian fire.
Nor do the lovers of our day esteem her less highly, adopting
Her plaintive and humble accents, voiced in like varied measures.[110]

[110] Ibid., X, 81ff.

FUNCTIONAL MUSIC

If the somber Petrarch has left so few descriptions of Art Music, it comes as no surprise that he barely mentions the lower aesthetic representatives. Considering the fact that he became absorbed with spiritual matters late in life, we might have expected some expression of interest in Church music. Certainly, the one comment he made, which is at all descriptive, makes us wish for more discussion. Only in his first *Eclogue*, do we find this reference to Church singing, which he describes as 'deep reaching into souls with mysterious sweetness.'[111]

[111] Ibid., I, 103.

Ceremonial music is mentioned in Petrarch only in a passing reference to 'the trumpet blasts of soldiers,'[112] and in a description of a pastoral procession in his third Eclogue.

[112] Letter to Giovanni Colonna, in *Letters from Petrarch*, 35.

> Multitudes cheered as they marched 'midst the triumphant blare of the trumpets ...
> Hither came other singers, too many to mention, among them
> He of the threefold reed, your dearly cherished Parthenias.[113]

[113] *Petrarch's Bucolicum Carmen*, III, 137, 156.

There are two references to occupational music, one of the 'plowmen singing in the fields'[114] the other of the 'poor hoer.'

> When the sun turns his flaming wheels to give place to night and the shadows descend more widely from the highest mountains, the poor hoer takes up his tools and with words and mountains tunes lightens his breast of all heaviness.[115]

[114] Letter to Guido Sette, in *Letters from Petrarch*, 268.

[115] 'Ne la stagion che 'l ciel rapido inchina,' in *Petrarch's Lyric Poems*, 116.

ENTERTAINMENT MUSIC

In all the writings of Petrarch there is little enthusiasm to be found for traditional entertainment. Even in the case of banquets, which are frequently mentioned in all early literature, one gathers the impression that Petrarch didn't have much fun, finding them ostentatious and boring, 'Trumpets blare and cymbals crash, and it seems that everything serves pomp and circumstance.'[116]

For those who had to make their living providing entertainment, Petrarch had little sympathy.

> One law holds for entertainers and parasites: both of them chase after the rich with alluring flatteries. For lowly hangers-on it is sufficient to fill their bellies. But entertainers, to whom the very mention of food is an insult, have to satisfy in other ways their greed, which is bottomless and everlasting.[117]

In another reference to this environment he places Entertainment Music above other forms of entertainment.

> A nobler amusement [than entertainers] is provided by well-modulated music, created, as you know, according to a certain liberal art—while the environment produced by entertainers appeals only to vanity and shamelessness.[118]

We conclude with Petrarch's attack on dancing, a form of entertainment for which he subscribes to the strong moral objections of the Church.

> Joy: I enjoy dancing.
> Reason: I would be surprised if the sound of stringed instruments and pipes did not suggest dancing to you, and, according to

[116] *Remedies*, I, xix, 55.

[117] Ibid., I, xxviii, 85.

[118] Ibid., I, xxviii, 84.

established rule, one vanity would not be followed by another greater and more disgraceful one. Because in song there is a certain sweetness, often profitable, even saintly. Yet dancing offers nothing but sensuous and worthless exhibition, hateful to decent eyes and unworthy of a man ...

[Imagine dancing without music playing] just the silly girls and their partners, softer than girls, turning around and prancing forward and backward in the silent room. Tell me, have you ever seen anything more absurd and inane? In reality, the ugly motions are, of course, accompanied by the sound of strings and pipes, as one mindless folly view with another one ...

There is less immediate pleasure in dancing than anticipation of pleasure to come. Dancing is the foreplay of Venus: to lead around the simpering girls dazed by music, to touch them and squeeze them, and, under the guise of being sociable, fondle them. Licentious hands, licentious eyes, licentious whisperings, the stamping feet, the dissonance of the singing and the blaring brasses, the to-and-fro of bodies ... all drive off restraint and modesty, they all arouse lechery and wanton indulgence ...

Since you are afflicted in this way ... as long as you cannot go without dancing altogether, indulge in it sparingly and with the utmost restraint; do not act in any way over dainty and like a woman, but let, at all times, manly rigor show itself, even beyond its usual limits ...

I cite Seneca ...

> Scipio would disport his triumphal and soldierly person to the sound of music, moving not with the voluptuous contortions that are now in fashion, when men even in walking squirm with more than a woman's voluptuousness, but in the manly style in which men in the days of old were wont to dance during the times of sport and festival, risking no loss of dignity even if their own enemies looked on.[119]

[119] Ibid., I, xxiv, 73ff.

3 BOCCACCIO

GIOVANNI BOCCACCIO (1313–1375), reared in Florence and Naples, was destined by his family for a career in finance, but like his great friend, Petrarch, he abandoned his profession for poetry. A biography written in the generation after Boccaccio's death quotes him as saying,

> Later on, having almost reached maturity, and making my own decisions, I was not the least bit hesitant to concentrate on the poets, without having consulted anyone or being persuaded by a teacher.[1]

Boccaccio also once expressed the wish that his father would have allowed him to begin the study of poetry in his youth.

> If my father had only been favorable to such a course at a time of life when I was more adaptable, I do not doubt that I should have taken my place among poets of fame. But while he tried to bend my mind first into business and next into a lucrative profession, it came to pass that I turned out neither a business man nor a lawyer, and missed being a good poet besides.[2]

Today, of course, we recognize him as a famous poet after all. Like Petrarch, much of his poetry was inspired by a woman he could not have, whom he also met in church on an Easter Sunday. In this case, at least, we know she was a real person, Maria d'Aquino, a natural daughter to King Robert of Naples. Boccaccio called her Fiammetta (little flame) and dedicated many of his large works to her, including *Filocopo*, *Teseide* (the basis of Chaucer's 'The Knight's Tale') and the *Amorosa Visione*.

She appears as well as a character in his masterpiece, one of the supreme masterpieces of all literature, *The Decameron*. There is no greater testimonial to the new spirit of humanism than the fact that Boccaccio could write this work, so filled with joy, humor, beauty and the zest for living, on the heals of the great plague, the Black Death.

---

1 Giannozzo Manetti (1396–1459) *The Life of Giovanni Boccaccio*, quoted in *The Decameron*, trans. Mark Musa and Peter Bondanella (New York: Norton, 1977), 193. In the dedication of his *Concerning Famous Women*, Boccaccio identifies himself not as a poet, but as 'a scholarly man.'

2 *Genealogia Deorum Gentilium*, XV, x, quoted in Charles Osgood, trans., *Boccaccio on Poetry* (New York: The Liberal Arts Press, 1956).

Again like Petrarch, Boccaccio became obsessed with ancient literature, saving works from oblivion and promoting them. Upon the ominous urging of a dying cleric, Boccaccio returned to religion late in life and contemplated selling all his books and becoming a monk. A letter from Petrarch helped prevent the destruction of his writings. He died in poverty and, indeed, when Petrarch died the previous year he left in his will money to buy a mantle for Boccaccio. A biographical note written by an author born during Boccaccio's lifetime paints a rather unhappy portrait of his life.

> I will not write Boccaccio's biography at this time, not because he does not deserve greatest praise, but because I do not know the particulars of his birth or his personal condition and life. Without knowledge of such things, one should not write. However, his works and books are well known to me, and it is clear to me that he had a great mind and was extremely cultured and hardworking. It is amazing that he wrote so many things ... He was greatly hindered by poverty, and was never content with his life; on the contrary he continually wrote complaints and moaned about himself. Sensitive and disdainful by nature, he had many problems because he could neither bear to be with his own peers, nor in the company of princes and lords.[3]

3 Leonardo Bruni (1369–1444), quoted in *The Decameron*, trans. Musa, 188.

With our greater perspective today, Boccaccio's contribution can be more accurately judged and we appreciate the assessment given by the modern scholar, Thomas G. Bergin.

> Italian literature is built firmly and enduringly on the great triangular base of Dante, Petrarch and Boccaccio. These are figures of such authority and magnetism as not only to have affected the course of Italian letters but to have left as well visible traces of their inspiration and example on the thought and creative fancy of the Western world ... As not infrequently happens in families where the youngest brother is overshadowed by his talented siblings, Boccaccio is commonly thought of as ranking third, so far as distinction is decent among giants. Yet if he lacks the grandeur of Dante and the grace of Petrarch, it may fairly be claimed for the youngest brother that he is the most versatile and inventive of all of them.[4]

4 Thomas G. Bergin, 'An Introduction to Boccaccio,' in ibid., 151.

ON THE PHYSIOLOGY OF AESTHETICS

It is interesting that neither Petrarch nor Boccaccio, although they were well read and had good inquisitive minds, seemed to have much inclination to contemplate on the complex late medieval Scholastic theories of how the mind is organized. These theories, in some cases with layers of kinds of intelligence, had their root in the desperate attempt by some philosophers to build a bridge between a Church based on faith and the rediscovery of the brilliant works on logic and reason by the early Greeks.

For Boccaccio, it seemed enough to simply accept the idea that Reason must rule over the other faculties, and if it doesn't one has difficulties.

> Therefore the vice of the noble spirit is this, that it wishes to ascend to higher things by another way than reason allows, but from where it usually falls.[5]

In his later years, when Boccaccio turned to spiritual thoughts, he distinguished between 'natural' and 'divine' Reason.

> Natural reason cannot perceive the matters revealed to me by Cybele—nor can any other keen capacity you might possess—if the mind does not pass into divine reason, where I often dwell with firm faith, without seeking the cause of the how; and there I clearly discern what I believe certain among men.[6]

It does seem odd, for a poet, that Boccaccio wrote so little of the value of sensory information and experiences. In one passage, although the final line suggests that he was angry at getting advice from uninformed persons, like an early Church father he assigns Reason to man and the senses to animals.

> Animals show their feelings by a movement of their heads, by a whistle or a roar, but to man alone was it granted to express thoughts in words. Nor was this without cause; for how could nature in any other way more wisely separate mankind, endowed with a divine soul, from the beasts, controlled only by sensuality. Servants of their senses, the thoughts of the latter are only on earthly things, and they take pleasure only in these. For the beast it seems superfluous to have a tongue for easy speech. We conclude, and rightly, that unintelligent beings had far better exist without tongues.[7]

---

5 'In Defense of Alcibiades,' in Bocaccio, *The Fates of Illustrious Men*, trans. Louis Hall (New York: Ungar, 1965), 103.

6 Boccaccio, *L'Ameto*, trans. Judith Serafini-Sauli (New York: Garland, 1985), 130.

7 'Against the Detractors of Rhetoric,' in *The Fates of Illustrious Men*, 165.

In the same spirit, in another place he warns of the dangers, not the virtues, of the senses.

> Since the eyes are the gates of the spirit, through them lust sends messages to the mind, through them love sighs and lights blind fires. Through them the heart sends sighs and shows its shameful affections. If one knew them well, he would either keep them closed or turn them heavenward or fix them upon the ground. No other ways but these are safe.[8]

One reference to the senses is very curious. During his description of the plague, Boccaccio mentions that some persons walked around holding flowers or strong smelling herbs to their noses believing it an excellent way to 'fortify the brain.'[9]

In only one place, in his *Corbaccio*, does Boccaccio admit that it is the senses which are the source of aesthetic delight. Here, during a dream, he relates,

> I seemed to enter upon a delightful and beautiful path, more pleasing to my eyes and all my other senses than anything I had seen before. I did not seem to recognize the place, wherever it was; and I did not seem to care about recognizing it once I felt its delight.[10]

Regarding the value of experience, Boccaccio maintains that it is a man's personal experience, not merely knowledge, which makes him productive. In this passage he seems to infer that experience and the man become one.

> It is difficult for anyone to accomplish anything in which he has not had any experience ... This is the reason a worker is able to use his tools—a man is known according to his inner nature.[11]

Unlike Petrarch, Boccaccio writes little of education. In one interesting discussion, he first joins the observation of many early writers, that philosophers tend to be poor. Then, in one of several places where he defends the virtues of poverty, he suggests that poverty is 'the distinguished mother of all laudable study.'[12]

---

8 'Medea,' in Boccaccio, *Concerning Famous Women*, trans. Guido Guarino (New Brunswick: Rutgers University Press, 1963), 37.

9 Boccaccio, *Decameron*, trans. John Payne, (Berkeley: University of California Press, 1982), I, 11.

10 Boccaccio, *The Corbaccio*, trans. Anthony Cassell (Urbana: University of Illinois Press, 1975), 6.

11 'A Warning against Credulousness,' in *The Fates of Illustrious Men*, 25.

12 'Poverty Applauded,' in ibid., 37.

ON THE PSYCHOLOGY OF AESTHETICS

Boccaccio's discussion of the emotions is limited to the poet's despair of Love. He observes, following most early philosophers, that the stronger emotions, in particular Love, have the negative effect of depriving one of Reason. In his *The Corbaccio*, he cries out to the lover, 'Oh, poor fool! Where is the meager power of your reason (no, rather, the expulsion of your reason) leading you?'[13]

In a passage in his *Concerning Famous Women*, Boccaccio, sounding very much like a medieval Church father, argues at length on the dangers of Love, how it enters through the senses and how lovers lack Reason. Boccaccio finds virtue only in the first stages of love, when it tends to improve a man's behavior—including the inspiration to study music.

> This must instill great fear in men who are solicitous of their wellbeing and must shake them out of their lethargy, when it is clear what a strong and powerful enemy threatens them. We must therefore be vigilant and arm our hearts with great strength, so that we are not overcome against our wishes. First a man must resist. He must curb his eyes so that they do not see vain things, close his ears like an asp, and tame lust with continual toil, because love seems alluring to men who are not wary, and at first sight it is pleasing. If it is well received, when it first enters it pleases a man with happy hopes, makes him adorn himself, encourages good behavior, *savoir-faire*, dances, songs, music, games, conviviality, and similar things. But after love through foolish consent has seized the entire man, conquered freedom, and chained and bound the mind and the fulfillment of desires is delayed beyond what had been hoped, it awakens sighs, forces the mind to make use of wiles without differentiating between vices and virtues as long as it achieves it desires, and it numbers among its enemies anything which is contrary to this ... If the lovers do not attain their desires, then love, lacking reason and using his spurs and whip, increases their worries, heightens desire, and brings almost intolerable pain, which cannot be cured by any remedy except tears, laments, and at times death.[14]

In his *The Corbaccio*, we find an even more extensive catalog of the dangerous effects of Love.

> Love is a blinding passion of the spirit, a seducer of the intellect, which dulls or rather deprives one of memory, a dissipator of earthly

13 *The Corbaccio*, 2.

14 'Iole,' in *Concerning Famous Women*, 46ff.

wealth, a waster of bodily strength, the enemy of youth, and the death of old age, the parent of vices, and the inhabiter of inane breasts, a thing without reason or order, without the least stability, the vice of unhealthy minds, and the stifler of human liberty.[15]

¹⁵ *The Corbaccio*, 23.

In this same work he concludes that this deprivation of Reason reduces man almost to the state of animals.

> There were two things which had nearly led me to utter despair: one was the recognition that, whereas I believed I had some understanding, I realized I was almost a beast without intellect (and certainly this is something to be more than a little distressed over, considering that I have spent the best part of my life trying to learn something, only to find then, when the need arises, that I know nothing).[16]

¹⁶ Ibid., 20.

In one place in *The Decameron*, Boccaccio reverses this thought and concludes that one must simply set aside the faculty of Reason before engaging in thoughts of Love. In the seventh story of the eighth day, we read,

> The learned scholar, laying aside philosophical speculations, turned all his thoughts to her …[17]

¹⁷ *The Decameron*, II, 589.

Regarding Pleasure, one passage in *The Decameron* might serve as a symbol for the concept of Pleasure which Boccaccio would have comfortably endorsed: that which is tempered by Reason. Here, as the group of young people are preparing to seek a retreat outside of town to escape the perils of the plague, Pampinea gives their purpose, in part, to,

> there take such diversion, such delight and such pleasure as we may, without in any way overpassing the bounds of reason.[18]

¹⁸ Ibid., I, 19.

Clearly he would not have endorsed the aim of making the pursuit of Pleasure the purpose of life. In speaking of the goal of living a long life, he observes,

> There is a great difference between enduring for a very long time to delight in pleasure, and enduring to strive ardently that we might make our fame known through a great many centuries.[19]

¹⁹ 'Against Sardanapalus and his Ilk,' in *The Fates of Illustrious Men*, 62.

Boccaccio makes the observation that Pleasure is an important component of the successful choice of a profession. One is by nature, he suggests, attracted to the profession in which he finds pleasure.

> While there is one kind of person, there are still many kinds of interests, and each person decides where he can achieve his own happiness as he wishes. For this reason a soldier chooses the wars, the lawyer the court, the farmer the fields—the examples can be infinite. The poet seeks out a solitary place and lives there. The soldier enjoys the tumult of battle, the lawyer enjoys the argumentation and litigation, the farmer the beauty and greenery of the fields, the poet the harmonious sound of verses. The first is accustomed to combat, the second to judgments, the third to the progress of the seasons, and the last to contemplation. To the soldier the final goal is victory, to the lawyer it is money, to the farmer it is harvest, and to the poet it is reputation. This arises from a great complexity of professions, though each has only one end. What pleases one person is justifiably unattractive to another.[20]

Boccaccio offers a final general warning regarding pleasure. One can never be content in pleasure, because Fortune can in a moment reverse it.

> When your mind is filled with joy and something disturbs you, remember that you have risen by the same law as others and that you too will fall into insignificance and be punished for your offenses, if it so pleases Fortune. And so you are not deceived by any kind of belief in the stability of satisfaction, fix this in your mind: Whenever anyone's situation seems to be taken for granted by everturning Fortune, then in the midst of this unfortunate credulity, she is preparing a trap.[21]

Regarding the pleasures of Love, Boccaccio joins nearly all early writers and philosophers in concluding that in the end there is more pain than pleasure resulting from the experience.

> The person who works toward virtue finds that the object of pleasure is his greatest concern. He finds that he cannot break the chain which he forged himself, and very often he is rushing to his own downfall. Woe is me![22]

20 'The Author Acquitted and Poetry Commended,' in ibid., 104ff.

21 'A Last Few Mourners and the End of the Book,' in ibid., 242.

22 'Against Women,' in ibid., 43.

Nowhere does he make this more personal than in the introduction to his *The Corbaccio*, itself an extended attack on women.[23]

> I happened, as I had often done before, to begin thinking very hard about the vicissitudes of carnal love; and pondering over many past occurrences and musing to myself about every word and deed, I concluded that through no fault of mine I had been cruelly ill-treated by her whom I had chosen in my madness as my special lady and whom I honored and revered above all others and loved far more than life itself. Since it seemed to me that I had received abuse and insult in this affair without deserving it, after many sighs and lamentations, driven by resentment, I began not merely to weep bitterly but to cry out loud. I suffered so much, first bemoaning my stupidity, then the insolent cruelty of that woman, that by adding one grief to another in my thoughts, I decided that Death must be far easier to bear than such a life.[24]

In his dedication of *Theseus* to Fiammetta, however, he seems to find, through the memory of his lover, some solace for the pain of Love.

> Although departed joys which return to my memory in my present unhappiness are the unmistakable cause of heavy sorrow, it does not on that account displease me, O cruel lady, to revive in my weary soul from time to time the charming picture of your perfect loveliness … And its effect on me is the clearest proof that what I believe is true, because when the eyes of my mind behold it, a hidden sweetness, I know not how, beguiles my tormented heart, almost making it oblivious of its unremitting pains.[25]

ON THE PHILOSOPHY OF AESTHETICS

While delight has always been given, even in the fourteenth century, as an important purpose of aesthetics, Boccaccio stresses an exception. Delight, in speaking, can often mask deception.

> Countless tragedies known in every hamlet proclaim that it was the honeyed phrase, the deceptive tongue believed too easily which brought about the downfall of the credulous, the ruin of cities, the destruction of whole regions and their inhabitants, and the subversion of kingdoms. This kind of polished speech does not bring truth

---

[23] Among other things in this work he maintains that women were born to be slaves [*The Corbaccio*, 25], in addition to this extraordinary passage:

No other creature is less clean than woman: the pig, even when he is most wallowed in mud, is not as foul as they. If perhaps someone would deny this, let him consider their childbearing … [Ibid., 24].

[24] *The Corbaccio*, 2.

[25] Boccaccio, *Theseus*, trans. Bernadette McCoy (New York: Medieval Text Association, 1974), 335.

to the credulous, but in an instant it excites them, sways them, delights them, accuses them, soothes them, and irritates them.[26]

In the writings of Boccaccio one can find a number of clues to his general philosophy of aesthetics. First, oddly enough, is a defense of style over content. At the conclusion of his *The Decameron*, Boccaccio felt compelled to answer some criticism which had been leveled at this work, specifically that he had placed topics in the mouths of aristocratic women which were not appropriate to women of that class. He says, in effect, that it is not what you say, but the style in which you say it which supplies the necessary sophistication.

> This I deny, for there is nothing so unseemly as to be forbidden to anyone if only he express it in seemly terms, as it seems to me indeed I have here very aptly done.[27]

He follows this by observing that, of course, these stories must be read 'with the rational eye of a person of understanding.'

With regard to the ancient debate regarding the ability of Art to imitate Nature, Boccaccio, speaking of the attempts of early painters to capture the beauty of Helen, doubts that any artist could capture Beauty equal to that which Nature bestows.

> For who, with brush and paint in a painting or with chisel in a statue, could describe the happiness of the eyes, the calm pleasantness of her whole face, her heavenly smile, and the various expressions of her face according to what she heard and saw, since this is the prerogative of Nature alone?[28]

The pastoral romance, *L'Ameto*, contains lyrics for several songs, one of which similarly doubts the ability of music to describe Beauty created by Nature.

> Deserving of all song, your beauty cannot be touched by my meter, which is unworthy of such a task; and yet I shall sing of it for a while.[29]

Boccaccio also recognized the role of skill in the production of aesthetic works of art. In speaking of paintings in his *Theseus*, Boccaccio complements them only by speaking of their 'consummate skill.'[30] In another place, in describing an ancient painter, Lala of Cyzicus, he seems to equate speed with native skill.

---

26 'A Warning against Credulousness,' in *The Fates of Illustrious Men*, 25.

27 *Decameron*, II, 795.

28 'Helen, wife of Menelaus,' in *Concerning Famous Women*, 73.

29 *L'Ameto*, 19.

30 *Theseus*, VII, 62.

And what is far more marvelous, writers say not only that she painted excellently, which is something done by many, but that her hands were so swift in painting that no one else's were ever their equals.³¹

[31 'Marcia, daughter of Varro,' in *Concerning Famous Women*, 144.]

For Boccaccio, the concept of skill also included the taste which leads to the polishing of that which had been produced.

> Who is so lacking in good sense that he would not prefer something artistically produced to something which is not? And this holds especially true when artistry is added to something great already. Is not the man senseless and foolish who would disapprove when someone undertakes the effort to cleanse his writing of whatever crudeness he finds there and beautifies it with graceful elegance?³²

[32 'Against the Detractors of Rhetoric,' in *The Fates of Illustrious Men*, 166.]

Boccaccio wrote much more extensively on the subject of poetry than did Petrarch. In particular, in the fourteenth and fifteenth books of his *Genealogy of the Gods*, Boccaccio presents an extensive defense of poetry. Much of this discussion, dealing with his defense of those ancient Greek poets who no longer need a defense, is not terribly useful to us today. There are some passages, however, which offer insights into Boccaccio's concepts of aesthetics, culture and education which we should like to mention here.

He begins by attempting to categorize some of the types of men who criticize poets and poetry. First, there are those 'madmen' who are simply arrogant and criticize everything in sight. Such men, Boccaccio finds, are usually uneducated in the subjects they profess to judge, thus his prescription for them:

> If they really are impelled by this desire for glory, and seek a reputation for wisdom, let them go to school, listen to teachers, pore over their books, study late, learn something, frequent the halls of brilliant debaters; and lest they rush into teaching with undue haste, let them remember the Pythagorean caveat, that no one who came to his school to speak on philosophical subjects should open his mouth until he had listened for five years. When they shall win praise in this respect, and earn genuine title, then, if they wish to come forward, let them lecture, or dispute, or refute, or inveigh, and vigorously press their opponents. But any other course is proof rather of madness than wisdom.³³

[33 *Genealogia Deorum Gentilium*, in Osgood, *Boccaccio on Poetry* XIV, 1ff.]

Another who criticizes the poet is the lawyer, who, being interested only in money, cannot understand why anyone would desire a profession where they are destined to be poor. Boccaccio answers that the poet's reward is rather in wisdom and immortality.

> I readily grant therefore their contention, that poetry does not make money, and poets have always been poor—if they can be called poor who of their own accord have scorned wealth. But I do not concede that they were fools to follow the study of poetry, since I regard them as the wisest of men …
>
> ……
>
> Furthermore, if the privilege of long life is not granted a man in any other way, poetry, at any rate, through fame vouchsafes to her followers the lasting benefit of survival—rightly enough called a benefit, since we all long for it. It is perfectly clear that the songs of poets, like the name of the composer, are almost immortal. As for lawyers, they may shine for a little while in their gorgeous apparel, but their names in most cases perish with the body.[34]

[34] Ibid., XIV, ivff.

Next, Boccaccio turns to defining the virtues of poetry, among which he points to divine inspiration, reflection, creativity and the ability to move men to action.

> This poetry, which ignorant triflers cast aside, is a sort of fervid and exquisite invention, with fervid expression, in speech or writing, of that which the mind has invented. It proceeds from the bosom of God, and few, I find, are the souls in whom this gift is born; indeed so wonderful is a gift it is that true poets have always been the rarest of men. This fervor of poesy is sublime in its effects: it impels the soul to a longing for utterance; it brings forth strange and unheard-of creations of the mind; it arranges these meditations in a fixed order, adorns the whole composition with unusual interweaving of words and thoughts; and thus it veils truth in a fair and fitting garment of fiction. Further, if in any case the invention so requires, it can arm kings, marshal them for war, launch whole fleets from their docks, nay, counterfeit sky, land, sea, adorn young maidens with flowery garlands, portray human character in its various phases, awake the idle, stimulate the dull, restrain the rash, subdue the criminal, and distinguish excellent men with their proper need of praise: these, and many other such, are the effects of poetry.[35]

[35] Ibid., XIV, viiff.

He adds to this argument, a defense of poetry as an art.

> Now since nothing proceeds from this poetic fervor, which sharpens and illumines the powers of the mind, except what is wrought out by

art, poetry is generally called an art. Indeed the word poetry has not the origin that many carelessly suppose, namely *poio, pois*, which is but Latin *fingo, fingis*; rather it is derived from a very ancient Greek word *poetes*, which means in Latin exquisite discourse (*exquisita locutio*). For the first men who, thus inspired, began to employ an exquisite style of speech, such, for example, as song in an age hitherto unpolished, to render this unheard-of discourse sonorous to their hearers, let it fall in measured periods …

He follows this defense by quoting Cicero,

> We have it on the highest and most learned authority, that while other arts are matters of science and formula and technique, poetry depends solely upon an inborn faculty, is evoked by a purely mental activity, and is infused with a strange supernal inspiration.[36]

To the attacks of those who say that poetry is mere fiction, among his answers Boccaccio makes an observation similar to that we have quoted by Petrarch and Mozart in the previous chapter: poetry has the ability to educate the listener, even if he does not know why.

> Such then is the power of fiction that it pleases the unlearned by its external appearance, and exercises the minds of the learned with its hidden truth; and thus both are edified and delighted with one and the same perusal.[37]

In another book, Boccaccio again felt obligated to answer the attacks on poetry as fiction.

> Actually I do not want people to think that poets seek out mountainous caves, shady forests, clear fountains, murmuring streams, as well as the joyful and withdrawn silence of the country … so they can better fill their stomachs and satisfy their passions. This is not true … These places have been called places of repose which were removed from all the noise of people. Often I have praised such places, and I desire them very much when they are available to me …
>
> Many ignorant persons have the opinion that the summit of poetry can be reached very easily. Although they do not have any idea what poetry is, with sour faces they claim that poets are liars, are men addicted to the use of fables, and like entertainers who make use of knowledge not their own. These people are the liars if they really believe what they say.

36 Ibid.

37 Ibid., XIV, ix.

> In reality poetry is a celebrated body of knowledge, elevated and beautiful, requiring skill. Only by the aid of poetry is it possible, within the limits of human weakness, to follow in the footsteps of the Holy Writ … If the highest type of man is a poet, then his poetry is the highest achievement.[38]

Boccaccio also sets forth some important basic aesthetic principles of poetry. First, that the highest art has no purpose.

> Artistic embellishment acquires value though it is of no practical use whatever.[39]

He follows this by pointing to the example of Nature, which embellishes birds with their colorful plumage.[40] A second aesthetic principle he gives is that poetry raises the reader's mind to 'higher feelings.'[41]

Finally, Boccaccio, like Petrarch, did not associate himself with the broad public. In his dedication of his *Concerning Famous Women*, for example, he mentions that he wrote the work 'while away from the crude multitudes.'[42] In another book, he elaborates on his general distrust of the public.

> Envy tortures, but the multitude deceives. The first drives a man to destroy others; the second destroys him by his own conceit. The one inflames the mind; the other mocks hope … No one should ever put his faith in the praises of the common people. It is in the nature of the multitude to be ever changeable and perverse, preferring always conjecture to truth, crying always for activity, then deserting in times of danger. The crowd follows where Fortune goes, serves her humbly, but rules severely. And after bestowing its gifts, it kills those unfortunates who had trusted it.[43]

[38] 'The Author Acquitted and Poetry Commended,' in *The Fates of Illustrious Men*, 105ff.

[39] *Genealogia Deorum Gentilium*, in Osgood, *Boccaccio on Poetry*, XV, i.

[40] Today, of course, we understand that Nature *has* a purpose, having to do with reproduction.

[41] Ibid.

[42] *Concerning Famous Women*, xxxiii.

[43] 'Against the Faithlessness of the Common People,' in *The Fates of Illustrious Men*, 115ff.

ON THE AESTHETICS OF MUSIC

Boccaccio seems to stress, as the first aesthetic purpose of music, that it offer solace to the listener. At the end of the fourth day, in *The Decameron*, when customarily the group listens to one of its members sing a solo song, Phylostrato, the singer, is instructed,

> It is our pleasure that, so no more days than this one be troubled with your ill fortunes, that you sing such one thereof as most pleases you.[44]

[44] *Decameron*, I, 364.

It is also most interesting that, when the song is finished, the narrator indirectly gives us another purpose of music, 'The words of this song clearly enough discovered the state of Phylostrato's mind.'

In the seventh story of the tenth day, a song intended to provide solace has quite a different effect.

> … and then sang her sundry songs, the which were fire and flame to the girl's passion, whereas he thought to solace her.[45]

45 Ibid., II, 737.

In the *Filostrato*, a kind of testimonial to medieval courtly love, a character is sent music for the specific reason of lifting his spirits.

> They immediately sent messages to their ladies that each of them should go and visit him and make entertainment for him with melodies and singers, so that he should forget his irksome life.[46]

46 Boccaccio, *Filostrato*, vii, 83, here trans. Nathaniel Griffin and Arthur Myrick (New York: Bilbo and Tannen, 1967), 469.

Finally, in the romantic epic, *Theseus*, two disappointed lovers sing for their own comfort.

> Then, when she left, they returned to their earlier madness and often composed measured verse [songs] to comfort themselves in singing of her high worth. In this way they took some delight in their misfortune.[47]

47 *Theseus*, III, 38.

Another potential purpose of music is to fuel the flames of love. In his *Amorous Fiammetta*, Boccaccio wonders who is immune to this influence of music?

> There the cool Sea banks and most pleasant gardens, and every other place besides, with divers feasts, with new devised sports, with most fine and curious dancing, with all kinds of amorous songs and [canzonets], made, played and sung by those lusty youths and sweet Nymphs, did resound forth marvelous and pleasant Echoes. Who is he therefore that can, amongst so many enticing pleasures there, keep himself free from Cupid?[48]

48 Boccaccio, *Amorous Fiammetta*, trans. Edward Hutton (Westport: Greenwood Press, 1926), 157.

There was an element of this purpose of music which Boccaccio clearly disapproved of. In describing an early Roman woman, he mentions that 'with dancing and singing, which are instruments of sensuality, she turned to wantonness.'[49]

49 'The Roman Sempronia,' in *Concerning Famous Women*, 173.

But, on the other hand, Boccaccio finds a virtue in the power of Love for encouraging the study of music for the refinement of manners. In *The Decameron*, in the first story of the fifth day, we are given of list of the accomplishments necessary to turn a young man into a gentleman. Here we find he must learn to both sing and play an instrument ('song and sound').

> Then, consorting with young men of condition and learning the fashions and carriage that befitted gentlemen and especially lovers, he first, to the utmost wonderment of everyone, in a very brief space of time, not only learned the first elements of letters, but became very eminent among the students of philosophy, and after … he not only reduced his rude and rustical manner of speech to seemliness and civility, but became a past master of song and sound and exceedingly expert and doughty in riding and martial exercises, both by land and by sea.[50]

Boccaccio also presents one example of the use of music therapy. In the seventh story of the tenth day, in *The Decameron*, one sings a song, accompanied by a viol, to a girl with the result that,

> she was so rejoiced and so content that she straightaway showed manifest signs of great improvement.[51]

The purpose of music which we would regard as most important today is to communicate feeling. We know that what the common listener responds to in music is not the music itself, which would require everyone to be educated in music to appreciate it, but the communication of feelings. Boccaccio mentions this with regard to a love song.

> Love, heed not what my voice sings, but rather how much my heart, your subject, is filled with desire.[52]

In another place, Boccaccio turns this around and writes of the power of music to recreate feelings.

> And … giving a willing ear to the skillful music, and the silver sounds of those instruments, which with passing sweet notes entered deeply into my mind, and, thinking of my Panphilus, I did at one time cover and hide, discord, feasts and grief because, listening to the pleasant noise made, every demi-dead spirit of love did regain their former vigor and force in me again: and the remembrance of those merry times did return again to my mind, in which the heavenly harmony of these instruments, touched with rare skill, was wont in presence of my Panphilus to work divers commendable and sweet effects.[53]

50 *Decameron*, I, 371.

51 Ibid., II, 740.

52 *L'Ameto*, 40.

53 *Amorous Fiammetta*, 161.

One passage suggests that Boccaccio would have agreed that aesthetic music must be inspired.

> Now let the Muse who concerns me most compose her verses through me. Let her now sing through me.[54]

As Boccaccio mentions the importance of skill in painting, quoted above, so he apparently would have recognized the importance of skill in music. In his Theseus he refers to 'songs so well written, that they would have been lovely to Calliope.'[55]

ART MUSIC

Unlike Petrarch, there is much in Boccaccio which offers clues to actual performances of music he must have heard. Sometimes he displays a knowledge of music by using it in analogy, as in his *Genealogy of the Gods*, when he mentions in passing the tuning of the harp and the variety of tones which make up an interesting melody.[56] But his works also contain numerous references to actual songs, and often with the lyrics as well, sung by various characters. In one place he even mentions the enjoyment of music by those rowing on the water.

> We ploughed the gentle waves of the calm Sea, singing sometimes, and with playing sometimes on divers Instruments, went rowing up and down.[57]

Although once Boccaccio describes a song as 'ingenious,'[58] usually such music is described as 'sweet,' the term used in ancient lyric poetry to denote the most pleasing music. In the pastoral romance, *L'Ameto*, for example, the 'sweet voice of a ringing bagpipe' played by a shepherd, 'reached [the women's] ears.'

> So, moved by the pleas of the women, Teogapen put his mouth to the pierced reed, and entreated by them, following upon the music, he began to sing.[59]

Soon after, Boccaccio gives a more complete description of this musician as he accompanies another singer.

[54] *Theseus*, VIII, 2.
[55] Ibid., XII, 72.
[56] *Genealogia Deorum Gentilium*, in Osgood, trans., *Boccaccio on Poetry* XV, x.
[57] *Amorous Fiammetta*, 182.
[58] *Theseus*, XI, 63.
[59] *L'Ameto*, 24ff.

Thus, giving full breath to the waxed pipe with swollen throat and riotous cheeks, he resolved it into sound with quick fingers which now opened and now closed the holes, making pleasant music; and with gestures he commanded that Acaten respond to Alceste, who began by singing his verses.[60]

60 Ibid., 31.

A particularly interesting reference to art music is found at the beginning of his *The Decameron*, where Boccaccio gives a detailed account of the great plague under which so much of Italy suffered in the middle of the fourteenth century. In describing the different strategies by which people tried to avoid the plague, he mentions that some shut themselves up and eating only the most delicate meats and the finest wines 'they abode with music' and other diversions. This we take to be the private performance of art music, due to the description of what must surely be popular music performed by those of an alternate lifestyle, those who 'carouse and make merry and go about singing and frolicking.'[61]

61 *Decameron*, I, 10.

Throughout ancient literature, one finds descriptions of banquets where music is heard after the eating has finished, when the tables have been cleared. We take this to be art music, often in the form of a brief 'concert,' as distinguished from the functional music played while the guests were eating. In *The Decameron*, the group of young aristocrats which people this book are often described as participating in this type of music after the evening meal. On the evening before the stories of the first day, for example, we find,

the tables being cleared away, the queen (the person in charge for the day) bade that instruments of music be brought, for all the ladies knew how to dance, as also the young men, and some of them could both play and sing excellently well. Accordingly, at her bidding, Dyoneo took a lute and Fiammetta a viol and began softly to sound a dance; whereupon the queen and the other ladies, together with the two young men … struck up a round and began to dance with slow pace a roundelay; which ended, they fell to singing amorous and merry tunes. They continued thus till it seemed to the queen time to go to sleep.[62]

A similar description is found at the end of the first day.

Supper ended, the queen called for instruments of music and bade Lauretta leap up a dance, while Emilia sang a song, to the accompaniment of Dyoneo's lute.[63]

62 Ibid., I, 25ff.

63 Ibid., I, 74. Boccaccio provides here the lyrics for this song, a ballad, the first of a number of such lyrics he provides. On the evening before the eighth day, 'they ate with mirth and delight and *afterwards* sang.' [Ibid., II, 554] and at the end of the eighth day, they again sang *after* the meal [Ibid., II, 646]. At the end of the tenth day, the company, again *after* dinner, 'fell to singing and caroling and making music' [Ibid., II, 793].

At the end of the second day, they again danced and sang, but also played instrumental works.[64]

Before the commencement of the stories of the third day, the group sang 'half a dozen canzonets' and danced *before* the meal, and again *after* the meal they 'gave themselves anew to music making and singing and dancing.'[65] At the end of the third day, again 'as soon as the tables were taken away,' Lauretta is asked to sing a song, for which Boccaccio again provides the lyrics and also an interesting aesthetic clue, 'in a somewhat plaintive style.'[66]

> No maid disconsolate
> Hath cause as I, alas!
> Who sigh for love in vain, to mourn her fate …

Some additional interesting aesthetic descriptions are found in the singing before the tales of the sixth day. Here we are told that the company sang 'goodly and pleasant' canzonets and then later four people sang 'in concert,' implying perhaps a four-part song.[67] Another clue to the style of these songs is found in the description of the singing after 'the food and tables were removed' before the tales of the seventh day. Here the company sang 'more blithely than ever.'[68]

Most of these references to art music clearly imply that people were carefully listening to the music, as opposed to hearing background music. Indeed, in these books, we have made the presence of the contemplative listener a central feature of art music. A particularly vivid portrait of such a listener is found in Boccaccio's pastoral romance, *L'Ameto*.

> … as if beside himself, he gazed fixedly at the singer. At this point her song ended, and after a long pause he gave a start—like one suddenly recalled to consciousness from a deep sleep.[69]

In this same work, a contemplative listener says he 'remained beside myself for a good time in a happiness never before known' and at the conclusion of the performance he begins by saying, 'when I returned to my senses.'[70] Yet another listener is captured by the music.

> Ameto lingered, listening to the song of the ladies, graced with a happy spirit … and feeling surrendered his ears and his heart to sweet thoughts.[71]

---

64 Ibid., I, 193.

65 Ibid., I, 197. Performing music before the meal is described again at the beginning of the fifth day (Ibid., 367).

66 Ibid., I, 283. Afterward, 'diverse other songs were sung.'

67 Ibid., II, 445.

68 Ibid., II, 488.

69 *L'Ameto*, 10.

70 Ibid., 143.

71 Ibid., 139.

Another description of the contemplative listener is found in *Theseus*, where a Venus hears 'delightful singing and every musical instrument' and is described as 'rapt out of herself'.[72] And surely the contemplative listener is implied in a comment describing the conclusion of a song sung by Dyoneo, at the end of the fifth day in *The Decameron*.

> Dyoneo, *by his silence*, showing that his song was ended …[73]

There are a number of other specific references to contemplative listeners in *The Decameron*. At the conclusion of Elissa's song, at the end of the sixth day, we are told that the listeners 'all marveled at the words.' Elissa, herself, ended her song 'with a very plaintive sigh.'[74] Similarly, for the song sung at the conclusion of the eighth day, we are told the company listened with 'attentive solicitude.'[75] Likewise, in the sixth story of the tenth day, a canzonet is sung for a king, 'who beheld and listened to them with ravishment.'[76]

In a performance of a song, for which Boccaccio provides the words, in the seventh story of the tenth day, we find the listeners enchanted, still and attentive.

> These words Minuccio forthwith set to a soft and plaintive melody, such as the matter thereof required … King Pedro being still at table, he was bidden by him to sing somewhat to his viol. Thereupon he fell to singing the aforesaid song so sweetly that all who were in the royal hall appeared enchanted, so still and attentive were they all to listen.[77]

Finally, at the end of his *The Decameron* Boccaccio correctly observes that the receptive listener is part of the chain of aesthetics, not just the material and its performance.

> Again, such as they are, these stories, like everything else, can work both harm and profit, according to the disposition of the listener.[78]

In another place, Boccaccio reflects on the mysterious way in which both music and speech draw in the listener.

> Why do we neglect eloquence, by the cultivation of which we delight our ears and at the same time gratify our intellect? So certain moderate sounds of stringed instruments bring their delights into the minds. At first they seem with their sweetness to lead the mind into

72 *Theseus*, VII, 53.

73 *Decameron*, I, 444.

74 Ibid., II, 486.
75 Ibid., II, 647.

76 Ibid., II, 732.

77 Ibid., II, 739.

78 Ibid., II, 796.

relaxation; then from all sides the sound finally collects everything into itself.

In the same way well-polished speech flows into the mind by way of the ears, and it first soothes the mind by its brilliance. Then after it has driven away all other ideas, this skill so draws its audience to it that if you observe the audience, you will see that they are transfixed and unable to move, and that they all agree with the ideas of the speaker.[79]

By way of contrast, in one of his stories Boccaccio presents a musician who cannot find the necessary inspiration, resulting in listeners who are clearly not caught up in the experience.

At the same time they lent their ears to Ameto's song; but it seemed to him as if the gods had not given him heed—for [the listeners] hindered him with pleasant quips, jeering now and then.[80]

As we have seen in the previous chapter, the spirit of the troubadours was clearly still present in fourteenth-century Italy. In the case of Boccaccio, this presents a curious problem. On one hand he left poetry which has many of the characteristics of that style. But on the other hand, there are many passages in his works, especially among his later works, which treat women, generally, in a manner no troubadour would have understood. A typical example of the latter attitude is found in his book, *Concerning Famous Women*, where he observes, 'these things cannot be accomplished without a great deal of talent, which in women is usually very scarce.'[81] In this same book, in fact, he gives a rather clear description of his view of women's place, which includes avoiding singing!

If a woman is to be considered completely chaste, it is necessary above all for her to curb her lustful and wandering eyes and confine them to the fringe of her dress. Her words must be not only respectable but brief, and she must speak only at the proper time. She must avoid idleness as a sure and deadly enemy of chastity, and she must abstain from feasting, for Venus is weak without food and wine. She must avoid singing and dancing as arrows of lasciviousness, and attend to temperance and sobriety. She must take care of her house, close her ears to shameful conversation, and avoid roaming from place to place. She must reject paint, superfluous perfumes, and ornaments. She must trample with all her strength on harmful thoughts and appetites, persist in sacred thoughts, and be vigilant.

---

79 'Against the Detractors of Rhetoric,' in *The Fates of Illustrious Men*, 167ff.

80 *L'Ameto*, 42.

81 'Irene,' in *Concerning Famous Women*, 131.

And, not to discuss the entire subject of real chastity, she must love only her husband with great affection and scorn others, unless it is to love them with brotherly love. She must not go without shame in her face and breast to her husband's embrace, even when it is for the sake of procreation.[82]

82 'Sulpicia,' in ibid., 147.

It is no surprise, then, that in the introduction to the fourth day of his *The Decameron*, he pretends that the tradition of praising women, found in the troubadour repertoire of the thirteenth century, is now no longer in fashion. 'Others, making a show of wishing to speak more maturely,' he says, 'have said that it now ill sorts with my age to [write] of women or to [try] to please them.'[83] He writes that it is good to be inspired by the [women] gods, the 'Muses on Parnassus,' whereas contemporary women, while they look like the women gods, do not match them in worth. Nevertheless, he admits that contemporary women have inspired him to write poetry in the earlier style.

83 *Decameron*, I, 287.

If they pleased me for nought else, for this they would please me; because women have ere now been to me the occasion of composing a thousand verses, whereas the Muses never were to me the occasion of making any.[84]

84 Ibid., I, 291.

In his works inspired by ancient literature, such as his romantic epic *Theseus*, women are more kindly characterized. When these women sing, we are inclined to think Boccaccio's description may reflect singing he had actually heard.

Barefoot and clad in her shift, she entertained herself by singing amorous songs ... Singing and taking her delight ... she wove her garland with many flowers, all the while lightheartedly singing charming love lyrics with her angelic voice.[85]

85 *Theseus*, III, 8 and 10.

FUNCTIONAL MUSIC

Boccaccio mentions Church music only in passing. One type is funeral music, as for example in his discussion of the plague in *The Decameron*, where Boccaccio mentions the 'funeral pomp of chants and candles.'[86] Funeral music is mentioned again in *Theseus*, where he also provides a few adjectives to describe the actual music.

86 *Decameron*, I, 13.

The kings arrived there and the mournful trumpet with its melancholy music was made ready … They ordered the trumpet played and the sad laments of the mourners … found their voice.[87]

Another passing reference to Church music is found in the first story of the seventh day of *The Decameron*, where Boccaccio mentions the 'Laudsingers of Santa Maria Novella,' an order centered in Florence. They were particularly active during Lent, when their *laude* were even set to popular melodies. In this same story there is a reference to a hymn attributed to St. Ambrose, the 'Te lucis,' sung at the end of the day to protect one from evil dreams.[88]

The most revealing of these brief references to Church music is found in the context of a discussion in the defense of Rhetoric. Again, it is only in passing that Boccaccio mentions what appears to be a criticism of chant:

> It is not becoming to reveal the spirit of our thoughts to the Creator of all things in a disorganized way, or to sing His praise in words that are not melodious.[89]

Boccaccio also makes a few passing references to the music of the theater. In his *Theseus*, Boccaccio mentions the audience of the theater 'awaiting the third blast of the Tyrrhenian sound,'[90] which is a reference to the medieval tradition of the playing of three trumpet fanfares to signal the beginning of the play. The extended fanfare in the seventeenth-century *Orfeo*, which Monteverdi specifies is to be repeated three times, is in recognition of this long tradition. In this same book, Boccaccio mentions a painting of a theater scene showing the 'joyful sound of the different musical instruments, and the likenesses of all of them.'[91]

ENTERTAINMENT MUSIC

We have mentioned above that music performed at banquets, when the eating was concluded and after the tables had been cleared, was usually Art Music. Boccaccio does, however, give us in one instance a description of music being performed while the guests were eating, thus entertainment music.

---

87 *Theseus*, X, 5.

88 *Decameron*, II, 489, 491; see also, III, 881, 882.

89 'Against the Detractors of Rhetoric,' in *The Fates of Illustrious Men*, 166.

90 *Theseus*, VIII, 1.

91 Ibid., XI, 85.

The silver trays offered abundant food and the fine gold gave delicious wines to the thirsty; indeed the royal halls were soon to be seen filled with noble youths at every table; and the many and various musical sounds often caused the glittering hall to tremble.[92]

In another book, he mentions the entertainment music of banquets of a much lower order, 'we may … hear entertainers sing their dirty songs at banquets.'[93] Needless to say, our serious Boccaccio seems not to have enjoyed such scenes.

Do you think those who spend their time at great banquets and drinking are happy? Far from it. They are weak and soft from their indolence.[94]

In *The Decameron*, at the end of the ninth day, we find *after dinner* music which appears to have been songs of an entertainment nature, described as,

perhaps a thousand canzonets, more amusing in their words than masterful in their music.[95]

On several occasions, Boccaccio mentions the general entertainment to be found in great palaces, which we have no doubt still continued in his time. In *Theseus*, he speaks of the families of ancient Athens, of whom 'nothing was heard in their houses except songs, music, and merriment,'[96] as well as a great hall of the gods, where 'there were jongleurs and minstrels with a great number of different acts.'[97]

Boccaccio also describes elaborate entertainment music performed as part of the celebration of weddings.

And after that the new Bride was come home, and the magnificent pomp used at the Tables was ended, and everyone with his passing dainty cakes and heavenly Nectar had cheered up their frolic minds, as divers brave dances, sometimes directed by the tuned voice of some cunning and singular Musician, and other some led and footed by the sound of divers sweet instruments, were begun, every place of the espousal house resounding with a general applause of mirth and joy.[98]

92 *L'Ameto*, 103.

93 *Genealogia Deorum Gentilium*, Osgood, trans., XIV, xviii.

94 'Against Riches, the Frenzy of Many,' in *The Fates of Illustrious Men*, 109ff.

95 *Decameron*, II, 698.

96 *Theseus*, VI, 8.

97 Ibid., VII, 99.

98 *Amorous Fiammetta*, 169.

It turns out, however, that our narrator was himself not in the mood for such joyous celebration.

> And it grieved me no less to see myself deprived of the occasion of making such kind of joy, and enjoying such content, than I was sorrowful for the pleasure which I lost by [not hearing the] performance of the same. But from thence applying my ears to amorous delights, songs and sundry tunes, and remembering those with myself that were passed, I sighed, and marvelous desirous to see the end of such tedious feasts, being malcontent in the meantime, and sorrowful with myself, I passed them away.[99]

Another kind of entertainment music mentioned by Boccaccio was the 'noise of Trumpets, and of other martial instruments,' played during tournaments while the riders rode toward their targets.[100]

Finally, in the writings of Boccaccio there is an occasional reference to genuine popular folk music. He mentions common people singing 'ribald songs' in *The Decameron*,[101] and, in fact, actually gives us the title of one, 'Alas! who can the ill Christian be, that stole my pot away?'[102]

99 Ibid., 168.

100 Ibid., 196.

101 *Decameron*, I, 18.

102 Ibid., I, 331. The editor of this translation notes, without source, that three versions of this song are extant from this period.

4 FOURTEENTH-CENTURY FRANCE

IT IS ONLY APPROPRIATE, in this chapter, that we focus our attention on a very special poet and musician, Guillaume de Machaut.[1] His is the name written on every blackboard following the chalk line which symbolizes the beginning of the Renaissance, in part, no doubt, because he was born on the chalk line, in 1300 (and died in 1377). But we have always to remind ourselves that no one saw a chalk line in the sky in that year and the changes in style were not so clean cut. Stylistically, in fact, Machaut straddled the line. Much of his poetry praising nobles and their ladies is entirely in the tradition of the thirteenth-century troubadour. On the other hand, he was in some ways quite different and emphasized new ideas which would come to be associated with all the ways we think of Renaissance music as being different from that of the Middle Ages. At the very heart of these new ideas was feeling. Machaut goes beyond the troubadour being inspired by the lady. He talked about the importance of his feelings being genuine and heart-felt and he was concerned about the listener to a degree we have not seen in many centuries.

Machaut was the first artist–composer, as we think of that term. He collected his music and carefully indexed it—he was thinking of posterity. 'This is the order which G. de Machaut wishes his book to have.'

Vesci l'ordenance que G. de Machau wet quil ait en son livre.[2]

We see another expression of this concern when, late in life, he sends a copy of a poem to his lover, Peronnelle. He pleas that she take good care of it, since he has no copy and would be distressed if it were lost, and were not 'in the book where I put all my things.'

As his official duties required him to travel, he became the first internationally known musician of modern Europe. We have the testimony of this from his student, Eustache Deschamps (ca. 1346–1406):

[1] Machaut was probably educated at the cathedral school at Rheims and at the University of Paris. While still a young man be became associated with an important noble, John of Luxembourg, King of Bohemia. Machaut's reputation with other nobles can be seen in the fact that when Charles v visited Rheims a few years before the coronation, he advised the aldermen of the town to meet him 'chez maistre Guillyaume de Machault.' [Guillaume de Machaut, *Oeuvres*, ed. Ernest Hoepffner (Paris: Firmin-Didot, 1908–21), I, xxv, xxxvff.]

[2] In this index, Mauchat lists separately by incipits each of his *lais*, *motes*, *balades notes*, *rondeaulz* and *virelais* in the music section and includes several hundred lyrics for ballades which have no music.

Les balades ou il n'a point de chant

> All your works are with great honor
> Received by all in many a far-off place,
> And there no one, to my knowledge,
> Speaks anything of them but praise.
> Guillaume, the great lords hold you very dear,
> And take pleasure in what you write.[3]

Machaut's name was sufficiently well-known that even a century later, the author of a fifteenth-century hunting book in Portugal praised the noise of the hounds by stating that not even Guillaume de Machaut made such beautiful concordance of melody.

> Guilherme de Machado nom fez tam fermosa concordança de melodia, nem que tam bem pareça como a fazem os cañes quando bem correm.[4]

ON THE PHYSIOLOGY OF AESTHETICS

During the Middle Ages a frequent observation by philosophers was that we share our senses with lower animals, but not intellect. From this observation it followed that the senses must be a lower animal function, while intellect must be a special gift of God. Some writers under the influence of the Church even stated that certain kinds of intelligence are implanted in us before we are born. They were right, of course, but the answer is found in Darwin and not Deuteronomy.

When the first signs of humanism appear in the late Middle Ages, especially through the efforts of the troubadours who focused on the beauty of Nature and Love, the role of the senses began to be appreciated more. It is a hallmark of the fourteenth century, and the Renaissance, that the senses are understood to have a role in the formation of intelligence itself. Thus, even that hesitant modernist, Jacques de Liège, could admit, 'What is in the intellect was in the senses beforehand.'[5] Machaut symbolizes this nicely in a passage in which he points to the contribution of the senses to speech itself, which by its very nature is rational and not sensory.

---

3 Quoted in Machaut, *Oeuvres*, I, iv.

4 Quoted in Guillaume de Machaut, *Musikalische Werke*, ed. Friedrich Ludwig (Leipzig, 1926), II, 32.

5 Jacques de Liège, 'Speculum Musicae,' quoted in F. Joseph Smith, 'Ars Nova—A Re-Definition?' in *Musica Disciplina*, XVIII (1964), 34.

I summoned up all my senses together and then forced myself to speak …

'My dear and revered lady, worthy of praise and honor, perfect in every quality heart can imagine, eyes see, ears hear, hand draw, mouth say … taste savor, touch feel, desire or will or heart sense …[6]

On the other hand, the fourteenth century remained consistent with earlier philosophers in the firm belief that of our various faculties, Reason must rule. In Machaut's 'Remede de Fortune,' for example, the character Hope contends that Reason must still rule, even over states like happiness.[7] Happiness here perhaps is meant in the context of the result of moral behavior, for in another poem Machaut defines the determination of good and bad as the chief concern of Reason.

> I agreed to Reason's counsel,
> And sweetly I importuned her
> Henceforth to keep me company
> So I might never go amiss,
> But follow all her precepts and
> Thus live in wisdom and in peace.
> Reason then responded frankly:
> 'I will do it, but I tell you,
> When you come to know me better,
> You'll know all about my power,
> And know how I'm received, and how
> Well I pay those who pay me heed;
> All goodness I receive as good:
> But treat as ill, if such it proves.
> For goodness I give my reward,
> But badness earns severe reproof
> For I am judge of everything.'[8]

Similarly, in 'The Judgment of the King of Navarre,' where Machaut, himself a character in the poem, is introduced to a number of allegorical characters, the first, Understanding, specialized in the differences between virtue and vice and between good and evil. Discretion brings the Lady to a mirror, which is held in the right hand of Reason[9] (she holds a scale in her left hand). In this mirror the Lady sees,

> How Reason justly rules
> Through fair and good and loyal precept.[10]

6 Guillaume de Machaut, *Remede de Fortune*, trans. James Wimsatt and William Kibler (Athens: The University of Georgia Press, 1988), 294.

7 Ibid., 304–306.

8 Guillaume de Machaut, *The Tale of the Alerion*, trans. Minnette Gaudet and Constance Hieatt (Toronto: University of Toronto Press, 1994), lines 4403ff.

9 This is another of numerous unconscious references in early literature to the workings of the twin hemispheres of the brain—here the correspondence of the left hemisphere (Reason) with the right hand.

10 Guillaume de Machaut, *The Judgment of the King of Navarre*, trans. Barton Palmer (New York: Garland Publishing, 1988), lines 1155ff.

More characters appear, including Temperance, Peace, Harmony, Faith (escorted by Constancy), Charity, Honesty, Prudence (who carried Wisdom in her heart), Generosity (who sees nothing) and Sufficiency. Now Machaut points out that Reason must also rule over the senses,

> For I made use of the counsel of Discretion,
> Who made my attention return
> In the proper way through Reason,
> Who is always ready at the proper moment
> To bring true hearts back to themselves,
> Those who have wandered off too far.
> Just then Reason took charge of me
> So that afterward in her keeping she had
> My heart, my senses, and my thoughts,
> And thus they could resist
> And struggle against false ideas,
> And expel the temptations
> Which thought to have the victory
> Of making me think falsely.[11]

[11] Ibid., 1343ff.

The final four lines are a reference to something which earlier philosophers, in particular Boethius, loved to point out, that our senses can misinform us. It is for this reason that Machaut specifies,

> And I should also be pleased for Reason
> To be present, she who deceives no one …[12]

[12] Ibid., 1589–1590.

Another argument for Reason runs,

> Don't you know who judges
> The right when parties argue
> Who desire a decision and await it?
> Certainly you should be well aware
> That Reason is in charge of this.[13]

[13] Ibid., 1776ff.

In Machaut's 'Le Jugement du roy de Behaigne,' a similar group of allegorical figures appear in the castle of the king of Bohemia, including Sincerity, Honor, Courtesy, Beauty, Desire, Cheerful Happiness, Bravery, Valor, Love, Loyalty, Generosity, Will, Thought, Wealth, and Youth, followed by the observation, 'and then Reason who was mistress over all.'

Et puiz Raison, qui de tous fu maistresse.[14]

In another poem, Machaut makes it clear that he agrees with earlier philosophers that Reason must in particular control the emotions. In the following passage when the lover's desire, called here Presumption, took over the lover's mind, Reason intervened.

> Presumption was indeed at work,
> Convincing me that Love had deemed
> That right away she would be mine.
> Presumption overcame my mind.
> Then Reason made it clear to me
> That it could never be quite so,
> And that my thoughts were foolish ones.[15]

Later in this same poem Machaut presents Reason's argument from the lady's perspective.

> Now it possibly can happen
> That the lady may refuse him,
> Not because she is capricious
> Or really wants him to depart,
> But for the sake of Reason, which
> Leads her to know that Abstinence,
> Seated next to Moderation,
> Will allow her liberty
> Provided that she guard herself.[16]

We are relieved when Machaut allows one allegorical character to disagree. When the debate is over love and its consequences, Loyalty stipulates, 'A lover would be a fool to listen to you, Reason.'[17] This no doubt reflects a common observation: no matter how much you want to believe that Reason rules our actions, the ordinary experience of Love proves otherwise. Nothing demonstrates this more clearly than speech. In complimenting good speech, Machaut describes it as 'moderate, well-chosen, and appropriate, based wholly on Reason.'[18] But, what happens to Reason-dominated speech when Love is present? It can, Machaut observes, force one,

> to cut short his words and interrupt them with sighs, drawn from the depths of his being, that render him mute and silent, and he has no choice but to remain speechless.

14 Guillaume de Machaut, *Le Jugement du roy de Behaigne*, trans. James Wimsatt and William Kibler (Athens: The University of Georgia Press, 1988), 160.

15 *The Tale of the Alerion*, lines 570ff.

16 Ibid., 1881ff. In 'Chanson Amoureuse 3,' in Kristen Figg, *The Short Lyric Poems of Jean Froissart* (New York: Garland Publishing, 1994), 69, Froissart recommends as the lady's guardians, not Abstinence and Moderation, but Wisdom and Fear!

17 *Le Jugement du roy de Behaigne*, 154.

18 *Remede de Fortune*, 180.

Even the lover's song is interrupted in the same way.

> But some strange heat that turned to cold surprised me and gripped my heart so suddenly that there's no way I could relate how I feel or how it stings me, for I'm hot and cold together and am sweating and shaking at the same time, and I've lost all strength, and was struck speechless in the middle of my song like a dumb beast; wherefore my laughter, my joy, and my song are ended and I must remain silent.[19]

In fact, concludes Machaut, when it comes to expressing Love, speech seems to be beside the point.

> Do you think that an esteemed, intelligent, loyal and prudent lady would care for someone who implores her love with polished, deceitful words and who, in begging her, colors his speech to play the sage?[20]

And in another poem, Machaut advises the lover that too much talk can even turn joy into lament.

> My advice will suit the task
> And properly accomplish it:
> To hold his peace and mind his task—
> For too much talk, they say, does harm.
> I say, whomever it annoys
> That he whose custom is to talk
> May find himself, to his dismay,
> Discomfited by excess talk,
> His song changed to a sad lament.[21]

Another hallmark of the Renaissance and its movement toward humanism is a new sense of recognition of the importance of secular education. We find this expressed several times in the poetry of Machaut, as for example in the 'Remede de Fortune.'

> … for he who doesn't learn in his youth regrets it in his old age, if he could have learned: for learning is a most noble endeavor.[22]

And in 'The Judgment of the King of Navarre,' he adds Happiness and Honor to the rewards of Education.

19 Ibid., 340ff.
20 Ibid., 262.
21 *The Tale of the Alerion*, lines 847ff.
22 *Remede de Fortune*, 400.

> Though Happiness by nature,
> By fortune or according to custom,
> Is evident in the deeds of chivalry,
> She appears also in learning:
> There she holds honor in her hands.[23]

[23] *The Judgment of the King of Navarre*, lines 3925ff.

From our point of view, the most interesting discussion of education by Machaut is his description of the ideal student, in particular the skills and attitudes the student must have. It is especially interesting that he observes that education must begin at an early age, before the student acquires too much experience. And when he speaks of the importance of honoring and serving one's profession, and that learning is easily forgotten if not put into practice, we cannot help but feel that some of these thoughts were with the music student in mind.

> He who wishes to learn any skill must take heed of twelve things: first, he must choose something to which his heart most leads him and for which he has a natural inclination, because a person does not willingly finish what he seeks to do contrary to his will, since Nature stands against him. He should love his master and his profession above everything; and he must honor, obey, and serve them; and he must not feel he is enslaving himself, for if he loves them, they will love him; and if he hates them, they will hate him; he can gain nothing otherwise. He must receive instruction meekly; and he must be careful to follow it, for learning is difficult to retain and easily forgotten when it is not put into practice. He should be diligent, assiduous, and eager for knowledge, for thus can he attain wisdom. And he should seek it at an early age, before his heart turns to wickedness through too much experience; for the true state of innocence is like the white and polished tablet that is ready to receive the exact image of whatever one wishes to portray or paint upon it. And it is also like wax that can be written upon, and which retains the form and imprint exactly as one has imprinted it. Truly it is the same with human understanding, which is ready to receive whatever one wishes and can apprehend whatever one sets it to: arms, love, other art [*autre art*] or letter. For there is nothing so difficult that it cannot master it if it so chooses, providing it is willing to work and toil in accordance with what I have said above.[24]

[24] *Remede de Fortune*, 168ff.

ON THE PSYCHOLOGY OF AESTHETICS

Emotions

As we have shown above, Machaut perceived that Love had the capacity to somehow interrupt the composure of Reason. Now he adds the observation that strong emotions can also interfere with the senses and cause them to behave 'irrationally.' He introduces this idea in the context of a large group of singing birds, which is important because bird song is a frequent metaphor in early literature for the most beautiful music.

> And in more than thirty thousand places the birds, wide-throated, were trying to out-sing one another, as if it were a contest, making the whole orchard ring; and it's no lie that prior to Hope's visiting me in my need, my senses had been so distorted that I'd not noticed the birds or their music, or how merry they all were. But this should not be held against me, because there are two things that falsify the senses and cause them to react irrationally: these are great joy and great sadness.[25]

Today we would say this differently, understanding as we do that we have a left brain rational side of us and a right brain non-rational side, which includes the 'great joy and great sadness' of which Machaut speaks. Since, hopefully, we have learned to give both sides equal merit, we might simply say that the emotions speak for a different side of us. Machaut, in another poem, seems to reflect this in a passage which reminds us of an old popular song, 'Your lips say No, but your eyes say Yes.'

> Thus she subjects him to reproach
> That she speaks to him with her mouth:
> Yet when she utters this aloud,
> A sweet glance says the opposite.[26]

Froissart seemed to recognize *both* sides, when he describes a lady as consisting of 'reason, sense, desire and thought.'[27] But, for Froissart as with earlier writers, it was more typical to simply point out that Reason cannot explain the emotions.

> For the actions of people in love are of such great consequence
> That they cannot be properly valued or explained.[28]

---

25 Ibid., 334.

26 *The Tale of the Alerion*, lines 371ff.

27 'Ballade 1,' in Figg, *The Short Lyric Poems of Jean Froissart*, 231.

28 'Chanson Amoureuse 2,' in ibid., 63.

Similarly,

> In looking upon her, often
> Prudence, good sense, purpose and reason fail me.[29]

And,

> On an island in the sea, far from people,
> Where no one can get in except by chance,
> My passions dwell, which makes no sense at all.[30]

29 'Ballade 13,' in ibid., 239.

30 'Rondeau 48,' in ibid., 268.

Pleasure and Pain

The medieval writers, concerned with mortal sin, wrote at length on the definitions of Pleasure and Pain. The thirteenth- and fourteenth-century writers seem more inclined to assume the definitions are self-evident and generally confine themselves to focusing on their function as opposite states. Mauchaut does this in the most vivid language. First a lady speaks of the joy of love:

> In him were my hope and my joy, my pleasure, my heart, my love, my thoughts and my desires. My heart could enjoy every good simply by seeing and hearing him. He was my every consolation; he was my every pleasure, my every solace, my joy, my treasure ...[31]

31 *Le Jugement du roy de Behaigne*, 66ff.

He then paints an equally vivid picture of the pain which can follow joy.

> Alas! Unhappy me! Now all's reversed, for my pleasures have become grief-filled toils and my joys are bitter grief; my thoughts, which once brought consolation to my heart and comforted it sweetly in its sorrows, are and will always be painful, sad, and bitter.

In 'The Judgment of the King of Navarre,' Machaut considers in more detail the contrasting natures of joy and sorrow.

> For we have a saying
> Which the good philosopher devised:
> He affirms, and I believe well what he says,
> That all illnesses whatsoever—
> And there are no exceptions—

> Are cured by their contraries.
> Now we can infer one thing and one thing alone
> From this principle
> In regard to this particular illness.
> For such sudden maladies
> Can arise from two emotional states:
> That's to say, so God guide me,
> From great sorrow or overwhelming joy.
> And as a cause joy requires
> That she be made angry and irritated,
> And sorrow asks for just the opposite:
> One should make merry
> In her presence, do whatever would please her
> And whatever she asks for,
> And also minstrels should be summoned
> To entertain her and make her laugh.[32]

32 *The Judgment of the King of Navarre*, lines 1928ff.

Machaut joins in the opinion of much ancient literature in observing that when it comes to Love, its very definition is a blending of pleasure and pain.

> Thus I felt many wounds, at one moment sweet, at another bitter, at one pleasant, at another disagreeable, at one sad, at another joyful. For the heart that feels Love's wound is not always in one mood, nor sure of joy or tribulation; rather, it is subject to the whims of the fortune of Love. But with head hung like a bear, I accepted her sweet biddings, whether for joy or for sorrow, meekly like a perfect lover, loyal in word and in deed.[33]

33 *Remede de Fortune*, 188. Machaut returns to this theme in *The Tale of the Alerion*, lines 1010ff and 1465ff.

34 Ibid., 214ff.

In another place he points out that what Love gives man is not of the nature of 'discipline, rules, order or Reason.'[34] Rather, he says, he has learned from his own *experience*, and not otherwise, that,

> the heart of a lover who loves deeply is now joyful, now mournful, now laughing, now crying, now singing, now lamenting, now happy in its plaint, now trembling, now sweating, now hot, now cold.

Froissart, in his poetry, focuses mostly on the pain of love, very much in the style of the troubadours of the previous century.

35 'Ballade 17,' in Figg, *The Short Lyric Poems of Jean Froissart*, 242. In 'Ballade 33,' Froissart maintains that only sleep relieves this pain.

> Love makes me suffer greatly,
> For I am ardently led by just such a desire
> Which I can neither part from nor enjoy
> Nor be glad of because I suffer pain.[35]

And again,

> I've pledged my whole heart with such intensity
> That I don't understand and can't get it back again.
> I've lost a great deal more than I have gained
> In pursuit of love, that I can clearly see.[36]

In all fairness, Froissart found this pain equally present for the lady as for the lover.

> Well, Cupid, how you have made me suffer,
> Since the day when Venus first assailed me!
>
> ……
>
> Helen endured many pains for Paris,
> And for Tristan Isolde suffered much woe.[37]

In the end, however, Froissart thought the pain was worth it!

> Even if he must not yet enjoy mercy,
> Yet he considers his pain worthwhile.[38]

Similarly, the young poet, Jehan de Lescurel, concluded that if one must die for love, at least it is a pleasant death!

> Mourir ne puis plus doucement.[39]

Machaut took the presence of pain in love a little more philosophically. This, he observed, is what 'Fortune' deals out with respect to Love, and that the lover has no choice but to learn to accept it.

> If pain or suffering were to come to me from loving, or melancholy or sadness, I should welcome it submissively and not consider myself aggrieved.[40]

And in another place,

> … the suffering that Love and Desire caused me, who gave me many a painful blow for which I don't lament or complain, since I feel no pain or suffering, but receive them meekly, simply, and joyfully.[41]

---

36 'Rondeaux 7,' in ibid., 263.

37 'Ballade 9,' in ibid., 236–237.

38 'Chanson Amoureuse 2,' in ibid., 63.

39 Jehan de Lescurel, 'Amour, voulés vous acorder,' in Nigel Wilkins, *One Hundred Ballades, Rondeaux and Virelais* (Cambridge: University Press, 1969), 13. Unfortunately for this poet, a wealthy student cleric at Notre Dame, it was not a pleasant death: he was hanged for rape in 1304.

40 *Remede de Fortune*, 176.

41 Ibid., 182.

ON THE PHILOSOPHY OF AESTHETICS

Aside from music there is little reference among the fourteenth-century French writers regarding the influence on man by the aesthetic ideas in Art. This awareness must have been present, however, and is perhaps reflected in Froissart's comment, 'Whoever lacks what delights him, he has nothing.'[42]

When Machaut mentions Beauty, as a general aesthetic concept, it is often inseparable from what we might call aristocratic taste. Thus, when a knight describes the beauty of his lover, he includes her ability to dance gracefully and sing prettily.[43] It follows, that one can profit from Beauty, 'if one can imitate it well.'[44] With regard to dress, Machaut returns to the 'Golden Mean' of the ancient Greeks in saying, one should dress well, but not extravagantly, rather 'the best thing to do is to attain the happy mean.'[45]

Perhaps, as in the case with love, Machaut felt that words could not describe the highest form of Beauty. He says of a lady, 'her beauty surpassed all comprehension.'

> Si c'on ne puet sa grant beauté comprendre.[46]

Machaut was also familiar with the ancient Greek's discussion of art imitating Nature. Thus it was the highest compliment when Machaut has a knight describe the beauty of his lover by saying she 'was in perfect accord with Nature.'[47]

ON THE AESTHETICS OF MUSIC

Fourteenth-century writers speak of a much broader range of purposes of music, which is in itself another reflection of the new sense of humanism. Nothing is more characteristic of fourteenth-century thought than a new emphasis on the importance of feeling in music, therefore it is no surprise to find, as a purpose of music, the very modern idea that music can express what nothing else can.

> So I decided that I would compose, according to my feelings towards you and in praise of you, a lai, a *complainte*, or original song; for I did not dare or know how to tell you otherwise how I felt, and it seemed to be better to tell in my new song what was oppressing and wringing my heart than to try by some other method.[48]

---

42 'Ballade 3,' in Figg, *The Short Lyric Poems of Jean Froissart*, 233.

43 *Le Jugement du roy de Behaigne*, 74.

44 *Remede de Fortune*, 186.

45 Ibid., 184.

46 *Le Jugement du roy de Behaigne*, 122.

47 Ibid., 78.

48 *Remede de Fortune*, 368. The lover is recalling why he wrote the first song in this poem.

For the composer of art music, this feeling is inseparable from the inspiration to compose. Thus Machaut confides, 'you alone who inspired my song, rhyme, and joyful subject.'[49] Similarly when Machaut is 'on trial' in 'The Judgment of the King of Navarre,' for his writings against women, the Lady says of his poetry,

> You know if you did good therein or wrong,
> Since you put your heart into them.[50]

And where such feelings are genuine, Music becomes a form of Truth, Truth, moreover, which cannot be hidden.

> And if it please you, my dear lady, to consider the last little song I sang, of which I composed both words and music, you can easily tell whether I'm lying or speaking the truth.[51]

This is a very fundamental aesthetic principle, for in general the right hemisphere, which contains our feelings and all of music (except for notation, which we do not regard as music), cannot lie, in the normal sense of the word—because it cannot write or speak. The left hemisphere, the intellectual, speaking and writing side of us, as everyone knows can, and does, lie!

> Indeed my replies were very far from what I was thinking, for I constantly made white black.[52]

Machaut returns to this idea in 'The Judgment of the King of Navarre,'

> The words you've uttered here
> Are nothing but frivolity.
> They are pretty to mouth in private,
> But they contain no substance.[53]

Machaut also mentions one of the most traditional purposes of music, to express joy:

> and for the joy I felt I composed this rondelet as I went along.[54]

Similarly,

> So I went along singing and so happy in my song …[55]

49 Ibid., 376.

50 *The Judgment of the King of Navarre*, lines 875–876.

51 *Remede de Fortune*, 374.

52 Ibid., 386.

53 *The Judgment of the King of Navarre*, lines 3988ff.

54 *Remede de Fortune*, 398.

55 Ibid., 338.

This, and the closely related purpose, to solace the listener, were obviously the most important purposes of music for Machaut. In the Prologue to his collected works which he made at the end of his life, Machaut dwells on this at length. First, he promises the allegorical figure of Love not to write anything sad or difficult to understand, but only pleasant and sweet works which will soften and nourish hardened hearts.[56] He says he can bear witness to this from his own experience, for when he is in this joyous state, his only thought is the making of an appropriate poem or song.[57] Even if his subject is sad, the poet's manner must be gay, for a heart full of sadness cannot sing gaily. The melancholy man, on the other hand, is to be censured, nor could he possibly create anything so prettily. The very nature of Music, says Machaut, requires the artist-lover to be joyful.[58] 'Music is a science which asks that one laugh, and sing, and dance. It does not care for melancholy, nor for the man who is melancholy.'

> Et Musique est une science
> qui vuet qu'on rie et chante et dance.
> Cure n'a de merencolie
> Ne d'homme qui merencolie.[59]

Again, in 'The Tale of the Alerion,' Machaut observes that 'melancholy is a condition of no value.'[60]

'Wherever Music is, she makes men rejoice.' In the closing section of the Prologue, Machaut says this is his mission: music and poetry are meant to enlighten and soothe troubled mankind, as one can see in the example of David and his harp and Orpheus. We find the same philosophy mentioned in a letter to his lover, Peronnelle, where Machaut tells her, 'Singing is born of a cheerful heart, and tears come from sadness.' And in the 'Remede de Fortune,'

> I'll sing you a balladelle in my limpid voice, with new words and music, which you'll carry off with you, singing it to cheer up your heart as you go along, if it's troubled by any concern.[61]

In only one place, does Machaut admit that music fails to solace. Although he is speaking of the music of birds, he echoes the thirteenth-century troubadours who often voiced the thought that even music cannot cheer the sad lover.

---

56 Prologue, IV, 21ff.

57 Ibid., IV, 36ff.

58 Froissart, in 'Rondeau 97,' in Figg, *The Short Lyric Poems of Jean Froissart*, 276, says singing birds must also be joyful.

> Why do people find the song of the bird
> Called nightingale to be so full of grace?
> Because it is happy and it is amorous.

59 Ibid., IV, 85ff.

60 *The Tale of the Alerion*, lines 3764.

61 *Remede de Fortune*, 326.

I went there this morning to listen to their beautiful service and their merry singing, although my heart, which nothing can console, could take little pleasure in them.⁶²

62 *Le Jugement du roy de Behaigne*, 136.

Froissart goes beyond solace, attributing to music the virtue of renewing the spirit.

By what sights and sounds
My spirit is renewed.⁶³

63 'Ballade 34,' in ibid., 248.

Machaut's student, Eustache Deschamps, speaks of the purpose of music renewing the spirit in terms of the poor tired scholar!

Music is the final, and the medicinal science of the seven [liberal] arts; for when the heart and spirit of those applied to the other arts … are wearied and vexed with their labors, Music, by the sweetness of her science and the melodiousness of her voice, sings them her delectable and pleasant melodies with her six notes in thirds, fifths, and octaves. These she performs sometimes with *orgues* and *chalumeaux* by blowing with the mouth and touching with the fingers; otherwise with the *harpe, rebebe, vielle, douçaine*, with the noise of *tabours*, with *fleuthes*, and other musical instruments, so much so that by her delectable melody the hearts and minds of those who were fatigued, weighed down, and troubled with the said arts by thought, imagination or labor are revived and restored. Thus they are afterwards more able to study and labor with the other six arts.⁶⁴

64 Eustache Deschamps, 'L'Art de Dictier,' quoted in Christopher Page, 'Machaut's "Pupil" Deschamps on the Performance of Music,' *Early Music* 5 (1977): 488ff.

Finally, Deschamps offers as additional purposes of music several practical considerations of an economic and social nature.

Learning to play the recorder well is the path to better profits, money, clothes, heritage, friends, and access to the Prince, who is always happy to hear the recorder well played.⁶⁵

65 Eustache Deschamps, 'Du metier profitable,' in Hoepffner, ed., *Oeuvres complètes*, 6:128.

On Composition

In the writings of Machaut we find the first composer of the Christian Era who speaks at length of his compositional process. The entire discussion is, at the same time, a statement of his personal philosophy with regard to the aesthetics of music.

In his famous Prologue, Machaut first meets the allegorical figure of Nature. Here he is not only associating his art with Nature in the Greek sense, but he is making the point that Nature supplied his inspiration.

> I, Nature, by whom all things take form,
> All that there is above and on earth and in the sea,
> Have come to you, Guillaume, a man I have formed
> For my part, in order for you to create
> Some new and pleasant love poems.[66]

With regard to inspiration, in Machaut's *Voir Dit*, his 'true story,' he speaks of this subject in several of his letters to his lover, Peronnelle. He tells her his work is often interrupted by the demands of his noble patrons, but more important if he does not hear from her, he stops working for lack of inspiration.[67] But if he is inspired he says he can write one hundred lines a day.[68]

But composition requires more than inspiration, it also requires skill. Therefore Nature loans Machaut her three children, Reason [*sense*], who will make him clever; Rhetoric, who will instruct him in meter and rhyme; and Music, which will give him many, various and pleasing songs.[69]

'Thus,' Nature says, 'you cannot fail at all.'[70] Here, in part, is a reference to having skill sufficient for 'correctness,' clearly another virtue of aesthetics in music. Nature promises, 'your works will be more renowned that those of any other because there will be nothing in them to criticize, and thus they will be loved by everyone.'[71] We can see how important the aspect of his technique was to Machaut in a remark he makes in 'The Remede de Fortune' regarding a poet and his work.

> I dared not refuse her, but rather read it from beginning to end, with trembling heart and bowed head, fearing there might be some mistake, since I had composed it.[72]

Before leaving the subject of Nature, we should mention that Machaut attributes the power of music in part to the fact that all musical instruments are formed according to her laws, and her works are more perfectly proportioned than any others.

> Tous ses fais plus a point mesure
> Que ne fait nulle autre measure.[73]

66 Prologue, I, 1ff.

67 Quoted in Sylvie Bazin-Tacchella, *Le Livre du Voir-Dit de Guillaume de Machaut* (Paris: Société des bibliophiles français, 1875), 262 and 342.

68 Ibid., 202.

69 Prologue., I, 10ff.

70 Ibid., I, 17.

71 Ibid., I, 19ff.

72 *Remede de Fortune*, 206.

73 Prologue, I, 99ff.

But in addition to inspiration and skill, experience is also necessary to art. This is provided to Machaut by another allegorical figure, Love, who offers her three children, Sweet Thought, Pleasure, and Hope. It should also not escape our attention that Love (experience) is not introduced to Machaut by Nature (skill), but rather she comes independently. Love promises that from her children 'you can derive great assistance, and this will help you invent and compose many a pretty poem about them.'[74] Machaut responds that Love and her children have 'greatly clarified for me the themes I have to treat.'[75]

Thus it is with the combination of skill and experience that Machaut is promised the necessary ability to compose 'tales and songs, double hoquets, pleasant lais, motets, rondeaux and virelais, complaints, ballades, in honor and praise of all ladies.'[76]

But there is another requirement for composition which was clearly of the greatest importance to Machaut. The composer's work must come from the most genuine, heart-felt feelings. In a letter to Peronnelle, he explains, 'There is nothing so just and true as experience ... He who does not create out of real feeling, counterfeits his words and songs.'

> Qui de sentement ne fait, Son dit et son chant contrefait.[77]

Machaut returns to this stipulation again in his poem 'Remede de Fortune.'

> And since I was not always in one mood, I learned to compose chansons and lais, ballades, rondeaux, virelais, and songs, according to my feelings, about love and nothing else; because he who does not compose according to his feelings falsifies his work and his song.[78]
>
> [Et pour ce que n'estoie mie
> Tousdis en un point, m'estudie
> Mis en faire chansons et lays,
> Baladez, rondeaus, virelays,
> Et chans, selonc mon sentement,
> Amoureus et non autrement;
> Car qui de sentement ne fait,
> Son oeuvre et son chant contrefait.]

The character in this same poem now composes a song to express his feelings [*fait un lay de son sentement*]. Among the words for

74 Ibid., III, 17ff.
75 Ibid., IV, 13ff.

76 Ibid., II, 12ff.

77 *Le Livre du Voir-Dit*, 61.

78 *Remede de Fortune*, 188.

this song, one finds Machaut once more stressing the acceptance of varied emotions of Love.

> And if I experience any sorrow
> from Desire, I don't complain,
> for her sweet laughing eye
> completely soothes
> the sorrow born of Desire.[79]

[79] Ibid., 196.

At the end of the song, Machaut once again returns to feeling.

> But I composed it to her praise in accord with the skill I possessed, and as near to my feelings as I well could.[80]

[80] Ibid., 206.

We gain some insight into what 'feeling' meant to Machaut in the following passage. While the thirteenth-century troubadour also mentioned the pain of love, one does not find in that literature the emphasis on the feelings themselves that we read here—it is a distinction of the Renaissance.

> Then, like one accustomed to sighing, I uttered a lament and sigh from the depths of my heart, accompanied by weeping and washed in tears; and with great effort I turned toward her my flushed, pale, sad, sorrowful, and weeping face, full of suffering. But I said nothing to her because I was unable to speak; instead, I gazed fixedly at her.[81]

[81] Ibid., 254.

A similar thought is expressed by Froissart.

> Pleasure sets him on fire so forcefully
> And true love has such power over him
> That, when he wishes to express his feelings,
> He cannot move his mouth or bring forth words.[82]

[82] 'Chanson Royale,' in Figg, *The Short Lyric Poems of Jean Froissart*, 211.

Finally, in another letter to Peronnelle, Machaut reveals one more important vital characteristic of the good composer—one must always double-check one's work!

> My sweetheart, I have composed the rondel which contains your name and I would have sent it by this messenger; but by my soul, I have never listened to it and I am not accustomed to sending off anything I compose before I have listened to it.[83]

[83] *Le Livre du Voir-Dit*, 258.

Comments of the Theorists on Aesthetics in Music

By the fourteenth century, the university had replaced the Church as the center for debate on the principles of music and foremost among the universities in this regard was the University of Paris. Here the study of music remained under its medieval Scholastic definition as a branch of mathematics and was a required course for all students of the arts faculty.[84] French theorists of the fourteenth century continued to divide music into *musica theoretica* and *musica practica*, although the former clearly dominates their treatises.[85] One encounters these terms everywhere, and perhaps they had passed into the common language, as we can see in Machaut, where, with respect to a lover's ability to heal his pain, he notes that she was 'like one who knew all the theory and practice needed to heal me.'[86]

We call these *music* treatises, but they were written by mathematicians. On the subject of aesthetics, therefore, one has to be disappointed that they made so few comments on what is the most important subject from our perspective today, the stylistic distinctions in *musica practica* between the *ars antiqua* and the *ars nova*.

The most famous representative of the *ars antiqua* in Paris was Jacques de Liège, who wrote his *Speculum Musicae* in about 1313. In this treatise, of which the first five of seven books are concerned with mathematics, we have a man crying out for the respect which he feels is due the older practice.

> Now in our day have come new and more recent authors, writing on mensurable music, little revering their ancestors, the ancient doctors; nay, rather changing their sound doctrine in many respects, corrupting, reproving, annulling it, they protest against it in word and deed …
>
> ……
>
> Should the men who composed and used these [older] sorts of music, or those who know and use them, be called rude, idiotic, and ignorant of the art of singing?
>
> ……
>
> I do not deny that the moderns have composed much good and beautiful music, but this is no reason why the ancients should be maligned and banished from the fellowship of singers.[87]

---

84 Carpenter, *Music in the Medieval and Renaissance Universities*, 54, 68.

85 Although the labels have changed, this distinction exists in all its prejudice today. F. Joseph Smith in 'Ars Nova—a Re-Definition?' makes the kind of absurd, let alone misinformed, remark characteristic of some educators today who think of music as only a cerebral affair, and not a performance reality.

> It is only in relatively recent times that instrumentalists have come to be called musicians. But then it is only in relatively recent times that we have come to realize that one can think with his fingers as well as his head.

It reminds us of a remark once made by a University of California professor: The study of the clarinet is to the study of Music, as the study of typing is to the study of English Literature!

86 *Remede de Fortune*, 256.

87 Quoted in Oliver Strunk, *Source Readings in Music History* (New York: Norton, 1950), 181, 185, 189.

Aside from some specific objections to changing the old rules of notation, de Liège unfortunately does not describe in aesthetic detail the new music. His choice of words to describe the new style is very interesting:

> What profit can there be in adding to a sound old doctrine a wanton and curious new one.
>
> ......
>
> To some, perhaps, the modern art will seem more perfect than the ancient, because it seems subtler and more difficult: subtler, because it reaches out further and makes many additions to the old art.[88]

'Wanton, curious, subtle,' what is he talking about? Everything he finds offensive, we find good, positive steps forward. When we hear a Church work by Machaut, it sounds to us more expressive, more genuine and certainly more pleasing because the interval of the third is beginning to sneak in the back door, unnoticed as yet by the doctors of the university. We also have to remember that for several hundred years popular music had advanced far ahead of Church music, with respect to modern sounding melodies and rhythms. It's no wonder one Church prelate said, 'Why does the devil have all the good melodies?' To de Liège, then, a Church work by Machaut may have simply sounded like popular music. We would guess this is what he means by 'wanton.'

One also has to remember that de Liège was carrying a lot of heavy Scholastic baggage. For him music was not just an aesthetic experience, music was an expression of Reason, a cornerstone in a Church structure carefully constructed on order, mathematics and other tangible earthly manifestations of God. He was being asked to give all this up for the pleasure of the senses.

> There must be a place for what accords with Reason and with Art, since this lives by Art and Reason in every man. Reason follows the law of nature which God has implanted in rational creatures.[89]

A perfect example of his worry was the tendency of much of the new music to move away from perfections, constructing music on the principle of three, after the trinity, etc., a concept arrived at solely by Reason.

[88] Strunk, *Source Readings in Music History*, 181, 183.

[89] Ibid., 182.

> Should the ancients be called rude for using perfections, the moderns subtle for using imperfections?
>
> ……
>
> The art of singing of the moderns seems to compare with the ancient art as a lady with a bondswoman or a housemaid, for now the new art seems to be mistress, the old art to serve; the new art reigns, the ancient is exiled. But it is contrary to Reason and the art which uses perfections should be reduced to subjection and the art which uses imperfections should dominate, since the master should be more perfect than the slave.[90]

Therefore, he says, let us return to Reason, 'let the well reasoned art [*refloreat rationabilis ars*] of the ancients flower forth again.'[91]

From his various comments and protests, we can deduce a few principles of aesthetics in music. First, a valid purpose in music is for the delight of the listener, and he admits of the new music that he has delighted in their 'song, singers, music, and musicians.'[92]

Second, economy of means was important to de Liège and he criticized the new music that it accomplished 'by many means what can be conveniently accomplished by few.'[93]

Third, art must be judged on moral grounds.

> For though art is said to be concerned with what is difficult, it is nevertheless concerned with what is good and useful, since it is a virtue perfecting the soul through the medium of the intellect.[94]

From this it follows that the value of art is in its influence on the character of man.

> For, if I may say so, the old art seems more perfect, more rational, more seemly, freer, simpler, and plainer. Music was originally discreet, seemly, simple, masculine, and of good morals; have not the moderns rendered it lascivious beyond measure? For this reason they have offended and are offending many judicious persons skilled also in music as Thales the Milesian offended the Spartans and Laconians.[95]

Next, reaching back to a basic tenet of Church music maintained by most of the early Church fathers, de Liège reaffirms the principle that in Church music it is the *words* which are most important.

> Wherein does this studied lasciviousness in singing so greatly please, by which, as some think, the words are lost, the harmony of conso-

90 Ibid., 184ff, 186ff.

91 Ibid., 189.

92 Ibid., 182.

93 Ibid., 181.

94 Ibid., 184.

95 Ibid., 189.

nances is diminished, the value of the notes is changed, perfection is brought low, imperfection is exalted, and measure is confounded?

In a great company of judicious men, when motets in the modern manner were being sung, I observed that the question was asked, what language such singers were using, whether Hebrew, Greek, Latin, or some other, because it could not be made out what they were saying.[96]

And de Liège observes, 'consonance pleases; dissonance displeases.'[97]

Finally, there was a part of de Liège which was more modern than he consciously realized. Music, he says, is properly called *Musica sonora*, a subdivision of *musica divina*. Further,

> Instrumental music is also called *sonora* because it has to do with sound, which furnishes the material of sensible musical consonances and is expressed by both artificial and natural instruments.[98]

He goes on to point out that he believed Aristoxenus was wrong in stressing the senses too much and that Ptolemy was correct in saying we should judge by both Reason and the senses.[99] In other words, some part of de Liège was listening to music in a new way, to its performance as sound (*sonora*) and no longer as a rational, mathematical concept.

He also reveals a modern tendency when he admits,

> I think in all fairness that the modern musical instruments are by far more perfect [*perfecciores*] than those that were used in the past when simple and modest music was the rule. I also think that modern singers and performers are much better than former ones.[100]

Another who represented the old view, of course, was Pope John XXII, who, in 1324–1325, issued an attack against the *ars nova* in his bull, 'Docta Sanctorum.' Aside from his reference to the thirteenth-century Motet, which had become so great an embarrassment to the Church with its hidden bawdy songs in French hidden in the upper voices, we find his strongest concerns here are the faster moving note values (probably he was hearing improvisation), the movement away from the old Church Modes, his recognition of hearing more emotions in performance, including some form of movement by the singers and generally abandoning the duty to soothe the worshiper. It is also particularly interesting that he approved some limited improvisation above the chant.

---

96   Ibid., 189ff.

97   Quoted in Smith, 'Ars Nova—A Re-Definition?,' 24.

98   Ibid., 23, 25.

99   Ibid., 35.

100   Walter Grossmann, *Die einleitenden Kapitel des 'Speculum Musicae'*, (Leipzig, 1924), 91.

Certain disciples of the new school, much concerned with measured rhythms, write in new notes, preferring to devise methods of their own rather than to continue singing in the old way. The music therefore of the divine offices is now performed with semibreves and minims, and with these notes of small value every composition is pestered. Moreover, they truncate the melodies with hoquets, they lubricate them with counterpoints [*discantibus*], and sometimes they even stuff them with upper parts [*triplis et motetis*] made out of secular songs. So that often they must be losing sight of the fundamental sources of our melodies in the Antiphoner and Gradual, and may thus forget what that is upon which their superstructure is raised. They may become entirely ignorant concerning the ecclesiastical Tones, which they already no longer distinguish, and the limits of which they even confound, since, in the multitude of their notes, the modest risings and temperate descents of the plainsong, by which the scales themselves are to be known one from another, must be entirely obscured. Their voices are incessantly running to and fro, intoxicating the ear, not soothing it, while the men themselves endeavor to convey by their gestures the sentiment of the music which they utter. As a consequence of all this, devotion, the true end of worship, is little thought of, and wantonness, which ought to be eschewed, increases. Thus, it was not without good reason that Boethius said: 'A person who is intrinsically sensuous will delight in hearing these indecent melodies, and one who listens to them frequently will be weakened thereby and lose his virility of soul.'

This state of things, hitherto the common one, we and our brethren have regarded as standing in need of correction; and we now hasten therefore to banish those methods, nay rather to cast them entirely away, and to put them to flight more effectually than heretofore, far from the house of God. Wherefore, having taken counsel with our brethren, we straightly command that no one henceforward shall think himself at liberty to attempt those methods, or methods like them, in the aforesaid Offices, and especially in the canonical Hours, or in the solemn celebrations of the Mass.

And if any be disobedient, let him, on the authority of this Canon, be punished by a suspension from office of eight days; either by the Ordinary of the diocese in which the forbidden things are done or by his deputies in places not exempt from episcopal authority, or, in places which are exempt, by such of their offices as are usually considered responsible for the correction of irregularities and excesses, and such like matters.

Yet, for all this, it is not our intention to forbid, occasionally—and especially upon feast days or in the solemn celebrations of the Mass and in the aforesaid divine offices—the use of some consonances, for example the octave, fifth, and fourth, which heighten the beauty of the melody; such intervals therefore may be sung above the simple ecclesiastical Chant, yet so that the integrity of the Chant itself may remain intact, and that nothing in the authoritative music be changed. Used in such sort the consonances would much more than by any other method both soothe the hearer and arouse his devotion, and also would not destroy religious feeling in the minds of the singers.[101]

101 Quoted in H.E. Wooldridge, *The Oxford History of Music*, 2nd edition (London: Oxford University Press, 1929), 294ff.

The first two theorists who are identified with the *ars nova* have again written treatises on notation, from the perspective of mathematics, and offer very little in the way of their views on aesthetics. To us, these two treatises, in spite of the reputation they have been given by modern musicology, seem very old-fashioned in their thought processes. Perhaps this is best explained by simply supposing that then, as now, the theorists were far behind actual music practice.

Philippe de Vitry's treatise, *Ars Nova*, is particularly disappointing with regard to performance practice. It is certainly a very dated viewpoint, when he defines music as 'the knowledge of accurate singing, or an easy means of achieving perfection in singing.'[102] The only real indication that he is thinking of more contemporary music practice (leaving notation aside) is his comment on *musica ficta*. While earlier Church fathers were very hesitant regarding any changes in the music of the Church, de Vitry seems to be using his ear.

102 Philippe de Vitry, 'Ars Nova,' trans. Leon Plantinga in *Journal of Music Theory* 5 (1961), 211.

> Clearly, the question arises of what occasions the necessity in regular music of musica falsa, or of false mutation, when nothing governed by rule ought to accept that which is false, but rather the true. To this it is to be answered that false mutation or musica falsa is not useless; indeed it is necessary in order that good sounds may be achieved, and bad ones avoided.[103]

103 Ibid., 212.

Similarly, Jean de Muris's (ca. 1290–1350) treatise, *Ars nove musice*, although it soon replaced Boethius as the standard university text, is again basically a treatise in the old Scholastic mathematical style. It is the old mathematical basis of music, as part of the Liberal Arts, which enables de Muris to say, 'no [other] science is hidden from him who knows music well.'[104]

He seems particularly old-fashioned in his condemnation of the new musical practice as abandoning the foundation of perfection.[105]

104 Strunk, *Source Readings in Music History*, 179.

105 Ibid., 173.

> All music, especially mensurable music, is founded in perfection, combining in itself number and sound. The number, moreover, which musicians consider perfect in music is … the ternary number. Music, then, takes its origin from the ternary number.[106]

106 Ibid., 174.

As his rational support of this, he offers an extensive list of 'proofs,' including not only the Trinity, but the three aspects of time of celestial bodies, the three attributes of the stars and sun, the three attributes of the elements, the three intellectual operations, the three terms in the syllogism and many more.[107]

107 Ibid., 173.

In discussing what shapes the notes should be, de Muris again looks to the past, observing, 'the wiser ancients long ago agreed and conceded that geometrical figures should be the symbols of musical sounds.'[108] This he follows with an extraordinary omission, which, had he filled it, would be worth more to us than the rest of his entire treatise.

108 Ibid., 175.

> For reasons which we shall pass over, their symbols did not adequately represent what they sang.

Eustache Deschamps, being a musician–poet like his teacher, Machaut, in his treatise *L'Art de Dictier*, goes back to the lyric poets of ancient Greece for his definition of music. Music, he says, consists of *musique artificiele*, by which we mean music, and *musique naturele*, by which he means poetry. He finds these two so closely related as to be nearly inseparable.[109]

109 His views on the influences of music on man, we have quoted above.

> It must be understood that we have two kinds of music: one is *artificial* and the other is *natural*.
> *Artificial* music is … called *artificial* as an art for by its six notes, which are called *us, ré, my, fa, sol, la*, one may teach the most uncultivated man in the world to sing, make harmony and an octave, fifth and third, make a tenor, and descant by the form of notes, by clefs and by staves. Or at least one may do so much, supposing now he did not have a voice suitable for singing or making harmony well, that he would know and be able to recognize accords and discords with all the art of this science by which, and by the notes mentioned above, one tunes and gives diverse sound to steels, irons, woods and metals, by various additives of tin, lead, bronze, and copper, as may be evident in the sounds of bells enclosed in various clocks. These, by the touch of hammers, give harmonious sounds according to the said six notes, uttering sequences and other things of the melodies of Holy Church. This harmony may be heard on other musical instru-

ments such as *rebebes*, *guiternes*, *vielles*, and *psalterions* by the variety of their size, the nature of the strings and the action of the fingers. Also on *fleutes* and on similar loud instruments, with the breath that is introduced into them.

Also these two musics [music and poetry] are so consonant with one another that each may well be called 'music,' as much for the sweetness of both the melody and of the words which are all pronounced and articulated by the pleasantness of the voice and the opening of the mouth. It is with these two as a marriage, that is, a conjunction of science, through the melodies which are more ennobled and are more seemly with the words and the fluency of the texts than they would be alone. Similarly, poems are made more delightful and embellished by the melody and the tenors, trebles and contratenors of music. However, each of these two [music and poetry] is pleasant to hear by itself. One may be sung with the voice in an artistic way without the words; also the texts of chansons may often be recited in many places where they are very willingly heard, and where their music would not always be appropriate as among lords and ladies remaining in private, where poetry may be recited by a single person, or where some book of these pleasant thing may be read before one who is ill. There are other similar cases where music would have no place because of its loudness, and because of the three voices for the tenors and contratenors that are necessary to perform the said music perfectly with two or three people.[110]

110 Quoted in Christopher Page, 'Machaut's "Pupil" Deschamps on the Performance of Music,' 489. Page devotes a substantial portion of his article to discussing the enigmatic final sentence.

ART MUSIC

In all early literature the most conspicuous hallmark of art music, as compared to functional or entertainment music, is the presence of the contemplative listener, one who is actively listening to the music. When one considers how strongly Machaut emphasizes the importance of genuine, deeply felt feelings on the part of the composer, it is no surprise that we find him concentrating on the receiving end of those feelings—the listener—to a degree that is almost entirely missing in Medieval literature. Nowhere in Medieval literature do we find a composer so fervently interested in the reaction of the listener as we do in Machaut's 'Remede de Fortune.'

> How do you like it? What do you say? … What do you think of my song? … What do you say? … Won't you tell me if I sing well or poorly?[111]

111 *Remede de Fortune*, 280.

Later in this same poem a listener is described.

> When she had finished her ballade, which was very pleasant and agreeable to my ears and in my heart, since I'd never before heard such sweet harmony, I was overjoyed. But if the sweet music pleased me, the words brought me more joy than anyone could conceive. So I made a great effort to learn it, and memorized it so quickly that before she'd left the place or had even finished singing it, I knew both the words and the music.[112]

Machaut's 'Le Jugement du roy de Behaigne' begins with an allusion to the 'sweet' singing of birds, a topic found in so much literature in the thirteenth and fourteenth centuries, but here the observer not only really seems to be listening to one, but takes pleasure as a listener.

> I dropped gently to the ground and hid myself as best I could beneath the trees, so it could not see me there, to listen to the very sweet melody of its delightful song. And I took more pleasure in listening to its sweet singing that ever I could tell.[113]

Since contemplative *listening* to the music is one of the essential aspects of what we mean by 'concert' music, we have often pointed out in these pages that the brief concert *after* the dinner, as opposed to dinner music, is one of the earliest forms of concerts in the modern use of the word. And there is no reason to doubt that these nobles were informed listeners. Christine de Pisan wrote of the fourteenth-century French King Charles V,

> The King understood so well every aspect of music, which is the science of harmonizing sounds by slow and fast notes ... that no discord could pass unperceived by him.[114]

Machaut, in his 'Remede de Fortune,' describes one of these after dinner concerts, not only making the point that the musicians appear after the dinner, but he even suggests that they arrive dressed for a concert, as it were. We should also mention here that, just as it was an artistic challenge for painters to portray one of each possible instrument in similar canvases, the poets loved to list one of each instrument. We should not believe such an ensemble really played together.

112 Ibid., 328ff.

113 *Le Jugement du roy de Behaigne*, 60.

114 Christine de Pisan, *Le Livre des Fais et Bonnes Meurs du Sage Roy Charles V*, ed. S. Solente (Paris: H. Champion, 1936), II, 34.

And after the meal you should have seen the musicians arrive, all combed and comfortably attired. They played various harmonies, for there all in a circle I saw vielle, rebec, guitar, lute, Moorish guitar, small psaltery, cittern, and the psaltery, harp, tabor, trumpets, nakers, portative organs, more than ten pairs of horns, bagpipes, flutes, musettes, douçaines, cymbals, bells, timbrels, the Bohemian flute and the large German cornett, willow flutes, a fife, pipe, Alsatian reed pipe, small trumpet, busines, psaltery, a monochord (which has a single string), and a straw pipe all together. And it certainly seemed to me that such a melodious sound had never been perceived or heard; because I heard and perceived each one of them, according to the pitch of his instrument—vielle, guitar, cittern, harp, trumpet, horn, flute, pipe, bladder pipe, bagpipe, naker, tabor, and whatever could be played with finger, pick or bow—performing in perfect harmony there in the little park.[115]

115 *Remede de Fortune*, 390ff. A poem of 1340, 'Parfait du paon,' by Jean de la Motte mentions 'cor, buisines et calimiaus menus, trompes, timbres, nacaires, tabours, estives, cor a doix, flagot et frestiaux.' See André Pirro, *Histoire de la Musique de la fin du XIVe siècle a la fin du XVIe* (Paris: Librarie Renouard, 1940), 8.

[Mais qui veïst aprés mangier
Venir menestreuls sans dangier,
Pigniés et mis en puré corps,
La firent meins divers acors;
Car je vi la tout en un cerne
Violle, rubelle, guiterne,
Leü, morache, micanon,
Cytolle, et le psalterion,
Harpe, tabour, trompes, nacaires,
Orgues, cornes, plus de dis paires,
Cornemuses, flajos, chevretes,
Douceinnes, simbales, clocettes,
Tymbre, la flëuste brehaingne,
Et le grant cornet d'Alemaingne,
Flajos de Scens, fistule, pipe
Muse d'Assay, trompe petite,
Buissines, eles, monocorde
Ou il n'a c'une seule corde,
Et muse de flef tout ensemble.
Et certainement, il me samble
Qu'onques mais telle melodie
Ne fu veüe në oÿe,
Car chascuns d'eaus, selonc l'acort
De son instrument, sans decort,
Viole, guiterne, cytolle,
Harpe trompe, corne, flajole,
Pipe, souffle, muse, naquaire,
Tamboure, et quanquë on puet faire
De dois, de penne, et de l'archet
Ouÿ je et vi en ce parchet.]

It is also interesting to note that after this post-dinner concert concluded, instruments were made available for the guests to play as part of their own entertainment. And, no doubt as an obvious compliment to the aristocrats, Machaut attributes to them knowledge of both *ars antiqua* and *ars nova* styles.

> After they had performed an estampie, the ladies and their company went off by twos and threes, holding hands, to a very beautiful room; and there all the men and women alike who wanted to relax, dance, sing, or play at backgammon, chess or parsons found all they needed at hand and ready for games, singing, and music [*par notes, ou par sons*]. And there were musicians more skilled and knowledgeable in both the new and old styles.[116]

116 Milleurs assez et plus scïens / En la vieus et nouvelle forge

In another poem, 'La Prise d'Alexandrie,' Machaut describes the events surrounding a visit of the King of Cyprus to Prague. The castle there was 'paradise on earth. There they had all instruments,' among which Machaut lists no fewer than thirty-five. The visiting king, listening to this performance, 'marveled very much and said that in his life he had never experienced such great melody.'[117]

117 Guillaume de Machaut, *La Prise d'Alexandre*, ed. L. de Mas Latrie (Geneva, 1877), 69.

Under the French King, John II (1350–1364) the minstrels of his household are defined as those who play,

> naquaires ou timbales, canon ou demi-flûte, du cornet, de la guiterne ou guitare Latine, de la flûte Behaigne ou bohemienne, de la trompette, de la guiterne Moresche ou guitare mauresque, et de la vielle.[118]

118 M.B. Bernard, 'Recherches sur l'histoire de la Corporation des Ménétriers ou Joueurs d'Instruments de la Ville de Paris,' in *Bibliothèque de l'École chantes* (April, 1842), 5.

One continues to find much poetry and love song in fourteenth-century France which is reminiscent of the troubadour repertoire of the previous century. A poem by Jean Froissart, singing the praises of a lady, is a perfect example.

> I will serve my lady always,
> For truly I cannot spend
> My time or youth
> In any better way.
> And so with happy heart,
> Awaiting her desire,
> Most joyously
> I will sing both night and day.[119]

119 'Lay 4,' in Figg, *The Short Lyric Poems of Jean Froissart*, 59.

Similarly, in the Prologue to his collected works, Machaut has Love warn him,

> But above all else, take care that you are not emboldened
> To write anything full of disrespect,
> And never slander any of my ladies.
> Rather in every case you are to praise and exalt them.
> Know well that if you do otherwise,
> I will most cruelly take away your standing.
> Instead, do everything in honor and thus advance yourself.[120]

[120] Prologue, III, 21.

It is in the context of the frequency of this theme that 'The Judgment of the King of Navarre,' by Machaut, is understood. In his poem, at the end of Machaut's 'trial' for having written unkindly about women, he is given the following sentence.

> You must—the thing is certain—
> Compose a lay for the first,
> And agreeably, without resisting;
> For the second, a song
> Of three stanzas and a refrain
> —Listen how I qualify this—
> A song which begins with the refrain
> Just like the ones sung at a dance;
> And for the third, a ballade.
> Now don't act like you're sick about this,
> But respond happily,
> As we have commanded.[121]

[121] *The Judgment of the King of Navarre*, lines 4181ff.

It is also enlightening that Machaut stipulates these love songs might also be appropriately performed as instrument works.

> By God, it is a long time since I have made such a good thing to my taste; and the melodies [*tenures*] are as gentle as fine pap. Whoever performs it on organs, bagpipes, or other instruments, that is its proper nature![122]

[122] *Le Livre du Voir-Dit*, 69.

It is surely another clue to art music, when Machaut says here that he has composed these love songs 'to my taste.' That others heard this repertoire as art music is reflected by Deschamps' comment, after the death of Machaut, that his death will be mourned by princes and kings because 'his song gave much pleasure to nobles, ladies, and bourgeois.'[123] And Deschamps himself sang of Machaut,

[123] Machaut, *Oeuvres*, I, iiiff.

> O flower of the very flowers of melody itself,
> So sweet master of such great talent,
> O Guillaume the earthly god of harmony …
>
> [O flour des flours de toute melodie,
> Tres doulz maistres qui tant fuestes adrois,
> Guillaume, mondains diex d'armonie.]

As for the value Machaut himself placed on these love songs, we have his comments in letters written to his lover, Peronnelle. He tells her not to circulate copies of what he sends her, for he is thinking of making music for them,[124] and he says that some nobles who have learned of their affair have requested copies.[125]

Among the poems of Froissart one is surprised to find some pastoral poems in the spirit of the ancient Greek lyric poets. As in their models, these poems often mention rustic music and instruments, as for example,

> And little bells from Saint Remy,
> Pipes, reed instruments, and little flutes,
> And bagpipes with droning bass,
> Drums and carved out fiddles.[126]
>
> [Et clokettes de Saint Remi,
> Pipes, canemiaus et flaios
> Et musettes a bourdons gros,
> Tamburs et esclifes trauwés.]

Or the small horn, bagpipe and little flute [*cornuelle, le musette et le flahutelle*] in another pastoral poem,[127] and panpipes, bagpipes and reed instruments [*freteaus, nos muses et nos canimeaus*] in yet another.[128]

Finally, Froissart, in a word, defines art music as being noble.

> And they were singing with noble words
> To the sound of a low bagpipe:
> 'Would you dare to ask for more?'[129]
>
> [Et chantoient par mos gentieus
> Avoec une basse musete.]

124 *Le Livre du Voir-Dit*, Letter VI.

125 Ibid., Letter XXV.

126 'Pastourelle 7,' in Figg, *The Short Lyric Poems of Jean Froissart*, 95.

127 'Pastourelle 2,' in ibid., 215.

128 'Pastourelle 14,' in ibid., 230.

129 'Pastourelle 4,' in ibid., 104.

FUNCTIONAL MUSIC

In view of the fact that Machaut's education was that which might ordinarily lead to the priesthood, it is somewhat surprising that he so rarely refers to the music of the Church. One passage is particularly interesting, however, where he describes a group of flagellants and their music, a bizarre form of religious piety stemming from the thirteenth century, but which continued in Bohemia during the 1340s.

> At this time a company arose
> At the urging of Hypocrisy, their lady,
> Who beat themselves with whips
> And crucified themselves flat on the ground,
> While singing to an instrument
> Some new song or other,
> And according to them, they were worth more
> Than any saint in Paradise.
> But the Church attended to them,
> Forbidding them to beat themselves,
> And likewise condemned their song,
> Which little children were singing,
> And excommunicated all of them
> By the power God had granted it,
> Because their self-abuse
> And their song were heresy.[130]

130 *The Judgment of the King of Navarre*, lines 241ff.

A horn or trumpet signal for the guest to wash their hands was the first announcement for dinner in a castle. Here we read 'the horns sounded the call to wash, and the loud trumpets too.'

> Et il estoit prez heure de souper.
> Et a ce mot on prist l'yaue a corner
> Par le chastel, et forment a tromper.[131]

131 *Le Jugement du roy de Behaigne*, 160.

This signal which calls the guest to dinner is frequently mentioned in literature of the Renaissance and Baroque. But since this literature is nearly always concerned with the aristocracy, we almost never read of what this signal means to the servants. Machaut's words are so vivid it seems as if we really are standing watching.

> When Mass was over, I heard a chamberlain sounding a trumpet loudly. You should have seen all the servants! Each hurried to his

station, one toward the pantry, another to the wine cellar, the others to the kitchen, according to what each prepared. Messengers and stable boys set up benches, trestles, and tables. It was quite a sight to see them hurrying to and fro, bringing rushes, spreading rugs, shouting, hollering, and sweeping—it was bedlam to hear them call to one another in French, Breton, German, Italian, English, Occitan and Norman, and in many other unusual languages. It was a marvel to see elsewhere the carvers arranging, polishing, decorating, and straightening things, readying the water, slicing bread for their masters, preparing the plates, calling for tablecloths, removing cheeseskins with their own hands, one sitting down, the other scurrying along, yet another scrubbing off dirt, others washing and cleaning their hands, one more and the other less, before going to sit down. They were making quite a racket, with everyone shouting and exclaiming: 'Hurry up! Mass is ended and they've sounded the trumpets for dinner long since!'[132]

It is in the fourteenth century in France that we begin to have extant documents regarding musicians employed by various towns, who primarily performed functional music. In most places the medieval 'watch' musician was still needed and a Parisian police document of 1372, in hope of guarding against false alarms, made 'unofficial' trumpet playing after the curfew hour a crime.

A fourteenth-century account of a civic procession in Lille mentions the various guilds and civic officials, including the civic 'trompet' players, all in special dress, with the visiting minstrels following at the end of the procession.[133]

A French civic document of 1391 again speaks of trumpets and drums in an official procession.

> Quae guidem processio facta in dicta villa cum omnibus mimmis, tam cordarum grossorum instrumentorum tromparum et taborellorum.[134]

It was on 14 September 1321, that thirty-seven minstrels (male and female!) formed the minstrel guild of Paris, called 'Confrérie de St. Julien.' In 1331 they constructed a chapel and a hospital in the rue St. Martin, a building which existed until the late eighteenth century.[135]

The original by-laws of this guild are very informative. They refer to 'the science and music of minstrelsy' and have their purpose in limiting public music in Paris to members of the guild. Much of the document deals with the ethics of performance contracts: one

132 *Remede de Fortune*, 388.

133 L. Lefébre, *Histoire du théâtre de Lille* (Lille, 1907), I, 38.

134 Quoted in B. de Toulmon, 'Dissertation sur les instruments de musique,' in *Memoires de la Société des antiquaires de France* (1844), 69.

135 A reproduction of a painting of this building can be seen in José Subirá, *Historia de la Música* (Barcelona: Salvat, 1947), 600.

may not leave an engagement to take another until the first one is finished; once one is contracted to play a particular job, one may not have another minstrel take his place—unless he is ill or in prison; and if one is hired to play for a wedding, one can not—on the side—also contract to cook or supply food, thus depriving a third person of his commission.

There were restrictions on advertising, as for example one could not walk through the streets of Paris advertising his availability—a restriction no doubt aimed at the wandering minstrel.

The subject of apprenticeship is also discussed in the original by-laws. The apprentice could not accept a performance without his master's knowledge and any apprentice caught playing in a tavern was to be expelled.[136]

New statutes in 1372 exempt minstrels from having to play 'serenades' at night, unless they are inside, in order to protect the musicians from robbers. In 1395 a statute reveals that singers ('mouth-minstrels') were now admitted into the guild. This statute forbids them to sing songs which satirize the pope, king, or any of the great men of France, under penalty of prison with bread and water!

136   Bernard, 'Recherches sur l'histoire de la Corporation des Ménétriers ou Joueurs d'Instruments de la Ville de Paris,' 24ff.

ENTERTAINMENT MUSIC

In the indoor entertainment music for the aristocracy, the medieval distinctions of 'loud' and 'soft' music remained in use, a distinction which probably had more to do with the size of room than for aesthetic reasons.[137] Thus in Eustache Deschamps' 'Echecs amoureux' the 'loud' wind band is designated for a dance in the large hall ('a crowd' of dancers).

137   Eustache Deschamps, in his 'Ballade pour Machaut,' includes the shawms in the 'soft' ensemble, which is unusual for this time.

> Whenever that they were fain to dance
> And frolic, gathered in a crowd,
> The dancers called for music loud—
> It was this that always pleased them best,
> And ever added to their zest.
> One could hear each instrument
> That sounded forth its merriment.
> Trumpet, tabor, drum and bell
> Cymbals (which played so well)
> Cornemuse and shawm
> And horns that they did loudly blow.[138]

138   Translation by Curt Sachs, *World History of the Dance* (New York, 1937), 287.

Trompez, tabours, tymbrez, naquaires,
Cymballes (dont il n'est mes guaires),
Cornemusez et chalemelles
Et cornes ....

This same poem lists flutes, cromornes, rebec and rote as 'soft' instruments employed when 'less noise' is desired and which are pleasing for the appropriate entertainment.

The wandering jongleur still existed and no doubt he was found in temporary employment in numerous noble venues. Such an example is found in an early miracle play, *La Nonne qui Laissa son Abbaie*, where there is a brief discussion of the jongleurs performing in the castle.[139]

Genuine popular entertainment music is almost never mentioned in this literature. An exception is found in Froissart's 'Pastourelle 5,' where he speaks of the peasants drinking until they were drunk, and then composing a song called 'Of Poitevin and Gasconne.'[140]

[139] 'La Nonne qui laissa son abbaie,' ed. Nigel Wilkins in *Two Miracles* (Edinburgh: Scottish Academic Press, 1972), lines 727ff.

[140] Figg, *The Short Lyric Poems of Jean Froissart*, 221.

5 FOURTEENTH-CENTURY ENGLAND

IN ONE OF THE MOST IMPORTANT POEMS of fourteenth-century England, 'Piers Plowman,' William Langland makes passing reference to the two major positions of the Church against which the intellectual life of the late Middle Ages and early Renaissance is positioned. In the early centuries when the Church had finally won its battle against pagan Rome, the basic attitude of the Church was to abolish formal secular education and say to the faithful, in effect, 'you don't need to question, or think for yourselves, just believe what we tell you.' Thus the line which Langland attributes to St. Augustine, 'Know no more than is necessary.'[1]

By the sixth century, finding itself unable to keep people uneducated, the Church accepted the teaching of the seven Liberal Arts, of which Music was one,[2] under the argument that it was necessary to educate the faithful in order for them to understand the Scriptures. Thus, in a reference to Church education, Langland mentions,

> Who is sib to the seven arts; she is called Scripture …
> She learned logic from me, and all the law after,
> And with all the measures in music I made her acquainted.[3]

And regarding these monastic schools themselves, Langland notes,

> For in cloister no man comes to quarrel or to fight,
> But there all is obedience and books, to read and to learn.
> There is scorn in school if a clerk will not learn.[4]

This was followed in the late Middle Ages, after the rediscovery of the works of the great ancient Greek philosophers, principally Aristotle, by a period called Scholasticism, which attempted to prove the medieval Church dogma through the rational arguments of the older philosophers. It is against this intellectual background that the Renaissance philosophers began to turn in a more humanistic direction.

---

1 William Langland, *Piers Plowman*, trans. E. Talbot Donaldson (New York: Norton, 1990), X, 121.

2 In addition to Grammar, Rhetoric, Logic, Arithmetic, Geometry and Astronomy.

3 Langland, *Piers Plowman*, X, 155 and 176ff.

4 Ibid., X, 307ff.

ON THE PHYSIOLOGY OF AESTHETICS

The most important philosopher of fourteenth-century England was William of Ockham (ca. 1300–1349). A member of the Order of Friars Minor, he probably thought of himself as a theologian first and a philosopher second, but the influence of his philosophy was far reaching. He mortally wounded Scholasticism, weakened the foundations of the Church, thus becoming a fugitive of the pope, but was perhaps the first important philosopher of the modern era.

In terms of our subject, one can see here the seeds for how many people think about and teach music to this day. In this regard, in particular, is Ockham's concept of knowledge. First, Ockham says, there is a form of knowledge consisting of evident things which are known to us on the basis of trust, on the basis of our having been told.[5] Philosophers today sometimes call this 'spectator' knowledge, and it is the form of knowledge most suited to the left hemisphere of our brains.

By far the most evident, and most important, form of knowledge to Ockham is that based on our own experience of what we have observed by our senses. We would call this 'experiential' knowledge, understanding innately the province of the right hemisphere. But we part company with Ockham with regard to what he says next, a viewpoint conditioned both by centuries of Church teaching and the lack of access which all early philosophers had to our knowledge of how the twin hemispheres process information.

> No act of the sensitive part of the soul is either partially or totally the immediate and proximate cause of the intellect's own act of judgment.[6]

Similarly, with regard to natural science, he wrote,

> The fact is that the propositions known by natural science are composed not of sensible things or substances, but of mental contents or concepts that are common to such things.[7]

The thought here is one of the most fundamental pillars of all of Ockham's philosophy. He is saying that although what we intake through the senses or experience is real, and the necessary first step to knowledge, this is not *real* knowledge. Real knowledge is when this input is considered, and judgments are made, by the intellect

---

5 William of Ockham, 'Epistemological Problems,' in Philotheus Boehner, *Ockham, Philosophical Writings* (Edinburgh: Thomas Nelson, 1959), 4ff.

6 Ibid., 19.

7 Ibid., 11.

itself. So knowledge is what the intellect thinks, not what our senses think. To put this in modern medical terms, one would have to phrase it as meaning only the left hemisphere has *real* knowledge.

Having based so much of his philosophy on this contention, that real knowledge is what our intellect concludes and judges from sensory and experiential input, he must also attempt to explain how such things as the emotions, love, pleasure and pain (which we would call *non*-rational) can be part of this same intellect. His difficulty in doing this is self-evident.

> Whenever an intelligible thing can be known only by intellect and in no way by sense, if there can be one non-complex cognition of the thing that suffices for evident knowledge of a contingent truth and another that does not suffice, then the two cognitions are specifically distinct. But acts of intellect, emotions, pleasures, griefs and the like, can be apprehended only by the intellect and not by the sense-faculty. Now some non-complex knowledge of them suffices for evident knowledge of whether they exist or not, and whether or not they exist in such and such a subject. Yet not all non-complex knowledge of them suffices for this. The first part of the minor premise is shown thus: Everyone experiences in himself that he understands, loves, is pleased, is sad. Since such knowledge concerns contingent facts, it cannot be obtained from necessary propositions …
>
> There is no inconsistency in the supposition that someone does not know whether a certain intelligible thing exists or does not exist, and has nevertheless a non-complex cognition of it; this is no more inconsistent than the corresponding supposition about a certain sensible thing. If, therefore, someone's intellect should directly perceive another person's love and he were thus as certain of this other person's love as of his own love, then there would not be any difficulty about supposing that later on he could still think of this love and nevertheless not know whether it continued to exist, even though it did still exist; just as may happen with some sensible thing which is first seen and then thought of.
>
> This second argument proves that it is possible for the intellect to have this twofold cognition and to have it about purely intelligible facts, whereas the first proves that our intellect actually has this twofold cognition in the present life, and has it even as regards sensible facts.[8]

The third type of knowledge, according to Ockham, consists of a general category of intuitive knowledge. Although he raises the doubt that, 'intuitive cognition is not proper knowledge,'[9] it was

8 Ibid., 20ff.

9 Ibid., 29.

necessary as a theologian to recognize some vehicle for information supplied by God. Of most interest to our subject is his belief that it is possible to have an intuitive cognition of *non-existent* things, due to the supernatural help of God.[10] Thinking of an intuitive, previously non-existent idea is what we would say today a composer does, which is perhaps why some early composers, Bach in particular, gave God credit for their composition. But with regard to Art, Ockham seems to have missed this point. He only attributes to the artist the ability to see something, store it in his memory and then later imitates it—not create something which has never existed.

> For just as the artist who sees a house or building outside the mind first pictures in the mind a similar house and later produces a similar house in reality which is only numerically distinct from the first, so in our case the picture in the mind that we get from seeing something outside would act as a pattern ...
>
> Again, works of art do not seem to inhere in the mind of the craftsman as independent subjects any more than the creatures did in the divine mind before creation.[11]

Finally, Ockham explores the relationship of conceptual thought to our *expression* of that thought, a topic which has great indirect relevance to music. He correctly recognizes that words are only a symbolic language which represent something else, the rational concept itself.

> Words are applied in order to signify the very same things which are signified by mental concepts.[12]

He also correctly observes that a symbolic language, including all its words, is simply a societal agreement that a particular written or spoken symbol will *represent* a particular rational concept.

> Hence the concept signifies something primarily and naturally, whilst the word signifies the same thing secondarily ... Some words may also primarily signify impressions of the mind, or concepts; these may in turn signify secondarily other intentions of the mind.
>
> What has been said about words in regard to impressions or contents or concepts holds likewise analogously for written words in reference to spoken words.
>
> Certain differences are to be found among these sorts of terms. One is the following: A concept or mental impression signifies natu-

10 Ibid., xxvii.

11 'Epistemological Problems,' in ibid., 41ff.

12 'Logical Problems,' in ibid., 48.

rally whatever it does signify; a spoken or written term, on the other hand, does not signify anything except by free convention.

From this follows another difference. We can change the designation of the spoken or written term at will, but the designation of the conceptual term is not to be changed at anybody's will.[13]

13 Ibid.

Now, what *really* bothered Ockham, and others before him, was the recognition of the common difficulty we all have in expressing our ideas to another person. Why is this? Conceptual information (left hemisphere of the brain) should be *perfectly* capable of communication through conceptual symbolic language, providing the speaker/writer is capable of using this symbolic language correctly, and the listener/reader has an equal background in the subject and understands the agreed conventional meaning of the symbolic language.

The *problem* is that the speaking/writing part of us, the left hemisphere, cannot express *non*-rational concepts very well, as anyone knows who has ever tried to write a love letter. This is why we have retained, since earliest man, a separate non-rational language, which today we call Music.

The importance of all of this to the present subject has to do with the origin of the teaching of music in academic environments, which began with the first modern universities of Western Europe, foremost among which was Oxford.

The Scholastic doctors who taught at Oxford and Paris, beginning in the thirteenth century, were accustomed by long precedent to discuss music as a *conceptual* subject. For a thousand years it had been a branch of mathematics and a member of the seven Liberal Arts, the other six of which are abstract sciences. But these professors were very much aware that the actual performance of music which they *heard* included elements, such as feeling, which were not easily represented or explained by numbers, or any other conceptual symbols.[14]

14 Even today we have no independent symbols of music notation dedicated to feeling.

Hence they simply separated the discipline of Music at this time into two branches: *musica speculativa* and *musica practica*. They said, in effect, 'We will teach the first, and leave to you, the performers, the second.' The roots for this division of music can be found to some degree in the medieval music treatises, in Boethius in particular, but with the appearance of the new, modern universities the idea became institutionalized and proposition became dogma. Thus, for example, at the university in Oxford, one finds in the fourteenth century new treatises by Walter Odington and Simon Tunstede which are organized on the basis of *musica speculativa* and *musica practica*.¹⁵ Of the six books which constitute Odington's treatise, by the way, the first three are purely mathematical.

Thus we have inherited two forms of 'Music,' a *speculativa* form, which includes notation and all of 'theory' and music education, which we can talk and write about, and which we learn by eye, and a *practica* form which is mostly learned by ear (the private studio teacher says, 'No, it goes like this').

But in truth, the *speculativa* form does not exist. It is *only* a conceptual symbolic language which represents the *practica* form, which is the *real* music! Thus, when music schools teach the conceptual form, while they call it music, they are not really teaching music. Harmony as it is usually taught, for example, is not music and might better be identified as another symbolic language.

Ockham was also thinking along these lines. He thought there *should* be a non-conceptual form of knowledge, an experiential knowledge analogous to 'musica practica,' but he had no insights, as we do from clinical brain research, to suppose that it exists.

> We note that [natural science] is a theoretical science for the most part. For a science that does not treat of what we do is speculative. But this science is the kind that is not about what we do; therefore it is speculative. But should there be some part of the philosophy of nature that provides a directive knowledge for the performance of actions, this part would be practical, not theoretical.¹⁶

An important fourteenth-century anonymous English poem, 'The Pearl,' addresses the second of the three types of knowledge which Ockham discusses above. A jeweler looking at a pearl, says he only believes what he sees with his eyes. This is a 'presumption,' says the poem, 'our Lord would not lie.' Rather we must only believe what Reason alone can judge.

> To believe no tale be true to trust
> Save that which his reason alone may judge.¹⁷

With regard to this emphasis on Reason, or left hemisphere understanding, the fourteenth-century theologian–poet, Richard Rolle, goes further and reminds the faithful that you can get to heaven *only* by wisdom.

15 Carpenter, *Music n the Medieval and Renaissance Universities*, 86.

16 Ockham, 'Epistemological Problems,' in Boehner, *Ockham, Philosophical Writings*, 15.

17 Anonymous, *The Pearl*, trans. Mary Hillmann (Convent Station, NJ: College of Saint Elizabeth Press, 1959), 301ff.

Ffor tylle the kyngdom of heven may no man com
Bot he ga bi the way of wisdom.[18]

On the other hand, one anonymous writer wonders, on a subject such as life after death, if one can know either by experience or Reason.

Who knoweth by dede oughte, bote by thought?[19]

The last important English philosopher of the fourteenth century, John Gower (1330–1408), shares some curiously retrospective views with English and French writers of the early fifteenth century. These views might be characterized as a return to some aspects of the philosophy of the medieval Church, as if there was a need felt by some to create a Counter-Humanism movement. It is astonishing, for example, to read Gower reaching back a thousand years to say, in effect, 'don't think, you don't need education, just believe what we tell you,' when he suggests that it is helpful for a man to be ignorant!

Submit your mind to faith, for a mortal creature cannot understand the mysteries of eternal judgment …
Since it is certainly not for us to understand the circumstances of the world, to what purpose does man labor to understand creation? For us to experience faith tested by reason—that task is not for human powers. It is not a human task to mount up to the stars; mortal man does not grasp that by his reason … It is helpful for man to be in ignorance about a great deal; most facts offend the senses. Therefore, a man should acquire knowledge prudently. Let him entrust to faith what he would not have been able to trust to reason.[20]

It is not a surprise to read earlier in this same book that Gower complained that the young were not paying attention to his teaching.

Knowing very little used to be a great disgrace for an old man … But nowadays if old age is wise in any way or teaches what it has learned earlier, its voice hardly receives the welcome of a youth's. Even if they are fervent in their zeal, the words which old men write are, as a rule, acceptable to young men only quite rarely. Yet no matter how much the voices of the dogs may bark in objection, I shall not run away, but instead I shall sing out my words. Imbibe oil from the rocks and honey from the stones for yourself, and single out the sweet notes from my harsh song.[21]

18 Richard Rolle, *The Pricke of Conscience* (Berlin: A. Asher, 1863), 7541.

19 'The World an Illusion,' quoted in R. T. Davies, *Medieval English Lyrics* (Evanston: Northwestern University Press, 1964), line 47.

20 John Gower, *The Voice of One Crying*, trans. Eric Stockton in *The Major Latin Works of John Gower* (Seattle: University of Washington Press, 1962), II, ix.

21 Ibid., II, Prologue.

Perhaps he was aware that this approach did not work, for in another book Gower tries a different approach, observing that reading a book entirely devoted to wisdom dulls a man's wit. He goes on to say he proposes to write a book that includes as well, lust, love and women, so 'man may like of that I write.'

> But for men sain, and soth it is,
> That who that al of wisdom writ,
> It dulleth ofte a mannes wit
> To hem that shall it al day rede.[22]

In his *The Voice of One Crying*, Gower is especially critical of the clergy he knew at the end of the fourteenth century. He finds them being satisfied with 'natural knowledge,' rather than sacred theology.[23] When they treat 'the subject of pregnancy, and in order to bear fruit he is highly repetitious about it' (too many illegitimate children!). He also finds a similar lack of enthusiasm among the clergy in their role as Church singers.

> A priest of God rarely rises sober from the table or chaste from a bed. When exhilarated by taverns his voice sings on high, but in churches it is all too mute.[24]

Finally, Gower's writings also retain the medieval Church's negative characterization of women.

> Neither learning nor understanding, neither constancy nor virtue such as men have flourishes in woman.[25]

His view of Art also reflects the old Church definitions.

> Was not all the world first founded for you, and its treasures laid out for your enjoyment? The world was not made for adoration but for use; it was made to be your servant, not your god. Therefore, does reason urge you that what the artisan melts in the fire or carves on smooth wood is a god? ... This insanity of worshiping mute gods while they themselves know nothing is worse than all vices ... The sculptor is worthier than his sculpture; it is therefore conclusive that the worker who worships his own work is all too foolish.[26]

The concept of the soul, which to the medieval Church was more important than mind or body, is now little discussed. In 'Piers Plowman,' it is presented as a poetic symbol for nearly everything else.

---

[22] John Gower, 'Prologue to *Confessio Amantis*,' quoted in *Survey of British Poetry* (New York: Poetry Anthology Press, 1988), I, 82.

[23] Gower, *The Voice of One Crying*, III, xvii.

[24] Ibid., III, xx.

[25] Ibid., IV, xiii.

[26] Ibid., II, x.

The soul [*Anima*] is distinguished by various names according to
its various actions:
> When it vivifies the body it is Life;
> When it wills it is Soul;
> When it knows it is Mind;
> When it recollects it is Memory;
> When it judges it is Reason;
> When it feels it is Sense;
> When it desires or consents it is Conscience;
> When it loves it is Love;
> When it expires it is Spirit.[27]

This seems very much like an observation of Richard Rolle, who, while he recognizes both the soul as the inner man and the body as the outer man, nevertheless calls the soul 'the life of the body.'

> The saule the lyfe of the body es.[28]

Finally, we have pointed out in the previous volumes of this series a long and constant prejudice in literature for the right hand over the left. The origin for this, while unknown to these writers, actually lies in the fact that the right hand is an extension of the left hemisphere, or 'Rational,' brain which alone can talk or write and tends not to recognize the very existence of the right hemisphere. Hence, the speaking brain favors the right hand. Thus we find, in the 'The Pricke of Conscience,' Rolle observing that as all clergy understands, the world fights us with two hands: the right bringing wealth and the left sorrow and poverty.

> For the worlde assayles sum men awhile,
> With the right hand tham to bygile;
> That es welth, als I sayde before,
> Of worldly riches and tresore;
> And assayles men, nyght and day,
> With the left hand tham to flay;
> That es with angre and tribulacion,
> And povert, and persecucion.[29]

Similarly, in 'Sir Gawain and the Green Knight,' an older woman, held in high honor by all, leads the young queen by the *left* hand, as a subtle means of distinguishing their relative status.[30]

---

27 Langland, *Piers Plowman*, XV, 39ff.

28 Rolle, *The Pricke of Conscience*, 3028.

29 Rolle, *The Pricke of Conscience*, 1257ff. See also 6147ff where he discusses Christ's dealing with those on his right and left hand.

30 Richard Rolle, *Sir Gawain and the Green Knight*, trans. Marie Borroff (New York: Norton, 1967), 947.

ON THE PSYCHOLOGY OF AESTHETICS

Emotions

There is surprisingly little discussion of the emotions in the literature of fourteenth-century England. The most frequently mentioned emotion, joy, is most often associated with music. This sounds very much in the tradition of the troubadour of the previous century, as does the knight finding joy in deserving the praise of a lady.

> To the plesaunce of your pris; hit were a pure joy.[31]

[31] Ibid., 1247.

The pessimistic Richard Rolle, in another place, concludes one can find little joy on this earth.

> He suld fynd ful litel matere
> To mak joy whilles he here duelles.[32]

[32] Rolle, *The Pricke of Conscience*, 895.

Rolle also addresses a familiar theme of the Church, that Reason must control the passions. He says that if our attention is turned to the senses, uncleanness enters the soul. But if Reason concentrates on spiritual things, meditations, sermons and reading holy books, then we experience a form of delight which has none of the 'inordinate stirrings.' Thereafter, the 'goodness of our Lord' rewards our soul by a form of comfort in our sensuality, to which the flesh joins in its joy.

> Twa thynges makes our delyte pure. Ane es, ternynge of sensualite to [Reason]. For, when any es tornede to delite of hys fyve wittes, alsonne vnclennes entyrs into his saule. Another es, that the Reason mekely be vssede in [spiritual] thynges, als in medytacyons, and orysouns, and lukynge in haly bukes. For-thy the delyte that has noghte of vnordaynde styrrynge …
> ……
> And this es the gudnes of oure Lorde, that sen the saule is puneschede in the sensualite, and the flesche es partynere of the payne, That eftirwarde the saule be comforthede in hir sensualite, and the flesche be [a companion] of the Joye and comforthe with the saule, noghte fleschely, bot [spiritually], als he was [companion] in tribulacione and payne.[33]

[33] Richard Rolle, 'Of the Vertu,' in *English Prose Treatises of Richard Rolle* (London: Humphrey Milford, Oxford University Press, 1866, 1921), 14 and 16.

John Gower makes two observations regarding the communication of emotions. First, he suggests that emotions have no value if they cannot be applied, 'the feeling in the heart accomplishes nothing when the lips refuse to speak.'[34] Second, he correctly identifies the role of the face in expressing emotions, whereas earlier philosophers incorrectly assigned this role to the eyes alone.

> For whatever a man is afflicted with, his inner agitation affects his outer emotions in token of it.
> The face expresses the state of one's mind and displays the wrath of a heart strongly aroused. For in the event that one express himself silently, no index of the mind can be more reliable than the face.[35]

Curiously, he appears not to recognize the direct role music plays in expressing the emotions.

> Outwardly, their voice sings in chorus, yet inwardly their spirit grumbles.[36]

34 Gower, *The Voice of One Crying*, II, Prologue.

35 Ibid., IV, iii.

36 Ibid.

Pleasure and Pain

The fourteenth-century English writers also omit much discussion of Pleasure and Pain, generally only pointing out that they are opposites. A frequent device is to equate sorrow with hell and joy with heaven.

> And als sorow es ay in the lawest place,
> Swa es ay in the heghest, joy and solace.[37]

We also frequently find the observation that pain can turn to pleasure, and pleasure to pain. Thus, in an anonymous 'Adult Lullaby,' we find the line,

> It turneth woe to wel, and ek wel to wo.[38]

John Gower similarly writes, 'Sadness often comes after joys'[39] and,

> Not one single day provides a man with so many joys but that during some part of it grief will afflict him.[40]

37 Rolle, *The Pricke of Conscience*, 7757.

38 Quoted in R. T. Davies, *Medieval English Lyrics* (Evanston: Northwestern University Press, 1964), line 21.

39 Gower, *The Voice of One Crying*, I, i.

40 Ibid., II, i.

In another place he attributes this to Fortune, 'Fortune does not know how to give honey without gall.'[41]

Richard Rolle writes that joy is like the new hay, now fair and green which soon withers away.

> The joy that men have seen is likened til the hay,
> That now is fair and green, and now wites away.[42]

This topic of joy turning to sadness was frequently expressed during the late Middle Ages as seen in the effects of Love. Thus, an anonymous writer bemoans the fact that love has turned to anger.

> Me thinketh that love to wrathe is went.[43]

No more agitated exposition of the contrasting qualities and emotions of Love was ever written than that by John Gower in the following:

> O, if a knight were to think of the ways of love, which are changed so suddenly, he would not suffer them. Love is not of one hue, but is conflicting within itself; it tempers its vicissitudes intemperately. Love conceals and reveals, disunites and reunites, and often drives happy hearts mad with grief. Love is an unjust judge; marrying opposites, it makes the very natures of things deteriorate. In love, discord is harmonious, learning is ignorant, anger makes jests, honor is base, a poor man has plenty, joys grieve, praise reproves, despair hopes, hope is afraid, harms are helpful, assets are harmful. In love chills perspire, sickness is strengthening. So take greater heed, knight, of the dangers you see. Read what forms love's sickness takes.
>
> Love is sickly health, troubled rest, pious sin, warlike peace, a pleasant wound, a delightful calamity, anxious happiness, a devious path, dark light, gentle harshness, a light lump of lead, both a flowery winter and a withered, flowerless spring, a thorny rose, a capricious law without justice, weeping laughter, laughing lamentation, intemperate temperance, a hostile ally and a gracious enemy, fickle constancy, a wish opposed to itself, hope despairing of itself, doubting faith, black whiteness, bright blackness, bitter honey, delicious gall, a prison offering pleasures, irrational reason, foolish discretion, an untrustworthy judge, an ignorant person reflecting upon everything, food never digestible and drink ever thirsty, an insatiable mental hunger, a living death, a dying life, harmonious discord, a garrulous mind, mute speech, a secret fever, poor prosperity, prosperous poverty, a slavish prince, a subject queen and destitute king, drunken

---

[41] Ibid., II, iv.

[42] From 'Love is Life that Lasts Ay,' quoted in Frances Comper, *The Life of Richard Rolle* (London: Dent, 1929), 252.

[43] 'Love unlike Love,' quoted in Davies, *Medieval English Lyrics*, line 6.

sobriety, demented clemency, the port of Scylla, a pestilential cure, a way of health; love is a delightful serpent, a ferocious lamb, a gentle lion, a timid hawk and a rapacious dove, a fatuous school turning out an even more fatuous pupil, whose mind applies itself the more diligently as a result.[44]

44   Gower, *The Voice of One Crying*, IV, ii.

ON THE PHILOSOPHY OF AESTHETICS

Aesthetics as a general subject is also little discussed in fourteenth-century English literature. Since 'delight' is a frequently given purpose for aesthetics, we should mention that Richard Rolle defines the highest form of delight as that which is pure and 'not blended with anything else.'

> It is pure, when it es noghte blendid with na thynge that es contrayrie thareto. And it is firm, when it es certeyn and stabill, delitande by itselfe.[45]

45   Richard Rolle, 'Desyre and Delit,' in Hope Allen, ed., *English Writings of Richard Rolle* (Oxford: Clarendon Press, 1963), 58.

We shall see references below to the importance of correctness in the performance of music. This seems to have been an important value in poetry as well, for in another place Rolle prays the reader will have charity towards his errors in rhyme.

> Bot I pray yhou alle, par charité,
> That this tretice wil here or se
> Yhe haf me excused at this tyme,
> If yhe fynde defaut in the ryme.[46]

46   Rolle, *The Pricke of Conscience*, 9581ff.

Similarly, we read in 'Sir Gawain and the Green Knight' that a high value was given to the art of eloquence in speaking among nobles.[47]

47   Rolle, *Sir Gawain and the Green Knight*, 917. See also 1013.

ON THE AESTHETICS OF MUSIC

The writers of fourteenth-century England continue in an aesthetic tradition unbroken since the early Greeks of referring to the *most* pleasing music as being 'sweet.' A typical expression, found in the anonymous poem, 'The Pearl,' is,

> Yet never imagined I so sweet a song.[48]

48   Anonymous, *The Pearl*, 19.

And we find in the same poem another common theme, no doubt as a form of tribute to Nature and God, the observation that earthly musicians cannot equal the perfect joy of the sweet harmony of birds.

> There in the woodland birds flew in flocks,
> Of flaming colors, both small and great;
> But citole string and gittern player
> Could not reproduce their perfect mirth,
> For when those birds their wings did beat,
> With a sweet harmony they sang.[49]
> Joy so gracious could no man attain
> As to hear and see their splendor.[50]

We find many of the traditional purposes for music also given in this literature. The most common is to express joy, and often the joy of love, as we read in a poem attributed to Richard Rolle, when he exclaims, 'Love can sing for joy'.[51]

For the faithful, the joy expressed through music is rather associated with the joy of salvation. Thus, in the *Fysshers and Marynars* play, of the York Cycle of Mystery Plays, Noah says,

> More joy in heart never I had.
> We may be saved, now may we sing.[52]

A similar expression is found in the 'Second Shepherds' Play.'

> GIB. Come forth, now are we won!
> DAW. To sing are we bound:
>   Let take on loft [Let's raise our voices].[53]
>   [*They sing*]

Another form of joy is that of celebration and we find an indirect reference to the celebration of the harvest in the anonymous poem, 'The Farmer's Complaint,' where men are complaining that the good harvest years and good corn crops are gone and one no longer hears the farmers sing any songs of celebration.[54]

A rare instance of singing of pain, other than in the context of love, is found in the *Spurriers and Lorimers* play, when Mary sings,

> Of sorrows sore shall be my song.[55]

---

[49] 'songen wyth a swete asent.'

[50] Anonymous, *The Pearl*, 85ff.

[51] 'Love is Life,' quoted in Celia and Kenneth Sisam, ed., *The Oxford Book of Medieval English Verse* (Oxford: Clarendon Press, 1970), 77.

[52] J.S. Purvis, *The York Cycle* [London: S.P.C.K, 1957), 55.

[53] Quoted in *The Norton Anthology of English Literature* (New York: Norton, 1968), the final three lines of the play.

[54] 'The Farmer's Complaint,' quoted in Celia and Kenneth Sisam, *The Oxford Book of Medieval English Verse*, 111.

[55] Purvis, *The York Cycle*, 141.

One of the most frequent purposes of music given in ancient and medieval literature is rather to soothe those who are sad. We find such an example in another play, the *Drapers* play, where Jesus says,

> And bring me my mother to the highest of heaven,
> With mirth and with melody, her mood for to mend.[56]

56 Ibid., 358.

In the *Second Shepherds' Play* three shepherds sing a three-part song to cheer (to 'mirth') them up during the long night.

> COLL. That is right. By the cross, these nights are long!
>   Yet I would, ere we went, one gave us a song.
> GIB. So I thought as I stood, to mirth us among.
> DAW. I grant.
> COLL. Let me sing the tenory.
> GIB. And I the treble so hee [high].
> DAW. Then the mean falls to me.
>   Let see how you chant.[57]

57 Quoted in *The Norton Anthology of English Literature*, 182.

We also find some interesting clues in this literature of contemporary values in good musicianship or good performance. In 'The Pearl' there is a passage which describes the new music (*a note full new*) which will be sung by the 44,000 souls permitted to enter heaven, as mentioned in the book of Revelations. In this ideal music we find the goals of a full and clear performance, noble (*gentle*) character, in tune and something beyond what one might expect from earthly performers. We might also point out here that the fourteenth-century English writers use 'craft' as we would use 'art,' which is again a reflection of the definition of art given in much ancient Greek literature.

> I heard them sound forth a note quite new.
> To hear that was most pleasingly dear!
> As harpers harp upon their harps,
> That new song they sang full clear,
> In resounding tones—a gentle utterance!
> Full fair in unison they caught the modes …
> Nevertheless, none was ever so skilled,
> Despite all the crafts that ever they knew,
> Who of that song might sing a note
> Except that company.[58]

58 Anonymous, *The Pearl*, 877ff.

Similar objections to singing out of tune can be found in the *Second Shepherds' Play*,⁵⁹ and in the famous 'Piers Plowman.' In this latter passage, aside from the objection to out of tune string playing, there is also a general complaint against musicians who waste their time and talents playing in taverns.

> He does best who desists, day and night,
> From squandering any speech or any space of time.
>   *Who offends in one point is guilty in all.*
> And Truth knows what's true: time that is wasted
> On earth is most hated by those who are in Heaven,
> And then the squandering of speech, which is the sprout of grace,
> And God's music-maker, and a merriment of Heaven.
> The faithful father would never wish that his fiddle were untuned!
> Nor his gleeman a gadabout, a goer to taverns.⁶⁰

Near the beginning of this same poem is an accurate observation on the current state of the minstrel. Beginning with the thirteenth century the general concept of the wandering musician had begun to disappear to be replaced by a number of new names which not only reflected the wide variety in skills of the musicians, but, and more important, offered the hope for the more respectable to be recognized by the Church. It is in the thirteenth century that we begin to find higher levels of 'minstrels,' the troubadours, trouvières and Minnesingers, many of whom included nobles.

By the fourteenth century the instrumental musicians also began to separate in their nomenclature. The better performers, often now with real jobs working for cities or nobles, were called minstrels, while the true wandering musicians, often followed by questionable reputations, were the jongleurs.

Thus, as we noted, it is this distinction which one finds near the beginning of 'Piers Plowman,' the minstrel, who plays for money in an honorable fashion, and the jongleur, who is quite castigated here.

> And some make mirth as minstrels can
> And get gold for their music, guiltless, I think.⁶¹
> But jokers [*jongleurs*] and word jugglers, Judas' children,
> Invent fantasies to tell about and make fools of themselves,
> And have whatever wits they need to work if they wanted.
> What Paul preaches of them I don't dare repeat here:
> *Qui loquitur turpiloquium*⁶² is Lucifer's henchman.
> Beadsmen and beggars bustled about

---

59 Quoted in *The Norton Anthology of English Literature*, 476.

60 Langland, *Piers Plowman*, IX, 99ff.

61 In ibid., X, 159, we also read, 'Merrier than a minstrel whom men have given gold,'

62 'Who speaks filthy language.'

Till both their bellies and their bags were crammed to the brim;
Staged fights for their food, fought over beer.
In gluttony, God knows, they go to bed.
And rise up with ribaldry, those robber boys.
Sleep and sloth pursue them always.[63]

63 Langland, *Piers Plowman*, Prologue, 33fff.

And in another place, Langland adds,

Minstrelsy and mirth among men nowadays
Are filthiness, flatteries, and foolish tales.[64]

64 Ibid., X, 49.

At this time many of the lower wandering musicians were string players, the 'beer fiddlers.' This is the musician Langland refers to when he writes,

And not fare like a fiddler or friar seeking feasts,
At home in other men's houses and hating his own.[65]

65 Ibid., X, 95.

Langland provides a major sketch of one of these less than admirable minstrels, a man named Hawkin, although when we first meet him he calls himself 'Active Life,' a reference to the practical versus Scholastic theoretical definitions of music which were being formulated by the universities. In spite of his siding with the practical musicians, when Hawkin first describes himself, he presents a picture of a musician who simply doesn't have the skills to be successful. He hasn't even acquired the hand-down garments which even the wandering musicians often received.

They met with a minstrel as it seemed to me then.
Patience approached him and prayed him to tell
Conscience what craft he practiced, and to what country he was bound.
'I am a minstrel,' said that man, 'my name is *Activa Vita*.
I hate everything idle, for from "active" is my name.
A wafer-seller, if you want to know, and I work for many lords,
But I've few robes as my fee from them, or fur-lined gowns.
If I could lie to make men laugh, then I might look to get
Either mantel or money among lords' minstrels.
But because I can neither play a tabor nor a trumpet nor tell any stories
Nor fart nor fiddle at feasts, nor play the harp,
Joke nor juggle nor gently pipe,
Nor dance nor strum the psaltery, nor sing to the guitar,
I have no good gifts from these great lords'.[66]

66 Ibid., XIII, 221ff.

To make up for his lack of skills, Hawkin appears to have earned his living by talk, primarily as an impostor of one kind or another (although some of this is surely Langland's picture of the prima donna musician). In fact, we next meet him in the habit of the clergy. Here, as the reader will recognize, the author is using a humorous analogy of the minstrel to actually represent his objections to the clergy.

> I took close heed, by Christ, and Conscience did too,
> Of Hawkin the Active Man and how he was dressed.
> He had a coat of Christendom, as Holy Kirk believes,
> But it was soiled with many spots in sundry places,
> Here a spot of insolent speech, and there a spot of pride,
> Of scorning and of scoffing and unsuitable behavior;
> As in apparel and deportment proud among the people;
> Presenting himself as something more than he seems or is;
> Wishing all men would think him what he is not,
> And so he boasts and brags with many bold oaths;
> And impatient of reproof from any person living;
> And himself so singular as to seem to the people
> As if there were none such as himself, nor none so pope-holy;
> In the habit of a hermit, an order by himself,
> A religious *sans* rule or reasonable obedience;
> Belittling lettered men and unlettered both;
> Pretending to like lawful life and a liar in soul;
> With inwit and with outwit to imagine and study,
> As it would be best for his body, to be thought a bold man;
> And interfere everywhere where he has no business;
> Wishing every one to be assured his intellect was the best,
> Or that he was most clever at his craft, or a clerk of greatest wisdom,
> Or strongest on steed, or stiffest below the belt,
> And loveliest to look at and most lawful of deeds,
> And none so holy as he, nor any cleaner of life,
> Or fairest of features in form and in shape,
> And most splendid at song, or most skillful of hands,
> And glad to give generously, to get praise thereby,
> And if he gives to poor people, proclaims what he's giving;
> Poor of possession in purse and in coffer;
> And like a lion to look at, and lordly of speech;
> Boldest of beggars; a boaster who has nothing,
> In town and in taverns telling his tales,
> And speaking of something he never saw and swearing it true.[67]

---

[67] Ibid., XIII, 271ff.

And, finally, our minstrel/clergyman could be seen pursuing the girls.

> For every maid that he met he made her a gesture
> Suggesting sin, and some he would savor
> About the mouth, or beneath begin to grope,
> Till their wills grow keen together and they get to work,
> As well on fasting days as Fridays and forbidden nights
> And as [well] in Lent as out of Lent, all times alike;
> Such works with them were never out of season.⁶⁸

68 Ibid., XIII, 344ff.

Conscience tries to reform Hawkin, promising him success if he will follow the ethics of the Church.

> No herald nor harper will have a fairer garment
> Than Hawkin the Active Man, if you act according to my teaching,
> Nor any minstrel be held more worthy among poor and rich
> Than will Hawkin the waferer, who is *Active Vita*.⁶⁹

69 Ibid., XIV, 25ff.

Patience now joins in and, taking bread from his bag, offers some to Hawkin in an impromptu Mass.

> 'Have some, Hawkin,' said Patience, 'and eat it when you're hungry,
> Or when your teeth chatter for chill, or you chew your cheek for thirst.
> Shall never handcuffs harm you, nor anger of great lords,
> Prison or pain, for *patientes vincunt*.'⁷⁰

70 Ibid., XIV, 51ff. *Patientes vincunt*, means 'the patient overcome.'

Finally, Langland balances this by making reference to the most respected minstrel, the one who has been fortunate to be hired by a noble.

> A lewd man should not have audience in hall nor in chamber
> Where wise men are, God's words witness,
> Nor any light-minded man be allowed among lords.
> Clerks and knights welcome king's minstrels,
> And for love of their lord listen to them at feasts;
> Much more, it seems to me, rich men should
> Have beggars before them, who shall be God's minstrels
> As he says himself; Saint John bears witness:
>   *He who despiseth you despiseth me.*
> Therefore I remind you rich men, when you make your revels.
> To solace your souls have such minstrels:
> A poor person for a fool-sage placed at your table,

And a learned man from whom to learn what our Lord suffered
To save your soul from Satan your enemy,
And without flattering fiddle for you Good Friday's story,
And a blind man for a banterer, or a bedridden woman
To ask alms for you before our Lord, to exhibit your good fame.
A man is made to laugh by minstrels like these three,
And in his death-dying they do him great comfort.
Who in his lifetime listened to them and loved to hear them.[71]

71 Ibid., XIII, 433ff.

CHURCH MUSIC

In the fourteenth-century English poet, Richard Rolle, we have one of those leftover Medieval types who was so focused on the next life that there is little trace of his living the present one. When he speaks of music and joy, mirth or bliss, it is all in the context of the love of Jesus.

Sa that I may thi mercy syng in thi blys withowten ende.[72]

......

Jhesu, my myrth and melody, when will thow com, my keyng?[73]

......

And when thou spekes til hym, and says 'Jhesu,' thurgh custom, it sal be in thi ere joy, for thi mouth hony, and in thi hert melody. For the sall thynk joy to here that name be named, swetnes to speke it, myrth and sang to thynk it.[74]

72 Richard Rolle, 'A Song of Mercy,' in Hope Allen, ed., *English Writings of Richard Rolle* (Oxford: Clarendon Press, 1963), 40.

73 'Ego Dormio,' in ibid., 71.

74 'The Form of Living,' in ibid., 108.

For Rolle, the purpose of music is the comforting of a soul by angel's song. The nature of this song, he says, no one can describe, for it is spiritual and thus above man's imagination or reason.

Also oure Lorde comforthes a saule by Aungells sange. Bot what that sange es, it may noghte [be] dyscryuded be no bodyly lyknes, for it es [spiritual], and abown all manere of ymagynacyone and mans reson.[75]

75 'Of the Vertu,' in ibid., 17.

Only those with a pure soul can hear this song, but if they can, then they can sing a new song, of heavenly bliss, without deceit or pretending.

> Than [truly] may he synge a newe sange, and [truly] may be here a blysfull heuenly sown and Aungells sange, with-owtten dessayte or feynynge.[76]

76 Ibid., 18.

And therefore, he warns, if you see a man spiritually occupied fall into any of these sins, deceits or 'frensyes,' you will know he never heard angel's song or heavenly sound. For truly, hearing the angel's song makes one so wise he cannot succumb to the sins of fantasy, indiscretion or tricks of the devil.

> For [truly], he that verreyly heres Aungels sange, he es made so wyse that he sall never erre by fantasye, ne by indiscrecyon, ne by no sleghte of the deuelle.[77]

77 Ibid., 19.

Rolle now turns his attention to heaven, where he promises there will be more joy than the 'heart can think' or the tongue can tell.

> Than salle mare joy be in heven,
> Than hert may thynk or tong kan neven.[78]

78 Rolle, *The Pricke of Conscience*, 7783.

Rolle paints a long and dismal portrait of hell, where, among other things there will be filth and stink, darkness, vermin, beatings by devils and dragons, etc. Then he presents a lengthy picture of heaven and among the joys to be found there are rest, goods, peace, pleasure, twenty-four hours of daylight (a reference to the dangers of medieval towns which had no lights), wisdom without folly,[79] Beauty[80] and 'melody and angel's song.'[81]

79 Ibid., 7855.
80 Ibid., 7857.
81 Ibid., 7841.

With regard to the music in heaven, Rolle gives much detail. The righteous there will find great joy and liking in what they hear: angels singing, holy men singing praises, voices *delightful and clear*, all manner of melody, *delectable* wind bands, and all kinds of *sweet* tones of music that any man's *heart* might like.

> Alswa ilkan sal haf in pair heryng,
> Grete joy in heven and grete lykyng,
> For thai sal here thar aungel sang,
> And the haly men sal ay syng omang,
> With delitabel voyces and clere;
> And, with that, thai sal ay here
> Alle other manere of melody,
> Of the delytable noys of mynstralsy,
> And of alkyn swet tones of musyke,
> That til any mans hert mught like.[82]

82 Ibid., 9252.

Finally, with regard to musical references in context with the Church, one of the most familiar symbols in early church dramas was the association of the trumpet with the Day of Judgment. In a typical example, from the *Merceres* play, God says,

> Therefore mine angels will I send
> To blow their trumpets, that all may hear
> The time is come when I make end.
> Angels, blow your trumpets high,
> Every creature for to call.[83]

ART MUSIC

In fourteenth-century England we continue to find love songs in the spirit of the earlier troubadour repertoire. A typical example is found in the anonymous poem, 'The White Beauty,' where a singer sings, 'The joy of her is never gone while I can sing.'

> Hir gladshipe n'is never gon
> Whil I may glewe.[84]

Even in the poetry of Richard Rolle, we find an occasional love song.

> Thou make my sawl dear,
> for love changes my chere,
> how long shall I be here
> oft to hear song
> that is lasting so long;
> thou be my loving
> that I [of my] love may sing.[85]

In a religious love song, he sings, 'My song is in sighing.'[86] Similarly, a good man in 'Piers Plowman' is said to sometimes weep when he sings.[87]

A special form of very heart-felt song is the Christmas songs described in 'Sir Gawain and the Green Knight.'

> When burnes blithe of his burthe schal sitte
> And syng.[88]

---

83 Purvis, *The York Cycle*, 374.

84 'The White Beauty,' quoted in Sisam, *The Oxford Book of Medieval English Verse* (Oxford: Clarendon Press, 1970), 117.

85 From 'Ego Dormio,' quoted in Comper, *The Life of Richard Rolle* (London: Dent, 1929), 230.

86 Ibid., 231. The same line occurs again in the poem, 'Ihesu, God's Son, Lord of Majesty,' ibid., 242.

87 Langland, *Piers Plowman*, IX, 99ff.

88 Rolle, *Sir Gawain and the Green Knight*, 922.

One of the important roots of concert music, as we know it, were the brief performances sung after the meal was finished, when the listeners could concentrate on listening. In this same poem we read of the company, 'at the supper *and after*,' singing many noble songs, part-songs of Christmas and new carols.

> At the soper and after, mony athel songes,
> As coundutes of Cristmasse and caroles newe.[89]

[89] Ibid., 1654.

An anonymous poem, 'Orfeo and Heurodis,' also mentions the after dinner brief 'concert.' Here we read of the usual dinner music, but the performance in question was presumably a special one, after the meal. This performer waited until the guests were all silent and carefully tuned his instrument before he played. And, we are told, everyone liked his performance!

> In the castel the steward sat atte mete,
> And many lording was by him sete.
> Ther were trumpours and tabourers,
> Harpours fele, and crouders;
> Miche melody they maked alle;
> And Orfeo sat stille in the halle,
> And herkneth. When they been al stille
> He took his harp and tempred shille;
> The blissfulest notes he harped there
> That ever any man y-herd with ere;
> Ich man liked wel his glee.[90]

[90] Quoted in Sisam, *The Oxford Book of Medieval English Verse*, 95.

This same poem also portrays an individual artist, in a passage which is probably descriptive of many fine harpists of the time.

> Orfeo most of any thing
> Lovede the glee of harping;
> [Sure] was every good harpòur
> Of him to have muche honòur.
> Himself loved for to harpe
> And layde theron his wittes sharpe.
> He lerned so, ther nothing was
> A better harper in no plas;
> In the world was never ban born
> That ones Orpheo sat beforn,
> And he might of his harping here,
> He shulde thinke that he were

In one of the joys of Paradis,
Suche joy and melody in his harping is.[91]

[91] Ibid., 77.

The earliest king of England for whom we can document permanent musicians employed for art music is Edward III (1327–1377). His official household in 1348 included five shawm players and two string players, in addition to the instruments used for ceremonial music. There are also records of this king sending his shawm players abroad to minstrel schools, where they learned new repertoire.

Richard II (1377–1399) also sent his musicians to the minstrel schools and also rewarded visiting musicians who came to play for him, such as two musicians of the king of Aragon in 1392. But Richard himself was also a talented musician and his playing is described in an early chronicle.

And so playing balades and songs
Rondeleau and laix
Very well and beautiful: so it was
No one left him [when he played].[92]

[92] Quoted in Gerald Hayes, *King's Music* (London: Oxford University Press, 1937), 34.

This musician–king also loved books, helped Chaucer and opened schools. It was of Richard, murdered at age thirty-three, that Shakespeare wrote,

For God's sake let us sit upon the ground
and tell sad stories of the death of Kings.[93]

[93] *Richard II*, III, 3.

EDUCATIONAL MUSIC

There is an exceptional extant poem about the teaching of singers for the performance of church music which contains interesting hints of the performance expectations of these singers, including perfect intonation, knowledge of *musica ficta* and accuracy in the reading of rhythmic and melodic notation.

Unfit for the cloister I cower full of concern;
I look like an idiot and, well listen to my tale.
The song of the *si–sol–fa* makes me sick and sore
And I sit stuttering over a song a month and more.

I go wailing about as does a cuckoo.
There is many a sorrowful song I sing in my book;
I am held so hard at it, I scarcely dare look up.
All the mirth of this world I gave up for God.

I wail over my gradual and rore like a rook;
Little I knew when singing I undertook!
Some notes are short and some are long,
Some bend a-wayward like a meat-hook.

When I can sing my lesson, I go to my master
He hears my performance and doubts I have done well.
'What have you been doing, Master Walter, since Saturday noon?
You don't hold a single note, by God, in tune!

'Oh my dear Walter, your performance is a shame,
You start and stumble as though you were lame!
Your tones are not the tones which are named;
You bite asunder the B-natural, for a B-flat you are blamed.

'Oh my dear Walter, your work leaves much to wonder!
Like an old cauldron you begin to rumble!
You don't hit the notes, you sing under them.
Hold up, for shame! you sing flat.'

Then is Walter so woeful his heart nearly bleeds,
And he goes to visit William and wishes him luck.
'God knows,' says William, 'that I need it!'
Now I know how *judicare* was set in the Credo!

'I am as woeful as a bee that flounders in the water:
I work on the Psalms until my tongue tires.
I have not performed since Palm Sunday.
Are all songs as miserable as the psalms?'

'Yes, by God! you've said it, and it is worse.
I practice solfege, and sing afterwards, but I'm never better;
I hurl at the notes and heave them out of here!
Everyone who hears me knows that I error.

'Of B-flat and B-natural I knew nothing
When I left the secular world and, well listen to my tale—
Of *ef-fa-ut* and *e-la-mi* I knew nothing before;
I fail strongly in the *fa*, in it my fortune fails more.

'And there are other notes, *sol* and *ut* and *la*,
And that troublesome wretch men call *fa*:
Often it makes me ill and makes me full of woe;
I can never get it in tune when it is *ta*.[94]

94 A rule of musica ficta is that *ti* is sung like *fa* (*ta*, as our singer says), or B natural becomes B flat, when it is the top of a phrase.

'And there is a held note with two long tails;
For it our master has often knocked down my skittles.
How little you know what sorrow ails me:
It is but child's play what you do with the psalms!

'When one note leaps to another and causes riot,
That we call motion in high *ge–sol–re–ut*.
You were better not born if a mistake you would;
For then our master says "You're no good".'[95]

The discipline demanded of choral singers apparently made it difficult to recruit boys for the Chapel Royal, during the reign of Richard II. Therefore an order went out to one, John Melynek, to kidnap ('Impress') boys for this purpose.

> ... to take and seize for the king all such singing-men expert in the science of music as he could find and think able to do the king's service, within all places of the realm ... .[96]

FUNCTIONAL MUSIC

In 'Sir Gawain and the Green Knight,' we read of the king and his company entering the great hall, after the chanting in the chapel, to celebrate the Christmas season.

Fro the kyng was comen with knightes into the halle,
The chauntry of the chapel [came] to an ende,
Loude cry was there cast of clerkes and other.[97]

William Langland criticizes those clerics who take money on the side for the private Masses they sing[98] and another who after thirty years still can't sing!

I've been a priest and parson passing thirty years now,
Yet I can't either sing or chant *sol–fa*.[99]

A very common form of Functional Music was that used to welcome visitors to the town. Thus, in the *Tapiters and Couchers* play, the character Beadle says, 'And made mirth and melody this man for to meet.'[100] And an anonymous poem speaks of welcoming music with many players, while the observers 'wept for joy with their eyes because they saw them come back safe and sound.'

---

95 'Choristers Training,' in our modern English from the original quoted in Sisam, *The Oxford Book of Medieval English Verse*, 184ff.

96 Quoted in Edmonstoune Duncan, *The Story of Minstrelsy* (Detroit, 1968), 85.

97 Rolle, *Sir Gawain and the Green Knight*, 43.

98 Langland, *Piers Plowman*, III, 253.

99 Ibid., V, 415.

100 Purvis, *The York Cycle*, 230.

> The brought the queen into the town
> With al maner minstralcy.
> Lord! the was grete melody!
> For joye they wepe with her eighe
> That hem so sounde y-comen seighe.[101]

Some welcome festivities were rather ritualized, as for example in the tradition which remained consistent throughout the Renaissance—the association of trumpets with the highest nobility, the king. Thus, Froissart in his chronicles mentions that a lesser Scottish noble, Lord James Douglas, maintained trumpets and timpani, '*as if* he were king of Scotland.'

> ... son tinel honnerablement à trompes et à nakaires comme se ce fuist li rois d'Escoce.[102]

For important civic processions, such as the Lord Mayor's Procession in London, additional musicians would be hired. There was a growing supply of good musicians to be found in the civic wind bands which were beginning to be founded outside of London during the fourteenth century, including Leicester (1314), Exeter (1362) and York (1369). Thus an extant receipt for the Lord Mayor's Procession of 1369 lists payments to nine minstrels 'for playing, for their hoods and for drink.'[103]

At this time the important trade guilds in London also hired musicians to represent them on ceremonial occasions. An eyewitness report of the coronation procession for Richard II, reads,

> Nor did these great guilds lack a large company of clarions and trumpets: for every guild is led by its own trumpeters. Trumpeters had been stationed by the Londoners above the tower in the same street, which had been built in the king's honor, to sound a fanfare on his approach.[104]

There must have been many forms of music specific to various occupations, although it is little mentioned in the literature of this time. One interesting reference, in 'Piers Plowman,' mentions the songs of the ditch diggers and provides us with an actual title of one such song while complaining about the slow work.

> Such as diggers of ditches that do their jobs badly,
> And dawdle away the long day with '*Dieu save dame Emme*.'[105]

[101] 'Sir Orfeo,' quoted in Sisam, *The Oxford Book of Medieval English Verse*, 98.

[102] Jean Froissart, *Chroniques de Froissart* (Osnabrück: Biblio Verlag, 1967), II, 204.

[103] Maurice Byrne, 'Instruments for the Goldsmiths Company,' *The Galpin Society Journal* 24 (July 1971): 63.

[104] T. Walsingham, *Historia anglicana* (London: Longman, 1863), I, 331.

[105] Langland, *Piers Plowman*, Prologue, 224.

Hunting was, of course, a familiar activity among nobles and 'Sir Gawain and the Green Knight' mentions it often. In a typical reference we read 'the hunters blew many strong hunting signals.'

Strakande ful stoutly mony stif motes.[106]

Finally, numerous accounts of the use of music in battle can be found in the Chronicles of Froissart. Having said that, his primary interest was in accounting for the various nobles, and one must regret that his perspective was so limited. Thus, even the military descriptions are brief in detail. The following, for example, is all he left us of what must have been an unusually festive occasion, the entrance of Edward III into Calais.

> The King mounted his horse, as did the royalty, barons, and knights, they rode forward toward Calais and entered into the city to an abundance of trumpets, tabours, nacaires and buccines.[107]

Froissart also describes Edward's musicians performing on board ship in 1350.

> On embarking, the King gave orders as to the plan of fighting, and then seated himself in the bow of his ship, waiting for the Spaniards. He was dressed in a black velvet jacket, with a beaver hat of the same color, which became him well; and, according to those who were there, he was never more joyous. He made his minstrels play to him, on the horn, a German dance which 'Master John Chandos,' who was with him, had brought over from Germany; and he made 'Master Chandos' sing with his minstrels, 'which gave him great pleasure.'[108]

A final Froissart excerpt provides a striking description of the war music of the Scots. This passage, which reminds us of the accounts of the Crusades when the armies of the East used music to frighten the soldiers of the West, once again disappoints us in his failure to tell us all he knew.

> After that they made all their minstrels blow a variety of tones at once, and made the greatest revel in the world. It was the custom of the Scots, when they were assembled as an army, to have the foot soldiers, who had horns of all kinds, some small and some large, around their necks like hunters, to blow them all at once so that they make such a noise they can be heard four miles away; thus do they frighten their enemies and rejoice themselves. When the bishop of

---

106   Rolle, *Sir Gawain and the Green Knight*, 1364 See also 1362, 1428, 1446, 1465, 1698, 1910, 1913 'they all played at once,' and 1923.

107   Quoted in Georges Kastner, *Manuel Général de Musique Militaire* (Paris, 1848), 90.

108   Quoted in William Longman, *The History of the Life and Times of Edward the Third* (London: Longsman, Green & Co., 1869), 325.

Durham, with his banner and men approached within a league, the Scots blew their horns in such a manner that it seemed that all the devils in hell had been among them and those who heard them, and did not know of their custom, were much frightened. This blowing and noise continued for a long time and then ceased. And by that time the English were within a mile away. Then the Scots began to blow again, and made a great noise for as long as they did before. Then the bishop approached with his troops well arranged and came within sight of the Scots, who blew their horns again for a long time.[109]

Even lesser lords maintained impressive bands of military musicians for their personal use. The earl of Arundel took with him for the battle of Crecy, in 1376, four shawms, two trumpets and a clarion player.[110]

ENTERTAINMENT MUSIC

The most frequently mentioned form of entertainment music in early literature is the music of the banquet. 'Sir Gawain and the Green Knight' gives a full account of these festive occasions, including one in which carols were sung in the course of a banquet which had been continuing for fifteen days!

> Sithen cayred to the court caroles to make.
> For there the fest was ilyche ful fiften dayes.[111]

Again the suggestion is made that on such festive occasions the nobles themselves participated, as 'Such craft [art] is becoming at Christmastide, laughing at interludes and singing appropriate carols.'

> Wel becomes such craft upon Cristmasse,
> Laykyng of enterludes, to laghe and to syng,
> Among these kynde caroles of knightes and ladies.[112]

At great banquets each food course was paraded out from the kitchen by musicians. In this same poem we are told the first course was served with the sounds of trumpets, bedecked with bright banners, and the noise of *new* nakers and noble pipes.

> Then the first cource come with crakkyng of trumpes,
> With mony baner ful bryght that therbi henged.
> Newe nakryn noyse with the noble pipes.[113]

[109] Jean Froissart, *The Chronicle of Froissart*, trans. John Bourchier [1523] (New York: AMS Press, 1967), V, 230. We have modernized the English.

[110] Francis William Galpin, *Old English Instruments of Music* (London: Methuen, 1910), 203.

[111] Rolle, *Sir Gawain and the Green Knight*, 62ff.

[112] Ibid., 471ff.

[113] Ibid., 116ff.

We also find here the wind band playing for the meal, while the guests, we are told, and 'all manner of meats, they made as much merriment as any men might.'

With mirthe and mynstralsye, with metes at her wille,
Thay maden as mery as any men myghten.[114]

And, of course, there was dancing, which in England was most frequently done while singing carols.

Daunsed ful dryly with dere caroles.[115]

It is somewhat surprising in these early accounts to read of the more noisy ceremonial instruments playing indoors, as for example during the Christmas banquet described above.

Trumpes and nakerys,
Much pypyng [was present][116]

We may presume the trumpets, in particular, were not as powerful as the modern instrument we know and could thus be tolerated indoors. An extant payment during the reign of Edward II, for 1321, rewards two trumpeters 'for minstrelsy before the king in his chamber in the castle of Devizes.'[117]

We cannot conclude these references to aristocratic Entertainment Music without quoting one of our favorite eyewitness accounts from this century. This account describes a 'mumming,' which was an entertainment in disguises, in which the guest of honor plays a dice game, rigged to insure he would win. This particular event occurred in 1377, shortly before the coronation of Richard II, and includes the performance of the wind band and trumpets.

> At ye same tyme ye Comons of London made great sporte and solemnity to ye yong prince: for upon ye monday next before ye purification of our lady at night and in ye night were 130 men disguizedly aparailed and well mounted on horsebacke to goe on mumming to ye said prince, riding from Newgate through Cheape whear many people saw them with great noyse of minstralsye, trumpets, cornets and shawmes and great plenty of waxe troches lighted and in the beginning they rid 48 after ye maner of esquiers two and two together clothed in cotes and clokes of red say or sendall and their faces covered with vizards well and handsomely made: after these

114 Ibid., 1952.

115 Ibid., 1026.

116 Ibid., 1016.

117 Quoted in Richard Rastall, 'Some English Consort-Groupings of the late Middle Ages,' *Music & Letters* 55, no. 2 (1974): 188.

esquiers came 48 like knightes well arayed after ye same manner: after ye knights came one excellent arrayed and well mounted as he had bene an emperor: after him some 100 yards came one nobly arayed as a pope and after him came 24 arayed like cardinals and after ye cardinals came 8 or 10 arayed and with black vizards like deuils appearing nothing amiable seeming like legates, riding through London and ouer London bridge toward Kenyton wher ye yong prince made his aboad with his mother and the D. of Lancaster and ye Earles of Cambridge, Hertford, Warrick and Suffolk and many other lordes which were with him to hould the solemnity, and when they were come before the mansion they alighted on foot and entered into ye haule and sone after ye prince and his mother and ye other lordes came out of ye chamber into ye haule, and ye said mummers saluted them, shewing a pair of dice upon a table to play with ye prince, which dice were subtilly made that when ye prince shold cast he shold winne and ye said players and mummers set before ye prince three jewels each after other: the first a balle of gould, then a cupp of gould, then a gould ring, ye which ye said prince wonne at thre castes as before it was appointed, and after that they set before the prince's mother, the D. of Lancaster and ye other earles euery one a gould ringe and ye mother and ye lordes wonne them. And then ye prince caused to bring ye wyne and they dronk with great joye, commanding ye minstrels to play and ye trompets to begin to sound and other instruments to pipe etc. And ye prince and ye lordes dansed on ye one syde, and ye mummers on ye other a great while and then they drank and tooke their leaue and so departed toward London.[118]

118 London, British Library (Harleian MS 247, f. 172v).

Finally, in 'Piers Plowman,' we read of the singing by the common folk, in the tavern.

They began to make bets and bought more rounds
And sat so till evensong and sang sometimes
Till Glutton had gulped down a gallon and a gill.[119]

119 Langland, *Piers Plowman*, V, 337ff.

6   CHAUCER

GEOFFREY CHAUCER (1340–1400) was the first great figure of English literature and certainly her greatest writer of the fourteenth century. Chaucer was also a composer and he tells us that he composed hymns, ballades, roundels and virelais.[1]

The man saw much of life, fighting in France in 1357 and making diplomatic journeys to Italy in 1372 and 1378. As a result, he gives us a broad view of fourteenth-century English life, including the role of music. Indeed, one is struck by the constant presence of music throughout all levels of society. Among the ordinary people of his famous 'Canterbury Tales,' which describes a group of people meeting in a tavern on their pilgrimage to the shrine of Becket at Canterbury, the Knight, Squire, Prioress, Friar, Miller, a Cook's apprentice, Pardoner, Sumner, a carpenter's wife, Nicholas the poor scholar and Absalom the parish clerk were all performing musicians. The Squire, in particular, attracts our attention. Described as a lover and soldier, but without reference to being educated, he stands as a symbol of the importance of music as part of being a cultured person in the Renaissance. We would not have found one such as him before the fourteenth century. How many young men today could equal his accomplishments? Leaving aside the fact that he could ride a horse well, dance and draw, he is described as singing or playing the flute all day and could compose and notate his own music!

> Syngynge he was or floytynge al the day
> He was a fressh as is the monthe of May.
> Short was his gowne, with sleves longe and wyde.
> Wel koude he sitte on hors and faire ryde.
> He koude songes make and wel endite [notate],
> Juste and eek daunce, and weel purtreye and write.[2]

[1] 'The Legend of Good Women,' 422. Unless otherwise indicated, the line designations correspond to the version of the *Canterbury Tales* issued in 1868–1877 by the Chaucer Society and were taken from Geoffrey Chaucer, *The Complete Works of Geoffrey Chaucer*, ed. F. N. Robinson (Boston: Houghton Mifflin, 1933).

[2] 'Prologue, The Canterbury Tales,' 91ff.

ON THE PHYSIOLOGY OF AESTHETICS

As the reader will see below, when Chaucer intends Art, as we use the term, he uses the word 'craft.' When he uses the word 'Art,' as a noun, he usually means the 'Liberal Arts.' In such references to scholars of the Liberal Arts, Chaucer nearly always adds that they are poorly paid—as they are today! In 'The Miller's Tale,' for example, we read of 'a poor scholar, who had studied the liberal arts.'

> With hym ther was dwellynge a poure scoler,
> Hadde lerned art, …³

[3 'The Miller's Tale,' 3189.]

And in another place he mentions the poor scholar's threadbare cape:

> With a thredbare cope, as is a povre scoler …⁴

[4 Prologue, 'The Canterbury Tales,' 260.]

The philosophers, being another type of scholar, were also ones with little money.

> But al be that he was a philosophre,
> Yet hadde he but litel gold in cofre …⁵

[5 Ibid., 297.]

Perhaps this contributed to Chaucer's saying, in 'The Reeve's Tale,' that he 'cares not a weed' for philosophers and their art!

> Of al hir art I counte noght a tare.⁶

[6 'The Reeve's Tale,' 4056.]

One of the hallmarks of the early Renaissance humanists was a renewed interest in the writings of the ancient Greek philosophers and among these writings they rediscovered the concept of the 'music of the spheres.' Chaucer was also interested in this idea and the music of the nine spheres, he contends, is the original source for melody and harmony in the world.

> And after shewede he hym the nyne speres,
> And after that the melodye herde he
> That cometh of thilke speres thryes thre,
> That welle is of musik and melodye
> In this world here, and cause of armonye.⁷

[7 'The Parliament of the Birds,' 59ff.]

Perhaps because of the disparaging remarks which Chaucer makes from time to time about philosophers, we should not be too surprised that he seems not inclined to address or define Reason at length. Only indirectly does he recognize this faculty, as for example when he states that good speech is based on Reason.

> And which a goodly, softe speche
> Had that swete, my lyves leche!
> So frendly, and so wel ygrounded,
> Up al resoun so wel yfounded …[8]

8 'The Book of the Duchess,' 919. 'My lyves leche' is 'my love is my physician.'

Chaucer does clearly distinguish between Reason and the emotions, almost as if he were aware of the existence of the right and left hemispheres of the brain. In 'The Romaunt of the Rose,' for example, a lover, after becoming lost in the feelings of Love, rediscovers his rational self.

> And hadde witt, and my felyng.[9]

9 'The Romaunt of the Rose,' 1738.

In an even more interesting passage, Chaucer seems to suggest that a character should use both halves of the brain, as it were, to fully comprehend.

> You must both perceive *and* feel that pride is a sin.[10]

10 Ibid., 2240.

Chaucer, following centuries of Church writers, also suggests that it is Reason which must keep the emotions under control. In 'The Merchant's Tale,' the advice is given that, in order not to hinder one's salvation, the lust of one's wife must be controlled by skill and reason. Not pleasing her *too* amorously keeps one from other sins.

> In mariage, ne nevere mo shal bee,
> That yow shal lette of youre savacion,
> So that ye use, as skile is and reson,
> The lustes of youre wyf attemprely,
> And that ye plese hire nat to amorously,
> And that ye kepe yow eek from oother synne.[11]

11 'The Merchant's Tale,' 1676.

This was possible because Chaucer understood both Reason and the emotions to be housed in the mind.

> Have pacience and resoun in youre mynde![12]
> ……
> And moche sorwe hadde he in his mynde …[13]

12 Ibid., 2369.

13 'The Legend of Good Women,' III, 946.

That being the case, it seemed to him to follow naturally that Reason could control emotion, for as he said in one case, 'If you don't think of pain, you will feel none!'[14]

But this is not to say that Reason can *explain* the emotions. Especially in the example of a man falling in love, Chaucer wonders, 'Who can find Reason or wit in this?'

> That men shulde loven alwey causeles,
> Who can a resound fynde or wit in that?[15]

On the whole, one gets the impression that Chaucer himself valued what he had learned by experience more than what he had gained by conceptual information, such as we would associate with Reason. Even when he mentions 'science,' it is usually a reference to some practical knowledge, rather than formal or speculative knowledge. In 'The Canon's Yeoman's Tale,' when a priest is working at alchemy, he makes fun of the philosopher's 'waxing' and adds that there are few philosophers he would share his practical information with.

> Of this quyksilver an ounce, and heer bigynne,
> In the name of Crist, to wexe a philosofre.
> Ther been ful fewe to whiche I wolde profre
> To shewen hem thus muche of my science.[16]

Going even further, Chaucer says we should trust books only in the absence of personal experience. 'We should honor and believe these old books, where there is no test other than experience.'[17] Indeed, in numerous places Chaucer clearly states that various kinds of knowledge is proven only by experience. For example, with regard to the fact that there is a limit to one's lifespan, Chaucer says we need no authority for this, as it is proven by experience.[18] Or regarding the significance of dreams, 'This has been well founded by experience.'[19] Even, Chaucer says, where the Bible does not suffice, experience will teach you.

> And yf that hooly writ may nat suffyse,
> Experience shal the teche.[20]

---

14 'Troilus and Criseyde,' IV, 466.

15 'The Parliament of the Birds, ' 590.

16 'The Canon's Yeoman's Tale,' 1121.

17 'The Legend of Good Women,' 27.

18 'The Knight's Tale,' 3001.

19 'The Nun's Priest's Tale,' 4168.

20 'L'Envoy de Chaucer a Bukton,' 21. For additional references to understanding being proven by experience, see 'The Wife of Bath's Tale,' 468; 'The Friar'sTale,' 1517; 'The Sumner's Tale,' 2057; 'The Merchant's Tale,' 2238; 'Troilus and Criseyde,' III, 1283; 'The House of Fame,' II, 370; and 'Romaunt of the Rose,' 5553.

However much Chaucer valued experience, he also recognized, in an almost Darwinian sense, that we are in some way programed by Nature. In 'The Squire's Tale,' for example,

> That Nature in youre principles hath set.[21]

It follows, as well, that one can act against these principles.

> It is agayns the proces of nature.[22]

Chaucer attributes this kind of understanding to a frequently mentioned goddess of Nature,[23] whom, in turn, is the 'vicaire of the almyghty Lord.'[24]

While Chaucer mentions, from time to time, the five senses, he does not discuss the senses in a philosophical manner, apart from a few lines in his translation of Boethius. Neither does he discuss the soul in a philosophical context. He mentions the soul frequently, but usually only as an expression, much as we would today say, 'Bless my soul.'

ON THE PSYCHOLOGY OF AESTHETICS

EMOTIONS

Chaucer's references to the emotions suggest that he viewed them as natural and common to every man, as when he says 'Every happy man has a full delicate feeling.'[25] Emotions are real, and can be expressed through speech, as in 'A Complaint to his Lady,' where a character says, 'For truly I *say*, as I *feel*.'[26] He also gives an example of non-verbal expression of emotions, when Troilus gives a gentle sigh as an expression of his internal emotions,

> That shewed his affeccioun withinne.[27]

It is interesting that twice in 'The Legend of Good Women,' Chaucer raises the question whether emotions can be pretended. First he says, yes, it is possible to 'counterfeit pain and woe.'[28] Later, however, in 'The Legend of Phillis,' a character doubts that anyone has the ability to fake 'such tears.'

> 'How coude ye wepe so by craft' quod she,
> 'May there swiche teres feyned be?'[29]

---

21 'The Squire's Tale,' 487. See also 'The House of Fame,' I, 490 and III, 276; 'The Legend of Good Women,' 975; and 'The Complaint of Venus,' 14.

22 'The Franklin's Tale,' 1345. See also 'The Romaunt of the Rose,' 4769.

23 For references to the goddess of Nature, see the first 'Parson's Tale,' 450–460; 'The Book of the Duchess,' 870; 'The Parliament of Birds,' 303, 368, 639; and 'The Romaunt of the Rose,' 4871.

24 'The Parliament of Birds,' 379.

25 'Boece,' IV, 108.

26 'A Complaint to his Lady,' 55. Birds also express emotions orally, as in 'The Squire's Tale,' 55, they 'Ful loude songen hire [their] affeccious.'

27 'Troilus and Criseyde,' III, 1364.

28 'The Legend of Good Women,' 1376.

29 Ibid., 2528.

For Chaucer, Love was the most strongly felt emotion, which we see in his lines 'Lo which a greet thyng is affeccioun!'[30] and 'here beganne the depe affeccioun.'[31] This emotion is so strong that one can entirely lose one's sense of self. In 'Troilus and Criseyde,' Criseyde kisses Troilus until he was 'so full of joy he knew not where his spirit was.'

That where his spirit was, for joie he nyste.[32]

Pleasure and Pain

Chaucer usually presents Pleasure and Pain as opposites, as in 'For joy is contrarie unto sorowe,'[33] but again he does not engage in philosophical discussion.[34] In a case where each emotion becomes its opposite, a character in 'The Book of the Duchess,' cries 'my song has turned to lamentation, my laughter to weeping, my glad thoughts to heaviness.'

My song ys turned to pleynynge,
And al my laughtre to wepynge,
My glade thoghtes to hevynesse.[35]

In another place he associates joy with heaven, which he opposes with pain and hell.

A thousand tymes have I herd men telle
That ther ys joy in hevene and peyne in helle,
And I accorde wel that it ys so.[36]

On the other hand, he adds his contribution to a thought frequently found in ancient literature, that Love consists of *both* pleasure and pain.

A peyne also it is joious.[37]

This admixture of Pleasure and Pain in Love sometimes leaves the lover suffering a confusion of his feelings, weeping in laughter and singing while lamenting.

Wepinge to laughe, and singe in compleynyng …[38]

---

[30] 'The Miller's Tale,' 3611.
[31] 'The Legend of Good Women,' 1229.

[32] 'Troilus and Criseyde,' III, 1351.

[33] 'The Romaunt of the Rose,' 348.
[34] We especially wish he had elaborated on his observation in 'The Nun's Priest's Tale,' 4169, that dreams have a significance in both the joy and tribulation that we endure in the present life.

That dremes been significaciouns
As wel of joye as of tribulaciouns
That folk enduren in this lif present.

[35] 'The Book of the Duchess,' 599ff. A similar list of opposites is found in 'Troilus and Criseyde,' V, 1375.

[36] 'The Legend of Good Women,' 1ff.

[37] 'The Romaunt of the Rose,' 4733, and again in 5252.

[38] 'The Complaint of Venus,' 28.

One poor lover is so confused he declares, 'joy or sorrow, whatsoever it be—I have no feelings [at all].'

> Joye or sorowe, wherso hyt be—
> For I have felynge in nothyng ...³⁹

39 'The Book of the Duchess,' 10.

Chaucer speaks often of pain, although usually it is in some religious context, regarding sin, guilt or hell. The most extensive descriptions of pain, however, have to do with love. A character whose lady has died, in 'The Book of the Duchess,' experiences 'sorrows so painful, [which] lay so cold on his heart ... he had well-nigh lost his mind.' To express his pain he composed 'ten or twelve verses of a complaint, the most piteous, the most rueful, that ever I heard; for, by my troth, it was a great marvel that nature could suffer any living being to have such sorrow and not die,' It was 'a kind of song, but without note or tune.'⁴⁰ Chaucer adds that bachelors, not having Love, often experience only pain and woe.⁴¹

Finally, in his references to Pleasure and Pain, Chaucer several times uses Music as a synonym for joy or pleasure, as if the comparison were not 'Pleasure and Pain,' but 'Music and Pain.' Thus, Troilus asks, 'Shall I now weep or sing?'⁴² Similarly, a girl in 'The Man of Law's Tale' is told she must depart, whether 'she wepe or synge.'⁴³

40 'The Book of the Duchess,' 458ff. Chaucer provides these verses of 'complaint.'

> I am with sorrows overrun,
> Happiness get I never none ...

41 'The Merchant's Tale, 1278.
42 'Troilus and Criseyde,' II, 952.
43 'The Man of Law's Tale,' 294.

ON THE PHILOSOPHY OF AESTHETICS

One cannot expect to find, by the fourteenth century, much definition of the aesthetics of Art as we think of it today. Except for music, Art was still what it was since the world of ancient Greece, something thought of as a craft. Nevertheless, in Chaucer we begin to see characteristics which clearly extend beyond 'craft.' First of all, in 'The House of Fame,' he makes it clear that Beauty is something which words cannot describe.

> So that the grete craft, beaute,
> The cast, the curiosite
> Ne kan I not to yow devyse;
> My wit ne may me not suffise.⁴⁴

44 'The House of Fame,' III, 1177.

In another place, he makes a similar complaint that he lacks the power, be it in poetry or in prose, to adequately describe flowers.

> Allas, that I ne had Englyssh, ryme or prose,
> Suffisant this flour to preyse aryght!⁴⁵

All the best poetic expressions have been taken by earlier poets, Chaucer protests, 'Others have garnered the corn and I, coming after, am lucky to find an ear.' And once again, a character, upon seeing the face of a lady, declares that he lacks both the language and the wit to describe such Beauty.

> But which a visage had she thertoo!
> Allas! myn herte ys wonder woo
> That I ne kan discryven hyt!
> Me lakketh both Englyssh and wit
> For to undo hyt at the fulle;
> And eke my spirites be so dulle
> So gret a thyng for to devyse.⁴⁶

But we do not believe that Chaucer understood his craft to be merely a skill. On one occasion,⁴⁷ for example, he indirectly seems to suggest that one can identify good craft, that there is something there which can be seen or identified. It is nearly how we would use the word art, as in 'the art of poetry,' and it begins to approach our concepts of aesthetics. In this case, he says he does not want to exert himself to *show* his craft, but rather simply to provide the meaning.

> And that I do no diligence
> To shewe craft, but o sentence.⁴⁸

We also note that he recognized the element of inspiration as something needed for attaining a success beyond that of mere craft. In his 'Troilus and Criseyde,' based on Boccaccio's *Filostrato*, Chaucer begs the Muse, Cleo, to inspire him to succeed in rhyming this poem in English, which he is taking from the Latin. 'I need here none other art but thine.'

> O lady myn, that called art Cleo,
> Thow be my speed fro this forth, and my Muse,
> To ryme wel this book til I have do;
> Me nedeth here noon other art to use.⁴⁹

Other than pointing out that Beauty is something which cannot be described in words, the most specific definition which Chaucer

---

45 'The Legend of Good Women,' 66.

46 'The Book of the Duchess,' 895ff.

47 'The House of Fame, III, 1099.

48 'o sentence' is 'only the meaning' in old English.

49 'Troilus and Criseyde,' II, 7ff.

offers for Beauty is that it is *Truth*. 'Truth,' he says, 'is the crown of Beauty.'[50] This relationship between Beauty and Truth is, we believe, closely related in Chaucer's thinking on the ancient association between Art and Nature, for he also points out 'Nature does not lie.'[51] This observation, found in his poem, 'The Parliament of Birds,' is part of a discussion relating to the marriages of birds. The recommendation which Nature makes, in this regard, we might take as including two characteristics of the highest values in Nature, and hence, perhaps, in Chaucer's view of Art. Nature recommends that a bird marry the royal falcon, because it is the 'noblest [*gentilleste*] and most worthy.'

Chaucer pays tribute to the thought of the ancient Greeks, that Art imitates Nature, however, he generally implies that this cannot be perfectly done—hence, for example, his choice of a word to mean 'imitates.'

    As craft countrefeteth kynde.[52]

Indeed, in 'The Physician's Tale,' Nature herself addresses this point. 'I,' says Nature, 'can form and color a creature—who can imitate me?' Not Pygmalion, not Apelles or Zeuxis, for 'the Principal Former [God] has made me his vicar-general to form and paint earthly creatures as I will.'

    Lo! I, Nature,
    Thus kan I forme and peynte a creature,
    Whan that me list; who kan me countrefete?[53]

Thus, Chaucer reminds us that if Art imitates Nature, it is also something *less* than nature. Echo died because Narcissus would not love her!

    And Ecquo died, for Narcisus
    Nolde nat love hir.[54]

In one instance, Chaucer, in 'The Squire's Tale,' has the squire describe a perfect horse, of which he says *neither* 'Nature nor Art could improve, as all the people deemed.'

    Fro his tayl unto his ere,
    Nature ne art ne koude hym nat amende
    In no degree, as all the peple wende.[55]

50 'A Complaint unto Pity,' 75.

51 'The Parliament of Birds,' 629.

52 'The House of Fame,' III, 1212.

53 'The Physician's Tale,' 11ff.

54 'The Book of the Duchess,' 755.

55 'The Squire's Tale,' 196.

Finally, after the rediscovery of the ancient Greek Tragedies, there was some speculation among the humanists as to the role of music in these plays—some even contending that the entire plays were sung. Chaucer also refers to the importance of music in the original productions of Greek Tragedy, when he says Tragedy is nothing other than crying and bewailing *in song*, Fortune's attacks upon proud thrones.

> Traagediës noon oother maner thyng
> Ne kan in syngyng crie ne biwaille
> But that Fortune alwey wole assaille
> With unwar strook the regnes that been proude.[56]

56 'The Monk's Tale,' 3951.

ON THE AESTHETICS OF MUSIC

Chaucer makes the point that music is not just sounds made on musical instruments, but rather music is something beyond those sounds. He does this in 'Troilus and Criseyde,' where Pandarus observes that an ass hears the sound of a man playing the harp, but it, being a beast, does not hear the *music*, 'no melody can sink in to his mind to gladden him.'

> Or artow lik an asse to the harpe,
> That hereth sown whan men the strynges plye,
> But in his mynde of that no melodie
> May sinken hym to gladen, for that he
> So dul ys of his bestialite.[57]

57 'Troilus and Criseyde,' I, 731ff.

58 'The Book of the Duchess,' 1172.

Regarding the purpose of music, we find a very interesting comment in 'The Book of the Duchess,'[58] especially in view of the growing division in the Renaissance between *speculative* music (conceptual) and *practical* music (performance). When a character is speaking of whether Jubal invented music, as related in the Old Testament, or Pythagoras, another character responds that none of that matters and as for himself, 'I put my feeling into songs, to gladden my heart.' Chaucer touches here upon the very essence of music—expression of feelings. The use of music to 'gladden,' is, of course, one of the most frequently given purposes of music in all ancient and medieval literature.

Another reference to the importance of *feeling* in music is very interesting because Chaucer, for the knowing reader, makes fun of earlier philosophers, in particular Boethius for his emphasis on the mathematical aspects of music over feeling. Found in the 'Nun's Priest's Tale,' where a fox who has come to hear a rooster sing and declares that the rooster sings with more feeling in his music than Boethius or any singer.

> Therwith ye han in musyk moore feelynge
> Than hadde Boece, or any that kan synge.[59]

59 'Nun's Priest's Tale,' 4483

Later in this same passage, Chaucer observes that the best singer is one who sings from the heart.[60]

60 Ibid., 4491.

In this regard, since the importance of the expression of feeling and emotions in music is associated in more modern times with the fact that music can express what words cannot, it is interesting that the miller, in 'The Miller's Tale,' could play on his gittern and sing in a loud voice, yet was 'bashful of speech.'[61]

61 'The Miller's Tale,' 3333.

Another interesting reference to music as an expression of feeling is found in 'The Romaunt of the Rose,' where a musician's feelings toward unfaithful women is expressed by *discordant* music.[62]

62 'The Romaunt of the Rose,' 4247ff.

Returning to the purpose of music, earlier in the passage cited above from 'The Book of the Duchess,' another purpose for music is given as, 'to keep me from idleness.' Here the speaker makes the interesting observation that he had made many songs, but could 'not make them so well, nor knew all the art,' which, of course, carries the suggestion that there was a recognized 'art' to this form of composition.

> Althogh I koude not make so wel
> Songes, ne knewe the art al …[63]

63 'The Miller's Tale,' 1160.

Another frequently given purpose for music in both ancient and medieval literature is for the purpose of solace. Thus in 'The Romaunt of the Rose,' a singer specifically sings to 'solace the folk,'

> To syngen first, folk to solace.[64]

64 'The Romaunt of the Rose,' 756.

In 'Troilus and Criseyde,' Troilus begins a song which also has the purpose of overcoming sorrow.[65]

65 'Troilus and Criseyde,' I, 389.

On the other hand, sometimes sadness is so great that even music cannot 'gladden the heart.' When Criseyde was away, Troilus was so sad that he could not bear to hear (instrumental) music and thought no one should make music.

> Syn that he saugh his lade was aweye,
> It was his sorwe upon him for to sen,
> Or for to here on instruments so pleye.
> For she, that of his herte berthe the keye,
> Was absent, lo, this was his fantasie,
> That no wight sholde maken melodie.[66]

66 Ibid., V, 456.

A similar thought is expressed in a poem known as 'A.B.C.,' in which a plea is addressed to the Virgin Mary for solace, as 'no music or song can aid us in our adversity.'

> We han noon oother melodye or glee
> Us to rejoyse in oure adversitee.[67]

67 'A.B.C.,' 100.

Additional examples can be found in 'The Knight's Tale,' where even music can not cheer up a sad lover,[68] and in 'The Book of the Duchess,' when a character tells us that not even Orpheus, the god of music, can make his sorrow pass.[69] The same god of music, Orpheus, appears under his alternate name, Phoebes, in 'The Manciple's Tale,' where in his sadness he actually destroys his musical instruments!

68 ' 'The Knight's Tale,' 1367.

69 'The Book of the Duchess,' 569.

> For sorwe of which he brak his mynstralcie,
> Bothe harpe, and lute, and gyterne, and sautrie ...[70]

70 'The Manciple's Tale,' 267.

Another purpose of music given by Chaucer is to express sadness, by which he makes reference to a 'new' French song, *I have wasted my time and labor*.[71] Yet another purpose of music is to celebrate one's good fortune. In 'Troilus and Criseyde,' Pandarus says to Paranuter, 'thow hast cause for to synge.'[72]

71 'The Parson's Tale,' 245–250.

72 'Troilus and Criseyde,' I, 854.

Given this broad view of the purposes of music, one can appreciate the fact that Chaucer also believed variety was an important value in performance. In one place he observes that even the best harpist alive, with the best sounding harp and the most pointed plectrum, would never play on just one string or play just one song, for everyone's 'ears would grow dull.'[73]

73 Ibid., II, 1030.

As was the case with the ancient Greeks, the adjective 'sweet' is found in Chaucer as a synonym for the most beautiful music. In

'The Parliament of Birds,' we read of string instruments playing music of 'ravishing sweetness.'

> Of instruments of strenges in accord
> Herde I so pleye a ravyshyng swetnesse.⁷⁴

74 'The Parliament of Birds,' 197.

In this same passage, however, birds are given an even higher compliment, for their music is the voice of angels.

> On every bow the bryddes herde I synge,
> With voys of aungel in here armonye.

In 'The Books of the Duchess,' Chaucer again speaks of birds singing, some low and some high, with 'sweetness,' in tune, with 'so merry a harmony, so sweet strains' and observes 'nowhere was ever heard instrument or melody yet half so sweet or of half so well in accord.' When he also mentions that none merely pretended to sing, but all did not spare their voices, not to mention the reference to 'the most solemn service,' we are inclined to wonder if this passage were intended to reflect, not really a description of birds, but a representation of the best choral singing Chaucer had heard.

> With smale foules a gret hep
> That had affrayed me out of my slep,
> Thorgh noyse and swetness of her song.
> And, as me mette, they sate among
> Upon my chambre roof wythoute,
> Upon the tyles, overal aboute,
> And songen, everch in hys wyse,
> The moste solempne servise
> By noote, that ever man, y trowe,
> Had herd; for some of hem song lowe,
> Som high, and al of oon acord.
> To telle shortly, att oo word.
> Was never herd so swete a steven,—
> But hyt had be a thyng of heven,—
> So mery a soun, so swete entewnes,
> That certes, for the toun of Tewnes,
> I nolde but I had herd hem synge;
> For al my chambre gan to rynge
> Thurgh syngynge of her armonye.
> For instrument nor melodye
> Was nowhere herd yet half so swete,

Nor of acorde half so mete;
For ther was noon of hem that feyned
To synge, for ech of hem hym peyned
To fynde out mery crafty notes.
They ne spared not her throtes.⁷⁵

Finally, we treat separately the remarkable poem, 'The House of Fame,' for it offers some of Chaucer's most extensive descriptions of fourteenth-century musical practice.

The House of Fame

The general musician of the thirteenth century, the *jongleur*, gives way in the fourteenth century to the more specialized *minstrel*, who is usually a wind player.⁷⁶ The jongleur remains the lesser, wandering musician, whom Chaucer in one place equates with the golliard, the unemployed, wandering students and clergy of the thirteenth century.⁷⁷ The general disfavor in which these wandering musicians were now held can be seen in Chaucer's declaration that 'a jongleur is abominable to God!'⁷⁸

During the fourteenth century, the institutions called *scolae ministrallorum* appear and can be documented in considerable numbers. During Lent, when performances were not allowed, the more respected minstrels from throughout Europe would gather each year in a town willing to be host, usually in the Low Countries, in great numbers—one Italian town in 1324 is said to have hosted 1,500 minstrels.⁷⁹ It was in these gatherings, 'schools,' that the minstrels traded instruments and especially learned new, international repertoire, '*pour apprendre des nouvelles chansons*.'⁸⁰

Other than a number of references of various nobles sending their minstrels to these schools, and documentation of the various towns which hosted them, there is no literature which describes them—these were players, not writers. It is with this perspective, then, that our attention is drawn to a passage in Book III of Chaucer's *House of Fame*.⁸¹ We believe this passage, which has been overlooked by musicologists, is a rare description by someone who had actually observed one of these minstrel schools. While this poem takes the form of a dream, it is our contention that he could *only* have imagined such a description of a large gathering of wind instrument minstrels if he had at some point witnessed one of these

75 'The Book of the Duchess,' 295ff.

76 String players are sometimes called, 'string minstrels,' and singers 'mouth minstrels' (*ménétriers de bouche*).

77 'Prologue, The Canterbury Tales,' 560.

78 'The Manciple's Tale,' 343.

79 Romain Goldron, *Minstrels and Masters* (N.p.: H.S. Stuttman, 1968), 38.

80 Walter Salmen, *Der Fahrende Musiker im Europäischen Mittelalter* (Kassel: J. P. Hinnenthal-Verlag, 1960), 181ff.

81 House of Fame, 1197ff.

'schools.' And it is the extraordinarily large number of instrumentalists in particular which first attracts our attention. Of the wind instrument players, he says he saw 'many thousand times twelve!' There were others, playing instruments whose names he did not know, and they were more numerous 'than there be stars in heaven.' These he says he won't bother to name because it would take too much time and 'time lost can in no way be recovered.' He concludes his description of players with the lowly jongleurs, some of whom were also famous and whose name he knew. But, again, to list them all, he says, 'would take from now until doomsday!'

The contention that this description was inspired by his having observed a minstrel school is strengthened by his reference to the presence of famous players, as well as foreign visitors ('Pipers of the Duche tonge') and his specific mention that they all came 'to lerne.' It may be our only first-hand description of one of these schools.

> Ful the castel alle aboute,
> Of alle maner of mynstralles
> And gestiours that tellen tales
>   ……
>
> Tho saugh I stonden hem behynde,
> Afer fro hem, al be hemselve,
> Many thousand tymes twelve,
> That maden lowde mynstralcyes
> In cornemuse and shalemyes,
> And many other maner pipe,
> That craftely begunne to pipe
> Bothe in doucet and in rede,
> That ben at festes with the brede,
> And many flowte and liltyng-horne,
> And pipes made of grfene corne
>   ……
>
> Ther saugh I famous, olde and yonge,
> Pipers of the Duche tonge,
> To lerne love-daunces, sprynges,
> Reyes, and these strange thynges.
>   ……
>
> There saugh I sitte in other seës,
> Pleyinge upon sondry gleës,
> Whiche that I kan not nevene,
> Moo than sterres ben in hevene,

> Of whiche I nyl as now not ryme,
> For ese of yow, and los of tyme.
> For tyme ylost, this knowen ye,
> Be no way may recovered be.
> There saugh I pleye jugelours,
> ......
>
> What shuld I make lenger tale
> Of alle the pepil y ther say,
> Fro hennes into domes day!

Following this passage, Chaucer then begins a long section which addresses the entitlement of various members of society to 'Fame,' or lasting reputation. Since music and several kinds of musicians also figure in this section we should also consider them as well, for their possible insights into his views on the aesthetics of music.

The narrator begins walking up a hill covered with the tombstones of 'famous folk,' but in every case the inscriptions had been worn by time and the names could no longer be read. The narrator observes that these names have been 'melted away by heat, and not worn away by storms.' He does not identify these people, but we cannot help but wonder if they were troubadours, those who melted away by heat [Love], as compared to the wandering jongleurs who were out in the 'storms.'[82]

At the top of the hill are more tombstones, but on these the names can still be read, as they were protected against the elements by the castle. Do these represent those most fortunate of all minstrels, those hired, and thus protected, by nobles?

In another location, apart from the rest, is a space reserved for famous trumpeters, including some named in ancient literature and the Old Testament. These he associates with war, for in bloodshed one gladly uses trumpet playing.

> Of hem that maken blody soun
> In trumpe, beme, and claryoun;
> For in fight and blod-shedynge
> Ys used gladly clarionynge.

Now he comes across a group of the lowest class of musicians, the true wandering beggar musicians. They are crying for handouts, yet the narrator mentions how ironic it is to see them clad in royal coats, with coat-of-arms from all over the world (castoff

---

82 As in the *De Saint Pierre de du jongleor*:

But quite often in his shirt
Was exposed to wind and blast …

clothing being a common gift to such musicians). The whole class of thirteenth-century jongleurs and troubadours had often been criticized for being available to sing praise of a nobleman, for a fee, so here Chaucer also mentions those 'That crien ryche folkes laudes.'

Now, in this allegorical dream, we come upon the goddess of Fame herself who sits in judgment of various groups of people making their pleas for lasting fame.[83] To help dispense her judgments, she calls upon Æolus, the god of the winds, to bring his trumpets [*clarioun*]. One of these is a trumpet of gold, called 'Clear Praise' [*Clere Laude*], and the other is black, made of brass by the devil, and is called 'Slander.' When this black trumpet is blown, the sound, coming out as fast as a ball from a gun, is described as a foul noise, a kind of black, blue, red, greenish smoke, such as comes from the chimney where men melt lead.

83 Among these are poets and historians and one, whom is mentioned by name, the 'Englyssh Gaufride,' is thought by some scholars to be Chaucer himself.

> What dide this Eolus, but he
> Tok out hys blake trumpe of bras,
> That fouler than the devel was,
> and gan this trumpe for to blowe,
> As al the world shulde overthrowe,
> That thrughout every regioun
> Wente this foule trumpes soun,
> As swifte as pelet out of gonne,
> Whan fyr is in the poudre ronne.
> And such a smoke gan out wende
> Out of his foule trumpes ende,
> Blak, bloo, grenyssh, swartish red,
> As doth were that men melte led …

For a group of people who have done good works, but never received credit, the golden trumpet is blown. Presumably the golden trumpet was also blown for the next group, those who don't want credit, their good works having been done for goodness and for no other reason. 'I grant your wish,' says the goddess of Fame, 'let your works die!'

The following group also wanted no fame, for their works were done for God. 'What! are you mad?,' the goddess responds, 'You think you will do good and have no glory for it?' She has the golden trumpet 'ring out in music' their deeds for all the world to hear.

The next group is surely troubadours, for their 'good works' have all been done for women, for which 'women loved us madly,' but often rewarded only with brooches or rings. For all this hard work, they felt they deserved renown and the goddess agreed and had the golden trumpet play again.

Another group, though they were 'gluttonous swine and idle wretches full of the rotten vice of sloth,' thought they deserved fame on the same basis as the previous group, but the goddess had them condemned by the black trumpet. The following group of 'treacherous' people received the same reward.

In concluding this dream, the narrator provides the theme, 'I knew ever that folk have desired fame and glory and renown diversely. But truly till now I knew not how or where Fame dwelt; nor yet what manner of weight she is, in look or quality, nor the manner of her judgments, till the time I came hither.'

Finally, in this same poem, Chaucer makes several interesting observations on the acoustics of music and sound.[84] Sound, he says, is nothing but broken air, thus all speech is nothing but air. Similarly, when a player strikes the harp strings, whether hard or lightly, 'the air breaks apart with the stroke.' When a pipe is blown 'sharp' [strongly?], what we hear is the air 'twisted and rent with violence.' And, lastly, all sound tends to rise.

ART MUSIC

Chaucer refers to songs or singing a great number of times in his poetry and many of these references remind one of the troubadour, trouviére and Minnesinger traditions of the previous century. In particular, we think of the character in 'The Legend of Good Women'[85] who composes songs for the lady, sends her letters, tokens, brooches and rings and attends to her at dances and banquets, or the one who composed songs 'for the worship of Love' found in 'The House of Fame.'[86] In 'The Clerk of Oxford's Tale,' the clerk declares 'with heart fresh and lusty I will sing you a song to gladden you,'[87] which is all the more interesting to us for Chaucer provides the lyrics for this love song. In 'Troilus and Criseyde,' we find the lyrics for another love song.[88]

The troubadours also often sang welcome songs for the return of spring and summer, and Chaucer gives us the lyrics for such a song, although here sung by birds. Interestingly enough, he mentions that the melody of this song came from France.[89]

---

84 'The House of Fame,' II, 765ff.

85 'The Legend of Good Women,' 1268ff.

86 'The House of Fame,' 622ff.

87 'The Clerk's Tale,' 1173ff.

88 'Troilus and Criseyde,' I, 400ff.

89 'The Parliament of Birds,' 675ff.

> Now welcome, somer, with thy sonne softe,
> That hast this wintres wedres overshake,
> And driven away the longe nyghtes blake!

In the allegorical story of the goddess of Fame, the description of accompanied songs which made the palace walls ring, is also quite similar to many such scenes in the troubadour poetry.

> And, Lord! the hevenyssh melodye
> Of songes, ful of armonye,
> I herde aboute her trone ysonge
> That al the paleys-walles ronge![90]

An even more ancient tradition is the epic song, in which the singer sings of the deeds of heroes of the past. We find him in the tale of 'Sir Thopas,' where a minstrel is called for to sing tales of royalty, popes and cardinals.[91] In this same tradition are nineteen ladies who sing and dance a ballade, in 'carol style,'[92] the lyrics of which include reference to music in the Old Testament, Greece and Rome and Cleopatra.

A characteristic of the solo song which we do not find in the thirteenth century is 'loud' singing, which we take to mean enthusiasm. In the 'Canterbury Tales,' the carpenter's wife sang 'loud and lively'[93] and we are told that even a trumpet was not half so loud as the two-part songs sung by the Pardoner and the Sumner.[94] The parish clerk, Absalom, sometimes sang in a 'loud treble,'[95] but when he was thinking of love he sang in a small and gentle voice with good harmony from his gittern.

> He syngeth in his voys gentil and smal,
> 'Now, deere laady, if thy wille be,
> I praye yow that ye wole rewe on me,'
> Ful wel acordaunt to his gyternynge.[96]

We begin to find in the fourteenth century hints of performance which begin to have characteristics of 'concert' music. The Prior, when singing, appears to have enjoyed his listeners as much as they enjoyed his music, for 'his eyes twinkled in his head as the stars on a frosty night.'[97] Certainly we have a little concert by the wind minstrels when we are told 'it was like heaven to listen to them.'

---

90 'The House of Fame,' III, 1395.

91 'Sir Thopas,' 845ff.

92 'The Legend of Good Women,' 200ff.

93 'The Miller's Tale,' 3257.

94 'Prologue, The Canterbury Tales,' 669.

95 'The Miller's Tale,' 3332.

96 Ibid., 3360. This musical parish clerk could also serve as a barber, surgeon, lawyer and dance twenty different ways in the 'Oxford manner.'

97 'Prologue, The Canterbury Tales,' 266.

> Toforn hym gooth the loude mynstralcye,
> Til he cam to his chambre of parementz,
> Ther as they sownen diverse instrumentz,
> That it is lyk an heavene for to heere.⁹⁸

Another place where one finds something similar to 'concert' music as we know it, is *after* the meal. Music played when the food is brought out, or when the people are eating, must be considered functional music. But often brief 'concerts' followed a meal and the key is if the guests are *listening* to the music. We find such a description in 'The Squire's Tale,' where after the third course, the king 'sat … listening to his minstrels play their things deliciously before him at the table.'

> Whil that this kyng sit thus in his nobleye,
> Herknynge his mynstralles hir thynges pleye
> Biforn hym at the bord deliciously.⁹⁹

A singer we find especially attractive is Nicholas, the 'poor scholar' of Oxford. He sang only at night, in his room, for himself, sweetly singing to the accompaniment of his psaltery. But he sang a varied repertoire, some sacred songs and some secular ones, such as 'The King's Note.'

> And al above ther lay a gay sautrie,
> On which he made a-nyghtes melodie
> So swetely that all the cyhambre rong;
> And *Angelus ad virginem* he song;
> And after that he song the kynges noote.¹⁰⁰

98 'The Squire's Tale,' 268ff.
99 Ibid., 78.
100 'The Miller's Tale,' 3213.

EDUCATIONAL MUSIC

We find only one mention of true educational music in Chaucer, but it is a rather interesting one. It is a reference to the use of music to learn the Latin prayers of the Church.¹⁰¹ A child in the church school hears the older students singing the *Alma redemptoris* daily. After repeatedly hearing this, the child himself soon knows the music and the first verse by heart, but, of course, he has no idea what it means. When he asks an older child, one of the singers, what the words mean, the older child says he has heard that it is a salute

101 'The Prioress's Tale,' 516ff.

to 'our blessed Lady and pray her to be our help and succor when we die.' But, he brings into question the effectiveness of using music to teach Latin by observing that he really can't say more about it, for 'I learn singing, but know little grammar.'

> I kan namoore expounde in this mateere;
> I lerne song, I kan but smal grammeere.

FUNCTIONAL MUSIC

Chaucer provides descriptions for the full range of fourteenth-century functional music. References to church music include the singing of the friars,

> Til that the belle of laudes gan to rynge,
> And freres in the chauncel gonne synge.[102]

and the prioress, Madame Eglantine, who sang the divine service 'intoned full seemly in her nose.'[103]

Chaucer describes in several places the music performed for marriage celebrations. First, we see the bachelor arriving with minstrels hired for the occasion.

> And of his retenue the bachelrye,
> With many a sound of sondry melodye,
> Unto the village of the which I tolde,
> In this array the righte wey han holde.[104]

During one marriage ceremony the music is described as,

> And thus with alle blisse and melodye
> Hath Palamon ywedded Emelye.[105]

and in another place the following wedding celebration included flowers, torches and 'the place full of the sound of minstrelsy, of the amorous songs of marriage.'[106]

In 'The Man of Law's Tale,' Chaucer seems to tire of such description. 'Why,' he asks, 'should I speak of the royal array at the marriage, what course went first at the banquet, who blows a horn or trumpet?

102 'The Miller's Tale,' 3655.

103 'Prologue, The Canterbury Tales,' 122.

104 'The Clerk's Tale,' 270ff.

105 'The Knight's Tale,' 3097.

106 'The Legend of Good Women,' 2615.

Only the cream of every tale is to be set forth; there was eating and drinking, and folk danced and sang and made merry.'[107]

In 'The Knight's Tale' we find a description of an entire day on which a tournament is held. Since the tournament was, among other things, a form of practice for battle, it was usually the musical instruments used in battle which accompanied the tournament as well. In this case, the tournament is announced at the beginning of the day by,

> Pypes, trompes, nakers, clariounes,
> That in the bataille blowen blody sounes …[108]

Next, these instruments lead the participants through the city in a procession to the lists where the tournament will be held.

> Up goon the trompes and the melodye,
> And to the lystes rit the compaignye,
> By ordinance, thurghout the citee large …[109]

Now, as the trumpets announce the start, there is no more to say—we will see, he says, who can joust and who can ride.

> Now ryngen trompes loude and clarioun.
> There is namoore to seyn, but west and est
> In goon the speres ful sadly in arrest;
> In gooth the sharpe spore into the syde.
> Ther seen men who kan juste and who kan ryde …[110]

And the winners are greeted by all the wind instrument minstrels in a joyous celebration.

> The trompes, with the loude mynstralcie,
> The heraudes, that ful loude yelle and crie,
> Been in hire wele for joye …[111]

We might mention here that in his poem, 'The Former Age,' Chaucer imagines some former 'blissful life, peaceful and sweet,' where there was no war. Consequently, these people also did not know the trumpets of war.

> No trompes for the werres folk ne knewe …[112]

---

[107] 'The Man of Law's Tale,' 703.

[108] 'The Knight's Tale,' 2511. The Naker was an early timpani-type percussion instrument.

[109] Ibid., 2565.

[110] Ibid., 2600.

[111] Ibid., 2671.

[112] 'The Former Age,' 23.

Music for hunting is also mentioned by Chaucer. In 'The Nun's Priest's Tale,' we read of horns made of brass, wood and bone in which the hunters blew and bellowed.'[113] In 'The Book of the Duchess' a specific hunting horn signal is mentioned: 'three mots,' for the uncoupling of the hounds.[114]

The medieval tower watchman–musician, here the 'keeper of the fourth gate,' is also present.[115]

A final form of functional music which Chaucer includes is the bagpipe music of the miller, to which the pilgrims of the 'Canterbury Tales' walk.

> A baggepipe wel koude he blowe and sowne,
> And therwithal he broghte us out of towne.[116]

[113] 'The Nun's Priest's Tale,' 4588.

[114] 'The Book of the Duchess,' 375. See also 345.

[115] 'The Romaunt of the Rose,' 4236ff.

[116] 'Prologue, The Canterbury Tales,' 564.

ENTERTAINMENT MUSIC

In ancient and medieval literature the most frequently mentioned form of Entertainment Music is that performed for the banquet. The reference by Chaucer to 'The mynstralcye, the service at the feeste,'[117] must have been a common occurrence. For a great banquet additional musicians would be needed and it is here we find the wandering jongleurs earning a few coins.

> As jogelours pleyen at thise feestes grete.[118]

It was the normal tradition at banquets with important guests to have the food brought out from the kitchen, a course at a time, in a procession led by the wind instrument minstrels. This is exactly what Chaucer mentions in describing a wedding feast.

> Biforn hem stoode instrumentz of swich soun
> That Orpheus, ne of Thebes Amphioun,
> Ne maden nevere swich a melodye.
> At every cours thanne cam loud mynstralcye.[119]

And for entertainment at such banquets, the guests sang and danced.

> There feste they, there daunce they and synge.[120]

[117] 'The Knight's Tale,' 2197.

[118] 'The Squire's Tale,' 219.

[119] 'The Merchant's Tale,' 1715. The 'loud' minstrels were exclusively wind instruments.

[120] 'The Legend of Good Women,' 2157

7 FIFTEENTH-CENTURY ITALY

Nothing so marks the progress of humanism in Italy, not to mention the distance traveled by the Church since the Middle Ages, than a pronouncement made by Pope Nicholas v (1447–1455) shortly before his death. He urged Church officials to follow his example in supporting the arts and learning for the good of the Church. He even went so far as to proclaim the humanities as an essential part of the education of the clergy.[1] This pope, in fact, not only provided large stipends to leading scholars to make translations of ancient Greek literature, and to scribes to make copies, but he himself had personally made discoveries of important manuscripts.[2]

Gradually, during the course of the fifteenth century, painting, sculpture and architecture began to be accepted as members of the Liberal Arts and distinguished from the manual arts. It had taken two thousand years since the ancient Greeks to reach this point and yet to come was the concept of the 'Fine Arts,' which appears in the sixteenth century in the term *Arti di disegno*. Likewise the purpose of Art was becoming more defined. Alberti said the painter should please the crowd [*tutta la moltitudine*], but Leonardo raised the standard to pleasing the higher part of the crowd, speaking scornfully of those painters who aim to please the ignorant.[3]

The great scholar of Italian literature, Symonds finds, particularly in the poetry of Francesco Colonna, a deeper meaning which the arts had for the humanists.

> Thus Francesco Colonna makes us understand how Italy used both art and erudition as instruments in the liberation of human energies. For the thinkers and actors of that period, antiquity and the plastic arts were aids to the recovery of a paradise from which man had been exiled. They could not dissociate the conception of nature from studies which revealed their human dignity and freedom, or from arts whereby they expressed their vivid sense of beauty.[4]

---

1   D'Amico, *Renaissance Humanism in Papal Rome*, 122. The late fifteenth century cleric–philosopher, Gaffurio, agreed, 'For the belief that [the study of music] is preeminently suitable to clerics has long been accepted.' See Irwin Young, trans., *The Practica musicae of Franchinus Gafurius* (Madison: University of Wisconsin Press, 1969), 5.

2   Charles Stinger, *The Renaissance in Rome* (Bloomington: Indiana University Press, 1985), 283ff. Not all Church officials were so enlightened. The important philosopher, Giovanni Pico della Mirandola, was charged with heresy and had to flee to France in 1486 after he invited fellow scholars to Rome to debate his 'Nine Hundred Theses,' which he had deduced from his study of ancient and medieval philosophy. [Ibid., 301]

3   Anthony Blunt, *Artistic Theory in Italy, 1450–1600* (Oxford: Clarendon Press, 1959), 55ff.

4   Symonds, *Renaissance in Italy* (New York: Capricorn Books, 1964), I, 201.

During the course of the fifteenth century, as the powerful dukes took power in the various cities of Italy, the patronage of the arts passed from the town to the aristocracy. Thus Angelo Poliziano's (1454–1494) beautiful romantic epic poem, 'Stanze,' was written for the utilitarian purpose of celebrating a court tournament. Symonds, who calls Poliziano 'the greatest poet in Greek and Latin that Italy has produced,' finds this work a symbol of the change which had taken place.

> This marks the change effected by a century of prince-craft. Henceforth great poets were to care less for what they sang than for the style in which they sang. Henceforth poetry in Italy was written to please—to please patrons who were flattered with false pedigrees and absurd mythologies, with the imputation of virtues they never possessed, and with the impudent palliation of shame apparent to the world. Henceforth the bards of Ausonia deigned to tickle the ears of lustful boys and debauched cardinals, buying the bread of courtly sloth … It was the combined result of … court life, which had enfeebled the recipients of princely patronage … of social inequalities, which forced the poet to eat a master's bread, and turned the scholars of Italy into a crowd of servile and yet arrogant beggars. All these circumstances, and many more of the same kind, were slowly and surely undermining the vigor of the Italian intellect. Over the meridian splendor of 'Le Stanze' we already see their influences floating like a vaporous miasma.[5]

At the same time the commissioning of large polyphonic works by the Church began to decline. In fact, for the second half of the fifteenth century in Italy there is extant relatively little native polyphony. Did the art of music die? The great scholar of this period, Pirrotta, says no, rather the humanists moved away from this essentially Northern tradition.

> To humanists the *ars musicae* appeared irremediably tied to scholastic traditions, so they tended to reject it as something too close to medieval sophistry, outmoded, and far from the classicism and simplicity which they aspired to reestablish.[6]

One fifteenth-century writer, whom Pirrotta quotes, criticized the Northern polyphony, in particular the music of Isaac, Brumel, Compère and others, for being 'so florid that it more than satiates the ordinary capacity of the ear.'[7] The severe preacher, Savonarola, made the same objection late in the century.

---

5 Ibid., I, 352ff.

6 Pirrotta, 'Ars Nova and Stil Novo,' 75.

7 Paolo Cortesi, 'De cardinalatu libri tres,' quoted in Nino Pirrotta, *Music and Culture in Italy from the Middle Ages to the Baroque* (Cambridge: Harvard University Press, 1984), 104.

> These princes have their cappelle of singers which are a great confusion, because there stands one singer with a big voice who sounds like a calf, and the others howl around him like dogs, and no one understands what they are saying. So let these *canti figurati* go and sing instead the *canti fermi* ordered by the church.[8]

One of the main points Pirrotta makes is that there was in fact a great deal of musical activity, but it was outside the view of musical performance represented by most of the scholarly treatises of this period.

> One gets the impression that a humanist seldom read beyond the initial paragraphs; beyond the general concept of numerical proportions underlying musical phenomena, he had no use for a more detailed study of modes, rules of notation, or rhythmic proportions.

In this regard, he quotes a letter of 1429 by Ambrogio Traversari which clearly documents a broad musical knowledge quite apart from the scholarly perspective of the *musicus*.

> I have known for a long time that your agile and certainly golden mind has succeeded also in those matters that, contrary to ancient custom, are better known to common people than to scholars, such as the ability to sing very sweet arias [accompanied] with sound.[9]

In this letter Traversari praises a solo art song singer, Leonardo Giustiniani, for his ability in singing 'sweet songs.' Pirrotta adds that Giustiniani was only one of,

> a series of musicians whose names were better known to the fifteenth-century than those of Dufay, Ockeghem, or Josquin ... In the daily life of the fifteenth century they, not written music, were the elements of a resounding open-air stream, which gave pleasure ... to every layer of society.[10]

In another place, Pirrotta elaborates further on the importance of the 'unwritten' music. This music, he says, was,

> much more widely influential amongst the common people as well as amongst the wealthy. However, either because they were wholly or partially based on improvisation, or because they were transmitted without the use of written notation, much less evidence about these forms has survived. We cannot afford to overlook this

[8] Quoted in Lewis Lockwood, 'Strategies of Music Patronage in the Fifteenth Century: the Cappella of Ercole I d'Este,' in Iain Fenlon, ed., *Music in Medieval and Early Modern Europe* (Cambridge: Cambridge University Press, 1981), 243.

[9] Quoted in Pirrotta, *Music and Culture in Italy*, 145.

[10] Ibid., 167ff.

unwritten ... tradition ... however elusive it might prove. Indeed, it becomes especially important to consider it carefully when one is studying the different manifestations of humanist culture, for though we are better acquainted with the written tradition, the humanists themselves were almost suspicious of it, associating it as they did with scholasticism.

Poliziano and his contemporaries were quite right in seeing the works of musical theory on which polyphony was based as one of the most typical examples of that convoluted scholastic thought against which they were reacting.[11]

11 Nino Pirrotta and Elena Povoledo, *Music and Theatre from Poliziano to Monteverdi* (Cambridge: Cambridge University Press, 1982), 22.

ON THE PHYSIOLOGY OF AESTHETICS

Among the fifteenth-century Italian philosophers there was still some discussion of the problems which had concerned Church philosophers throughout the Middle Ages, in particular how the mind works and the nature of the soul.

The important early fifteenth-century Florentine philosopher, Leon Battista Alberti (b. 1404) believed strongly that Reason, and not the senses or the emotions, must rule man. He begins his book on the family, *I Libri della Famiglia* (1443), by promising 'I think about this matter objectively, with a mind detached and free of passion.'[12]

12 Leon Battista Alberti, *I Libri dela Famiglia*, trans. Renée Watkins (Columbia: University of South Carolina Press, 1969), 25. Alberti wrote treatises on ethics, love, religion, sociology, law, mathematics and the natural sciences.

During the fourteenth and fifteenth century in Italy the subject of the 'music of the spheres' again becomes a topic of discussion with the renewed interest in the writings of the early Greeks. The apparent organization of the heavenly bodies, and the possibility that they might be related to the proportions found in music, generated some discussion regarding music and the organization of the soul. For example, Marsilio Ficino, in his commentary on Plato's 'Timaeus,' takes Plato's reference to cosmic harmony and the 'soul of the universe' and projects the idea on the human soul.

> Musical consonance occurs in [air] and reaches the ears through motion, spherical motion: so that it is not surprising that it should be fitting to the soul, which is both the mean of things, and the origin of circular motion. In addition, musical sound, more than anything else perceived by the senses, conveys, as if animated, the emotions and thoughts of the singer's or player's soul to the listeners' souls; thus it preeminently corresponds with the soul.

He explains that the other senses only 'titillate the sense organs' but do not penetrate the depths of the soul like music. But music at once works on the senses, the soul and the mind, hence,

> it floods us with a wonderful pleasure: by its nature, both spiritual and material, it at once seizes and claims as its own, man in his entirety.[13]

13 Quoted in Palisca, *Humanism in Italian Renaissance Musical Thought*, 169.

The late fifteenth-century scholar and *maestro di capella* at the Duomo of Milan, Franchino Gaffurio, in his *De harmonia*, found that both cosmic and human harmony were the very basis of the purpose of music. The subsequent power of music on the soul he found due to his belief that the soul is organized according to musical ratios.

> The intellective part corresponds to the octave, the sensitive to the fifth, and the habitual to the fourth. The species of fourth are analogous to the motions of the habitual soul—increase, stasis, and decrease; the species of fifth, to the powers of the sensitive soul—sight, hearing, smell, and taste; the species of octave, to the function of the intellective soul—imagination, intellect, thought, reflection, opinion, reason and knowledge.[14]

14 Quoted in ibid., 177.

But Ugolino of Orvieto, in his *Declaratio musicae disciplinae* (ca. 1430–1435), found that it was human music, and not cosmic music, which harmonizes the parts of the soul and the sense's capacity to feel with the intellect's capacity to perceive. He also found that music permits the elements and parts of the body to be harmonized within itself.[15]

15 Quoted in ibid., 164.

Some humanistic philosophers, however, seemed no longer so interested in the process of knowledge, but rather preferred to extol the virtues of knowledge itself. Matteo Maria Boiardo, Count of Scandiano (1434–1494), wrote an epic romance, 'Orlando Innamorato,' which in many respects seems more characteristic of the romances of the thirteenth century. However, among the features which would not have been found in those earlier epics filled with chivalric love and battle is this humanistic argument on behalf of knowledge.

> I acknowledge, returned Orlando, that arms are the first consideration of a gentleman; but not at all that he does himself dishonor by knowledge. On the contrary, knowledge is as great an embellishment of the rest of his attainments, as the flowers are to the meadow before

us; and as to the knowledge of his Maker, the man that is without it is no better than a stock or a stone, or a brute beast. Neither, without study, can he reach anything like a due sense of the depth and divineness of the contemplation.[16]

For Alberti, both the first step toward knowledge and the first step in education was reading.

> Who does not know that the first useful thing to teach children is their letters? This is so basic that a gentleman, no matter how well born, will never be thought anything but a country dunce if he cannot read. I would like to see the young noble with a book in his hand more often than a sword. I have never liked the common saying of some people, that if you know how to sign your name and can figure out your balance, you have enough education.[17]

And by reading, Alberti, following his humanistic bent, meant only the finest of the ancient writers.

> The intellect, they say, is like a drinking vessel; if you first fill it with bad stuff it always retains something of the taste. This is why one should avoid crude and rough writers. One should follow the finest and most polished, keep them ever at hand, never tire of rereading them, recite them aloud frequently, and commit them to memory. I do not say anything against the knowledge found in any erudite and abundant source, but I decidedly prefer the good writers to the poor ones, and as there are enough whose work is perfect, I am sorry when people select the others.[18]

Giorgio Valla, a fifteenth-century music theorist, distinguished between science and art (one is immutable, the other not), but took the viewpoint of some earlier philosophers that the study of music must come first.

> A knowledge of music is necessary, without a doubt, to learning the [other] liberal arts, which are all dependent on speech.[19]

[16] Quoted in Leigh Hunt, *Stories from the Italian Poets* (London: Chapman and Hall, 1846), 63.

[17] Alberti, *I Libri dela Famiglia*, I, 80.

[18] Ibid., I, 83. He also recommends the exercises of antiquity, offering his opinion 'I think hardly any game which is played sitting down is proper to a really virile man.'

[19] Valla, 'De expetendis et fugiendis rebus' (Venice, 1501), quoted in Palisca, *Humanism in Italian Renaissance Musical Thought*, 67, 70.

ON THE PSYCHOLOGY OF AESTHETICS

The long period of Church discussion of, and condemnation of, feelings and emotions had long since ended. Following the thirteenth century troubadours, the emotion most frequently discussed was Love. Perhaps it is not an overstatement to say that no emotion so illuminated the feelings of man, nor played a greater role in bringing on the Renaissance, than did Love. Alberti gives a testimonial to the power of Love and, more significantly, points out that it is only by *experience* that one can understand such an emotion.

> Who would believe, except by the experience of his own feelings, how great and intense is the love of a father toward his children? Every kind of love seems to me no small matter. Many have been known to risk all their possessions, to give time and fortune, to undergo terrible hardships, dangers, and troubles only to display their loyalty and the quality of their love for a friend. And it is said that there have been men who, for desire of things loved which they thought they had lost, refused to continue living.[20]

In the play *Orpheus* (1471) by Angelo Poliziano, we find the familiar complaint of those earlier troubadours that there is more pain than joy in Love. He calls it the 'pain so sweet,' adding the interesting observation, 'He praises Love who suffers most from Love.'[21] This is followed by a song of a shepherd who complains that his 'fair Nymph' is deaf not only to his complaints, but the music of his pipe.

In this same author's romantic epic poem, 'Stanze,' a youth has not yet found pain in love and 'cannot put faith in the tears of others.' But another, 'consumed by ardent flames cried out to heaven,'

> Let just disdain move you, Love, let him at least believe by experience![22]

When this young man at length does fall in love, Poliziano makes the impact of this emotion most vivid.

> Ah! what a change came over him! Ah, how the fire rushed all through the young man's marrow! What a trembling shook the heart within his breast! He was soaked with an icy sweat.[23]

20 Alberti, *I Libri dela Famiglia*, I, 45.

21 Angelo Poliziano, *Orpheus*, trans. Louis Lord (Oxford: Oxford University Press, 1931), I, 78.

22 Angelo Poliziano, *Stanze*, trans. David Quint (University Park: Pennsylvania State University Press, 1993), I, xxii.

23 Ibid., I, xli.

Even the mighty Hercules, says Poliziano, is no match for the power of this emotion.

> Hercules puts aside the wild lion hide and clothes himself in a woman's skirt, he who has rescued the world from grave perils is now a lady's servant; and he is willing to suffer the unworthy pride of Love, he who once made his shoulders the column of heaven; and that hand accustomed to the ponderous club now turns a spindle.[24]

On the other hand, while the thirteenth- and fourteenth-century poets emphasized the pain which inevitably seemed to follow Love, now, perhaps reflecting the humanists' support of education in general, we find in Boiardo's 'Orlando Innamorato' an argument that Love improves a man.

> These feelings pursued him all the rest of the day, and still more closely at night. He did nothing but think and sigh, and find the soft feathers harder than any stone. Nor did he get better as time advanced. His once favorite pastime of hunting now ceased to afford him any delight. Nothing pleased him but to be giving dinners and balls, to make verses and sing them to his lute, and to joust and tourney in the eyes of his love, dressed in the most sumptuous apparel. But above all, gentle and graceful as he had been before, he now became still more gentle and graceful—for good qualities are always increased when a man is in love.[25]

Similarly, while the abstract concepts of Pleasure and Pain are no longer debated, the humanist philosopher, Paolo Cortesi, finds in this subject another opportunity to focus on learning. He emphasizes that the mere stopping of pain results in pleasure, but an ideal form of pleasure is one which also holds the potential for learning. Here he points to music as an example.

> We can easily establish that the stopping of anything from which sadness arises must be considered joyous by its own nature. Thus, if a discipline—which is a certain function of understanding something with the guidance of reason—is recognized to have a way of seeking not only a profit but also becoming pleasure, it is proper that whatever must be sought after for the sake of understanding and results by its own nature is a pleasure, this same should be sought after for the sake of both diversion and learning. Also, nobody who accords to music the faculty of contemplation, while its own nature is cheerful, should hesitate to confess that it must be rightly sought after for the sake of both pleasure and learning.[26]

---

24 Ibid., I, cxiv.

25 Quoted in Hunt, *Stories from the Italian Poets*, 74.

26 Cortesi, 'De cardinalatu libri tres,' quoted in Pirrotta, *Music and Culture in Italy*, 102.

ON THE PHILOSOPHY OF AESTHETICS

Apart from Leonardo da Vinci, there is relatively little extended discussion of the general philosophical concepts of aesthetics. Alberti defines Beauty as 'a certain regular harmony of all the parts of a thing of such a kind that nothing could be added or taken away or altered without making it less pleasing.' In saying this, however, he was not thinking of judging by an irrational delight, but rather by a rational, even mathematical,[27] standard.

> Beauty is a kind of harmony and concord of all the parts to form a whole which is constructed according to a fixed number, and a certain relation and order, as symmetry, the highest and most perfect law of nature, demands.[28]

Neither, he believed, is Beauty a matter of personal taste, although he took note of man's varying preference in women. He discusses this issue in writing about architecture.

> Many … say that our ideas of beauty and architecture are wholly false, maintaining that the forms of buildings are various and changeable according to the taste of each individual and not dependent on any rules of art. This is a common error of ignorance, to maintain that what [one] does not know does not exist.[29]

The traditional purpose given for Art is delight and for Alberti, the concept of delight in Art seems to have been a very realistic one.

> I may well stand looking at a picture … with no less delight to my mind than if I was reading a good history; for both are painters, one painting with words and the other with the brush.[30]

He also considered that one of the chief virtues of Art was found in the fact that in its practice it combined in a man both mind and body.

> There are other activities in which powers of body and mind function together to bring profit. Such are the occupations of painters, sculptors, musicians, and others like them. All these ways of making a living, since they depend mainly on our own personal powers, are what men call arts. They remain with us and do not go down in shipwrecks but swim away with our naked selves. They keep us company all our lives and feed and maintain our name and fame.[31]

---

27 Quite literally, he explains regarding the drawing of bodies:

> We have chosen a number of bodies considered by the skillful to be the most beautiful and have taken the dimensions of each of these. These we compared together, and leaving aside the extreme measurements which were below or above certain limits, we chose out those which the agreement of many cases showed to be the average.

28 Quoted in Blunt, *Artistic Theory in Italy*, 15.

29 Ibid., 17.

30 Ibid.,12.

31 Alberti, *I Libri dela Famiglia*, II, 145.

The familiarity with the ancient Greek philosophical treatises by the fifteenth-century humanists in Italy led to considerable discussion relative to imitation in Art. Cortesi, following the logic of Aristotle, placed great importance on the importance of imitation in the arts, reasoning that only that which we perceive by the senses can become part of the mind.[32]

For Alberti, the object in Art is not imitation of Nature, but Beauty. He observed that since Nature is rarely granted 'to produce anything absolutely perfect in every part,' one must 'always take what we paint from Nature and always choose from it the most beautiful things.' He mentions in this regard the ancient painter, Demetrius,

> who failed to obtain the highest praise, because he paid much more attention to making paintings which were true to nature than to making them beautiful.[33]

32 D'Amico, *Renaissance Humanism in Papal Rome*, 130.

33 Quoted in Blunt, *Artistic Theory in Italy*, 15.

ON THE AESTHETICS OF MUSIC

Above all, in the discussions of music during the fifteenth century in Italy, one is aware of a new emphasis on the importance of music. Carlo Valgulio, a late fifteenth-century writer who was drawn to music scholarship because of 'an incredible love for music and musicians,' wrote of the importance of music in his preface to his translation of Plutarch's 'De musica.'

> Since melos [also] signifies what someone cares about, and almost nothing ought to be of greater concern to a man than song and music, as it moves men and gods so much, they called song melos. Nor did they call absolutely any song thus but only that consisting of harmony.[34]

34 Quoted in Palisca, *Humanism in Italian Renaissance Musical Thought*, 88, 94.

One finds in the writings of Leonardo da Vinci an unprecedented discussion of numerous details of the technical aspects of painting and sculpture. The writers on music hardly mention this aspect of the performance of music. Indeed, for Cortese, mere technique for him hid from the listener the true virtues of music itself. Speaking of two organists he knew, he observes,

> Those who admire most highly Dominicus Venetus or Daniel Germanus usually in their praise omit the fact that they make intemperate

use of quick runs, by which the sense of the ear is filled with variety, but the artful modes cannot be knowingly discerned.³⁵

The only element of music which might be referred to as technique which was discussed at length, was relative to the organization of the score. The late fifteenth-century scholar, Franchino Gaffurio, in his *Theorica musice*, draws on a comment from Themistius' paraphrase of Aristotle's 'De anima' to suggest that delight in art comes from our recognition of order.

> When we receive something in sounds that is aptly and suitably put together, if it is intermingled and suitably in agreement with us, we take delight in it, recognizing it to be constructed in similitude with ourselves.³⁶

Thus, he concludes, all souls derive pleasure from music because it corresponds to the harmony within ourselves. In this regard, he quotes a remarkable passage from Cicero.

> A certain tuning pitch exists in one's body like that of the voice and instruments called harmony; just as sounds are made in singing, so out of the nature and form of the whole body issue various vibrations.³⁷

He mentions this passage from Cicero again in his *Practica musicae*.

> According to Marcus Tullius [Cicero] in the first of the Tusculan Disputations, Aristoxenus, a musician and philosopher, held that a certain tension of the body exists in the same way that a certain tension exists in vocal and instrumental music, a tension called harmony; so various vibrations are caused from the nature and configuration of the whole body like sounds in music.³⁸

The most recent research by physicists has demonstrated this is, in fact, the case. Every organ of the body produces a specific pitch!

While for centuries the discussion of individual tones had to be confined to their mathematical qualities, the music theorist, Giorgio Valla, now attempts to discuss the aesthetic qualities of tones.

> Some are straight, others round and reverberant; some rough, others flabby; some harsh, others grating; some are equal, such as unisons, others unequal, such as combinations of high and low pitch. Some are equal sounding, as are the diapason and disdiapason; others consonant, such as the diapente and diatessaron. Some are melodi-

35 Cortesi, 'De cardinalatu libri tres,' quoted in Pirrotta, *Music and Culture in Italy*, 103.

36 Quoted in ibid., 175.

37 'Tusculan Disputations,' 1.9.19–20, quoted in ibid., 177ff.

38 Young, *The Practica musicae of Franchinus Gafurius*, 11.

ous, such as the tone; others are dissonant and hard, like the tritone; others unmelodious, such as the semitone and ditone. There are transparent, yet not unpleasant, sounds; others are lean, like the voices of infants or sick persons; others are plump and dense, such as voices of men of warm temperament, or thin, as of boys, eunuchs, and women. Or they may be hard and bitter, harsh and violent, like thunder or hammering, or mute and raucous. Of voices some are strong and vigorous and at the same time pleasant, others broken and dissolute, weak and tremulant.[39]

Above all, among the humanists it is now the feelings and emotions in music which are emphasized. Gaffurio mentions this relative to his discussion of those elements of music which are established in nature and those through common practice.

> How does music exist? Partly by nature, partly through our practice. What sort of things by nature? Height and depth of pitch and the intervals. What sort of things through our practice? The rendering of emotion through the use of the pitches.[40]

Vincenzo Calmeta writes that while pleasure may be experienced from many kinds of music for its own sake, when music is used together with poetry it must give up some of its individuality and take on the primary responsibility of emphasizing the emotions and thought of the text.

> We must praise the good judgment of those, who in singing put all their effort into expressing the words well ... and have them accompanied by the music in the manner of masters accompanied by their servants ... not making the thoughts and emotions subservient to the music, but the music to the emotions and thoughts.[41]

The end of feelings in music is, of course, to move the listener. Among the numerous treatises on music extant from the University of Padua in the fifteenth century, is one by Prosdocimus de Beldemandis, 'Brevis summula proportionum,' which deals with both *musica speculativa* and *musica practica*.[42] In his 'Tractatus de contrapuncto,' he stresses that one must judge music by the ear as well as the intellect and recognizes the ability of *harmonia delectabilis* to move the listener.[43]

The fifteenth-century Italian philosophers continue to stress the long held purpose of music to offer solace to the listener. Thus, in Poliziano's play, *Orpheus* (1471), Orpheus prays to the gods to teach him a new kind of music, that he might soothe the cardinal of

---

39 Valla, 'De Musica,' quoted in Palisca, *Humanism in Italian Renaissance Musical Thought*, 79ff.

40 'Theorica,' (1492), II, i, quoted in ibid., 198.

41 Quoted in Pirrotta, *Music and Theatre*, 28.

42 Carpenter, *Music in the Medieval and Renaissance Universities*, 44ff.

43 Ibid., 46.

Mantua who was attending the first performance, 'one that may make serene my lord's brow, lighten his cares and charm his learned ears.'[44] Similarly, Gaffurio, in the final chapter of his *Theorica*, writes,

> Music soothes the human ears with wonderful sweetness derived as nowhere else from such measure, so much order, so much measured sonority.[45]

For Alberti, it was in particular the music of the Church which had a powerful soothing power.

> All other modes and kinds of singing weary with reiteration; only religious music never palls. I know not how others are affected; but for myself, those hymns and psalms of the Church produce on me the very effect for which they were designed, soothing all disturbance of the soul, and inspiring a certain ineffable languor full of reverence towards God. What heart of man is so rude as not to be softened when he hears the rhythmic rise and fall of those voices, complete and true, in cadences so sweet and flexible? I assure you that I never listen in these mysteries and funeral ceremonies to the Greek words which call on God for aid against our human wretchedness, without weeping. Then, too, I ponder what power music brings with it to soften us and soothe.[46]

There was one fifteenth-century Italian writer who spoke of music therapy as one of the purposes of music. Marsilio Ficino, the fifteenth-century founder of the Florentine Academy, was a philosopher who was an active musician in his leisure, playing the lyre for his own relaxation, but also in concerts in the Medici palace.[47] His combined interests in music and philosophy resulted in some very interesting conclusions on the virtues of music. Music, he believed, served man's 'spirit' in the same way medicine serves the body and theology the soul. The music one hears provokes a memory in the soul of the divine music found in the mind of God and in the music of the spheres.[48] Through affecting the spirit, Music also affects the body and soul. He says he personally found music valuable for ridding the body of disturbances and lifting his mind to a higher level of intellect.

Finally, one writer offers us an insight into the aesthetic value given contemporary music, when he observes, 'the song people praise is always the latest thing.'[49] Another singer is described as being careful 'to sing in well-ordered verses, to the *cythara*, the love stories of modern people that are [most] praised.'[50]

44 Poliziano, *Orpheus*, I, 84ff.

45 Quoted in Palisca, *Humanism in Italian Renaissance Musical Thought*, 197.

46 Quoted in Symonds, *Renaissance in Italy*, I, 188.

47 Paul Kristeller, 'Music and Learning in the Early Italian Renaissance,' *The Journal of Renaissance and Baroque Music* 1, no. 4 (June 1947): 269ff.

48 Ficino carries his belief in the 'music of the spheres' to an association of the signs of the zodiac with the tones of the scale.

49 Telemachos, 'Odyssey,' I, quoted in Nino Pirrotta, 'Music and Cultural Tendencies in 15th-Century Italy,' *Journal of the American Musicological Society* 19, no. 2 (Summer 1966): 140.

50 Ibid. Pirrotta in the following pages gives several more illustrations of such performance.

THE *PRACTICA MUSICAE* OF FRANCHINO GAFFURIO (1451–1518)

Gaffurio having done his duty to *musica speculativa*, with treatises on theory and harmony, in 1496 he published an important book on *musica practica*. Although this book is basically a text on composing, it nevertheless offers important first-hand observations on the actual performance of music in Italy in the second-half of the fifteenth century. This influential book was reprinted four more times before 1512 and material was taken from it by such later writers as Zarlino, Glarean and even John Dowland.

Gaffurio begins his book, by way of a dedication to Duke Ludovico Sforza of Milan, with a glowing tribute to the virtues of music.

> It is readily apparent, illustrious Prince, how much influence the profession of the art of music had and with what veneration it was held among the ancients. We know this both from the example of the greatest philosophers, who, when they were very old, devoted themselves to this discipline as if in it they put the finishing touch to their studies, and from the practice of the strictest governments, which with the utmost diligence saw to it that whatever was harmful to public morals should be eliminated. Not only did these states not banish the art of music; they cultivated it with the utmost zeal as the mother and nurse of morals. In a word, the position of music is firmly established by the unanimous and steadfast conviction of all people and all nations who have held this art in greater honor than any other.
>
> What other discipline has ever been accepted with so much approval? What other discipline has ever been accepted with so much unanimity by people of every age or sex, so that no one, in any condition of life, has yet been found who was not eager to soothe his cares with music.[51]

51 Young, *The Practica musicae of Franchinus Gaffurius*, 3.

Next Gaffurio states that the study of music has very practical benefits, even related to fields outside of music itself. In this regard he hastens to add that by music he is thinking only of noble music.

> Now music is not, like the other learned disciplines, merely a speculative pursuit: it reaches out into practice, and as was said previously, is connected with morality. I would not have fulfilled my duty if I had remained in the field of research only, serving a few without toiling diligently for the public good also.

Thus this field of music theory is valuable not only because of the knowledge it gives music itself, but also because its roots extend very far; it aids other disciplines. This has been verified by the testimony of very influential men who have acknowledged that they learned literature from music above all else. Fabius Quintilian declares, on the authority of Timagenes, that this art 'is the most ancient of all studies in liberal education.'

Now when I talk about music, I do not mean that theatrical and effeminate music which destroys rather than forms public morals, but rather that moderate, manly music celebrated by the ancient heroes, that music which was presented at the tables of kings and festive banquets when the guests, vying with one anther as the cithara circulated among them, sang of famous deeds of famous men, which was certainly a great inducement to kindle their eagerness for brave deeds. Truly this music rose even higher: she penetrates the heavens, and according to the testimony of the most celebrated bards, tells of the labors of the sun and the wandering moon and the titan stars, and as if not content to have filled the spaces of earth with merit, she invades the skies and takes her place among the mysteries of things divine.[52]

Gaffurio begins the main body of his text with the accurate observation that most previous theorists had concentrated on *musica speculativa*, rather than *musica practica*. Since it seems also to have been his observation that most practicing musicians had ignored the treatises on *musica speculativa*, and he seems to have forgotten that music is for the ear and not the eye, he is astonished that musicians could nevertheless understand such things as harmony. We know today that it is perfectly reasonable that one can know music without knowing about music, as is most perfectly demonstrated in the child prodigy and many popular artists who 'know nothing' about music.

> Even though the majority of scholars have pursued the science of harmony, while neglecting its practical application, far more extensively than those who have studied the practical application of the science—after all, the science of harmony is the domain of the theoretician—nevertheless, it is incredible that musicians could have attained the practical skill in harmony which they did attain without any study of theory.[53]

Gaffurio's explanation for this 'incredible' fact is the correct one: musicians learn the fundamentals of music experientially. It is this

52 Ibid., 5ff.

53 Ibid., 11.

same explanation, we might add, that accounts for the fact that the world is filled with musicians who have never taken our music classes! As a cleric, Gaffurio's discussion here is concentrated on vocal music.

> There are also those who hold things valueless if they are not put to use. These people feel that the practice of vocal music has contributed most to the development of harmony, not because of the multitude of possibilities inherent in practice, but because it exhibits perfection itself.
>
> The mechanics of music are found in the movement of sounds producing consonances and melody. It is true that these sounds are assembled in vain by theory and science unless they are expressed in practice. Hence one must become thoroughly conversant with the highness, lowness, and the combinations of these sounds not only through one's mind and reason but also through the habit of listening to and articulating them.[54]

Next, Gaffurio divides the field of vocal music into four categories,[55] the first being Church chant. Here he makes two interesting observations: first, that chant does not follow 'the nature of harmony,' but rather the Church modes, and second that he regards chant not so much music as 'a sonorous reading.'

The second category is poetry, the third is accompanied song and the fourth is song used in the theater. Here it is interesting that he testifies that some form of the ancient choral dance was still being performed.

In his following discussion of the nomenclature of notation, Gaffurio astutely recognizes that the notated material is not music, but only a symbol of the real music. Here he makes the fascinating suggestion that singers were singing some pitches which could not be notated.

> An interval, or space, can be understood to be the distance between a high and a low sound. Moreover, the mental concept of sound is symbolized in given notes. One must express the fixed, raised and lowered pitches of these notes arranged on a variety of lines and spaces vocally. Consequently, these notes are called vocal symbols. Further, sounds which cannot be written down are committed to memory by usage and practice so that they will not be lost, for their delivery flows imperceptibly into the past.[56]

54 Ibid., 12.

55 Ibid., 12ff.

56 Ibid., 18.

In his discussion of rhythm, Gaffurio suggests that the basic unit of pulse should correspond with the human pulse.

> Physicians agree that the correct measure of a short unit of time ought to be matched to the even beat of the pulse, establishing arsis and thesis as equal to that which they call [expansion] and [contraction] in the measurement of each pulse.[57]

57 Ibid., 69.

Regarding the expression of arsis and thesis in poetry, the rhythmic modes, Gaffurio makes a personal aesthetic judgment in placing elegance above following the rules.

> But it is not our province to prescribe rules and canons for everything that relates to this sort of structure and invention. We leave to the poets matters which are properly theirs. Yet I would have poets pay closest attention that they may attain this elegance in their poetry.[58]

58 Ibid., 70. He nevertheless offers some rules, as for example, 'The heroic hexameter loses most of its elegance whenever the second foot ends a part of the thought.'

Gaffurio also offers some very interesting aesthetics observations on the actual practice of singing as he knew it.[59]

59 Ibid., 160ff.

> Finally we are led to propose to young singers for the purpose of instruction and admonition that in performing they should not project their voices with an unusual and unsightly opening of their mouths, or with an absurd low bellowing when they strive after melodies, especially in the divine mysteries. They should also spurn excessive vibrato and voices which are too loud, for they are not compatible with other voices similarly pitched. In short, because of their own continual instability they cannot maintain harmonious proportions with the other voices.
>
> It is likewise fitting for one voice to be adjusted to another—a tenor to a cantus, for example—so that one may not be obscured by the other and succumb to its excessive clamor.
>
> ......
>
> Also an extravagant and indecorous movement of the head or hands reveals an unsound mind in a singer. The hand or head does not produce harmonious sounds; a well-modulated voice produces them. Those who sing imprudently are for the most part displeasing to those whom they expect to please. This was the principal reason by Guido himself, when he forsook florid, mensurable song, devoted himself to ecclesiastical modulation. For he says concerning these people, a fact which I painful report, 'In our times among all men singers are fools.'

In a note to composers, Gaffurio stresses the constant theme of both the Renaissance and early Baroque, that the music must emotionally support the words. It is interesting here that he associates Love with 'doleful sounds.'

> Let the composer of music strive to adapt the melody in its sweetness to the words of the song, so that when the words concern love or a longing for death or some lamentation, he will articulate and arrange doleful sounds so far as he can, as the Venetians are wont to do.[60]

Gaffurio concludes his treatise, *Practica musicae*, by once again observing that after having written two treatises on *musica speculativa*, he felt compelled to add a volume on *musica practica*.

> Now, most gracious reader, I have presented my thoughts on musical practice with perhaps no less talent and industry than you wished for, though your wish was unspoken. For of course, since you must have grown weary reading my books on theory, you needed this just as some sharp foods are needed to revive and refresh the taste. Nor did I think I could escape blame if, when I taught the art of music and unveiled its innermost secrets (if I may use the phrase), I held back in silence from this part as well, which is called *practica* and consists of and is perfected by the actual practice of music itself.[61]

ART MUSIC

The tradition of the civic band which had begun to flourish in Italy during the fourteenth century continued during the fifteenth. In Florence, for example, the ensemble now grew to include three shawms and two trombones. Beginning with the employment of a German shawmist in 1401, German musicians became a distinct preference in Florence throughout the century. One of these, the famous Augustine of Augsburg, served the city of Florence from 1489 to 1493 and then joined the wind band of Maximilian I.[62]

During the fifteenth century, in addition to a wide variety of performance functions, including horse races and archery contests, there is clear evidence that these civic bands had begun to perform regular concerts for the public. This was meant in a document of Florence which required the civic band to play every Sunday at the city hall.[63] Similarly, the civic players of Perugia at this time were

---

60 Ibid., 161.

61 Ibid., 266.

62 Keith Polk, 'Civic Patronage and Instrumental Ensembles in Renaissance Florence' (unpublished).

63 L. Cellesi, 'Documenti per la storia musicale di Firenze,' in *Rivista Musicale Italiana* (1927), 285.

also required by contract to play 'for the enjoyment of the public.'⁶⁴ An eyewitness from Turin describes such a concert, an hour-long concert from an arcade of the town hall.

64 Vessella, *La Banda*, 44.

> Ma che alegrezza se alde tutto il zorno de quel pifari de la signoria che sona in cima a un pergolo del palazzo un'ora de longo.⁶⁵

65 Andrea Calmo, *Lettere*, ed. V. Rosso (Turin, 1888), 331.

Some of the music played by these ensembles at civic banquets for visiting guests was also undoubtedly art music.

It is the fifteenth century, however, when we see the patronage of music shift from the towns to the newly powerful aristocrats—beginning with the pope, who now had his own wind band, known under the name '*i Musici Capitolini e i tamburini del Popolo Romano*.'

In Ferrara the employment of court musicians begins in earnest under Niccolò III (1393–1441) and continued under Borso d'Este (1450–1471) who maintained, in 1456, five trumpets, two shawms, a trombone, five players of keyboard and strings and one singer. Ten years later the size of the musical establishment was larger and now included an independent shawm ensemble. We gain a glimpse of the importance of this ensemble to the court in a letter of Borso's wife, written in response to a request by Bianca Maria Sforza to borrow the ensemble to help celebrate her daughter's wedding.

> Because the wedding will occur in April, which coincides with our own festival in honor of San Zorzo, the piffari are needed, indeed most needed to help honor our Saint. If the illustrious Bianca Maria Sforza would therefore accept our excuse we would be most content and if there are any other possibilities of repaying the declined favor we would be most happy.⁶⁶

66 Quoted in E. Motta, *Musici alla Corte degli Sforza: ricerche e documenti milanesi* (Milano, 1887), 22ff.

Under the next duke, Ercole I (1471–1505), the musical establishment grew to include separate ensembles of singers, 'musici, trombeti, piffari,' and 'tromboni.' Early in his reign he established the goal of creating 'a most celebrated cappella,' for which he mentions in a letter the 'excellent musicians, whom we are looking for everywhere.'⁶⁷ By 1474, this court, under Galeazzo, had an establishment of forty singers, of which eighteen were designated 'da camera.' The pay records indicate that one of the musicians was paid as much as a physician and all of them nearly twice the pay for court workers such as gardeners.⁶⁸ When his daughter, Lucrezia, was married to Annibale Bentivoglio of Bologna, in 1487, the procession to the

67 Quoted in Lockwood, 'Strategies of Music Patronage in the Fifteenth Century,' 231.

68 Werner Gundersheimer, *Ferrara* (Princeton: Princeton University Press, 1973), 293ff.

church of San Petronio included '100 trombita e 70 pifari e trombuni e chorni e flauti e tamburini e zamamele.'[69]

In Milan, the duke who was most active in the support of music was Galeazzo Maria Sforza (1466–1476), a man otherwise cruel and given to the seduction of the wives of his friends—which resulted in his murder. Court records prove that Galeazzo Maria was very active in competing with other dukes to acquire the best possible musicians. He paid very high wages to obtain the best winds from Germany and Flanders, as well as singers.[70]

When his successor, Giangaleazzo Sforza, was married in 1488 to Isabella of Aragon, an ensemble of fifty woodwind and brass participated. Another family wedding, that of Constanze Sforza to Camilla of Aragon in 1475, featured a performance of a large polychoral composition during the Mass.[71]

The most distinguished member of this family was duke Ludovico Sforza (1481–1499), famed for his building of numerous hospitals and universities and for his good fortune to marry one of the most extraordinary women of the fifteenth century, Beatrice d'Este (1475–1497). It was Beatrice who brought the Renaissance to Milan. A contemporary, Bernardino Corio, in his *Historia di Milano* (1500) recalled,

> Here was the learning of Greece, here Latin verse and prose flourished resplendently, here were the poetic Muses; hither the masters of the sculptor's art and those foremost in painting had gathered from distant countries, and here songs and sweet sounds of every kind and such dulcet harmonies were heard, that they seemed to have descended from Heaven itself upon this excelling court.

One of the artists attracted to the court was Leonardo da Vinci and one story is that he got the job by winning a music contest in Milan, singing to a lyre he had made. He was soon fulfilling a wide variety of requests for the court, including decorating stables, planning pageants, designing girdles for Beatrice, painting portraits for family members—not to mention his masterpiece, *The Last Supper*.

Beatrice herself was an accomplished singer and one eyewitness reports her 'spending day and night in singing and dancing.' A letter from Lodovico's son-in-law, Galeazzo, to Isabella d'Este, sister to Beatrice, describes Beatrice singing chansons while traveling.

---

69 L. F. Tagliavini, 'La Scuola musicale bolognese,' in *Musiciati della scuola emiliana* (Siena, 1956), 11.

70 Edmond Vander Straeten, *La Musique aux Pays Bas avant le XIXe Siècle* (New York, 1969), V, 26ff; Motta, *Musici alla Corte degli Sforza*; and F. Malaguzzi Valeri, *La Corte di Lodovico il Moro; La vita privata e l'arte a Milano nella seconda metà del quattrocento* (Milan: Ulrich Hoepli, 1913). A fascinating letter filled with details for his search for fine singers is quoted in William F. Prizer, 'North Italian Courts, 1460–1540,' in *The Renaissance*, ed. Iain Fenlon (Englewood Cliffs: Prentice Hall, 1989), 139.

71 Otto Kinkeldey, *Orgel und Klavier in der Musik des 16. Jahrhunderts* (Leipzig, 1910), 165ff., and *The New Grove Dictionary* (1980), 14:568.

> I started at ten o'clock with the duchess [Beatrice] and all of her ladies on horseback to go to Cuzzago, and in order to let your Highness enter fully into our pleasures, I must tell you that first of all I had to ride in a chariot with the duchess and Dioda, and as we drove we sang more than twenty-five chansons, arranged for three voices.

Beatrice, one of the greatest women of the Renaissance, died at age twenty-two.

In Mantua we encounter the sister to Beatrice, Isabella d'Este (1474–1539), who married Gianfrancesco Gonzaga in 1490. As extraordinary as her sister, when an ambassador said of Isabella 'I had heard much of her singular intelligence, yet I would not have believed the extent of it,' she was only six years of age!

By the age of sixteen she was an accomplished singer and performer on the clavichord. The distinguished poet, Pietro Bembo, who heard her sing some years later, left this account of hearing her singing.

> When she sings, especially to the lute, I believe that Orpheus and Amphion, who knew how to bring inanimate objects to life with their song, would be stupefied with wonder on hearing her, and I do not doubt that neither of them would have known how to do as well as she does in keeping the harmony most diligently so that the rhythm never falters, but rather measures the song, now rising, now falling, and keeps the harmony on the lute and at once according her tongue and both hands with the inflections of the song. Thus if you were to hear her sing even a single time, I am certain that you would be like those who heard the Sirens and forgot their native lands and their own homes.

Another eyewitness heard Isabella sing in 1502, reporting that 'with a lute in her hands she sang various canzonettes with [beautiful] tunes and utmost sweetness.'[72]

She also continued to maintain her proficiency on the clavichord as we see in an interesting letter she wrote to Lorenzo da Pavia, a maker of keyboard instruments.

> Honored Sir: We remember that when we were in Pavia we saw a very beautiful and flawless clavichord which you made for the illustrious duchess of Milan, our sister. We now wish to own an instrument of such perfection, and hold the view that there is nobody in all Italy who could satisfy us better than you. We therefore ask you

72 Zambotti, 'Diario ferrarese,' 327, in a report by Cagnolo, quoted in Pirrotta and Povoledo, *Music and Theatre from Poliziano to Monteverdi*, 52.

to make us a clavichord of such beauty and excellence as would be consonant with your talents and the confidence that we repose in you. We make only one condition: it must be light to the touch. Our hands are weak and we cannot play well if we have to press the keys hard.

She was as demanding of all the artists who worked for her, including the singers of the churches of her lands, as we see in a letter she wrote the abbot of one of these.

Kindly remember that we discussed your improving the singing of the nuns. I find it shameful that the Women's College performs in a disorderly fashion. If they learned to sing, they would not only offer greater glory to God but please me better … My ears are offended when I hear such discords.

Isabella also maintained a wind band and had her own children study the shawm and trombone privately.

Even a small court such as that of Federigo da Montefeltro of Urbino (1444–1482) maintained eight full-time wind players and two organists.[73] When Isabella of Urbino married Roberto Malatesta in 1475, the visiting musicians included fifty trumpets, one hundred shawms, twenty-two drummers and two cornett players from the service of the bishop of Ferrara.[74]

Finally, the court in Florence supported music as appropriate to the center of so much political activity in the latter part of the Renaissance in Italy. The best known personage of the fifteenth century in Florence, Lorenzo the Magnificent, maintained his own personal wind band. In an anecdote which reflects much on the life of the court musician at this time, he once decided, at two o'clock in the morning, to throw snow balls at the palace of Marietta Strozzi. This was accomplished by the light of flaming torches and the music of his trumpets and shawms.[75]

But he also loved singing[76] and was particularly associated with carnival songs, some of which he composed to be sung by characters on the magnificent chariots which rolled through Florence. A sixteenth-century scholar of these songs describes the custom,

to go forth after dinner, and often they lasted till three or four hours into the night, with a multitude of masked men on horseback following, richly dressed, exceeding sometimes three hundred in number, and as many men on foot with lighted torches. Thus they traversed the city, singing to the accompaniment of music arranged for four, eight, twelve, or even fifteen voices, supported by various instruments.[77]

---

73   Grove, 19:463

74   N. Bridgman, *La vie musicale au quattrocento* (Paris, 1964), 18, 46.

75   William Roscoe, *Life of Lorenzo de' Medici* (London, 1877), 118ff.

76   Pirrotta, *Music and Theatre*, 23.

77   Il Lasca, quoted in Symonds, *Renaissance in Italy*, I, 339.

After Savonarola, these events sometimes took on a grim satire of the earlier ones. A triumphal car in 1512 was covered in back cloth, with skeletons instead of art works painted on his sides. Now songs such as the following were heard:

> We too in the Carnival
> Sang our love-song through the town;
> Thus from sin to sin we all
> Headlong, heedless, tumbled down;
> Now we cry, the world around,
> Penitence, oh penitence!
>
> Senseless, blind, and stubborn fools!
> Time steals all things as he rides:
> Honors, glories, states, and schools,
> Pass away, and nought abides;
> Till the tomb our carcass hides,
> And compels grim penitence.[78]

From such fragmentary accounts it is difficult to judge with confidence the nature of Lorenzo's musical taste; perhaps the fact that he appreciated Heinrich Isaac is more revealing. In return, the composition Isaac wrote for Lorenzo's funeral in 1492, 'Quis dabit capiti meo aquam,' may have the exaggerated textual praise of a courtier,

> Who will give my head water,
> Who will give my eyes
> A fount of tears
> That I may weep at night,
> That I may weep by day?

but the music is different. It is a genuine, moving tribute to Lorenzo by Isaac.

Among the Art Music heard in these courts during the fifteenth century was the continued long tradition of the solo art song, the singer of poetry. Indeed, poets such as Cariteo, Tebaldeo and Poliziano hired singers to make their new poetry known to the public.[79]

An eyewitness to such a performance at the close of the century, Angelo Poliziano, was moved by what he heard.

> No sooner were we seated at the table than Fabio was ordered to sing, together with some other experts, certain of those songs which are put into writing with those little signs of music, and immediately he

78 A song by Antonio Alamanni, quoted in Symonds, *Renaissance in Italy*, I, 345.

79 Pirrotta, *Music and Culture*, 170.

filled our ears, or rather our hearts, with a voice so sweet that (I do not know about the others) as for myself, I was almost transported out of my senses, and was touched beyond doubt by the unspoken feeling of an altogether divine pleasure ... Now it was varied, now sustained, now exalted and now restrained, now calm and now vehement, now slowing down and now quickening its pace, but always it was precise, always clear and always pleasant.[80]

The power of song which Poliziano pays tribute to here can also be seen in his play, Orpheus, where he has Orpheus say, 'Perhaps my tearful song may change my bitter fate.'[81]

In an account of the 1441 wedding banquet of Francesco Sforza and Bianca Maria Visconti, a solo singer is introduced as 'whom the stars have endowed with the power of soothing and pacifying.'[82]

The fifteenth-century writer, Cortesi, mentions a specific singer for the beauty and power of his solo singing.

> Seraphinus Aquilanus was the originator of the renewal of this genre, by whom such a controlled conjunction of words and songs was woven that there could be nothing sweeter than the manner of his modes. And so, such a multitude of imitative court singers [*auledi*] emanated from him that whatever is seen to be sung in this genre in all Italy appears to be born out of the model of his sung poems [*carmina*] and modes. For which reason, it can be rightly said that the motions of the souls are usually appeased and excited with more vehemence by the *carmina* produced in this genre; for, when the rhythms of the words and sentences are combined with the sweetness of the melodic modes, nothing can prevent [the listener] from being exceedingly moved because of the power of the ear and of its similarity to the soul. And this usually happens quite often when either vehement motions are represented in the singing by the verses, or the spirits are exhorted to the learning of morals and knowledge, on which human happiness is dependent.[83]

This same writer also makes some interesting comments on the instruments which might have accompanied such singers. In mentioning the lutes, he speaks of their 'creeping easily into the minds of men with their exquisite sweetness.' Interestingly enough, he suggests that the ear rejects the 'Spanish lyre' as being almost too sweet.[84]

Finally, there was a broad repertoire of genuine popular solo singing, most of which has been lost to us in so far as the actual music is concerned. Symonds, however, finds that it lingers on as an echo in the Italian style.

---

80 Quoted in Pirrotta, *Music and Theatre*, 36.

81 Poliziano, *Orpheus*, III, 90.

82 Antonio Cornazano, 'La Sfortiade,' quoted in Pirrotta, *Music and Culture*, 90.

83 Paolo Cortesi, 'De cardinalatu libri tres,' quoted in ibid., 105.

84 Ibid., 103.

The popular poetry of the *quattrocento* is still more interesting than its prose. No period of Italian history was probably more fruitful of songs poured fourth from the very heart of the people, on the fields and in the city. The music of these lyrics still lingers about the Tuscan highlands and the shores of Sicily, where much that now passes for original composition is but the echo of most ancient melody stored in the retentive memory of peasants.[85]

85 Symonds, *Renaissance in Italy*, I, 208.

Symonds also adds that Poliziano, in a letter to Lorenzo de' Medici of 1488, mentions that he and his friends amused themselves by singing variations on peasant *rappresaglie* songs which they heard on the way.[86]

86 Ibid., 233.

Pirrota refers to some specific genre, such as the *tramesse*, *inframesse* and *tramezzi*, of banquet music played while the food was paraded out from the kitchen. But, he notes, the 'more elaborate performances were probably reserved for the end of the banquet.'[87] It was such after dinner performances which, as we have often pointed out in this series, were listened to as art music, as opposed to the 'background' music played while the food as being consumed.

87 Pirrotta, *Music and Theatre*, 10.

And above all, it is the presence of the contemplative listener which identifies art music. Thus, even in performance descriptions which otherwise seem to be of an entertainment genre, if the activity stops and people are reported to be intently listening we may suspect that a moment of art music was occurring. For example, in an allegorical pageant presented as part of the entertainment of the wedding of Annibale Bentivoglio and Lucrezia d'Este in 1487, an eyewitness reports 'the spectators, of whom there were a large number were asked to be silent, for the hall was full of the noise of their comments on the arrival of the floats.'[88]

88 Ibid., 14, fn. 16.

EDUCATIONAL MUSIC

During the fifteenth century in Italy, the humanists made strong arguments for a return to the practice of the ancient Greeks in using music to educate, to improve the character of the listener. Vittorino da Feltre (1396–1415), who established a humanistic school in the court of Gianfrancesco Gonzaga in Mantua, was a strong believer in the Greek ideals of music having a beneficial effect on character, and for this purpose he introduced music at meal times for his students.[89]

89 Carpenter, *Music in the Medieval and Renaissance Universities*, 44.

Another who believed in the use of music during meals for educational purposes was Paolo Cortesi. In a treatise on the organization of the household of a cardinal, *De cardinalatu libri tres*, he observes,

> The same must be said about the kind of all other passions, against which an adverse position must be taken always by the [cardinal] at other times, but more than ever at this time of recreation, lest his body be prevented from digesting the food by some intervening discomfort of his soul. Wherefore, since at this time those things must be sought after by which a cheerful mood is usually aroused, it may well be inquired whether the pleasure of music should be put to use particularly at this point, inasmuch as many, estranged from the natural disposition of the normal sense, not only reject it because of some sad perversion of their nature, but even think it to be hurtful for the reason that it is somehow an invitation to idle pleasure, and above all, that its merriment usually arouses the evil of lust. On the opposite side, however, many agree to resort to it as to a certain discipline that is engaged in the knowledge of concordance and modes.
>
> Indeed, we are convinced that music should be put to use at this time for the sake not only of merriment, but also of knowledge and morals …
>
> It must be said that music must be sought after for the sake of morals, inasmuch as the habit of passing judgment on what is similar to morals in its rational basis cannot be considered to be different from the habit of passing judgment on the rational basis of morals themselves, and of becoming expert in this latter judgment through imitation. Also, since the melodious modes of music appear to imitate all the habits of morals and all the motions of passions, there is no doubt that to be entertained by a temperate combination of modes would also mean to get in the habit of passing judgment on the rational basis of morals. This can also be proved, inasmuch as it is evident that all the habits and motions of the soul are found in the nature of the modes, in which nature the similarity to fortitude, or temperance, or anger, or mildness is exhibited, and it can easily be observed and judged that the minds of men are usually brought to those motions just as they are excited by the action of the modes.[90]

Carlo Valgulio, a secretary to the papal treasurer (1481–1485), and later to cardinal Cesare Borgia, believed that the performance of music was in a general state of decay. In the preface to his translation of Plutarch's *De musica*, dedicated to the singer Titus Pyrrhinus, he urges the latter to raise the level of performance and its ethical efficacy to that of the ancients.[91] He found that musicians have little

---

90 Cortesi, quoted in Pirrotta, in *Music and Culture*, 102.

91 Quoted in Palisca, *Humanism in Italian Renaissance Musical Thought*, 88ff. Valgulio also quotes, from Dicaearchus's lost treatise 'Concerning musical contests,' the interesting note that contest singers always held something in their hand while performing, such as a branch of laurel or myrtle. Today, it is a large handkerchief!

regard for these effects, 'filling their books with mere play of notes.' He recommends to this singer his interpretation of Aristotle's division of songs into three classes: edifying, purgative and recreational.

> Some songs were moral, others suitable for imbuing the soul with divine spirit, and still others active. The first category is suited to customs that are consistent with the most gentle virtue. The second class, songs which induce ecstasy, has the capacity to purge men who are disturbed by entering into subjects that are arousing and soft and by opening the affections to the purgation of fear and pity, which depress and afflict men's souls. Such melodies fill souls with a beneficial contentment.[92]

92 Ibid., 100.

Franchino Gaffurio, in his *Theorica musice*, also stresses the ethical potential of music.

> Socrates and Plato and also the Pythagoreans, attributing a moral resource to music, ordered by a common law that adolescents and youth, and young women too, be educated in music, not for inciting to desire, through which this discipline becomes cheapened, but for moderating the movements of the soul through rule and reason. Just as not every note is valid for a melody of sounds but only that which makes a good consonance, so also not all motions of the soul but only those that are suited to reason belong to the correct harmony of life.[93]

93 Ibid., 193.

Finally, Angelo Poliziano, in his 'Stanze,' finds an example of this purpose of music in the ancient tradition of solo singing, which was, for the humanists, another facet of their interest in ancient Greek culture.

> Then, once the stars had appeared in the sky, he would happily return to his house; in the company of the nine [muses] he would longingly sing celestial verses, and with his noble poetry he would awaken a thousand flames of ancient virtue in the breasts of his listeners.[94]

94 Poliziano, *Stanze*, I, xi.

FUNCTIONAL MUSIC

One of the most interesting aspects we find in accounts of fifteenth-century Church music in Italy is a suggestion that the *joy* of Church music had returned—the joy so often described in the early years of the Church, but so rarely mentioned during the Middle Ages. It is this new attitude, influenced by the humanists and amplified by the return of instruments to the Mass during the fifteenth century, which will result in the following century in the exuberant music of Gabrieli.

This new spirit even results in a new type of vernacular Church music, as we see in one of the important Church humanists of the fifteenth century, Ambrogio Traversari (b. 1386). As a monk he was of course trained to sing the necessary services, but in his correspondence with the Venetian humanist and composer, Leonardo Giustiniani (1388–1446), we learn he also delighted in singing vernacular songs in honor of God. Giustiniani had written such songs, with instrumental accompaniment, which were popular and when Traversari requested copies, the composer posed the question whether a humanist should be devoted to vernacular music. Yes, wrote Traversari, for,

> those ancients, whom we admire, hardly despised this as uncultured. As is well-known, Socrates as an old man sang, accompanying himself with a lyre, a skill he had not cultivated before.[95]

Traversari also mentions the joy of Church singing in a letter to Agostino da Portico, a monk at S. Maria degli Angeli.

> I cannot help but mourn being deprived of such joy, and the rich consolation which I experienced in the solitude of my heart when I celebrated with you the delightful Sabbath, when we sang to the Lord a new song and intoned psalms of joy.[96]

We begin to find, at this time, accounts of individual Church singers who were independently recognized as artists. When Matteo of Perugia was hired in 1402 by the cathedral in Milan, it was noted that he was recognized 'for his sweet and mellifluous songs and measures.' His successor in 1411, Ambrosio da Pessano, was hired 'that the church might be honored with mellifluous voices and sweet and beauteous songs.'[97]

---

95 Stinger, *Humanism and the Church Fathers*, 3. Part of Traversari's effectiveness as an humanist was that he had not studied in the university and was thus free of medieval scholasticism.

96 Stinger, *Humanism and the Church Fathers*, 4.

97 Larner, *Culture and Society in Italy, 1290–1420*, 169.

No doubt partly in competition with the festive celebrations organized by the town governments, special celebrations of the Church begin to make more use of music. In Rome, in 1462, a great Church celebration was held to honor the arrival of the relic, the head of Andrew, brother of St. Peter. On this occasion one heard the singing of children dressed as angels and the sounds of flutes and trumpets.[98] For some of the faithful, apparently, it was important as well for their funerals to reflect this expanding sense of ceremony. The 1412 will of Ludovico Cortusi, a professor of canon law at the University of Padua, stipulated that his funeral procession should include fifty musicians, performing on trumpets, string instruments and organs, together with twelve virgins singing and rejoicing.[99]

There are also a number of university documents which refer to musical performance, as for example a document of 1405 reveals that paid trumpeters were available at the University of Bologna to perform in university ceremonies.[100] Another document of 1435 tells us that each academic year began with a sung Mass and that students were no longer allowed to hire trumpets and other instruments to participate in their graduating ceremonies. He could hire instrumentalists to form a procession with him to the cathedral and one such payment mentions three shawms and four trumpeters.[101]

The romantic epic, 'Stanze,' by Poliziano contains a number of references to military trumpets, all reflecting the political turmoil of the latter part of the century. One of these, which portrays the inspiriting quality the military trumpet was supposed to have, reads,

> Already he seems to hear the sounding trumpets, already he becomes fierce in arms: all afire, he rises to his feet …[102]

[98] Stinger, *Humanism and the Church Fathers*, 177.

[99] Carpenter, *Music in the Medieval and Renaissance Universities*, 38.

[100] Ibid., 35.

[101] Ibid., 36.

[102] Poliziano, *Stanze*, II, xl.

ENTERTAINMENT MUSIC

Perhaps nothing in the literature of fifteenth-century Italy so clearly documents the rising aesthetic interests of the humanists as the fact that the usual descriptions of entertainment music, so frequently found in earlier literature because they make for fascinating reading, are almost entirely absent. Indeed, we cannot help but notice that a document of 1405 of the University of Bologna bans musical entertainment.[103]

[103] Carpenter, *Music in the Medieval and Renaissance Universities*, 35.

8 LEONARDO DA VINCI

LEONARDO DA VINCI (1452–1519) was perhaps the most broadly talented man who has yet lived. Apart from his drawings in his notebooks, which include not only virtually every machine known to the fifteenth century (and some not known, such as the helicopter), but also anatomy, zoology, optics and architecture, there is that extraordinary letter of job application which he wrote to Lodovico of Milan. After describing his abilities in designing instruments of war, from special cannons to armor plated vehicles and ships, he added,

> In time of peace I believe that I can give you as complete satisfaction as anyone else in architecture, in the construction of buildings both private and public, and in conducting water from one place to another.
>
> Also I can execute sculpture in marble, bronze, or clay, and also painting, in which my work will stand comparison with that of anyone else whoever he may be.

Were all those skills sufficient to convince Lodovico to hire Leonardo? Apparently not, for according to one sixteenth-century writer, Vasari, it was Leonardo's skill in music which won him the job![1] When he arrived he apparently won great applause by his performance on an instrument he had made, a silver lyre in the shape of a horse's skull.

Another contemporary, Paolo Giovio, reports that Leonardo's performances on the lyre were received by young and old with wonder and delight.[2] A sixteenth-century writer, Lomazzo, reports that his performance on the lyre 'surpassed all musicians of his time.'[3]

As with everything else the man was interested in, Leonardo's interest in music carried him into a study of the most remote corners of the subject, including sketches of numerous inventions and improvements of musical instruments and notes on acoustics. It is our great loss that Leonardo apparently wrote at least two books

1 Quoted in Jean Paul Richter, ed., *The Literary Works of Leonardo da Vinci* (London: Phaidon, 1970), I, 69.

2 Paolo Giovio, *Leonardi Vencii Vita* (1528).

3 Lomazzo, *Idea del Tempio della Pittura* (Milan: Per Paolo Gottardo Ponto, 1590).

on music which are no longer extant. One of these, on the voice, he mentioned in one of his notes.

> My book 'On Voice' is in the hands of Messer Battista dell' Aquila, steward-in-waiting to the pope.[4]

The note which follows this reference mentions a second book, on musical instruments.

> And I shall not enlarge on this as the subject is dealt with very fully in the book on musical instruments.[5]

Unfortunately, the extant written comments on music by Leonardo are not so extensive as we might have hoped, given his evident knowledge of the subject, but he did promise us that he would speak from personal experience.

> They will say that I, having no literary skill, cannot properly express that which I desire to treat of; but they do not know that my subjects are to be dealt with by experience rather than by words; and experience has been the mistress of those who wrote well. And so, as mistress, I will cite her in all cases.[6]

Most of Leonardo's remarks on music are by way of analogy to painting, but they are nevertheless revealing, taken together with his general comments on aesthetics.

ON THE PHYSIOLOGY OF AESTHETICS

The basis of Leonardo's approach to nearly every discipline was that of a true physical scientist.

> Science is an investigation by the mind which begins with the ultimate origin of a subject beyond which nothing in nature can be found to form part of that subject …
>
> No human investigation can be called true science without passing through mathematical tests; and if you say that the sciences which begin and end in the mind contain truth, this cannot be conceded, and must be denied for many reasons. First and foremost because in such mental discourses experience does not come in, without which nothing reveals itself with certainty.[7]

---

4   Richter, *The Literary Works of Leonardo da Vinci*, I, 113. Most references in this chapter are taken from this source, which also gives the original library and shelf-marks where the autograph documents may be found.

5   Ibid., I, 113.

6   Ibid., I, 116.

7   Ibid., I, 31ff.

By experience Leonardo meant that which has been confirmed by one's own senses. This becomes the basis of Reason and in those subjects which cannot be confirmed by Reason or experience, only the disagreement of varying opinions can exist.

> They say that knowledge born of experience is mechanical, but that knowledge born and consummated in the mind is scientific, while knowledge born of science and culminating in manual work is semi-mechanical. But to me it seems that all sciences are vain and full or errors that are not born of experience, mother of all certainty, and that are not tested by experience, that is to say, that do not at their origin, middle or end pass through any of the five senses. (For if we are doubtful about the certainty of things that pass through the senses how much more should we question the many things against which these senses rebel, such as the nature of God and the soul and the like, about which there are endless disputes and controversies. And truly it so happens that where reason is not, its place is taken by clamor. This never occurs when things are certain. Therefore, where there are quarrels, there true science is not; because truth can only end one way—wherever it is known, controversy is silenced for all time, and should controversy nevertheless again arise, then our conclusions must have been uncertain and confused and not truth which is reborn.) All true sciences are the result of experience which has passed through our senses, thus silencing the tongues of litigants.[8]

[8] Ibid., I, 33ff.

Leonardo addressed the importance of the role of experience through numerous observations, as the following will illustrate.

> Experience, the interpreter between formative nature and the human race, teaches how that nature acts among mortals; and being constrained by necessity cannot act otherwise than as reason, which is its helm, requires it to act.[9]
>
> ......
>
> Experience does not err; only your judgments err by expecting from her what is not in her power. Men wrongly complain of Experience; with great abuse they accuse her of leading them astray. Let experience alone, and turn your complaints against your ignorance, which causes you to be carried away by vain and foolish desires as to expect from it things that are not in her power; saying that she is fallacious.[10]
>
> ......
>
> Wisdom is the daughter of experience.[11]

[9] Ibid., II, 240.

[10] Ibid., II, 240.

[11] Ibid., II, 240.

On the Senses

Through Leonardo's personal study of anatomy he concluded from physical evidence that man's senses were inferior to those of the lower animals. This is no doubt true, although the correct reason lies in adaption and not the one he arrives at.

> I have found that in the composition of the human body as compared with the bodies of animals the organs of sense are duller and coarser. Thus it is composed of less ingenious instruments, and of spaces less capacious for receiving the faculties of sense.[12]

12 Ibid., II, 96.

One of Leonardo's fundamental beliefs, one which he writes of numerous times, is that among the senses of man, vision is the most valuable. In this passage he takes the opportunity to remind the other sciences of their debt to the eye.

> The eye, which is the window of the soul, is the chief organ whereby the understanding can have the most complete and magnificent view of the infinite works of nature; and the ear comes second, which acquires dignity by hearing the things the eye has seen. If you historians, or poets, or mathematicians, had never seen things with your eyes, you could report but imperfectly on them in your writing.[13]

13 Ibid., I, 56, 367.

For many centuries philosophers had wondered and argued over the question of the process by which we obtain the information of the senses. In the case of vision, it was clear to Leonardo that we actually capture the image itself. He took as proof of this the example that in looking at a bright light, when we close the eye we can still see the image in the eye.[14] He made no comparable analogy for the sense of hearing, but he did use the illustration of water making circles when a stone is thrown in it as a demonstration of the explanation for the nature of sound waves.[15]

14 Ibid., I, 132.

15 Ibid., I, 140.

It is also interesting that Leonardo seemed to find a relationship with the visual perspective of objects as they recede into the distance and the aural perspective of notes as they proceed in time.

> Although the objects seen by the eye do, in fact, touch each other as they recede, I will nevertheless found my rule on spaces of 20 braccia each; as a musician does with notes, which, though they can be carried on one into the next, he divides into degrees from note to note, calling them 1st, 2nd, 3rd, 4th, 5th; and has affixed a name to each degree in raising or lowering the voice.[16]

16 Ibid., I, 157.

Of Man's Faculties

The Church fathers had for centuries speculated on the location of the soul, an important necessity for a dogma based on life after death. Leonardo, in an analogy with music, first concluded the soul is in the body, but not of the body.

> The soul can never be corrupted with the corruption of the body, but is in the body as it were the air which causes the sound of the organ, where, when a pipe bursts, the wind would cease to have any good effect.[17]

17 Ibid., II, 238.

As for the location of the soul, Leonardo appears to have concluded that it is synonymous with the mind.

> The soul seems to reside in the judgment, and the judgment would seem to be seated in that part where all the senses meet; and this is called the Common Sense [*senso comune*] and is not all-pervading throughout the body, as many have thought.[18]

18 Ibid., II, 101.

Here also, Leonardo found the principal faculties of man.

> There are four Powers: memory and intellect, desire and covetousness. The first two are mental and the others sensual. The three senses: sight, hearing, and smell cannot well be prevented; touch and taste not at all.[19]

19 Ibid., II, 103.

While he did not emphasize the conclusion asserted by most philosophers that Reason must rule, he clearly set it apart in function.

> The senses are of the earth; Reason stands apart from them in contemplation.[20]

20 Ibid., II, 239.

On Knowledge and Education

In general, Leonardo regarded knowledge as so fundamental to man that he several times spoke of it as a kind of food.

> The knowledge of past times and of the places on the earth is both ornament and nutriment to the human mind.[21]

21 Ibid., II, 243.

......

Acquire learning in youth which restores the damage of old age; and if you understand that old age has wisdom for its food, you will so conduct yourself in youth that your old age will not lack sustenance.

He continued this analogy in recommending that education should seek to make the acquisition of knowledge palatable.

Just as food eaten without caring for it is turned into loathsome nourishment, so study without a taste for it spoils memory, causing it to retain nothing which it has taken in.[22]

Among the virtues of knowledge, Leonardo often points to their moral contribution.

The acquisition of any knowledge is always of use to the intellect, because it may thus drive out useless things and retain the good.[23]

Similarly, in the first of two reflections on culture in general, Leonardo found those who had not obtained knowledge to be little above animals.

It seems to me that men of coarse and clumsy habits and of small knowledge do not deserve such fine instruments or so great a variety of natural mechanism as men of speculation and of great knowledge ... for it seems to me they have nothing about them of the human species but the voice and the figure, and for all the rest are much below beasts.[24]

But, in this regard, the knowledge must be personally understood and absorbed, and not merely data which is employed in quotation.

Any one who in discussion relies upon authority uses, not his understanding, but rather his memory. Good culture is born of a good disposition; and since the cause is more to be praised than the effect, you will rather praise a good disposition without culture, than good culture without the disposition.[25]

With regard to traditional education, Leonardo several times mentioned his sensitivity to the fact that painting was not considered a member of the Liberal Arts.

22 Ibid., II, 244.
23 Ibid., II, 244.
24 Ibid., II, 235.
25 Ibid., II, 241.

> Painting has every right to complain of being driven out from the number of Liberal Arts, since she is a true daughter of nature and employs the noblest of all the senses. It was wrong, oh [ancient] writers, to leave her out from the number of Liberal Arts, because she deals not only with the works of nature but extends over an infinite number of things which nature never created.[26]

26 Ibid., I, 67.

ON THE PSYCHOLOGY OF AESTHETICS

Leonardo was perhaps the first important artist who talked about what we call today Expressionism, painting not merely the physical resemblance of the man but painting what he is thinking.

> The good painter must paint principally two things, which are man and the ideas in man's mind. The first is easy, the second difficult, because they can only be expressed by means of gestures and the movements of the limbs.[27]

27 Quoted in Blunt, *Artistic Theory in Italy, 1450–1600*, 34. A nice definition of the conductor, as well!

Above all in this regard, Leonardo was thinking of expressing the emotions of the subject and he advised the young artists to observe and take notes on the faces they see of persons expressing various emotions. He makes the additional remarkable recommendation that they study the dumb, who can express their emotions only by face and gesture, without the aid of the voice.[28]

28 Quoted in Ibid., 35.

In his various writings one can find very little speculation by Leonardo regarding the physical or psychological nature of the emotions themselves. With his usual emphasis on experience, it is no surprise to find him writing, 'For nothing can be loved or hated unless it is first known.'[29] The only other comment of this kind is a rather Darwinian observation.

29 Ibid., II, 244.

> Nature has ordained that animals, having motion, should experience pain in order to conserve those parts which by their motion might diminish or waste …[30]

30 Ibid., II, 258.

Beyond this, Leonardo's most vivid comments on emotions are all limited to pain. One passage seems a bit formal and was perhaps something intended for his students:

> Pleasure and Pain represent twins, since there never is one without the other; and as if they were united back to back, since they are contrary to each other.
>
> If you take Pleasure know that he has behind him one who will deal you Tribulation and Repentance.³¹

[31 Richter, *The Literary Works of Leonardo da Vinci*, I, 385.]

Still other comments appear very personal, as,

> The tears come from the heart and not from the brain.³²
>
> ……
>
> Where there is most feeling, there is the greatest martyrdom; a great martyr.³³

[32 Ibid., II, 93. Found together with notes on anatomy!]

[33 Ibid., II, 247.]

But, if this is a subject he was sensitive to, he would have us believe it did not carry over into his work.

> But the painter will move you to laughter and not to tears, because weeping implies a more violent agitation than laughter.³⁴

[34 Ibid., I, 64.]

ON THE PHILOSOPHY OF AESTHETICS

Leonardo wrote frequently of Beauty as found in Nature, but he does not attempt to define it as a philosopher might. For him it seems to have been sufficient to recognize that Beauty was of the realm of the artist. Here was his opportunity to argue against the members of Liberal Arts, which had omitted painting. 'Art,' he says, 'is not like mathematics, which one can learn by sheer application.' And of geometry and arithmetic in particular, he observed,

> these two sciences only extend to a knowledge of quantity … but they do not concern themselves with quality, which forms the beauty of the works of nature and the glory of the world.³⁵

[35 Quoted in Anthony Blunt, *Artistic Theory in Italy*, 36.]

To this he added one clear definition of Beauty, one of the traditional definitions of high art, that it can have no purpose.

> Beauty and utility cannot exist together, as seen in fortresses and in men.³⁶

[36 Ibid., II, 359.]

Leonardo gave more space to defining the concept that Art is found in the mind of the artist and not in the work of his hands. He seemed to have been sensitive to someone's suggestion that Art is only a 'semi-mechanical' discipline, and thus of a lower order than science. He answered this by first pointing out that all sciences, because they entail writing with the hand, are also mechanical. He expressed this once in the following way.

> Words are of less account than performances. But you, oh writer on the sciences, do you not, like the painter, copy by hand that which is in the mind?[37]

37 Richter, *The Literary Works of Leonardo da Vinci*, I, 78.

Second, since everything the artist understands about painting is understood first in the mind, before it is enacted manually, Art is as much of the domain of the mind as is science. Finally, since Art is in the mind of the artist, it is of a higher level of understanding than that of the observer or of the several disciplines which must be learned prior to engaging in painting.

> These are understood by the mind alone and entail no manual operation; and they constitute the science of painting which remains in the mind of its contemplators; and from it is then born the actual creation, which is far superior in dignity to the contemplation or science which precedes it.[38]

38 Ibid., I, 34.

In another place, Leonardo revealed his belief that the artist is not merely a scientist who copies Nature, but is a creator. Through imitation the artist's mind takes on,

> that divine power, which lies in the knowledge of the painter, transforms the mind of the painter into the likeness of the divine mind, for with a free hand he can produce [that which does not actually exist, including] different beings, animals, plants, fruits, landscapes, open fields, abysses, terrifying and fearful places.[39]

39 Quoted in Blunt, *Artistic Theory in Italy*, 37.

The skill, or craft, of the artist, in Leonardo's view, was first based on experience, and as anyone knows who has seen the meticulous notes and drawings of Leonardo's sketchbooks, his concept of experience included the most precise discipline of observation. From experience comes the knowledge and rules of the craft.

> Good judgment is born of clear understanding, and a clear understanding comes of reasons derived from sound rules, and sound rules are the product of sound experience—the common mother of all the sciences and arts.[40]

> ......

> Of the error of those who practice without knowledge; see first the *Ars poetica* of Horace.[41]

> ......

> Those who devote themselves to practice without science are like sailors who put to sea without rudder or compass and who can never be certain where they are going. Practice must always be founded on sound theory.[42]

In his notes, Leonardo also addressed two of the traditional topics associated with general theories of aesthetics, the first being Universality. Leonardo declared that painting is the most universal science, because it is perceived by the eye. In his following, in which he contrasts that which is perceived by the ear, he was no doubt thinking of poetry.

> That science is the most useful whose fruit is most communicable, and conversely, that is less useful which is less communicable. The result of painting is communicable to all generations of the universe, because it depends on the visual faculty; the way through the ear of our understanding is not the same as the way through the eye; because the latter way has no need of interpreters, for the various languages as letters have, and thus painting gives satisfaction at once to mankind, in the same way as things created by nature ...[43]

In another passage, he touches on the true nature of Universality in recommending to the student painter that he obtain an opinion of his work from everyone, even non-artists, for all men are familiar with the forms of Nature.[44] One example he gave is the image of man himself.

> Now tell me which is the nearer to the actual man: the name of man, or the image of the man. The name of the man differs in different countries, but his form is never changed but by death.[45]

Leonardo made extensive notes on the ancient question regarding the obligation of Art to imitate Nature. He seems to have come down rather firmly on the side of the affirmative, primarily because

---

40 Ibid., I, 119.

41 Richter, *The Literary Works of Leonardo da Vinci*, II, 373.

42 Quoted in Blunt, *Artistic Theory in Italy*, 28.

43 Richter, *The Literary Works of Leonardo da Vinci*, I, 35.

44 Ibid., I, 322.

45 Ibid., I, 368.

he viewed Nature as the ideal which could not be improved upon. It follows, he said, that 'That painting is the most to be praised which agrees most exactly with the thing imitated.'[46] Even the ugly, in the painting of a body, should be included, for it serves to point up the beautiful with greater intensity.[47]

In a brief history of painting, Leonardo suggests that this concept of the direct imitation of Nature had been abandoned during most of the Middle Ages until,

> Tomaso, of Florence, nicknamed Masaccio, showed by his perfect works how those who take for their standard any one but nature— the mistress of all masters—weary themselves in vain. And I would say about these mathematical studies that those who only study the authorities and not the works of nature are descendants but not sons of nature, the mistress of all good authors. Oh! how great is the folly of those who blame those who learn from nature, setting aside the authorities who were disciples of nature.[48]

For Leonardo, painting is the human activity most capable of illuminating the highest truths about Nature.

> Painting presents the works of nature to our understanding with more truth and accuracy than do words or letters; but letters represent words with more truth than does painting. But we affirm that a science representing the works of nature is more wonderful than one representing the works of a worker, that is to say, the works of man, such as words in poetry and the like, which are expressed by the human tongue.[49]

In another place he writes,

> Whosoever speaks ill of painting speaks ill of nature, because the works of the painter represent the works of nature, and therefore such a detractor lacks feeling.[50]

It is a great virtue of painting, according to Leonardo, that it not only imitates Beauty in Nature, but preserves its image forever 'which Nature with all its force could not keep.'

> How many paintings have preserved the image of divine beauty of which time or sudden death have destroyed Nature's original, so that the work of the painter has survived in nobler form that that of Nature, his mistress.[51]

46 Quoted in Blunt, *Artistic Theory in Italy*, 30.

47 Quoted in ibid., 31.

48 Richter, *The Literary Works of Leonardo da Vinci*, I, 372.

49 Ibid., I, 35.

50 Ibid., I, 38.

51 Ibid., I, 77.

Leonardo raised the question of the imitation of Nature again in a very interesting discussion of the study process of the young artist.

> The Adversary says that to acquire practice and do a great deal of work it is better that the first period of study should be employed in copying various compositions ... by diverse masters ... I reply that the method will be good, if it is based on works of good composition and by skilled masters. But since such masters are so rare that there are but few of them to be found, it is a surer way to go to natural objects than to those which are imitated from nature with great deterioration, and so form bad methods; for he who can go to the fountain does not go to the water-jar.[52]

An especially interesting reference to the imitation of Nature has to do with the imitation of emotions, 'That figure is most admirable which by its actions best expresses the emotions [*la passione*] that animates it.'[53] We get some idea how vividly he meant this in a passage in which he speaks of painting a hypothetical battle scene.

> Others must be represented in the agonies of death grinding their teeth, rolling their eyes, with their fists clenched against their bodies and their legs contorted.[54]

On a related topic, he recommends that 'the motions of men must be such as suggest their dignity or their baseness.'[55]

Finally, Leonardo included in his notes a little joke he no doubt used with his students when talking about the imitation of Nature.

> A painter was asked why, since he made such beautiful figures ... his children were so ugly; to which the painter replied that he made his pictures by day, and his children by night.[56]

[52] Ibid., I, 305.
[53] Ibid., I, 341.
[54] Ibid., I, 349.
[55] Ibid., I, 346.
[56] Ibid., II, 289.

On Painting

Leonardo wrote in many places of the superiority of painting over the other arts. In the following passage he goes further and sets painting above all other human activity, with regard to its value and uniqueness.

> Among the inimitable sciences painting comes first. It cannot be taught to those not endowed by nature like mathematics, where the pupil takes in as much as the master gives. It cannot be copied like letters where the copy has the same value as the original. It cannot be molded as in sculpture where the cast is equal in merit to the original; it cannot be reproduced indefinitely as is done in the printing of books. It remains peerless in its nobility; alone it does honor to its author, remaining unique and precious; it never engenders offspring equal to it; and this singleness makes it finer than the sciences which are published everywhere.[57]

57 Ibid., I, 35ff.

He was, nevertheless, keenly aware that not all writers share this view. His explanation of this has much in common with our understanding today of the twin hemispheres of the brain (for painting is of the right brain, while the domain of the writer is the left).

> As the writers have had no knowledge of the science of painting they could not assign to it its rightful place or share; and painting does not display her accomplishment in words; therefore she was classed below the sciences, through ignorance ...
>
> And it is not the fault of painting if painters have not described their art and reduced it to a science, she is not the less noble for that, since few painters profess to be writers because life is too short for the understanding of their art.[58]

58 Ibid., I, 37ff.

Finally, Leonardo made a few interesting observations on arts education. Young painters, he said, should always paint in the company of others and not alone. Not only will one be ashamed to be found behind the others, but one will be stimulated to work harder when observing the praise given the more skilled.[59] He warns the student, however, that it is much easier to recognize errors in the works of others, than in his own work.[60]

59 Ibid., I, 307.

60 Ibid., I, 321. Leonardo recommends to the artist looking at his work in a mirror, as, its images being reversed, it will appear as the work of another artist.

Leonardo also offers a thought which must be the prayer of every good teacher in the arts,

> He is a poor disciple who does not excel his master.[61]

61 Ibid., I, 308.

On Painting versus Poetry

Leonardo offered a number of arguments why painting is superior to poetry, beginning with its greater and more accurate ability to portray Nature. If, he proposes, painting and poetry were to compete in the description of a great battle,

> In that case the painter will be your superior, because your pen will be worn out before you can fully describe what the painter can demonstrate forthwith by the aid of his science, and your tongue will be parched with thirst and your body overcome by sleep and hunger before you can describe with words what a painter is able to show you in an instant ...
>
> It may be said, therefore, that poetry is the science for the blind and painting for the deaf. But painting is nobler than poetry inasmuch as it serves the nobler sense ...
>
> The painter can express an infinite variety of things which words cannot describe for want of appropriate terms.[62]

This is not understood, he says, because painters do not express themselves in words. Again, as we would say today, because the left hemisphere cannot describe the experience of the right.

> But as painters did not know how to plead for their own art she was left without advocates for a long time. For painting does not talk; but reveals herself as she is, ending in reality; and Poetry ends in words in which she eloquently sings her own praises.[63]

In another place, Leonardo discussed this with respect to the poet departing from the representation of Nature to become an orator.

> As soon as the poet ceases to represent in words what exists in nature, he in fact ceases to resemble the painter; for if the poet, leaving such representation, proceeds to describe the flowery and flattering speech of the figure which he wishes to make the speaker, he then is an orator and no longer a poet or a painter.[64]

Secondly, Leonardo believed painting is superior to poetry in its ability to portray Truth, which he found evident in the fact that lovers 'turn to the portraits of their beloved, [and even] speak to the painting which represents them.'[65] Third, and closely related to this, he says, is that while poetry can invent fiction, the painter's fictions give much greater satisfaction to the observer, due to their

62 Ibid., I, 53ff.

63 Ibid., I, 54ff.

64 Ibid., I, 371.

65 Ibid., I, 55ff.

greater detail.⁶⁶ Thus, he concluded, if poetry deals with moral philosophy, painting deals with natural philosophy.⁶⁷

Fourth, painting is superior to poetry because it appeals to a superior sense, a discussion he begins with a nice play on words.

> Painting is poetry which is seen and not heard, and poetry is a painting which is heard but not seen. These two arts, you may call them both either poetry or painting, have here interchanged the senses by which they penetrate to the intellect. Whatever is painted must pass by the eye, which is the nobler sense, and whatever is poetry must pass through a less noble sense, namely, the ear, to the understanding.⁶⁸

Fifth, he observed that the eye can immediately take in an entire painting, while in poetry the listener must follow a long series of individual details before understanding the whole. This Leonardo compared to hearing separate lines of music without hearing them performed together.

> The poet's way may be compared to that of a musician who all by himself undertakes to sing a composition which is intended for four voices and first sings the part of the soprano, then that of the tenor, then the contralto, and finally the bass. Such performances cannot produce the beauty of harmonious proportions set in harmonious divisions of time.⁶⁹

Sixth, Leonardo maintained that painting has the power to arouse stronger emotions than poetry. This he found particularly true in the example of Love, which he declared is 'the main motive of the species in the whole animal world.' He offers as a demonstration of proof the following anecdote.

> It once happened to me that I made a picture representing a sacred subject which was bought by one who loved it and who then wished to remove the symbols of divinity in order that he might kiss her without misgivings. Finally his conscience prevailed over his sighs and lust and he felt constrained to remove the picture from his house. Now let the poet go and try to rouse such desires in men by the description of a beauty which does not portray any living being.⁷⁰

Finally, Leonardo apparently desired to conclude this discussion by restoring some virtue to poetry, only to quickly change his mind and return to his principal argument!

---

66 Ibid., I, 57.
67 Ibid., I, 58 and 369.
68 Ibid., I, 58ff.
69 Ibid., I, 60, 79.
70 Ibid., I, 64.

> Let us therefore give praise both to him who delights our ears with words and to him who with painting delights our sight; but less praise is due to him who uses words, as they are but accidental designations created by man, who is inferior to the creator of the works of nature which the painter imitates.[71]

71 Ibid., I, 65.

On Painting versus Sculpture

Leonardo left no doubt that he regarded painting as a higher art than sculpture, but he left mixed signals regarding which is the more difficult. With regard to the range of skills needed, he clearly felt that painting was the more complex.

> After painting comes sculpture, a very noble art, but one that does not in the execution require the same supreme ingenuity as the art of painting, since in two most important and difficult particulars, in foreshortening and in light and shade, for which the painter has to invent a process, sculpture is helped by nature. Moreover, sculpture does not imitate color which the painter takes pains to attune so that the shadows accompany the lights.[72]

72 Ibid., I, 79.

On the other hand, in terms of physical labor he makes it clear, in humorously graphic detail, that sculpture is the more difficult.

> The sculptor in carving his statue out of marble or other stone wherein it is potentially contained has to take off the superfluous and excessive parts with the strength of his arms and the strokes of the hammer—a very mechanical exercise causing much perspiration which mingling with the grit turns into mud. His face is pasted and smeared all over with marble powder, making him look like a baker …
> How different the painter's lot … for the painter sits in front of his work at perfect ease. He is well dressed and handles a light brush dipped in delightful color. He is arrayed in the garments he fancies, and his home is clean and filled with delightful pictures, and he often enjoys the accompaniment of music.[73]

73 Ibid., I, 91.

In fact, Vasari reports that Leonardo painted his famous *Mona Lisa* to the accompaniment of music.[74]

74 Ibid., I, 72.

Finally, Leonardo acknowledged that mistakes, so easily painted over in painting, in sculpture cannot be corrected. This apparent demand for perfection, however, cannot be taken as meaning sculpture is a higher art. The postscript he adds to this thought appears to be a very personal confession.

> It is a poor argument to try to prove that a work is nobler because oversights are irremediable; I should rather say that it will be more difficult to mend the mind of a master who commits such errors than to mend the work he has spoiled.[75]

75 Ibid., I, 95.

ON THE AESTHETICS OF MUSIC

In view of the fact that Leonardo was reported to be a skilled and sensitive musician, it strikes the reader as very odd that his voice is not found joining the humanists in praise of the virtues of music. Instead, in his notes we find him focusing on the deficiencies of music as an art—for the purpose, as in the case of poetry and sculpture, of pointing to the superiority of painting.

The first deficiency of music, in his view, was that it was associated with one of the senses which he believed inferior to vision. In particular, he observed that the ear lacks the accuracy of sight.

> But the ear is apt to be misled in locating and judging the distances of its objects because the lines along which sound travels are not straight like those of the pyramid of sight, but tortuous and bent. And very often distant sounds seem nearer than those close by, owing to the transmission; although the sound of the echo travels to the ear by straight lines only.[76]

76 Ibid., I, 38ff.

Therefore it follows, as he wrote in several places, to be born blind is a much greater loss than to be born deaf.

> He who is born blind cannot replace this experience through the sense of hearing because he has never known what is the beauty of anything. There remains to him the sense of hearing whereby he hears [only] the voices and the speech of men which is composed of the names of all things that have been given names. But one can live happily without the knowledge of these names as is shown by those born deaf, who, being dumb, make themselves understood by drawing, which most of them enjoy.[77]

77 Ibid., I, 39.

......

Who would not lose his sense of hearing and the senses of smell and touch as well rather than his sight, because he who loses his sight is like a man chased from the world—for he no longer sees it nor anything of it, and such life is the sister of death.[78]

......

There is nobody so senseless who when given the choice of either remaining in perpetual darkness or losing his hearing will not at once say that he prefers to lose his hearing and his sense of smell as well rather than be blind. Because whoever loses his eyesight loses the beauty of the world with all the forms in creation, whereas deafness only brings the loss of sound, caused by motion arising from the percussion of the air, which is a very small matter.[79]

The second fundamental deficiency of music, which Leonardo found, was that it does not last, it disappears. This was an argument mentioned by a number of ancient Greek philosophers, as he had no doubt become aware through the general interest of the fifteenth-century humanists in ancient literature.

And from these shapes is born the proportionality called harmony, which delights the sense of sight with sweet concord just as the proportions of diverse voices delight the sense of hearing. But the harmony of music is less noble than the harmony which appeals to the eye, because the sound dies as soon as it is born, and its death is as swift as its birth, and this cannot happen with the sense of sight. For if you present to the eye the beauty of a human figure composed of fine proportions, these beauties will not be as transient nor will they be destroyed as swiftly as in music. On the contrary, beauty has a long life; it can be enjoyed and examined at leisure without having to be continually reborn like music which has to be played again and again, and it will not weary you …[80]

......

Music cannot be called otherwise than the sister of painting, for she is dependent upon hearing, a sense second to sight, and her harmony is composed of the union of its proportional parts sounded simultaneously, rising and falling in one or more harmonic rhythms. These rhythms may be said to surround the proportionality of the members composing the harmony, just as the contour bounds the members from which human beauty is born.
But painting excels and ranks higher than music, because it does not fade away as soon as it is born, as is the fate of unhappy music.[81]

......

78 Ibid., I, 40.
79 Ibid., I, 66.
80 Ibid., I, 61.
81 Ibid., I, 76.

> Music has two ills, one of which is mortal, and the other subjects it to deterioration. The mortal is ever linked to the instant which follows its creation, while the deterioration lies in its repetition making it hateful and vile.[82]

He must have known, but neglected to mention, that the ancient Greek philosophers held music to be a higher art than painting, which was relegated to the crafts such as carpentry. The Greeks held music in high estate in part because you cannot *see* music, hence they found it had characteristics similar to religion. Leonardo did mention this last aspect of music in passing.

> The poet ranks far below the painter in the representation of visible things, and far below the musician in that of invisible things.[83]

Leonardo also argued that for the true portrayal of Nature, painting, and not music, is the appropriate art.

> It is a sin against nature to want to give to the ear what is meant for the eye. Let music enter there and do not try to put in her place the science of painting, the true imitator of all the shapes of nature.[84]

In view of these arguments which he believed demonstrated the inferiority of music to painting, Leonardo could not understand why music was admitted as a member of the Liberal Arts, while painting was not.

> After giving a place to Music among the Liberal Arts you must place Painting there, too, or else withdraw Music.[85]

Among all the extensive autograph notes and letters by Leonardo, there is not a single reference to an actual performance of music which he heard. We are left with only a few clues from which to deduce his thoughts on performance.

First, one of his notes seems to be an oblique reference to performers who were not fulfilling their duties as he understood it.

> And if you say that there are vile painters, I reply that Music also can be spoiled by those who do not understand it.[86]

---

82 Ibid., II, 233.

83 Ibid., I, 80.

84 Ibid., I, 62.

85 Ibid., I, 79.

86 Ibid., I, 79.

Second, in speaking of how the eye takes in an entire painting at once, Leonardo provides an analogy with music whereby he reveals a striking awareness of the experience of the contemplative listener.

> And from painting which serves the eye, the noblest sense, arises harmony of proportions; just as many different voices joined together and singing simultaneously produce a harmonious proportion which gives such satisfaction to the sense of hearing that the listeners remain spellbound with admiration as if half alive.[87]

[87] Ibid., I, 59.

9 FIFTEENTH-CENTURY FRANCE

In the history of aesthetics in music, fifteenth-century France is a curious and ironic chapter. In the field of Church music there were some very gifted men, writing important music. But Dufay, Binchois, Dunstable, Ockeghem and the rest were already an anachronism. While the polyphonic style would continue to develop for another century, the humanists, particularly in Italy, who represented the new direction music history would take, were already condemning and abandoning this style. General music history texts still pretend this polyphonic activity was the sole and substance of Western European composition at this time, but the truth is that it was a style driven by scholastic principles of an era whose time had already passed. No matter how effective some of this polyphonic music is, it is music written from a premise of mathematics, and not feeling. Thus, it is no surprise that these composers,

> began to indulge in complicated rhythmic tricks and in the invention of highly involved methods of notating them.[1]

Interestingly enough, when these same composers wrote secular music the emotional quality is more evident. Martin le Franc, in a poem of 1441–1442, speaks of a 'newer style' in Dufay and Binchois.

> For these a newer way have found
> Of making pleasant concordance
> In loud and soft ensembles,
> With feigning, rests, mutatio.
> The English guise they wear with grace,
> They follow Dunstable aright,
> And thereby have they learned apace
> To make their music gay and bright.[2]

In general, however, the information on non-Church music is troublesome. Curiously enough, we find some writers in fifteenth-

[1] Gustave Reese, *Music in the Renaissance* (New York: Norton, 1959), 11, quoting Apel.

[2] Translated in ibid., 13, where the second and third line are incorrectly reversed.

century France who, taken by themselves, appear to reveal no awareness or influence of the great flowering of humanism in France during the previous century. There was still love poetry intended to be sung, and indeed Charles VI founded a Court of Love in 1401 in which members wrote poetry and music in the thirteenth-century trouvère manner.[3] The extant poetry praises love, but it no longer praises the power of music. And far from representing humanism, some writers appear to have reverted to medieval ideals. It seems incredible that Christine de Pizan (1364–1430) could write,

> The holy doctors of the Church prove it to us, that all the joys that one could want or wish in this world are nothing but mud, filth, and emptiness compared to those of the heavenly glory that those who die well receive at the end.[4]

As we can see in her choice of words, a certain pessimism hangs over French literature of this century and, indeed, the subject of music is rarely mentioned. In Christine de Pizan, it sometimes seems as if she deliberately omits music. For example, in one of her books, she describes, in a vision, visiting 'a noble university.' She finds there 'each separate branch of knowledge,' including grammar, dialectic, arithmetic, geometry, astrology, theology, philosophy, 'and so on with the other forbidden and liberal arts.' Music is conspicuously missing.[5] In another book, she quotes a story of Cyrus, king of Persia (ca. 550 BC), one often retold in early literature, which told of his concern over a conquered people and his decision to have the people instructed in music so that they might become effeminate and thus be unlikely to cause trouble. It is interesting that when Christine de Pizan tells this story, she omits 'music' and substitutes for it 'gambling and accustoming themselves to merchandise.'[6]

If music is a nearly forgotten subject in French literature of this century the reason must lie in two rather obvious explanations. First, the century was dominated by wars, both with England (1337–1453) and with the Burgundians, creating an intellectual environment inhospitable to the arts. Second, at a time when the arts were still supported primarily by the aristocracy, this society was led by a series of very weak kings. Just before the turn of the century there was Charles V, an idiot who was completely insane by 1392. Charles VI and VII were weak and overwhelmed by war. It was Charles VII who could not prevent the tragedy of Joan of Arc. Next comes Louis

---

3 Ibid., 7.

4 Christine de Pizan, *The Epistle of the Prison of Human Life*, trans. Josette Wisman (New York: Garland Publishing, 1984), 51. Christine de Pizan was perhaps the most prolific writer of the fifteenth century. Reared as the daughter of Charles V's Italian physician, from the age of five Christine lived in the Louvre and enjoyed an education as good as that available to that of any aristocrat in Paris.

5 Christine de Pizan, *Christine's Vision*, trans. Glenda McLeod (New York: Garland Publishing, 1993), II, ii.

6 Christine de Pizan, *The Book of the Body Politic*, trans. Kate Forhan (Cambridge: Cambridge University Press, 1994), I, xxviii.

XI, a strange man who dressed as an impoverished pilgrim. It would only be Charles VIII (1483–1498), by virtue of his aborted Crusade, who would bring the Renaissance back to France from Italy.

ON THE PHYSIOLOGY OF AESTHETICS

By this date nearly every philosopher understood that most of the information in the mind comes first from the senses. Christine de Pizan, in her *The Prison of Human Life*, departs from, and ridicules this view.

> Whatever we cannot see with our eyes, as the fools say, we cannot know, except what is given to us to hear. Indeed, whoever believes such reasoning, resembles those who have poor vision, and put the wrong medicine in their eyes in order to clear them, and thus become blind. Similarly, those who create these doubts, because they cannot see, are in this erroneous blindness because they search and want to ask too much …[7]

7 Pizan, *The Epistle of the Prison of Human Life*, 49.

Rather, she finds intelligence to be a gift from God, which is 'not at all bad to know and to feel in oneself,' but,

> this knowledge should not become vainglory, nor be attributed to one's own value and by doing so, render one proud: such a thing is presumption and sin which God dislikes very much.[8]

8 Ibid., 41.

In this same book, she equates the mind with understanding and finds three 'virtues' which are associated with understanding: Retention, Memory and Reason. Following the many earlier philosophers who contend that man must be ruled by Reason, she offers this explanation.

> Reason opens the way to put into practice what comprehension has understood and retention has kept and what memory has recorded. Therefore, reason is the administrator of works—like a bailiff or a provost marshal—of good and healthy comprehension, since the latter can be very different in one man or another, and whoever has a great deal of it, is enriched by no small treasure! But he must make good use of it, because there is none like it in this world. From reason comes and is born discretion, which some call prudence, and like the servant of reason, it sends off its orders to be put in the hearts of

men, and it distributes and imparts all that it commands. This discretion is called the mother of all virtues, and the reason why it is called this is because if virtues were not under its command they would become vices; for example, generosity is a virtue, but not when it is excessive and not checked by discretion, for then it becomes a foolish generosity that we call prodigality, which is a vice.[9]

Similarly, in another place she advises knights and nobles to base their actions on Reason, as a means of preventing 'foolhardiness.'[10]

Philippe de Commynes, whose *Memoirs* was written during a period of almost constant battle between the King of France and Duke Charles of Burgundy, developed a rather pessimistic view of mankind, finding neither Reason nor common sense sufficient to curb his instincts.

> One must conclude that neither our natural reason, nor our sense, nor fear of God, nor love of our neighbor will restrain us at all from doing violence to one another, or from keeping for ourselves what belongs to another, or from taking the possessions of others by all possible means.[11]

The subject of education is commented on at length by several writers of fifteenth-century France, but it is also a discussion with curious overtones. Christine de Pizan, in her *The Book of the Body Politic*, describes the nature of the education appropriate to princes. It is surprising to find a viewpoint here more characteristic of the Middle Ages than the Renaissance. She recommends that one should find a teacher 'who is wise and prudent more in morals than in lofty learning, despite the fact that in ancient times, the children of princes were taught by philosophers.' She then makes an even more surprising statement that, 'present princes do not desire to be educated in the sciences as they used to be,' before concluding,

> I believe that it would be better to have a very discrete and wise teacher who had good morals and loved God, rather than the most excellent and subtle philosopher.[12]

She recommends that the education of children include hearing, during meals, songs 'about the deeds of the noble dead and the good deeds of their ancestors,' in order to make them courageous.[13] Finally, she notes that it is the nature of children not to learn except out of fear of punishment, but she advises against 'severe beatings.'

---

9 Ibid., 35.

10 Pizan, *The Book of the Body Politic*, II, vii.

11 Philippe de Commynes, *The Memoirs of Philippe de Commynes*, trans. Isabelle Cazeaux (Columbia: University of South Carolina Press, 1969), I, 356.

12 Pizan, *The Book of the Body Politic*, I, iii.

13 Ibid., I, iv. She also recommends this practice for the 'wise princess,' in *Mirror of Honor; the Treasury of the City of Ladies*, trans. Charity Willard (Tenafly, NJ: Bard Hall Press, 1989), I, xii.

Strangely enough, when she is addressing 'the Common People,' she suddenly has a much higher regard for knowledge. Speaking to the students of the university of Paris, she most enthusiastically says,

> Oh well advised, oh happy people! I speak to you, the disciples of the study of wisdom, who, by the grace of God and good fortune or nature apply yourselves to seek out the heights of the clear rejoicing star, that is, knowledge, do take diligently from this treasure, drink from this clear and healthy fountain. Fill yourself from this pleasant repast, which can so benefit and elevate you! …
>
> There is nothing more perfect than the truth and clarity of things which knowledge demonstrates how to know and understand. There is no treasure of the goods of fortune that he who has tasted of the highest knowledge would exchange for a drop of the dregs of wisdom. And truly, no matter what others say, I dare say there is no treasure the like of understanding. Who would not undertake any labor, you champions of wisdom, to acquire it?[14]

14 Pizan, *The Book of the Body Politic*, III, iv.

She concludes this discussion by noting that she apparently knew some professors who did not practice what they preached. These she compared to 'people who die of hunger with food near them.'

Interestingly enough, Philippe de Commynes makes a statement about the education of nobles, which has the same half-hearted endorsement we have seen in de Pizan. He observes that 'great knowledge makes wicked men worse and good men better,' but admits,

> It is probable that knowledge does men more good than harm, if only because it makes them conscious of their bad actions and ashamed of them.[15]

15 Commynes, *The Memoirs of Philippe de Commynes*, I, 355.

In another book, de Pizan addresses the role of the parent in the education of the child and recommends a curiously cool role.

> If he has children, he must instruct them well and teach them to fear and to serve God; he must not appear too close to them when they are young, nor show too much love, but raise them in a moderate fear, make them learn or lead them into the sciences or the profession that he wants to give them.[16]

16 Pizan, *The Epistle of the Prison of Human Life*, 37.

As for herself, in another book, de Pizan regrets that she failed to take advantage of the educational opportunities available to her, especially the study of philosophy.

Alas! when I had masters of knowledge beside me, I neglected learning; and now the time has come when my mind and feeling are beggars, longing for that which they cannot have because of the failure to learn—your art, my mistress Philosophy. Ah learning: sweet, savory, and honeyed thing, supreme and preeminent among all other treasures! How happy are they who taste you fully![17]

François Villon, in his 'Great Testament,' similarly laments his failure to take advantage of his early educational opportunities.

> Good God, if I had studied
> in the days of my mad youth
> and been devoted more to virtue,
> I now would have a house with downy bed.
> But look! I ran away from school
> just like a naughty child.
> And now, as I write these words,
> my heart is close to breaking.[18]

ON THE PSYCHOLOGY OF AESTHETICS

Emotions, as an abstract subject, are rarely mentioned by writers of fifteenth-century France, apart, of course, to references to Love. We do note, nonetheless, an interesting, and rare, recommendation found in the *Memoirs* of Philippe de Commynes that one should openly express profound emotions.

> It is helpful to open one's heart to some close friend and to complain freely about one's fate; one should not be ashamed to show one's grief in the presence of a special friend, for it relieves one's heart and comforts it, and it revives one's spirits. It is unavoidable, since we are men, that such suffering should be accompanied by great emotion expressed either in public or in private, and therefore one should not follow the example of [Duke Charles of Burgundy], who chose to hide and remain alone.[19]

Pleasure and Pain are also not discussed much in a philosophical sense, but we are fond of the comparison found in a ballade by François Villon (ca. 1431–1463), apparently composed at the request of his mother, which includes the following,

---

17 Pizan, *Christine's Vision*, III, ix. In this vision, she encounters the Mistress of Philosophy behind an ivory door, behind which she can hear 'various women's voices in sweet and gentle song and conversation.' [Ibid., III, i.]

18 François Villon, 'The Testament,' in William Williams, ed., *The Complete Works of François Villon* (New York: David McKay, 1960), lines 201ff.

19 Commynes, *The Memoirs of Philippe de Commynes*, I, 313.

> I am a poor little old woman who knows nothing and has never read a letter; in my parish church I see Paradise painted, with harps and lutes, and a Hell where the damned are boiled: the one makes me afraid, the other joyful and happy.[20]

20 Quoted in Willard Trask, *Medieval Lyrics of Europe* (New York: World Publishing Company, 1969), 73.

Christine de Pizan repeats the old Church dogma that most pleasures lead to evil. She observes that she has heard some criticize old age because one is then deprived of bodily pleasures and delights.

> But, age is not to be blamed but greatly praised therefore, for it uproots the root of all evils … There is no evil that sensuality will not attract the human spirit to do. It is that which extinguishes the judgment of reason and blinds the human soul, and it has no affinity nor connection with virtue.[21]

21 Pizan, *The Book of the Body Politic*, I, xx.

She balances this, in another place, with a description of the pleasure enjoyed by the nun's contemplation which is fully emotional in character.

> The perfect contemplative often is so ravished that she seems other than herself, and the consolation, sweetness, and pleasure she experiences can scarcely be told, nor can any earthly joy be compared with them. She feels and tastes the glories and joys of Paradise.[22]

22 Pizan, *Mirror of Honor*, I, vi.

ON THE PHILOSOPHY OF AESTHETICS

Due to an environment dominated by war, one finds little discussion of aesthetics during the fifteenth century in France. The pessimistic strain in French literature, which we have mentioned, can be seen in a poem of Charles d'Orléans (1394–1465) in which he discusses Beauty.

> Put out my eyes! Let me not see! Too much I fear beauty everywhere.
> Beauty lies in wait to ravish all my joy out of the world.
> Put out my eyes! Let me not see!
> God keep me from beauty, may our ways never meet!
> Would not that be best? Put out my eyes? Let me not see![23]

23 Quoted in Trask, *Medieval Lyrics of Europe*, 71.

ON THE AESTHETICS OF MUSIC

Because of the more conservative artistic climate, one does not find, in fifteenth-century France, the open condemnation of polyphony, such as we see among the humanists of Italy. Indeed, there is one hint of criticism of the new style in a poem by Villon, in which he criticizes those 'singers singing at your pleasure, without rules.' Later he identifies these singers as those who 'write motets, rondeaux and lays.'[24]

A more progressive attitude would have been found in the university circles in Paris, of course. In a treatise, *Tractatus de Canticis*, by Jean de Gerson, Chancellor of the University of Paris, we find an important departure from the long held Church position that the artist was important, because God made him, but that the art work itself was not important. Gerson offers a new level of respect to the artist and craftsman.

> Happy is he who recognizes the mighty work of God not only in the things of nature … but also in the things of craft, how in the piercing of moderate sized pieces of wood as in the sambuca and fistulae, in beaten out metal as in the tubae and the cymbala, or in the dry wringing of sinews and intestines as in the cithara, so many sounds are varied.[25]

A comment on the importance of music in the education of the noble class can be seen in a Ballade of Charles of Orléans which mentions, in passing, that at least the young ladies were expected to have some level of musical culture.

> So well becometh the noble good princesses
> To sing or dance in all disport truly …[26]

Regarding the purpose of music, a passage in the manuscript, *Le Chevalier du Papegau*, in which a parrot, as a literary surrogate for a real singer, offers the traditional purpose of music to soothe.

> The parrot … began to sing and to comfort his lord and all the others who were there with a song so fine and beautiful that they soon forgot the grief they had suffered.[27]

Gerson also mentions this purpose of music in an interesting and curious reference to bells [*campanulae*] used in melodies, in particular as heard 'arranged in certain clocks.'

---

24 François Villon, 'Epistle to his Friends,' in Williams, *The Complete Works*, 153.

25 Jean de Gerson, 'Tractatus de Canticis,' trans. Christopher Page, in 'Early 15th-century instruments in Jean de Gerson's *Tractatus de Canticis*,' in *Early Music* 6, no. 3 (July 1978): 348.

26 'Ballade IX,' quoted in Robert Steele, *The English Poems of Charles of Orleans* (London: Oxford University Press, 1941), 16.

27 Thomas E. Vesce, trans., *The Knight of the Parrot* (New York: Garland, 1986), 84. This manuscript is thought to based on earlier works of unknown dates.

By these our inner dispositions of mind may be improved and stimulated, for it has been proved that he whose mind is agitated, weakened or tardy rejoices wholly in himself when this celebrated sound is made … This is the profusion of inestimable joy.[28]

28 Gerson, 'Tractatus de Canticis,' 348.

It is also interesting that Gerson, in describing various musical instruments, sometimes goes beyond the usual technical descriptions to provide more aesthetic characterizations. He describes, for example, the psalterium and cithara as 'smooth and serene' and the viella as producing 'sweet and delightful music.' Even the prototype timpani, the naquaires, he describes as consisting of one drum tuned to sound 'very dull' and the other 'very clear.'[29]

29 Ibid., 347.

ART MUSIC

Fifteenth-century French literature contains many examples of lyric poetry intended to be sung as love songs. Christine de Pizan mentions this tradition when a lover relates,

> I brought this new ballade to her, which pleased her greatly, and came away with one in return.[30]

30 Christine de Pizan, *The Book of the Duke of True Lovers*, trans. Thelma Fenster (New York: Persea Books, 1991), 107.

François Villon, in his 'Great Testament,' remembered the friends of his youth who were singers of love songs.

> Where are those laughing comrades
> that I was with in former days,
> who sang so well, talked so well
> and so excelled in word and deed?[31]

31 Villon, 'The Testament,' lines 225ff.

As an older man, he renounces his own participation in such love songs.

> I renounce and curse all loves
> and defy them with blood and fire.
> They send me to my death
> without a single thought.
> So I've put away my fiddle [*vielle*]; no longer
> will I spend my time with lovers.[32]

32 Ibid., lines 713ff.

Later, he mentions, humorously, a different kind of Love song.

> Item: to Master Ythier Marchand
> to whom I left my sword before,
> I now bequeath ten lines of verse
> which he must set for voice,
> and for the lute, a *De Profundis*
> for his old loves, whose names
> I will not mention, or otherwise
> he would forever hate me.[33]

A poem of Charles de Orléans shares this same pessimistic memory of love songs.

> Ballads, songs and laments
> Are put away and forgotten for me,
> For weariness and many thoughts
> Have held me long asleep.
> And yet, to pass the unhappy time,
> I should like to try whether I am able to
> Rhyme as I used to.
> At least I shall do what I can,
> Although I know and recognize
> That I shall find my language
> All rusted over with Nonchaloir …[34]

The 'Le Chevalier du Papegau,' twice describes art singers (once the surrogate parrot) which include references to the presence of the contemplative listener, an essential component of Art Music.

> The ladies were seated throughout the chambers in great comfort and delight, for a master of the viol, who knew how to perform very well indeed, sang them a courtly lay in a voice of very good tone that was in such harmony with the viol that it was truly a song to be listened to and enjoyed.[35]

> ……

> The parrot reached there by singing all along the way the many deeds of his lord to Flor de Mont. When he got near his lord and saw him coming forward to greet him, he began such a sweet melody that there were none there present who did not stop to tarry because of the sweetness of the song.[36]

---

33 Ibid., lines 970.

34 'Ballade LXXII,' quoted in Sally Purcell, *The Poems of Charles of Orleans* (Cheadle Hulme, Cheshire: Carcanet Press, 1973), 73.

35 Vesce, *The Knight of the Parrot*, 21.

36 Ibid., 82.

Another reference to the attentive listener is found in Crétin's 'Déploration,' in which Ockeghem is welcomed in heaven by Dufay, Busnois, Dunstable, and others.

> Full many folk about them listening drew,
> For good it was to hear such harmony …[37]

In another interesting reference to the performance of art songs, Craig Wright points out that the many duties of the boys in the choir school of Notre Dame included singing secular songs in the residences of the clergy.[38]

The singer of epic poetry was still to be found. We have mentioned above Christine de Pizan's recommendation that children hear songs of great deeds, etc., as part of their education. In another place she promises the prince that if he does his duty with virtue, then 'there would be songs of glory and praise about him.'[39]

Important additional references to secular music performance are found in the mystery plays, in particular in Arnoul Greban's *Mystère des Actes des apostres*. In one place we read,

> Bringing Dame Poetry to bear
> On sounds harmonious and sweet;
> Motets and chansons sing to us,
> Full of the sweetest melody;
> And let forthwith each render songs [lays]
> As sumptuous as may be found,
> And in your voices' harmony …[40]

The *Mystère de Saint Louis*, by the count of Provence, mentions the wind band performing 'a beautiful motet.'

The new statutes of 1407 for the minstrel guild of Paris, the *Confrérie de St. Julien*, indicate a new sense of professionalism, particularly with regard to the selection of membership. Now a candidate had to sign a formal contract in the home of one of the Masters before beginning a six-year apprenticeship. This period of study concluded with a performance of a 'chef-d'oeuvre' before the Masters.

It is reasonable to suppose that the higher professional requirements represented by this new statue were reflected in a higher standard of music heard by the public. Although documentation in France is rare, we must assume that these civic wind bands were

37 Quoted in Reese, *Music in the Renaissance*, 115.

38 Craig Wright, 'Antoine Brumel and Patronage at Paris,' in Iain Fenlon, ed., *Music in Medieval and Early Modern Europe* (Cambridge: Cambridge University Press, 1981), 45.

39 Pizan, *The Book of the Body Politic*, I, xxxiii.

40 Translated in Reese, *Music in the Renaissance*, 151.

beginning to perform some 'concerts' for the enjoyment of the public, as in other countries. Surely such a performance is intended in a document of 1480 referring to the four civic musicians of Lille playing 'for the honor of the city.'

> ... tous le jours, au matin, á la cloche du jour et au vespre ... sur le belfroy, bein et notablement á l'honneur de la ville.[41]

<aside>41 A. de la Fons-Mélicocq, 'Les ménstrels de Lille,' in *Archives historiques et littéraires du Nord* (1885), V, 62.</aside>

FUNCTIONAL MUSIC

We omit references to the style and composers of the great polyphonic Church music, of which so much has been written. We must mention, however, that the general music history texts discuss this music as having existed in an environment in which no accompanying instruments were to be found. Recent research, however, has clearly demonstrated that the long-banned instruments were finally beginning to find their way back into the Church during the fifteenth century. Gerson also makes reference to this changing tradition. After briefly discussing the organ, he adds,

> Ecclesiastical custom has retained only or especially this same musical instrument, to which, as we have seen, the tuba may be occasionally joined, but very rarely bombardae, chalemiae, cornemusae or other instruments which we will not name here, of which the Book of Daniel includes in the adoration of the statue with all kinds of instruments.[42]

<aside>42 Gerson, 'Tractatus de Canticis,' 348.</aside>

In a particularly curious reference to the trumpet [*tuba*], Gerson mentions its use in a truly pagan religious tradition, that of welcoming the new moon.[43]

<aside>43 Ibid., 347.</aside>

While by the end of the fifteenth century it was the rule, and not the exception, to find skilled musicians in the employ of towns and courts throughout Western Europe, it is possible that by this time the level of musician found singing in the Church in some towns was not nearly so high. Craig Wright has found among the documents for even a large cathedral such as that of Cambrai evidence of the employment of adult singers who could not read music. In one case in 1491 a man was hired as a vicar who not only could not read music, but was even married—which must surely suggest a difficulty in finding good voices.[44]

<aside>44 Craig Wright, 'Performance Practices at the Cathedral of Cambrai 1475–1550,' *The Musical Quarterly* 64, no. 3 (July 1978): 313.</aside>

Perhaps another clue to the quality of these singers may be inferred from documents which refer to disciplinary actions taken against them for various offenses committed during the actual church service. The most surprising of these is one of 1493 when the singers were admonished for,

> throwing meat and bones from one side of the choir to the other during the divine service.[45]

45 Ibid., 297.

Such a picture of fifteenth-century Church musicians helps frame a charming reference to two poor clerics associated with the University of Paris in the 'Little Testament,' by François Villon.

> They are Master Guillaume Cotin
> and Master Thibaud de Vitry,
> two poor Latin-speaking clerics,
> peaceful children, unquarrelsome,
> humble, good singers in the choir …[46]

46 François Villon, 'The Legacy,' in Williams, *The Complete Works*, lines 217ff.

An interesting reference to civic political music is found in the Memoirs of Philippe de Commynes, regarding an occasion after a defeat of Duke Charles of Burgundy by the king of France. Charles sent his ambassador, Contay, to the king, who was staying in Lyon, and the ambassador found himself,

> ridiculed by the townspeople; for songs were sung publicly, praising the conquerors and shaming the conquered.[47]

47 Commynes, *The Memoirs of Philippe de Commynes*, I, 304.

The same *Memoirs* frequently mentions the use of the trumpeter as an ambassador, to carry messages to the enemy. Because he had this recognized role, he was supposed to be given safe passage under all circumstances—something which, as he relates, did not always happen!

> The next morning I decided to continue with our negotiations for an agreement, as I was always desirous that the king should pass safely; but I could hardly find a trumpeter who was willing to go to the enemy camp because nine of their trumpeters, who had not been recognized, had been killed in battle.[48]

48 Ibid., II, 536.

A common form of functional music was that performed for the arrival of distinguished visitors. Upon the arrival of the Duke of Bedford in Paris, in October 1424, he was greeted by the clergy of Notre Dame, singing hymns 'so pure.' There were also players of organs and trumpets, joined by the ringing of all the bells.

> Les chanoynes de Notre-Dame le receurent à la plus grant honneur, en chantant hymnes et louages que ilz peurent, et jouait-on des sorgues et de trompes; et sonnoient toutes les cloches.[49]

When Louis IX visited Orléans in 1461, he was greeted by a wind band (*haut ménestrels*) and a children's chorus singing with an organ.[50]

A particularly interesting reference of this nature is relative to the 1457 visit to the court of Charles VII by ambassadors from King Ludislaus of Hungary. The envoys brought an instrument unknown to Paris, as an eyewitness describes,

> One had never before seen drums like big kettles, carried on horseback.[51]

A fifteenth-century French treatise on hunting suggests that the signal music used for this purpose was already fairly complex.

> You ought to blow after the unharboring two moots. And if your hounds do not come to your will as quickly as you would like, you ought to blow four moots to hasten the company to you, and to warn the company that the hart is unharbored [dislodged]. Then you ought to recheat on your hounds [call back from the wrong scent]. And afterwards, when they are gone ahead of you, you ought to call in the manner as I shall tell you, you ought to blow trout, trout, troutoutout, trout, trout, trourourourout, trourourourout, trourourourout.[52]

Finally, a rather unique example of functional music is found in an account one 'knight of the watch' in Paris, in 1418, who employed two or three minstrels, 'playing loud instruments,' to walk before him to frighten potential muggers!

> Il y avait alors à Paris un chevalier du guet nommé Messire Gautier Rallart, qui ne se rendait jamais au guet sans se faire précéder de deux ou trois ménétriers qui jouaient très fort, ce qui paraissait très étrange au peuple et lui faisait dire qu'il semblait annoncer aux malfaiteurs: 'Fuyez, car je viens!'[53]

---

49 Anonymous, *Journal d'un Bourgeois de Paris* (Paris, 1888), 200.

50 Y. Rokseth, *La musique d'orgue au XVe siècle et au début du XVIe* (Paris, 1930), 42.

51 Curt Sachs, *The History of Musical Instruments* (New York: Norton, 1940), 329.

52 Guyllaume Twici, *L'art de vénerie*, trans. A. Dryden (Northhampton, MA, 1908), 23.

53 *Journal d'un Bourgeois de Paris*, 50.

ENTERTAINMENT MUSIC

The most common form of entertainment music at this time was undoubtedly that performed for banquets. A visitor to a dinner given by René II of Anjou, in 1489, reports that the various courses were served with great ceremony with the music of trumpets, shawms [*fifres*] and tambours and that during the meal music was performed by 'all sorts of instruments.'[54]

By the fifteenth century the better musicians had been hired by towns and nobles, leaving the remaining true wandering musicians as a somewhat dishonorable class of entertainers. Christine de Pizan mentions one of these types, the goliards, remarking that the habits of 'such dubious characters are a sure road to damnation.'[55] François Villon, in his 'Great Testament,' mentions the musicians who waste their time playing in taverns.

> If you rhyme, jest, play cymbals or lute
> like a foolish and shameless impostor,
> or if you're a mummer, magician or flutist,
> or if in the towns and the cities
> you do farces, plays or moralities, or if
> you're a winner at dice, at cards or at ninepins,
> it soon is all gone (do you hear?)
> all to the girls and the taverns.[56]

Sometimes, no doubt, such behavior had ill results for these itinerant musicians, as we read in the text of a little ballade by Richard de Loqueville.

> When comrades sally forth to play
> In diverse countries here and there,
> They do not banquet every day
> On roasted capon or fat hare
> Save if with gold they are supplied.
> For just as sure it does betide
> That if a comrade lose his gains
> He ends with sorely wounded pride,
> His feet held fast by two stout chains.[57]

Christine de Pizan, in her *The Book of the Duke of True Lovers*, describes the activities of minstrels in the entertainments surrounding a great court tournament.[58] Six minstrels, with trumpets and

[54] Albert Jacquot, *La musique en Lorraine* (Paris, 1882), 8.

[55] Pizan, *Mirror of Honor*, III, ix.

[56] Villon, 'The Testament,' lines 1700ff.

[57] Translated by Gustave Reese, in *Music in the Renaissance*, 19.

[58] Pizan, *The Book of the Duke of True Lovers*, 60ff.

drums, greet the arrival of the nobles and 'blew so loudly that the hills and valleys resounded.'

> Menestrelz, trompes, naquaires
> y avoit plus de troys paires,
> qui si haultement cournoyent,
> que mons et vaulx resonnoyent.[59]

They performed for the banquet, 'lending luster to the festival.' After the meal was finished they performed again 'in gracious harmony.' During the course of the tournament itself, a piper played 'spreading cheer about' and 'minstrels trumpeted gaily.' The winners were greeted with music so loud 'that God thundering might not have been heard.'

> Lors menestrelz liement
> cournoient, hairaux crioent,
> Lances brisent, cops resonnent,
> et ces menestrelz haut sonnent
> si qu'on n'oïst Dieu tonnant.

Finally, Gerson makes a brief reference to the entertainment music of the common people.

> There are other tympana more used among the people, because they are louder for uncouth leaping and other dancing, and to these they customarily join two- and three-holed fistulae, and also a moderate sized tripos beaten on both sides.[60]

[59] Christine de Pizan, *Le livre du duc des vrais amants*, in *Oeuvres poétiques* (Paris, 1896), 79ff and 89ff.

[60] Gerson, 'Tractatus de Canticis,' 347.

10 THE LOW COUNTRIES IN THE FOURTEENTH AND FIFTEENTH CENTURIES

THE POLITICAL STORY OF BURGUNDY, an area so important to the cultural development of the early Renaissance, begins when the French King, John II, living in exile in London, gave a portion of these territories to his son Philip the Bold as a reward for his valor at the Battle of Poitiers. Philip, as duke of Burgundy (1363–1404), expanded the territory, adding Flanders, and it soon began to operate as a separate state, rather than as a province of France. It became the goal of Philip and the next three dukes to make their duchy a kingdom, something which could be granted only by the pope or the emperor of the Holy Roman Empire. Their basic political strategy was: 'If we live on a scale similar to kings, sooner or later they will call us a king.' Music was a beneficiary of this strategy, for these dukes, as part of 'living like kings,' began to spend freely on culture, thus making their court a magnet for the best musicians.

Philip the Bold began building his musical establishment immediately and by 1367 had twenty-eight musicians in his service.[1] Soon it was noticed that the court of Philip was more brilliant, with his musicians in greater number and chosen with greater care, than the court of the king of France.[2] Further evidence of Philip's interest in music can be seen in a number of documents relative to his sending his musicians to minstrel schools to acquire new repertoire.

Froissart heard Philip's musicians perform after the Battle of Tournai, in 1385, reporting a large ensemble performing in 'a very pleasing manner,'[3] and again on a voyage with the duke in 1390.

> Much great beauty and pleasure to hear from the resounding trumpets and clarions, sounding, and with other minstrels performing on bagpipes, shawm and timpani, as well as the sound of voices, resounding and echoing from the sea.[4]

The next duke of Burgundy, John the Fearless (1404–1419), was unsuccessful in battle, unscrupulous, dishonest and violent. He

[1] Edmund Bowles, 'Instruments at the Court of Burgundy,' *The Galpin Society Journal* 6 (July 1953): 32.

[2] Jeanne Marix, *Histoire de la Musique et des Musiciens de la Cour de Bourgogne sous le règne de Philippe le Bon* (Strasbourg: Heitz, 1939), 16ff.

[3] Kervyn de Lettenhove, 'Fragment inedit de Froissart,' in *Bulletin de l'Académie royale de Belgiques* (1886), XXV, 57.

[4] Jean Alexandre Buchon, *Chroniques de Froissart* (Paris: Verdière) III, iv, 13.

personally paid for the murder of Louis, Duke of Orléans, and was himself killed by an assassin. It was only because he was so bad, that his morally questionable son was called Philip 'the Good.' Nevertheless, he was a musician himself and maintained singers, ceremonial instruments and a six-member wind band, whom he dressed in scarlet robes. We can see their instrumentation in an order to the instrument maker, Pierre de Prost of Bruges, for two shawms, two bombards, a 'contre' and a slide trumpet (or perhaps trombone).[5]

Philip the Good (1419–1457) oversaw a complete separation from France and the annexation of large parts of what is now The Netherlands. His was a kingdom in everything but name and became the most important cultural center of the fifteenth century. We should pause for a look at this important figure, seen by one of his court chroniclers, George Chastellain.

> He had large bushy eyebrows which stood out like horns when he was angry ... His eyes varied considerably, sometimes looking fierce, at other times amiable. His face reflected his inner feelings ... He deserved a crown on the strength of his physical appearance alone ... He walked solemnly ... he sat but little, stood for long periods ... was always changing his clothes ... He was skillful on horseback, liked the bow and shot well, and was excellent at tennis ... he lingered over his meals. Though the best-served man alive, he was a modest eater.[6]

A more balanced assessment might add that he experienced flares of wrath, as when he once pursued his son through the palace with a sword, and cruelty—once drowning six hundred citizens of Dinant when they withheld taxes. He had twenty-four mistresses and sixteen illegitimate children.[7]

It seems safe to say that no aristocrat by this time devoted more personal attention to his musical establishment, which included Dufay and Binchois. Philip personally auditioned his musicians, sometimes more than once, as in the case a singer, Robert de la Magdelaine, whom he made sing for an entire week in 1448 before approving him.[8] To his wind band he began adding string players in 1433.[9]

Philip the Good was also generous in supporting music in many towns other than where his court resided. He built organs and established Church schools to teach singing and counterpoint.[10] No one was more generous in rewarding visiting minstrels, even those of the enemy during lulls in battle.

---

5 Vander Straeten, *La Musique aux Pays Bas avant le XIXe Siècle*, VII, 38ff.

6 Quoted in Richard Vaughan, *Philip the Good* (New York: Barnes & Noble, 1970), 127ff.

7 Following his model, the bishop of Cambrai had thirty-six illegitimate children and the bishop of Liege twelve!

8 Marix, *Histoire de la Musique*, 21.

9 Bowles, 'Instruments at the Court of Burgundy.'

10 Marix, *Histoire de la Musique*, 22.

Philip's son, Charles the Bold, was educated in music from an early age, learning to play the harp and sing by the age of seven. He also studied composition, as reported by Olivier de La Marche.

> He liked music, however he had a bad voice, but at the same time he had the art, and sang many songs well and composed well.[11]

11 Quoted in ibid., 19.

Charles continued the musical establishment of his father, adding the composer Busnois, but his constant battles left him little time to support the arts. One interesting document describes his meeting in 1473 with the emperor Frederick in Trier. For the occasion Charles outfitted the entire court in new robes, with 'cloth of gold' for the highest nobles down to the 'woollen cloths of different qualities' of the porters and humble servants. The musicians were somewhat below mid-point in this hierarchy, with the minstrels wearing 'short robes of damask and pourpoints of black satin' and his trumpeters 'robes of camlet.'[12]

12 Vaughan, *Philip the Good*, 143ff.

Otherwise, the last of these dukes was extraordinary, even to an age long inured to violence. When one of his own towns voted to join the French, Charles burned it to the ground and drowned hundreds of captives. His mad reign of ten years ended in 1477, when, defeated by the Swiss, his body was found in a pond with his face frozen in the ice. As Charles had no son, the territories passed through his daughter, Mary, to her husband Maximilian I and the Hapsburg empire.

During the fourteenth and fifteenth centuries there was also a tremendous expansion in the development of civic wind bands (*stad pijpers* or *scalmeyers*).[13] Until about 1480 the typical ensemble was a four-man band of shawms, bombard and trombone and after that date civic purchases began to also include recorders, crumhorns and cornetts, although evidence of the purchase of strings does not appear until the mid-sixteenth century. By the end of the fifteenth century the civic records begin to indicate the purchase of entire consorts, cases [*coker*] of instruments, anticipating the general practice of the sixteenth century.[14]

13 The sudden increase in competition in the weaving industry from England caused some decline in the wealth, and even population, in some towns at the end of the fifteenth century. Indeed, today Ieper has only one-half the population it had in 1350!

14 Keith Polk, 'Ensemble Instrumental Music in Flanders—1450–1550' [Unpublished], 17ff.

Some civic musicians were still found in the tower doing watch duty, thus in Mechlin applicants were given eye examinations as well as musical ones.[15] But there was also a wide range of performances, representatives of which are given below.

15 R. van Aerde, *Notes pour servir à l'histoire de la musique du theatre et de la danse à Malines* (Malines, 1925), 4, 14.

ART MUSIC

It is especially in the Low Countries where one finds accounts of performances by the civic wind bands which begin to have the characteristics of real concerts. By this, of course, we do not mean white ties, tails and programs, but simply performances where people actually *listened* to the music.

An annual event in many towns was the Ommegang, a celebration part religious and part civic in character. Often visiting civic bands would participate, as in the example of the Ommegang in Termonde in 1405 when seventeen separate ensembles performed. In addition to the official procession these bands also played concerts before the city hall.[16]

When important nobles visited they were often the guests of honor for a town banquet. On these occasions, after the meal was finished, a brief concert was often given by the town band. A typical example was the performance by the Brussels civic band in 1495 after a banquet honoring Philip, son to Maximilian I, in a concert reported to have consisted of various 'chansons de musique.'[17]

Some town bands were giving regular public concerts by the fourteenth century, such as those in Bruges by 1350 in the town plaza. A contract for this same town band of the fifteenth century gives interesting details of these concerts.

> Each [of the civic musicians] is obligated to play at the front of the old hall at the customary place on all Sundays and Holy Days at 11:00 before noon and at 6:00 in the evening from Easter to *Baefmesse* [Feast of St. Bava], and from *Baefmesse* to Easter at 3:00 in the afternoon; they are to play two chansons [*liedekens*] or motets [*moteten*] at each performance; each performer is to appear in uniform and sign the work book.[18]

When a group of musicians from Brabant were hired as the town band in Utrecht in 1489, their contract stipulated that they were to perform motets from the church tower on all Holy Days and to play in the Church for the Marian services.[19] In Bruges, the master of the children at St. Donaes, Casin de Brauwer, was commissioned by the city in 1484 to prepare a collection of motets for use by the city band in the Marian services.[20]

Similar concerts are described as being given in the market place in some towns, which, of course, was another focal point for the

---

16 Wytsman, *Anciens airs et chansons populaires de Termonde*, quoted in Vander Straeten, *La Musique aux Pays Bas*, IV, 198.

17 *Archives generales du royaume*, quoted in Vander Straeten, ibid., IV, 159ff.

18 Louis Gilliodts-Van Severen, 'Les ménestrels de Bruges,' in *Essais d'Archéologie Brugeoise* (Bruges, 1912), II, 111.

19 Polk, 'Ensemble Instrumental Music in Flanders,' 22.

20 Ibid., 23.

people. The *Chronik von Antwerpen* reports regular evening concerts by the six-member civic band[21] and a similar account from Michelin speaks of the performance of overtures [*overijasche*].

The opening of the annual town fair was perhaps another occasion for concerts by the civic bands. An account of the fair in Bergen-op-Zoom in 1499 speaks of 'singers and the town band performing motets during the night.'[22] A similar document for the Bruges civic band in 1481 required them to perform every evening 'tout la durée de la faire.'[23] A particularly interesting document regarding a performance at the Bruges market-fair of 1500 involves Obrecht, who, as chapel master at St. Donaes, was in charge. This document by the town fathers complains about the performance, mentioning 'great confusion … lack of communication … absence of singers … and the embarrassment to the city,' and demanding correction.[24]

Private concerts before the nobles are not so frequently documented, but Marix suggests that the receptions given by Philip the Good for visiting aristocrats were generally occasions for concerts.[25] A civic document of Brussels of 1495 describes that town band playing 'plusiers chansons' at a banquet for Philippe-le-Beau.[26]

FUNCTIONAL MUSIC

Regarding Church music, we notice the Mass for the marriage of Philip the Bold in 1385 was sung by 'many singers and musical *flusteurs*.'[27] We have brief references to the performances of Philip the Good's singers in the Masses associated with the meetings of his Order of the Golden Fleece. One in particular, referring to the Mass of St. Andrew, mentions '*cum una superba e suavissima musica*.'[28] Another account describes the performance of a Requiem, believed to be a lost work by Dufay, which was heard as 'mournful, sad and very exquisite.'[29]

All civic celebrations included a great procession through the town, which included local and visiting musicians. Michelin held an annual Procession of Peace from 1368, of which accounts speak of thirteen trumpeters and eighty-four minstrels in 1385, twenty-four trumpeters and fifty-eight shawms in 1414 and more than two hundred musicians in 1418.[30]

21 L. de Barbure, 'La musique à Anvers aux XIVe, XVe, et XVIe Siècles,' in *Annales de l'Académie Royale d'Archéologie de Belgique* (1906), 243.

22 Korneel Slootmans, 'De Hoge Lieve Vrouwe van Bergen-op-Zoom,' in *Jaerboek van de Oudheidkundige Kring de Ghulden Roos*, XXV, 212.

23 D. Van de Casteele, 'Préludes historiques sur la Ghilde des ménestrels de Bruges,' in *Annales de la Société d'Emulation* (3e série), III, 65ff.

24 Polk, 'Ensemble Instrumental Music in Flanders,' 22.

25 Marix, *Histoire de la Musique*, 22.

26 Polk, 'Ensemble Instrumental Music in Flanders,' 25.

27 Ibid., 18. *Flusteurs* was a term often used to mean 'winds' in general.

28 William Prizer, 'Music and Ceremonial in the Low Countries,' *Early Music History* 5 (1985): 124.

29 Quoted in ibid., 133.

30 E. Closson, *La facture des instruments de musique en Belgique* (Brussels: Degrace, 1935), 65ff. This procession in 1436 included elephants and camels!

Performances welcoming visiting nobles also were occasions for large numbers of musicians. On at least one occasion, a reception in Ghent in 1385, for the duke and duchess of Burgundy, included a performance in which all the players appear to have performed together, resulting in something 'enjoyable to hear.'

> … les trompettes, clarons et ménstreuls de toutes manières d'instruments commencerent à jouer et sonner tout à une fois que c'estoit chose plaisante et mélodieuse à ouyr.[31]

When Philip the Good was welcomed in Ghent on one occasion he was greeted by some thirty trumpets[32] and an allegorical pageant which featured four singers and two instrumentalists sitting on an elephant, performing a new chanson.[33] When Philip traveled he was first awakened by trumpeters, who then went into the stables to play for the horses—an important safety measure, accustoming the horses to the noise of the instruments. When the traveling party was ready, the trumpets would be joined by the *'haults instrumens,'* the shawms and bombards.[34]

Accounts of aristocratic weddings in the Low Countries are filled with references to music. Perhaps the most documented was the wedding of Philip the Good to Isabel of Portugal in 1430. When Isabel left Lisbon, it was to the music of 'a great number of trumpets, minstrels, players of organs, harps and other instruments.'[35] The problems of fifteenth-century travel being what they were, Philip had to wait impatiently for more than six months, while Isabel's ships were scattered by a storm, with some blown off course as far as England. Thus when she finally arrived in port, there was a great sense of celebration, as an eyewitness describes.

> On the feast day of Saint Estienne, before midday, the lady descended from her ship and at her descent were many barges and other small vessels decorated with flags, and many important siegneurs, squires and notable people from diverse lands to see, serve, and accompany her. There were also many trumpets, minstrels, and players of many musical instruments, and each tried to play the best he could, for the coming of the lady was much desired … Naturally there were heralds, trumpets, minstrels … more than 120 silver trumpets, plus other trumpets, minstrels, players of organ, harp and other instruments without number; the force of the music made the entire city vibrate.[36]

---

31 Quoted in Lettenhove, 'Fragment inedit de froissart,' 57.

32 J. du Clercq, *Mémoires* (Paris, 1838), 111.

33 Olivier de La Marche, *Mémoires* (Paris, 1883–1888), IV, 70ff.

34 Marix, *Histoire de la Musique*, 61.

35 L. P. Gachard, *Collection de documents inédits concernant la Belgique* (Bruxelles, 1833–1835), II, 65ff.

36 Anonymous Mss. (Archives générales du Belgique, Brussels), quoted in ibid.

Another eyewitness suggests at least one organized mass fanfare, '76 trumpets all played at the same time.'[37] And still another reporter heard one hundred and sixty-four trumpets which sounded 'very melodiously.'[38]

In 1440, Philip attended the marriage of Charles d'Orléans and Marie de Clèves held in Bruges. An eyewitness again reports 'the streets were filled with silver trumpets, clarions, minstrels and other instruments of music.'[39] Charles came from a musical family and his mother once had a gown upon which the chanson, 'Madame je suis plus joyeulx,' was notated with five hundred and sixty-eight pearls![40]

The marriage of Charles the Bold to Margaret of England in 1468 included a wedding procession which the Flemish chronicler, La Marche, describes as having included trumpets, clarions and 'minstrels from many lands.'[41] The wind band of Charles performed for the actual wedding service, which included a motet and a chanson performed by an ensemble of shawms, trombones and bombards, with 'excellent effect.'[42] During the several days of entertainments which followed the wedding there was an allegorical pageant which featured four rabbits playing flutes, four boars blowing trumpets, and four donkeys performing on shawms.[43]

Philip the Good's wind musicians accompanied him to battle, of course, and perhaps the most charming account involves a siege of Bouvignes in 1430. Philip had the citizens of Dinant construct an enormous wooden cat, large enough to contain two hundred soldiers, taking an idea from the famous horse of the Trojan Wars. The engineers forgot to oil the wheels of the cat and so we are told that the subsequent 'meowing,' together with Philip's trumpets, unfortunately alerted the citizens of Bouvignes of the approach of the cat![44]

Finally, we must not fail to mention that perhaps the most extraordinary instrumental music of the fifteenth century was the *basse danse*, played usually by two shawms and a slide trumpet. We know the two shawms engaged in florid improvisation above the melody in the slide trumpet, but because of the tradition of improvisation virtually nothing was ever written down. The two or three notated examples which are extant suggest an extraordinary level of virtuosity and invention and are a testimonial to our loss.

37 Jean Lefèvre, *Chronique* (Paris, 1876), II, 165ff.

38 E. de Monstrelet, *La Chronique d'Enguerran de Monsstrelet* (Paris, 1857–1862), IV, 371.

39 Ibid., V, 447.

40 Pierre Champion, *La vie de Charles d'Orléans* (Paris: H. Champion, 1911), 132.

41 La Marche, *Mémoires* (Paris, 1885), III, 109ff.

42 Wangermé, *Flemish Music* (New York, 1968), 213; Eric Simons, *The Reign of Edward IV* (London: F. Muller, 1966), 155; La Marche, *Mémoires*, III, 152ff; E. Dahnk, 'Musikausubung an den Hofen von Burgund und Orleans wahrend des 15. Jahrhunderts,' in *Archiv für Kulturgeschichte* (1934–1936), 210; and G. Thibault, 'Le Concert Instrumental au XVe Siècle,' in Jean Jacquot, *La Musique Instrumental de la Renaissance* (Paris, 1955), 31, which suggests several chansons which may have been used.

43 Léon de Laborde, *Les ducs de Bourgogne* (Paris, 1849–1852), II, 326ff.

44 Kervyn de Lettenhove, 'Chroniques relatives à l'histoire de Belgique sous la domination des ducs de Bourgogne,' in *Livre des trahisons de France* (Brussels, 1873), 201.

ENTERTAINMENT MUSIC

The most documented instances of entertainment music performed before the dukes of Burgundy are the accounts of music played for the banquets of the Order of the Golden Fleece [*Toison d'Or*], which had been created by Philip the Good in 1430 on the day of his wedding. For the first of these banquets, in 1431, we read of minstrels playing 'sweet music which lingered in the ears.'[45] In 1451 Philip's musicians were wearing 'robes of silver gilt linen cloth' and performed for the Mass associated with these meetings, as well as evening serenades for the noble members.[46]

The most famous of these gatherings was the one held in Lille in 1454, which Philip organized in the hope of attempting to convince the participating nobles to join in a crusade, Constantinople having fallen to the Turks the previous year. The banquet associated with this meeting of the Order is probably the most documented single banquet of the Renaissance. Gathering information from several eyewitnesses, we see three long tables inside the banquet hall, which was guarded by uniformed nobles and crossbowmen. Philip the Good's place was at the center table, beneath a canopy of velvet and gold. Here he sat 'with so many diamonds, rubies and fine pearls in his hat that there were no room for any more.' The tablecloths were of silk damask, touching the floor, with individual cushions embroidered with coats-of-arms on the benches. The service was of gold; the glassware of crystal with jewels encrusted.

The decorations included two statues, one the figure of a naked girl, leaning against one of the supporting columns of the hall with Hippocras spraying from her right breast and guarded by a live lion. She symbolized the city of Constantinople being protected by the lion of Flanders. Similarly, the other statue, that of a small boy, sprayed rose-water in 'the most natural fashion.'

The two major constructions in the hall also contained musicians. One was a model church, complete with stained glass windows and a bell in the steeple. It contained four singers and an organ. Across the room was a great pastry pie which contained twenty-eight musicians. One cannot be entirely sure of the instrumentation of the ensemble in the pie, as the eyewitnesses were somewhat confused by the resultant sound, but taking all the sources together there were mentioned bagpipes, cornetts, trumpets, lutes, dulcians, flutes and drums.[47]

---

[45] Lefèvre, *Chronique*, II, 201ff.

[46] Mathieu d'Escouchy, *Chronique* (Paris, 1863–1864), I, 350ff.

[47] Since Philip's colors were black and gray, we assume this must have been the inspiration for the song, 'Four and Twenty Black Birds Baked in a Pie.'

There were further tableaux: a replica of a Flemish ship in port, with rigging, sailors, bales and casks and a replica of a Flemish town, by a desert scene of tigers and snakes fighting (Christendom and the infidel again). There was a 'monster' in white and green silk, half man and half griffin, riding astride a boar, and a dragon spouting fire as it flew across the room and then mysteriously disappeared.

When all the guests were seated, a bell rang in the model church, followed by a chanson sung by the musicians inside. This was apparently the first of the musical selections performed as the food was being made ready. The chanson was followed with a performance by a musician of the bagpipe, dressed as a shepherd. Then a performing horse entered the hall, walking backward, and on its back were two trumpeters, sitting back to back and dressed in gray and black robes and wearing masks and 'surprising' hats. The organ in the church played next, followed by a 'German cornett' from the pie, 'sounding very strange.'

Now the food was ready to be served but due to the congestion, there was no room for the usual procession by which food paraded in at such events, so it had to be lowered from the ceiling by cranes. The duke, being an exception, was served by a 'two-headed horse' and later by 'a monster, consisting of a man riding on an elephant, with another man, whose feet were hidden, on his shoulders.' We may rest assured that the variety of food was adequate, as we are told each meat course alone consisted of more than forty different dishes!

As the banquet proceeded there was continual music. One heard the singers again in a motet and a three-part chanson, 'La saulvegarde de ma vie.' In through the doors of the hall came four trumpeters, in white robes playing gold trumpets, followed by more vocal music. Now a young boy (one account says a girl) seated on an artificial white stag with gilded antlers entered the hall. The boy wore a short costume of crimson silk, a little black hat and shoes of pony skin and sang Dufay's chanson, 'Je ne vis oncques la pareille,' accompanied by the stag (another hidden musician).

Next a play, *The Mystery and Adventure of Jason*, was performed on a stage, followed by more singing and organ playing from the model church. One heard a fanfare by the gold trumpets, from behind a green stage curtain, and then a four-part recorder performance from inside the pie. The duke's two blind vielle players performed with a young girl, followed by an instrumental work by pipe and tabor players inside the pie, and then another chanson.

Now a real elephant entered the hall, carrying a lady dressed in white, representing the captive Church begging for delivery by a crusade. At this time Dufay's 'Lamentatio sanctae matris ecclesiae Constantinopolitanae' was performed.

Finally the grand chivalric moment arrived, with the entrance of two knights of the Order of the Golden Fleece and a pheasant, which had a gold collar around its neck decorated with rubies and large pearls. The duke handed to the Golden Fleece king-of-arms a vow to read. It announced his intention to make the crusade, even going so far as to say that if challenged, he would accept single combat with the Turk! Everyone was amazed by this and one by one the other knights took the vow, although the crusade never took place.

A procession of torch-bearers and musicians now preceded the circulation of large bowls glittering with precious stones for the guests. A dance by the twelve actors brought the banquet to a conclusion. One of the guests reported he got tired and left just before four o'clock in the morning!

11 JOHANNES TINCTORIS

Gustave Reese calls Johannes Tinctoris (1435–1511) 'very much a man of his own time,' primarily because of the often quoted statement by Tinctoris that in his view only the compositions of the past forty years were worth performing.¹

    Be that as it may, and for all his brilliance and skill in observation of the current musical scene, he was nevertheless a theorist of the old Scholastic school. He was, after all, a canon of the church at Nivelles early in his career, which perhaps explains that for him (like many modern musicologists!) music meant Church music, with only token recognition of the wider world of music going on all around him. During his tenure in Naples under Ferdinand I, Tinctoris must have been exposed not only to Italian humanism, but to a wide variety of secular art music of high quality. Yet he assigns little space to these things in his treatises and concluded Jesus Christ to have been the greatest singer.

    Music, to Tinctoris, still belonged to the old medieval definition of the Liberal Arts, where it resided as a branch of mathematics. Contemporary information makes this association with Tinctoris irrefutably clear. A biographical note of 1495 calls him an outstanding mathematician, as well as a musician of the highest rank,² and in the Prologue to his own treatise *Concerning the Nature and Propriety of Tones*, Tinctoris identifies himself as one who professes 'the mathematical sciences.'³ In this same work, in speaking of Church modes he says these were named,

> according to arithmetic, without which it is obvious no famous musicians escapes.⁴

He also mentions, in this same treatise, that he has previously written a work on proportions, called *Proportionale Musices*, which had been criticized by one of 'the most ridiculous of all singers.' Indeed, he confides this man 'has not been afraid to menace me

1 Reese, *Music in the Renaissance*, 141.

2 Quoted in ibid., 138. This same 1495 biographical note recommends Tinctoris as 'worthy of memory to posterity,' which, as we have noted in an earlier chapter reflects one of the new characteristics of the Renaissance—thoughts of future life on earth, rather than just in heaven.

3 Johannes Tinctoris, *Concerning the Nature and Propriety of Tones*, trans. Albert Seay (Colorado Springs: Colorado College Music Press, 1976), 1. We reminding the reader that our purpose, as with our discussions of all early music treatises in this series of books, is to concentrate only on the writings which offer insights relative to the aesthetics of music and musical performance, while omitting technical discussion.

4 Ibid., 3.

with a violent meal of this little book if ever I should return to my native land.' We can only assume that it was a musician of more modern humanistic leanings who made this threat, the humanists in general being inclined to reject the old Scholastic concepts of composition represented by Tinctoris. The critic may have reacted to this passage in the earlier book, which both seems to recognize a new style, to the extent that even composers such as Okeghem are breaking the old rules, and testifies once again on behalf of a mathematical understanding of music.

> As a result of this tempest, the musical ability of our time has undergone such an increase that it seems to be a new art ...
>
> But alas! I wonder not only at these but even at many other famous composers, for while they compose so subtly and so ingeniously with incomprehensible smoothness, I have known them to ignore entirely musical proportions or to signify incorrectly those which they do know. I do not doubt that this results from a lack of arithmetic, without which no brilliant achievement in music escapes, for proportion is produced from its entrails.[5]

In another place he accounts for errors in proportions among composers he knew as being due to their failure in expertise in 'arithmetic.'[6] Here he also criticizes a group of composers for having followed an error of Dufay and attributes their lack of knowledge to their not being well read, an apparent reference to the numerous treatises of the Middle Ages which dwelt extensively with mathematics.

> I do not wonder at De Domarto, if Regis, Caron, Boubert, Faugues, Courbet and many others, as I have seen in their works, have imitated him in this error, since I have heard that they are but slightly read. And who can attain the truth of not only this or of any other liberal science without reading?[7]

One frequently discussed topic of the old Scholastic tradition which Tinctoris did not accept was the hypothesis of the 'music of the spheres.' However, because the topic was still being seriously advanced by some in the fifteenth century, he felt compelled to begin his treatise, the *Art of Counterpoint*, with a reference to, and rejection of, this two thousand-year-old notion.

> But although, as Boethius says, some assert that Saturn is moved with the deepest sound and, taking the remaining planets in proper

---

5 Johannes Tinctoris, *Proportionale Musices*, trans. Albert Seay in *Journal of Music Theory* 1, no. 1 (March 1957): 27.

6 Ibid., III, ii.

7 Ibid., III, iii.

order, the moon with the highest, while others, however, conversely attribute the deepest sound to the moon and the highest to the stars in their movement, I adhere to neither position. On the contrary, I unshakeably agree with Aristotle …, together with our more recent philosophers, who most clearly prove that there is neither real nor potential sound in the heavens. For this reason I can never be persuaded that musical consonances, which cannot be produced without sound, are made by the motion of heavenly bodies.

Concords of sounds and melodies, therefore, from whose sweetness, as Lactantius says, the pleasure of the ears is derived, are brought about, not by heavenly bodies, but by earthly instruments with the cooperation of nature.[8]

[8] Johannes Tinctoris, *The Art of Counterpoint*, trans. Albert Seay (American Institute of Musicology, 1961), 14.

ON THE AESTHETICS OF MUSIC

On the Purpose of Music

Tinctoris gives as the first purpose of music that it delight the listener, adding that he agrees with Boethius that 'consonances rule all the delight of music.'[9] He continues by expressing his feelings very clearly regarding music which offends the ear.

[9] Ibid.

> And, if I may refer to what I have heard and seen, I have held in my hands at one time or another many old songs of unknown authorship which are called *apocrypha* that are so inept and stupidly composed that they offended the ears rather than pleased them.[10]

[10] Ibid.

An additional purpose of music given by Tinctoris is quite interesting. For the first time since Aristotle we read of something quite similar to the famous philosopher's original concept of catharsis, a term he invented to describe the effect of Tragedy on the observer. With regard to music, Tinctoris describes the listener as being 'more refreshed and wiser.' He begins this passage with his observation, mentioned above, that he believed no composition more than forty years old was worthy of performance. He then lists composers he considered exemplary, including names familiar to musicians today, such as Dufay, Dunstable, Busnois, Binchois and Okeghem. After admitting he does not know whether the source of their excellence is 'some heavenly influence or to a zeal of constant application,' he gives the aesthetic purpose we have referred to.

> Almost all of these men's works exhale such sweetness, that, in my opinion, they should be considered most worthy, not only for men and heroes, but even for the immortal gods. Certainly I never listen to them or study them without coming away more refreshed and wiser.[11]

11 Ibid., 14ff.

In his treatise with regard to aesthetics Tinctoris acknowledges the effect of music on the listener, but here mostly in the context of rather practical results: music delights God, it excites the soul to piety, it elevates the mind, it makes work easier and it increases convivial pleasures.[12]

12 Reese, *Music in the Renaissance*, 146.

But on the other hand, for all his care in associating both the natural sweetness of consonance, and that dissonance which offends, with the musical materials themselves, Tinctoris was not quite willing to accept the position of both the ancient Greeks and the modern humanists that musical materials also affect character. No doubt his beliefs, like those regarding the mathematical nature of music, were conditioned by his adherence to the old Church dogma, which clearly had maintained for itself the role of character formation. At the same time, he seemed to share with the Greeks a genuine respect for the power of music.

> And how great was that melody by whose power the gods, shades, dread spirits, animals, including those capable of reason, and inanimate objects are read to have been moved! For (and this is the unbelievable part) it is not far from a mystery, since poets would not have conceived such things about music unless they had seen its power as something to be marveled at, with, at times, a divine invigoration of the soul.[13]

13 *Proportionale Musices*, Prologue.

For Tinctoris any ability musical performance had in reflecting a particular emotional quality was a characteristic not merely of the musical materials themselves, but of their performance or in the natural emotional makeup of the listener.

> To be sure, it will be possible for a song in one and the same [mode] to be plaintive and cheerful and stern and neutral, not only in regard to composers and singers, but instruments and sound-makers as well. For what person skilled in this art does not know how to compose, to sing and to perform some [melodies] plaintively, others cheerfully, some sternly and others neutrally, although their composition, singing and performance are carried out in the same [mode]?

> Also, certain kinds of voices and instruments are made or are naturally or artificially plaintive, certain cheerful, certain stern and certain neutral …
>
> Certain of these particular harmonies agree, are fitting and are useful for various ages and customs. There is not the same delight or a similar judgment to all people. A cheerful soul is delighted by cheerful harmonies and conversely stern ones are accepted by a stern soul.[14]

14 *Concerning the Nature and Propriety of Tones*, 4ff.

Modern clinical research has proven Tinctoris wrong, for we know today that emotions are universal and that the emotions communicated by music are also universal, at least on a general level. It follows, from common sense if nothing else, that ordinary listeners would not appreciate music as they do if it were necessary for them to understand the conceptual aspects of it. But for Tinctoris, the understanding of music by the listener was predicated on knowledge. Only musically educated persons can properly hear music.

> Although the Spartans may have said that they could judge without learning about good and bad harmonies, this position has not been completely defended, for as the universal opinion of all philosophers holds, a sense of hearing is too often lacking. If the truth is to be confessed I have known and put to the test many people, not deaf, but experts in the art of music, who, not admiring the size or beauty of the voice, prefer calflike bellowings to moderate rationalities and, as I say, to angelic songs. I think these people worthy to have their human faces with their stupid ears changed by divine intervention into those of an ass …
>
> Only musicians judge sounds correctly. Tullius has therefore written this to Hortensius: 'Many things escape us in song; only those trained in this field hear plainly.' Hence, Aristotle comes to this conclusion not uselessly in the eighth book of the *Politics*: 'The young should give themselves to the practice of the art of music so that, as old men, they can judge and enjoy it correctly.'[15]

15 Ibid., 5.

In another place, Tinctoris extends this view to the performer as well, paraphrasing an old Scholastic idea first advanced by Guido d'Arezzo.

> A musician is one who takes up the metier of singing, having observed its principles by means of study. Hence, someone has set down the difference between a musician and a singer in the following jingle:

> There is a big difference between musicians and singers.
> These know, those talk about, what music is.
> And he who doesn't know what he talks about is considered an animal.[16]

Finally, in another treatise, Tinctoris mentions the importance of music in increasing pleasures, observing that,

> singers and all types of instrumentalists—shawms, drummers, organists, lutenists, recorder and trumpet players—add to the magnificence of great banquets.[17]

He points to Obrecht, in his only reference to this composer, as being expert in such music. While never mentioned in general music history texts, Obrecht's father was the leader of a civic band and perhaps Obrecht was therefore more active in secular music than the student is led to believe.

On Melody and Harmony

The first interesting comment which Tinctoris makes regarding melody suggests that for him it still had its ancient association with poetry,

> A melodic interval is the immediate connection of one syllable after another.[18]

Next he makes two statements which may seem startling to the modern reader.

> Melody is the same as harmony.
> Melos is the same as harmony.[19]

Tinctoris, unfortunately, does not explain what he meant by this, but these statements make much sense in view of modern clinical research. Although in modern music schools melody and harmony are treated as if separate, but equal, elements of music, clinical research clearly demonstrates that melodic patterns have a strong genetic universality. All melody has harmonic character, of course. But beyond this fact, harmony probably has little impact on the listener, even with regard to feeling. The old 'major is happy and

---

16   Carl Parrish, *Dictionary of Musical Terms*, (New York: Free Press of Glencoe, 1963), 45.

17   Quoted in Reese, *Music in the Renaissance*, 146.

18   Parrish, *Dictionary of Musical Terms*, 17.

19   Ibid., 41.

minor is sad' cliché is neither borne out in either clinical research nor in actual practice by composers. Melody communicates happy or sad feelings, but our guess is that harmony probably contributes primarily to the awareness of motion through time.

In one other place, Tinctoris says 'Harmony is a certain pleasantness caused by an agreeable sound.'[20] Tonality (mode) he associates only with a single line, above all with the tenor, of a polyphonic work. Indeed, in one place he suggests that if one tries to sing a polyphonic work with the tenor part left out,

> the other parts would sound improperly discordant to each other and would bitterly offend our ears.[21]

[20] Ibid., 9.

[21] *Proportionale Musices*, III, iv.

On Time in Music

For the smallest element of time, the single note, Tinctoris quite correctly reminds the reader that notation is only a symbol of the real music.

> A note is the symbol of a sound, and is of either definite or indefinite time value.[22]

[22] Parrish, *Dictionary of Musical Terms*, 47.

The next level of time he associates with performance.

> Measure is the correct division of the notes, as far as their delivery is concerned.[23]

[23] Ibid., 41.

Perhaps the most impressive of all the treatises by Tinctoris is the *Proportionale Musices*, an extraordinarily complex exposition of the possibilities of this system of progressive metric changes in the individual line. Reese observes,

> We find him here a musical mathematician, at times explaining proportions that can have had little to do with actual practice, though they may have been studied for purposes of exercise.[24]

[24] Reese, *Music in the Renaissance*, 146.

We would go further and declare it impossible to imagine that any singer, then or now, could manage much of these abstract potentialities. Tinctoris himself seems to recognize this when he recommends a 'simple method' of approach to proportions in Church music to eliminate 'delay and doubt' in performance, for,

> When any compositions have been brought to a performing group, they ought to be performed without the slightest hesitation.[25]

Nevertheless, here Tinctoris was clearly on home ground and he is very outspoken regarding the errors he finds in even gifted composers. He does this, he says, not from arrogance, but for the purpose of fighting for truth.[26] In various places he criticizes 'the inexcusable error of Okeghem',[27] a 'bad use' by Dufay[28] (in another place, since he admired Dufay, he says the composer has 'most wonderfully erred'[29]) and with a 'ridiculous' practice by Pasquin, 'wanting in all art and melody'.[30]

On Form in Music

Among Tinctoris's observations regarding form, we find the following the most interesting:

> A canon is a rule showing the purpose of the composer behind a certain obscurity.[31]
>
> ……
>
> A cantilena is a small piece which is set to a text on any kind of subject, but more often to an amatory one.[32]
>
> ……
>
> A part-song is one which is produced by the relationship of the notes of one part to those of another in various ways, and which is commonly called 'composed' [written out].[33]
>
> ……
>
> A *cantus ut jacet* [the piece as it lies] is a piece which is sung entirely as it is written, without any diminution.[34]
>
> ……
>
> A hymn is the praise of God in song.[35]

25 *Proportionale Musices*, I, ii.
26 Ibid., Prologue.
27 Ibid., I, iii.
28 Ibid.
29 Ibid., III, vi.
30 Ibid., I, vi.
31 Parrish, *Dictionary of Musical Terms*, 13.
32 Ibid., 13.
33 Ibid., 13
34 Ibid.
35 Ibid., 37.

On Consonance and Dissonance

The careful attention Tinctoris gives to consonant and dissonant intervals is limited to his principal interest in Church music and his conclusions unfortunately do not reflect the broader world of secular music being performed all around him.[36] Nevertheless, one definition of consonance which he offers, in his *Dictionary*, would have been acceptable to all musicians, for he defines it as 'a blending of different pitches, which strikes pleasantly on the ear.'[37] In another treatise, he constantly prefers the simple definition, 'sweet,' but adds an important new insight. Here he clearly associates both consonance and dissonance with *feeling*, and not mathematical ratios. It is a truth almost completely forgotten in today's music theory classroom.

> A concord is the mixture of two pitches, sounding sweetly to our ears by its natural virtue; I think that the word, 'concord,' is derived metaphorically from 'con' and 'cor,' for just as a sweet friendship is brought about from the coming together of two hearts that are in mutual agreement, so is a smooth concord made from a mixture of two pitches that are mutually agreeable.[38]

With regard to the discussion by Tinctoris of the various intervals, we again focus only on those comments which carry aesthetic clues. Among the intervals which he considers, in general, 'concords,' he begins with the unison.

> The unison, because of its temperate sweetness is most carefully to be avoided, except when a composition is begun with it, or, for the sake of its charm.[39]

The fifteenth (two octaves apart) and twenty-second (three octaves), he finds 'most sonorous, sweet and perfect.'[40]

Both the third and the seventeenth (two octaves and a third) 'has the highest sweetness,' whereas the octave and a third he merely calls 'suave.'[41]

Regarding the fourth, Tinctoris admits this was favored 'by our ancestors,' but for his generation he says it produces 'an intolerable discord.' Here, also, he quotes Cicero as saying that 'learned ears cannot put up with a discordant harmony.'[42] The interval of the eleventh (octave and a fourth), he finds 'intolerably harsh to learned

---

36 Reese, *Music in the Renaissance*, 145.

37 Parrish, *Dictionary of Musical Terms*, 15. In the Brussels manuscript of this book, an additional definition is found: 'Symphony is the same as consonance.' [Ibid., 77]

38 *The Art of Counterpoint*, 17.

39 Ibid., 22.

40 Ibid., 60, 80.

41 Ibid., 25, 43, 65.

42 Ibid., 29.

ears.'⁴³ The eighteenth (two octaves and a fourth) he finds somewhat more interesting, for it 'offends learned ears in a wonderful way. Hence in counterpoint it is not allowed.' On the other hand, he notes that it is permissible 'if either a third or a fifth [above the highest note], by which it is made sweeter, will be placed beneath it.'⁴⁴

Interestingly enough, Tinctoris was not quite comfortable in calling the sixth a consonance. His reason, once again, was that, rather than 'sweetness,' for his ears it produced rather 'asperity.'⁴⁵ Similarly, the thirteenth (octave and a sixth), he states 'brings to the senses more asperity than suavity,' and in another place he calls it 'harsh,'⁴⁶ and the interval of the twentieth (two octaves and a sixth) he calls 'more of a discord than a concord.'⁴⁷

In his *Dictionary*, Tinctoris defines dissonance as 'a combination of different sounds which by nature is displeasing to the ears.'⁴⁸ In another place, using his same analogy above, in which this term is a metaphor for feeling, Tinctoris calls a dissonance that which is,

> a mixture of two pitches naturally offending the ears. And it is called discord metaphorically from 'dis' and 'corde,' for, just as the bitterness of enmity arises from the separation of two hearts from a mutual uniformity of sentiment, so the harshness of a discord is produced from two pitches not agreeing with each other.⁴⁹

One should never, he cautions, think of a dissonance as simply a bad consonance. He reserves his most aesthetically descriptive language for the tritone, which he declares 'is so unfriendly to nature that it not only offends the ears, but also, indeed, is impossible.'⁵⁰

The psychological states of tension and release familiar to the use of dissonance and its resolution in music of the period of functional harmony, and later, was an aesthetic concept not permissible for Tinctoris.

> There are some who approve the introduction of an integral discord for the reason that an immediately following concord would appear more suave, since it has been alleged that one quality placed beside its antithesis gleams forth more brightly. O most valid reasoning! Never ought any vice be committed by a man of commendable virtue so that his virtue may shine more clearly; never ought any inept ideas be inserted into a distinguished oration so that the other parts may seem more elegant. And which one of our learned painters striving to delight the sight, I ask, has considered introducing some kind of

43 Ibid., 48.

44 Ibid., 70.

45 Ibid., 34.

46 Ibid., 55ff.
47 Ibid., 76.

48 Parrish, *Dictionary of Musical Terms*, 25.

49 *The Art of Counterpoint*, 85.

50 Ibid., 88.

deformity into any lovely form so that the other members may appear more beautiful?[51]

51 Ibid.,127.

He quotes Cicero as pointing out that the trained listener hears even the most minute discrepancies in intonation in lyres or flutes, hence such an intentional discord would have the result,

> that the soul of the erudite listener falls into grief, contrary to the intention of music, which Aristotle claims to contain a natural delight within itself.[52]

52 Ibid.

Interestingly enough, he then seems to permit 'small discords,' presumably if they are what we call today passing tones. The most important principle, for Tinctoris, seems to be that the dissonance is not heard at the beginning of a principal tone. This corresponds with modern research which has demonstrated that it is the attack, and not the tone itself, which often influences listeners to decide if a given tone quality is good or bad.

> Nevertheless, small discords … are at times allowed to be used by musicians, just as reasonable figures [of speech] by grammarians, for the sake of ornament and necessity. For a song is ornamented when an ascent or descent is made from one concord to another by compatible means and by syncopations which cannot occasionally be made without discords. These particular small discords, therefore, do not represent themselves so vehemently to the hearing, since they are placed above the last parts of notes, as if they were used above the first [parts of notes]. Musical sounds, to be sure, are made from a violent motion; hence, if violent motion is their nature, so it is abated near the end. The consequence is that the second parts of notes are not of as violent [not as loud] a sound as the first.[53]

53 Ibid.,127ff.

On Performance Practice

Contrary to the view which has captured many university music professors in the United States during the past decades, Tinctoris correctly and categorically states: Music is Performance!

> Music is that skill consisting of performance in singing and playing, and it is threefold, namely harmonic [voice], organal [instruments], and rhythmical.[54]

54 Parrish, *Dictionary of Musical Terms*, 43.

As a Church official by training, music performance to Tinctoris meant first and foremost singing. Among the definitions in his *Dictionary* regarding singing, the following are the most interesting from an aesthetic point of view.

A *jubilus* is a melody delivered with a certain high exuberance.[55]

......

Pronunciation is the elegant delivery of the voice.[56]

......

There is also another semitone which is called the chromatic [*Cromaticum*]. It is used when, in singing, some note is raised for the purpose of a beautiful delivery.[57]

In general, Tinctoris says a good singer must have '*ars, mensura, modus, pronunciatio, et vox bona.*'[58]

Among Tinctoris's various discussions of Church singing, no doubt the most surprising topic for the modern reader is his rather frequent reference to improvisation [*super librum*]. But this is not only representative of the most ancient performance of music, but, as Reese observes 'the prominent role it played in the musical life of the time [of Tinctoris].'[59] In one of his more explicit references to this, Tinctoris suggests the improvisation was primarily done against the tenor and suggest some pre-agreement among the singers has a more profitable result.

> But, with two or three, four or many, harmonizing *super librum*, one is not subject to the other, for, indeed, it suffices that each of them make consonances with the tenor with those thing that pertain to the law and arrangement of concords. I do not, however, think it disgraceful, but rather most laudable, if, agreeing among themselves on a similarity of assumption and arrangement of concords, they sing prudently, or thus they make of their harmonizing a fuller and more suave [effect].[60]

Later in this same treatise, Tinctoris seems to suggest *variety in performance* as a primary virtue of improvisation.

> Variety must be most accurately sought for in all counterpoint, for, as Horace says in his *Poetics*: 'One who sings to the kithara is laughed at if he always wanders over the same string.' Wherefore, according to the opinion of Cicero, as a variety in the art of speaking most delights

---

55 Ibid., 37.

56 Ibid., 49.

57 Ibid., 57.

58 Quoted in Reese, *Music in the Renaissance*, 147.

59 Ibid.,143. Reese also suggests that much of the idioms of later style were first worked out in improvisation.

60 *The Art of Counterpoint*, 105.

the hearer, so also in music a diversity of harmonies vehemently provokes the souls of listeners into delight; hence Aristotle, in his *Ethics*, does not hesitate to state that variety is a most pleasant thing and human nature in need of it.

Also, any composer or improviser of the greatest genius may achieve this diversity if he either composes or improvises now by one quantity, then by another, now by one perfection, then by another, now by one proportion, then by another, now by one conjunction, then by another, now with syncopations, then without syncopations, now with *fugae*, then without *fugae*, now with pauses, now without pauses, now diminished, now as written. Nevertheless, the highest reason must be adhered to in all these, although I have kept silent about improvisation [*super librum*], which can be diversified by the will of those improvising; nor do so many and such varieties enter into one chanson as so many and such in a motet, nor so many and such in one motet as so many and such in one mass.[61]

61 Ibid., 139.

In his treatise, *De Inventione et Usu Musicae*, Tinctoris actually points to a tradition, called *cantus regalis*, in which some improvisation was done to plain chant.[62]

62 Reese, *Music in the Renaissance*, 147.

Finally, he suggests that the most successful musician is the one who 'composes with constant effort or sings *super librum*.' He concludes this discussion with the interesting observation that he has never known one successful composer or improviser who began his practice after the age of twenty.[63]

63 *The Art of Counterpoint*, 140ff.

On Instrumental Music

In his treatise, *De Inventione et Usu Musicae*, Tinctoris writes at length of the principal instruments, as well as the best performers known to him.

In book three he discusses the history of the early shawm, known first as *tibiae*, and in his time as *celimela*. Interestingly enough he mentions the continued existence of the double shawm [*duplici tibia*], which is surely the ancient aulos, but he calls this instrument the least perfect. The shawm he gives in three sizes, soprano, tenor [*bombarda*] and contratenor, the latter of which might be substituted by the trombone.[64] Together the ensemble is called *alta* [wind band]. The best player of the shawm he knew was Godefridus, a musician of Frederick III.[65]

64 Anthony Baines, 'Fifteenth-century Instruments in Tinctoris's De Inventine et Usu Musicae,' in *The Galpin Society Journal* 3 (March 1950): 20ff.

65 Reese, *Music in the Renaissance*, 147ff.

Books four and five Tinctoris devotes to a very detailed discussion of the wide variety of string instruments familiar to the Renaissance. The only string instrument he finds disagreeable is the Turkish *tambura*, which he calls a 'miserable and puny instrument which the Turks with their even more miserable and puny ingenuity, have evolved from the lyra.'[66] He later mentions that he heard this instrument in Naples played by Turks in captivity, to console themselves. To the ears of Tinctoris,

> The extravagance and rusticity of these pieces were such as only to emphasize the barbarity of those who played them.[67]

All of the strings he points out can play music in four parts and the lute, in particular, is used at feasts, dances and public and private entertainments. Among the most gifted players of the lute he points to Pietro Bono of Ferrara and Heinrich, a German in the service of Charles the Bold. The Germans, in particular, Tinctoris says 'improvise marvellously upon a treble part with such taste that the performance cannot be rivalled.'[68]

He speaks of the *viola* [viol] as being used in Spain and Italy to accompany the recitation of epic poetry and mentions the musicianship of two Flemish brothers, Charles and Jean Orbus.

> At Bruges, I heard Charles take the treble and Jean the tenor in many songs, playing this kind of viola so expertly and with such charm that the viola has never pleased me so well.[69]

The viol and rebec were clearly the favorite instruments of Tinctoris.

> I am similarly pleased by the rebec, my predilection for which I will not conceal, provided that it is played by a skillful artist, since its strains are very much like those of the viola. Accordingly, the viola and the rebec are my two instruments; I repeat, my chosen instruments, those that induce piety and stir my heart most ardently to the contemplation of heavenly joys. For these reasons I would rather reserve them solely for sacred music and the secret consolations of the soul, than have them sometimes used for profane occasions and public festivities.[70]

66 Baines, 'Fifteenth-century Instruments in Tinctoris's De Inventine et Usu Musicae,' IV, 23.

67 Ibid., IV, 25.

68 Ibid., 24.

69 Ibid.

70 Ibid., 24ff.

Gustave Reese emphasizes the importance of this reference by Tinctoris to the use of these instruments in sacred music as valuable 'supplementary evidence that instruments were used' in the performance of Church music.[71]

Finally, Tinctoris mentions the new guitar of Spain and found it played primarily by women to accompany love songs.

71 Reese, *Music in the Renaissance*, 148.

12 THE GERMAN-SPEAKING COUNTRIES IN THE FOURTEENTH AND FIFTEENTH CENTURIES

IN THE GERMAN-SPEAKING LANDS, during the fourteenth and fifteenth centuries one can see a rapidly accelerating force of intellectual ideas, but they are centered in a contest between Church and State. Several German towns were in open revolt against the Catholic Church during the fifteenth century, among them Madeburg, Passau and Erfurt. The Hussite revolt in Bohemia was having repercussions in Germany.

Germany had its humanists as well, including Jakob Wimpheling, Conradus Celtes, Johann Müller and Johannes Trithemius. The latter, the abbot of Sponheim, wrote in 1496, 'The days of building monasteries are past; the days of their destructon are coming.'[1] These men helped construct the explosive which Luther would ignite. It was not an environment likely to produce much philosophic contemplation on the arts.

But this is not to suggest an absence of actual musical activity, indeed as Polk's remarkable study of German civic music of the Renaissance[2] demonstrates, Germany was a leader in the field of instrumental music, both in instrument manufacture[3] and in quality of performance. The high pay[4] of these particular German musicians, and their status and influence in other countries, in Italy[5] and Spain in particular, are a testimonial to the quality of their music. Thus, nothing could be more misleading than Gustave Reese's statement that Germany was on the 'peripheral in relation to the main stream of musical developments.'[6] Of course, what Reese really meant was that Germany was on the peripheral of *polyphonic sacred music*. But the real question is, should we call this music the 'main stream of musical development?' We have the unsettling feeling that no one alive in the fifteenth century would have regarded Church music as the 'main stream of musical development.'

[1] James Thompson, *Economic and Social History of Europe in the Later Middle Ages* (New York: Century, 1931), 604.

[2] Keith Polk, 'Instrumental music in the Urban Centres of Renaissance Germany,' in *Early Music History*, VII, 159–186.

[3] As is evident already in the fourteenth-century poetry of Folgore da San Gimignano, quoted in ibid., 169.

[4] Polk's research is particularly startling on this subject. In the 1440s he found Augsburg civic musicians to be in the top 15% of the wealth of the city. Ibid., 179.

[5] A civic statute of 1445 in Florence said future civic hires *must* be German. Ibid., 176.

[6] Reese, *Music in the Renaissance*, 632.

ON THE PHYSIOLOGY OF AESTHETICS

There was one formidable intellectual in fifteenth-century Germany, Nicholas of Cusa (1401–1464), a man in equal parts mathematician and philosopher. Largely on the basis of Nicholas's familiarity with ancient Greek philosophy, Will Durant calls him a humanist, adding 'Had there been more such Nicholases there might have been no Luther.'[7] Durant must have been thinking of someone else, for whatever Nicholas was, he was certainly not a humanist. A cardinal in the Catholic Church, the writings of Nicholas are in fact completely in the spirit of the late medieval Scholastic philosophers. His goal, like theirs, was to find accommodation between modern intellectual ideas and God.

Because he had no knowledge of, nor did he deduce, the existence of the right hemisphere of the brain, it was necessary for him to attempt to explain everything in rational arguments, resulting in some conclusions which are simply wrong. For example, in discussing the circle, which can be defined precisely in rational terms, he was aware that one also has a separate awareness of a circle, arrived at through the senses. Nicholas is forced to recognize the spatial sensation, but simply write it off as being 'something other' from rationality.

> It is therefore not possible, that a circle outside of rationality is as it is in rationality. Therefore, a sensible circle participates in the unity of the rational circle in *otherness*.[8]

Today we would simply say that the right hemisphere understands the circle as a spatial object and the left hemisphere in terms of mathematical description.

Nevertheless, he wrote extensively on the nature of Reason, the intellect and the senses and therefore we shall attempt to summarize his views as they pertain to the subject areas we have been following in these books.

For Nicholas, knowing involved a distinct hierarchy of processes, beginning with God, the 'absolute, superdivine infinity.' Below this is man's intelligence and below that is Reason. The senses are the lowest, but through the senses one can climb to Reason, then to the intellect, then to God.[9] In another place he quotes St. Jerome as making the distinction that animals perceive by the senses, while man is 'endowed with logic, for logic is the power of reasoning.'

7 Will Durant, *The Reformation* (New York: Simon and Schuster, 1957), 257.

8 Nicholas of Cusa, 'On Conjectures,' XIII, trans. William Wertz, Jr., in *Toward a New Council of Florence* (Washington, D.C.: Schiller Institute, 1993), 81.

9 Ibid., 108.

Therefore, adds Nicholas, logic and philosophical investigation have nothing to do with the senses.¹⁰

Given this total reliance on the rational left brain, it is no surprise to find Nicholas observing,

> No one can ignore that the truth is attained in mathematics more certainly than in all other liberal arts.¹¹

He also quotes Boethius as saying that 'anyone who altogether lacked skill in mathematics could not attain a knowledge of divine matters.'¹² In another place he makes a revealing comment that one of his critics would have understood him, had he not been carried away by emotion.¹³

Regarding the nature of knowledge, Nicholas takes a statement attributed to Socrates, that he seemed to know nothing except that he did not know, and then coins his most famous phrase, 'learned ignorance.'

> If we can fully attain unto this [knowledge of our ignorance], we will attain unto learned ignorance. For a man—even one very well versed in learning—will attain unto nothing more perfect than to be found to be most learned in the ignorance which is distinctively his. The more he knows that he is unknowing, the more learned he will be.¹⁴

After another scholar, John Wenck, criticized this treatise as nonsense, Nicholas followed it with another, 'A Defense of Learned Ignorance,' in which he first dismisses his critic by contending that the famous ancient philosophers 'took great precautions that mystical teachings not come into the hands of the unlearned,' adding that this was the true meaning of the passage in the Bible about not 'casting a pearl before a swine.'¹⁵

This intellectual arrogance appears to be a hallmark of Nicholas. In this same treatise he mentions that the books of Meister Eckhart should be removed from public places, as only intelligent men can find them useful.¹⁶ And in yet another treatise he writes that 'the secrets of wisdom are not to be opened to everyone indiscriminately.'¹⁷

---

10 Nicholas of Cusa, 'A defense of Learned Ignorance,' trans. Jasper Hopkins in *Nicholas of Cusa's Debate with John Wenck* (Minneapolis: Banning Press, 1981), 52.

11 Nicholas of Cusa, 'Theological Complement,' II, trans. William Wertz, Jr., in *Toward a New Council of Florence* (Washington, D.C.: Schiller Institute, 1993), 274. He returns to the subject of the importance of mathematics in mind function in his treatise, 'On Actualized-possibility,' 43.

12 Nicholas of Cusa, 'On Learned Ignorance,' trans. Jasper Hopkins (Minneapolis: Banning Press, 1981), I, xi, 31.

13 Cusa, 'A defense of Learned Ignorance,' 52ff.

14 Cusa, 'On Learned Ignorance,' I, i, 4.

15 Cusa, 'A defense of Learned Ignorance,' 46.

16 Ibid., 59.

17 Nicholas of Cusa, 'De Sapientia,' trans. John Dolan, in *Unity and Reform* (Chicago: The University of Notre Dame Press, 1962), 105.

On Wisdom

In contrast with his complex explanations of Reason and intelligence, Nicholas seems to have regarded Wisdom as what we might call common sense today, something which might be found in the common man in the street. Here we find him, personified as a citizen, in a debate with an orator.

> ORATOR. If the food of wisdom is not to be found in the books of wise men, then where is it to be found?
> CITIZEN. I do not say that it is not found there but rather that one does not find in books the natural food of wisdom. Those who first endeavored to write of wisdom did not apply themselves to nonexisting books but rather by natural nourishment were brought to a state of perfection, and it is quite evident that they have surpassed all those who believe they have profited from books.
> ORATOR. Although it is perhaps possible that some things may be known without the study of letters, nevertheless, difficult and important matters cannot possibly be known since learning is increased by additions.
> CITIZEN. I have already pointed out that you are led by authority and in this way you are deceived. Someone writes something and you believe him. I wish to say that wisdom cries out in the very streets and her cry is how she dwells in the highest.[18]

Another fifteenth-century German writer, Sebastian Brant, seemed to agree that wisdom should be attainable by all men. Those who fail in this common sense are to be found in the most widely read book of the fifteenth century, after the Bible, his *The Ship of Fools* (1494), where he gives his purpose as the instruction and pursuit of wisdom, reason and good manners.[19] In his allegorical ship he places one hundred and ten examples of 'fools' to illustrate the fate of those who fail to follow wisdom. He is quick to point out, however, that his boat is too small.

> One vessel would be far too small
> To carry all the fools I know.[20]

Their fate, in Brant's traditional Catholic view, would find its full measure in the next life. Thus, it is his duty to speak the truth.

18 Ibid., 102.

19 Sebastian Brant, *The Ship of Fools*, trans. Edwin Zeydel (New York: Columbia University Press, 1944), Prologue.

20 Ibid.

> Naught else but truth the fool must hear,
> Although it pleases not his ear.²¹

21 Ibid.

Wisdom is Brant's principal theme, and he first defines it as follows, in his tale, 'of Bad Manners.'

> Real wisdom starts with modesty,
> It's decorous, acts peaceably,
> It is a friend of goodness too,
> Which brings God's blessing unto you.²²

22 Ibid., 9.

In another story he gives as an important virtue of wisdom,

> For wisdom glorifies the race,
> Enriches men in every place.²³

23 Ibid., 42.

In what is an apparent reference to humanism, Brant, in his 'Of Reward for Wisdom,' includes among those who fail to understand true wisdom both the scholars of his day and the Greek philosophers.

> Some fools seek knowledge high and higher,
> To M.A., Ph.D. aspire,
> Though people deem them very bright,
> These fools can't understand aright
> How they'd attain that knowledge rare
> Wherewith to heaven they may fare.
> And that all wisdom 'neath the sun
> To God is folly men should shun.
>   ......
>
> The Lord has given us the light
> Of wisdom, making all things bright.
> To darkness wisdom puts an end
> If but to wisdom we attend.
> It shows us too the difference
> 'Twixt folly's course and prudent sense.
> Such precious wisdom these did prize:
> Pythagoras, Plato the wise,
> And Socrates, who through their creed
> Won lasting fame and honor's meed
> Yet could not picture bright and clear
> The real wisdom dwelling here,
> Wherefore of them the Lord did say:
> 'Their knowledge, skill I'll toss away

> And wisdom too, who here are wise,
> Let children have it—this their prize.'
> To children only wisdom's taught,
> Which they from heavenly regions brought.[24]

The highest praise Brant reserves for those who naturally carry the wisdom of common sense, in contrast to those who must be taught.

> The best is he who'll always know
> What he should do and what forego,
> Whom no one needs to drill and teach,
> Since wisdom he himself does preach.[25]

On The Senses

Lacking any understanding of the separate, but equal, natures of the right hemisphere of the brain, as we said, Nicholas's writings are filled with prejudice toward the senses in general, as were the works of nearly all medieval Church fathers. In one place, he even suggests that the really intelligent person does not need the senses at all!

> The wealthy and more noble intelligent beings do not require the senses, since they are indeed as burning, inconsumable, and ever growing fires, which to burn do not require a wind, which stimulates them from the outside through a sensible blast into flaring up. For [in intelligent beings] they exist in actuality, although in a different manner. However, since our intellectual portion is, as it were, the spark … it requires this. And do not believe that we men, who are vigorous in the senses, attain [anything from them] which is hidden from intelligent beings.[26]

He follows this with an absurd argument for the superiority of the intellect over the senses by observing that in hearing a speaker the senses hear only the sound of the voice, while the intellect understands the meaning of what is heard.

Nicholas is completely in error regarding how the senses actually work. He says, for example, that it is the nose which has the sense of smell.[27] We know from modern clinical research that all feeling and sensation is actually perceived in the mind, as is vividly proved in the examples of 'phantom limb,' where a patient feels pain and

---

24 Ibid., 107.

25 Ibid., 108.

26 Cusa, 'On Conjectures,' XVI, 135.

27 Ibid., 126. Unlike the senses, which have a precise location, Nicholas can find no location for intelligence—like God, it is everywhere. [Ibid., 123.]

other sensations in a limb that no longer exists. Hence the following is simply incorrect:

> The points you have made will not seem surprising to anyone who experiences for himself how heat-in-the-domain-of-sensible-things is devoid of heat in the domain of the more abstract cognitive powers. In the senses, where heat is sensed, heat-which-is-not-devoid-of-heat is present; but in the imagination or in the intellect heat-without-heat is touched upon. A similar point must be made about all things with which the senses make contact. For example, [in the intellect there is contact with] a fragrance without fragrance, a sweet without sweetness, a sound without sound, and likewise for each distinct thing.[28]

He perhaps sensed that the problem was more complicated, for he proposes that intelligence then gives meaning to this sensation, however, since the intellect perceives intellectually, it does not 'intuit the entire sensible world in a sensible mode, but rather in an intellectual mode.'[29] For this reason, he adds, the cognition which is generated through vision is much superior to that generated by hearing.

Nicholas makes another attempt to define the relationship of the intellect and the senses in a work called 'On Not-Other.' (The premise of this 'negative theology' is introduced in the question, 'What is the sky?,' and the answer, 'Not other than the sky.')

> For although intelligible things are not perceptible things, nevertheless they are not other than perceptible things. For example, coldness is not other than cold; for when coldness is removed, there will neither be, nor be understood to be, cold. This is the way in which the intellect is related to the sense.[30]

Then Nicholas carries this idea into the realm of Scholastic double-talk.

> Whatever the mind sees, it does not see without Not-other. For example, it would not see other if Not-other were not the Other of other.
> ……
> Not-other shines forth more clearly in the intellect than in the senses; for the intellect is not other than what is understood—even as knowledge is not other than what is known. For [compared with the intellect] seeing is not as clearly not-other-than-what-is-seen; nor hearing, not-other-than-what-is-heard.[31]

28 Nicholas of Cusa, 'On Actualized-possibility,' trans. Jasper Hopkins in *A Concise Introduction to the Pyhilosophy of Nicholas of Cusa* (Minneapolis: Banning Press, 1978), 71.

29 Nicholas of Cusa, 'The Filation of God,' V, trans. William Wertz, Jr., in *Toward a New Council of Florence* (Washington, D.C.: Schiller Institute, 1993), 189.

30 Nicholas of Cusa, *Nicholas of Cusa on God as Not-Other*, trans. Jasper Hopkins (Minneapolis: University of Minnesota Press, 1979), XIV, 53.

31 Ibid., Proposition 9 and 19.

On Education

Brant argues that in Germany one now finds good universities and there is no longer justification for traveling to other countries for education.

> No need to foreign schools to turn.
> Who'd study here in native land
> Will now find many books at hand,
> You can't excuse yourself, you see,
> Without misleading shamefully.
> Once men thought learning could but ay
> Be sought at Athens far away,
> And then in Italy 'twas found,
> But now here too on German ground.
> Our only failing's love for wine,
> To it we Germans do incline,
> And good hard work is rarely done.[32]

32 Brant, *Ship of Fools*, 92.

At the same time, Brant observes that education and scholars are not honored at this time. Curiously, one reason he seems to suggest is that education has become too common and perhaps too easily attainable.

> The books are published ton on ton,
> Because there's too much printing being done.
> In our times all those books come forth
> Which long ago our parents wrought.
> So numerous are they here and there,
> They count for nothing anywhere
> And no one pays to them much heed,
> So 'tis with science, so with creed.
> In number schools were ne'er so great,
> As now are found in every state,
> And scarce a city now is known,
> That calls no higher school its own.
> There many scholars now are trained
> Who nowadays are quite disdained,
> And knowledge gets a scornful glance,
> Most men do look at it askance.
> The scholars needs must feel a shame
> For studies, gown, their very name.
> The peasants now attain the fore,

> And scholars hide behind the door.
> Men say: 'These lazy apes, these beasts,
> The devil's cursing us with priests!'
> That's ample evidence that science
> Lacks honor, love and breeds defiance.
> 'Tis thus that studies will be wrecked,
> For knowledge prospers through respect,
> And when no honor's paid to science
> Most men will view it with defiance.[33]

Another poem suggests that this disrespect may have followed the quality of teaching.

> And for his son Achilles hired,
> And Philip scoured Greece till he'd won
> The ablest teacher for his son;
> The greatest king that ever reigned,
> By Aristotle was he trained,
> And he did sit at Plato's knees,
> While Plato learned from Socrates.
> But fathers, oh, of nowaday,
> When greed and stringiness hold sway,
> Engage such teachers for a son
> Who'd made a fool of anyone
> And send him home again (for shame!)
> More foolish now than when he came.[34]

In spite of these problems in the universities, Brant was concerned for those who waste or do not take advantage of their opportunities for education. He begins with himself, as being among those 'fools' who own many books, but never read them.

> In dunce's dance I take the lead,
> Books useless, numerous my creed,
> Which I can't understand or read.
>   ……
> Of splendid books I own no end,
> But few that I can comprehend …
>   ……
> I, too, have many books indeed
> But don't peruse them very much;
> Why should I plague myself with such?[35]

[33] Ibid., 103.

[34] Ibid., 6.

[35] Ibid., 1.

Brant returns to a similar theme in his poem, 'Predestination of God.'

> Some fools display a wealth of wit
> Who hide behind the books and Writ,
> They think they're striped and famous sages
> When they have thumbed a volume's pages.
> They eat the Psalter, 'twould appear,
> As far e'en as *Beatus vir*,
> They think if God has blessed them all
> That then from grace they'll never fall.[36]

In his tale, 'Of Useless Studying,' Brant includes in his *Ship of Fools* the German student who fails to take advantage of the opportunity of education and thus ends up in a servile trade such as waiting on tables.

> Students should likewise not be skipped,
> With fool's caps they are well equipped,
> When these are pulled about the ear
> The tassel flaps and laps the rear,
> For when of books they should be thinking
> They go carousing, roistering, drinking.
> A youth puts learning on the shelf,
> He'd rather study for himself
> What's useless, vain—an empty bubble;
> And teachers too endure this trouble,
> Sensible learning they'll not heed,
> Their talk is empty, vain indeed.
> Could this be night or is it day?
> ......
>
> In Leipzig students act this way,
> In Erfurt, Mainz, Vienna, ay,
> Heidelberg, Basel, any place,
> Returning home in sheer disgrace.
> The money's spent in idleness,
> They're glad to tend a printing press
> And, learning how to handle wine,
> They're lowly waiters many a time.
> Thus money spent to train and school
> Has often gone to rear a fool.[37]

36 Ibid., 57.

37 Ibid., 27.

Finally, Brant's work contains much in the way of practical advice for his readers, as perhaps two examples will demonstrate. First, on the importance of advance planning, one can learn a lot from women, who do this all the time.

> But those who plan the while they act
> Must have experience in fact,
> Or must have watched the other sex,
> Who're very shrewd in these respects.[38]

38 Ibid., 12.

And, courts make decisions, but they do not necessarily find truth.

> Let judgment be a lesser care,
> For it alone does not make right,
> One must be searching, must be quite
> Inquisitive of evidence,
> Else right is wrong and bare of sense.[39]

39 Ibid. 2.

ON THE PSYCHOLOGY OF AESTHETICS

There is very little discussion in this literature of emotions as a part of the human mind and neither is there poetry praising Love. However we find a nice observation on the effects of Love in Brant.

> For lovers act like children too.
> They seldom speak a serious word,
> Their speech like children's is absurd
> ......
> Deprived are they of sense and wit,
> They dance about like fools insane.
> ......
> Who sees too much of woman's charms
> His morals and his conscience harms;
> He cannot worship God aright
> Who finds in women great delight.[40]

40 Ibid., 13.

Brant does address Pleasure and Pain more specifically. He finds life on earth as being mostly pain and in this passage he also appears to include a reference to the humanists, who were no longer as concerned with the next life.

> O fool, no pleasure here on earth
> Can evermore give joy and mirth,
> They're harsh and bitter through and through …
> A fool that person is from birth
> Who'd live long years upon this earth:
> Its nothing but a vale of tears,
> In joys brief, long in grief and fears …
> Has ever greater fool been born
> Than who'd stay here and heaven scorn?
> In God the Lord you'll not believe
> And from eternal life take leave,
> A drop of honey here, that's all
> You'd have and there a sea of gall,
> On earth a moment's jubilation,
> There endless joy, perhaps damnation.[41]

[41] Ibid., 43.

He gives similar warning against the influence of the humanists in his tale, 'Of Sensual Pleasure.'

> Like heathen king Sardanapalus,
> Who thought that men should live on earth
> In lust and joy and sensuous mirth,
> Because they're over when one dies.
> Such nonsense silly fools advise,
> To trust in pleasures ever fleeing.[42]

[42] Ibid., 50.

ON THE PHILOSOPHY OF AESTHETICS

Nicholas joins many earlier philosophers in defining the art existing in the artist's mind as being greater than that found in the art object. For Church philosophers, such as himself, the rationale behind this was the idea that since God created the artist, his accomplishment must be greater than that of the artist.

> Imagine a man who has mastery over mechanical art: He has the figures of this art in greater truth in his mental concept than they are figurable externally; just as a house, which arises through art, has a truer figure in the mind than in the wood. The form, which is made in the wood, is indeed a mental figure, an idea or exemplar. And thus it is with all such.[43]

[43] Nicholas of Cusa, 'On Beryllus,' XIV, trans. William Wertz, Jr., in *Toward a New Council of Florence* (Washington, D.C.: Schiller Institute, 1993), XXXII.

In his treatise, *On Not-Other*, Nicholas makes a surprising statement, in view of the Church inspired view that the importance of Art is in the mind of God. Here, he seems to be unaware of the goal, familiar to the observer today, of looking *through* the art object to see the more beautiful idea in the mind of the artist.

> We must not be surprised that God the Creator is invisible. Indeed, although in municipal buildings, in ships, artifacts, books, paintings, and countless other things we see the marvelous works of the intellect, nevertheless we do not make contact with the intellect by means of the sense of sight.[44]

[44] Cusa, *God as Not-Other*, XXIII, 104.

In another treatise, Nicholas speaks of Art as being in the soul, rather than the mind, and of being something which is learned. From this internal Art, he suggests, springs technique.

> In this world we see that some things are made by means of a human art and by the agency of those who have in their soul the art they have learned. Thus, the art is received in them and remains; and it is a word which teaches and governs those things which belong to the art.[45]

[45] Cusa, 'On Actualized-possibility,' 34.

Brant agrees that Art is created in the mind of the artist, in the form of noble ideas. Thus, he contends, Art tends to be produced by poor artists, because such persons are less concerned with greed.

> All arts by poverty were founded,
> Of evil poverty is bare,
> All honor takes its rise from there.[46]

[46] Brant, *Ship of Fools*, 83.

On the subject of Beauty, Nicholas takes the familiar phrase, 'Beauty is in the eye of the beholder' quite literally. He maintains that Beauty is a judgment of the eyes themselves, with 'the rational world [of] the intelligence' providing only 'vigor to the cognition of the true.'[47]

[47] Cusa, 'On Conjectures,' 124.

Brant only mentions Beauty with respect to humans, emphasizing that this beauty does not last.

> But beauty too's a great delight,
> Enduring scarcely over night …[48]

[48] Brant, *Ship of Fools*, 6.

The only significant discussion regarding the purpose of Art we find in Nicholas. This passage, in addition, is the only one we find in his writings which could be said to reflect humanism, for he contends that the purpose of Art is humanity itself. Behind this statement is his constant theme of the unity of everything in the universe.

> Therefore, there is no other end of the creative activity of humanity than humanity. When it creates, it does not go outside of itself, but rather when it unfolds its power, it comes to itself. Nor does it effect something new, but rather all that it creates through unfolding, it experiences to have existed in itself. Indeed, as the power of humanity is able to advance to everything in a human manner, so can the universe enter into it. That this wonderful power traverses and proceeds to everything, is not other than that it enfolds the universe in it in a human way.[49]

Brant mentions only functional Art, to which he attaches one of his basic themes, that one cannot successfully appear to be more than one is.

> A potter fashions out of earth
> A pot, to some of little worth,
> A jar, a jug of any style
> For any liquid good or vile.
> No pot will say to the potter's face:
> 'I should have been a lordly vase!'[50]

One of the fundamental points for discussion in all early philosophy dealing with aesthetics in Art was whether Art should imitate Nature. In a chapter entitled 'On Nature and Art,' Nicholas takes the position that this is not a valid question, for Nature and Art are one and the same.

> Since precision is unattainable, we are admonished to believe that there can be nothing which is only nature or art: Indeed, everything participates in both in its manner. One easily conceives that the intelligence, insofar as it emanates from divine rationality, participates in art. However, insofar as it exerts art from itself, we see it as nature. Indeed, art is, as it were, the imitation of nature. That some things are indeed natural sensible things, others [artistic] things, is obvious. But it is not possible that the natural sensible things are destitute of art, and likewise the [artistic] sensible things cannot be without nature.[51]

49 Cusa, 'On Conjectures,' XIV, 128.

50 Brant, *Ship of Fools*, 57.

51 Cusa, 'On Conjectures,' XIV, 121ff.

Next, in his attempt to explain further the relationship of Art and Nature, Nicholas reflects the anti-feminist views which had been so strongly expressed in the medieval (and present) Church.

> If you want to investigate the differences of nature and art and the connection of both, then return to the frequently revealed guidance of the figure. Nature indeed consists of masculine unity and feminine otherness. In intellectual masculinity femininity is absorbed. It is therefore fertilized unitively in itself. In vegetative femininity otherness determines the masculine nature in itself; hence it fructifies unfoldedly. The nature of animals distinguishes the sexes, the man generates in the woman, the woman gives birth externally. In intelligent beings nature engenders intellectual fruit, in animals animal fruit, in vegetation vegetative fruit. The sensible nature obeys the rational, the rational the intellectual, and the intellectual the divine. The sensibly formable thing obeys the rational art, the rational the intellectual, the intellectual the divine.

Nicholas concludes this discussion by returning to one of his fundamental themes: Reason is the unifying factor behind all things.

> Rationality is the unity of nature and of sensible art. Through the unity of rationality the sensible multitude of individuals is specified; just as also through the unity of rationality, which exists, for example, in the one art of shoemaking, innumerable shoes are produced. The unity of rationality therefore enfolds in itself the multitude of all natural and [artistic] sensible things. Therefore, it exerts from itself the rationality of natural and [artistic] things. The rationality of [artistic] things, however, is ordered to the end of the natural things. For the beginning and end of [artistic] things is nature.

In another treatise, Nicholas gives as the purpose for Art imitating Nature the fact that the observer finds joy in his unconscious perception of Art following the natural laws of Nature. Here Nicholas uses the example of music, referring to the often quoted, but completely impossible, story of the discovery of the overtone series by Pythagoras upon his overhearing the sounds made by a blacksmith.

> The considerations which calm wise men have found in connection with nature, they have sought to bring forth into general art by means of the equality of the rational ground; just as when, based on habit, they have experienced that the harmonies of certain notes

correspond to sounds, which blacksmiths produce as soon as they strike the anvil with the hammer. As a result they found the same proportionally in organs and chords, in great and small, and deduced the harmonies and disharmonies of nature in art. And this art, because it clearly imitates nature, is more pleasing. It incites the impulse of nature and helps in the vital motion, which is the motion of agreement and comfort, which is called joy. All art is therefore founded in the conclusions which the wise man has found in connection to nature, which he presupposes, since he does not know the cause, for whose sake it is. To that discovered he adds art, in that he extends it through the species of similitude, which is the rational ground of art, which imitates nature.[52]

ON THE AESTHETICS OF MUSIC

In the writings of the fifteenth-century Scholastic philosopher, Nicholas of Cusa, we find some strange notions about the origin of music. The medieval philosophers had kept education alive during the Dark Ages by endorsing the Liberal Arts as useful for helping the Christian understand the Scriptures. Now, Nicholas tells us, God used the Liberal Arts to create the world!

> In creating the world, God used arithmetic, geometry, music, and likewise astronomy. (We ourselves also use these arts when we investigate the comparative relationships of objects, of elements, and of motions.) For through arithmetic God united things. Through geometry He shaped them, in order that they would thereby attain firmness, stability, and mobility in accordance with their conditions. Through music He proportioned things in such a way that there is not more earth in earth than water in water, air in air, and fire in fire, so that no one element is altogether reducible to another. As a result, it happens that the world-machine cannot perish …
>
> And so, God, who created all things in number, weight, and measure, arranged the elements in an admirable order. (Number pertains to arithmetic, weight to music, measure to geometry.)[53]

In another place, Nicholas comes very close to the true essence of music, as the means by which we communicate feelings, as well as its being origin of speech, as all philologists today agree. Nicholas makes two important and accurate observations, that language

---

52 Nicholas of Cusa, 'Compendium,' XIV, trans. William Wertz, Jr., in *Toward a New Council of Florence* (Washington, D.C.: Schiller Institute, 1993), IX.

53 Cusa, 'On Learned Ignorance,' II, xiii, 175. Nicholas does not explain the reference of weight to music.

came first from sound and that animals, at least, communicate emotions by sound. But he failed to see the connection and makes the preposterous contention that Adam was created not only with a complete language, but that that language is the root of all modern languages—hence Adam would understand any language he heard today.[54]

From this unfortunate belief, Nicholas makes the conclusion that it is language, and not music, which expresses the senses, and from this the birth of Art follows.

> Therefore, as the first knowledge is designating things with names, which the ear perceives, so the second knowledge is in the visible symbol of names, which confront the eyes. This knowledge is by nature remote; children learn it more slowly and also only when the intellect begins to become vigorous in them. Hence it takes a greater part in the intellect than the first. Therefore, between nature and the intellect, which is the creator of art, these two arts fall, of which the one stands nearer to nature, the other to the intellect.
>
> However, the intellect forms in man this first art [language] in a sensuously audible symbol, i.e., in sound, because the animal endeavors by nature to make known its affections in this symbol. Hence, art articulates the formless symbol and modifies it in order to communicate better the various desires.[55]

Now he makes the fatal error of modern music education and many music theorists, who fail to find important meaning in the natural feeling content of music and turn instead to making it something it is not: conceptual data. Nicholas says, basically, you cannot know except by rational concepts.

> However, in all perfect animals one attains to those imaginative symbols which are the symbols of the symbols of the senses, so that the knowledge suitable to them is not lacking. Indeed, only man seeks a symbol which is free of all material connection and entirely formal and which represents the simple form of the thing. Which gives being to it. And although this symbol is very remote in respect to the sensible thing, it is nevertheless very near in respect to the intelligible …
>
> Therefore, since everything which is attained by the senses or the imagination is not known except in the symbols …[56]

54 Cusa, 'Compendium,' 539ff.

55 Ibid.

56 Ibid.

This representation of the senses by symbols, Nicholas concludes, distinguishes man from beast. We note here also that he thinks of 'art' as merely a 'craft.'

> Of all this and much more the brute animal is ignorant. Man is as man to animal as a learned man is to an unlearned one. A learned man and unlearned man see the letters of the alphabet. But the learned man assembles syllables from their various combinations, words from the syllables and sentences from the words, while the uneducated man is not able to do that, because he lacks the art, which, acquired through the exercise of his intellect, is in the learned man.[57]

Just as he saw God creating the world out of the Liberal Arts, Nicholas sought explanations which would reveal a unity of Reason behind all things. We see this clearly in the second part of the following passage. The first part reveals that he is still thinking of music from the medieval view of mathematics and had no better answer for the measuring of the half-step within the octave.

> All harmony therefore rests in these numbers 1, 2, 3, 4 and their combinations. The cause of every harmony arises therefore from the necessity of this rational progression. However, the fact that the precision of [the] semi-tone remains hidden to rationality, is because one cannot attain it without the coincidence of the even and the odd. You see that sensible combinations are unfoldings so to speak of rational unity, whence the harmonic rational unity; when it is closely contracted in the combination of sensible things, rationality takes delight in it just as though in its own work or in its close similitude.
>
> ......
>
> If you wish to assemble a more detailed treatment by means of these aforementioned principles of conjecture, then refer back to the figure of the universe, and take the maximum circle as rationality, and elicit from it the most lucid, more brilliant and more abstract rational art; the lowest more adumbral; and the median rational arts. If you inquire into mathematics, do the same, so that you constitute one as it were intellectual, another as it were sensible, and a median as it were rational; likewise with music. If you wish to know more about music itself, then take the circle of the universe as the rational nature of music; and you will intuit a music as it were more intellectually abstract, another as it were sensible, and a third as it were rational. You can effect the miraculous in all these things, if you devote yourself to them with diligent meditation.[58]

57 Ibid.

58 Cusa, 'On Conjectures,' XIV, 96ff.

In contrast to this rationally-based explanation for understanding music, in another treatise Nicholas seems to concede that the enjoyment in music lies in the domain of the senses.

> Consider also, how we have greater joy in a certain color; it is likewise with voice or song and the remaining sensory feelings. That is so because sensing is the life of the sensitive soul, which does not consist in sensing this or that, but rather in being in every sensible thing simultaneously. Therefore, it is more in that sensible thing, in which it apprehends more of the object in which therefore the sensible is in a certain harmonious union, just as if one color contains in itself many colors harmoniously or an harmonious song many different voices. It is likewise with the other senses.[59]

59 Cusa, 'On Beryllus,' XXXV.

The most frequently cited purpose for music in all ancient and early literature is its capacity to offer solace. The sole instance we find in this literature is a passing remark by Brant,

> The poor sing through the woods with cheer …[60]

60 Brant, *Ship of Fools*, 83.

Brant also offers an insight into the aesthetic perception of the instruments themselves. The bagpipe had been an aristocratic favorite during the Middle Ages, because of its ability to play a non-stop dance melody—the nobles fearing getting out of step if even a single beat were missing! In *The Ship of Fools* of the fifteenth century we now find the bagpipe ridiculed in several places as the despised instrument of the lowest classes. As part of the title of his tale, 'Of Impatience of Punishment,' Brant warns,

> If bagpipes you enjoy and prize
> And harps and lutes you would despise,
> You ride a fool's sled, are unwise.[61]

61 Ibid., 54. Bagpipes are again associated with fools in Tales Nr. 67 and 89.

In the main body of the story, he continues,

> A wise man lists to wise men's lore,
> Enriching thus his wisdom's store,
> Bagpipes are dunces' instrument,
> For harps they have no natural bent,
> And naught gives fools a greater joy
> Than wand and pipe, their favorite toy.

On Church Music

We have an important view of the aesthetics of Church music in the treatise, '*De modo bene cantandi*' (1474) by Conrad von Zabern, who was associated with Heidelberg University. His first observations have to do primarily with the more technical aspects of appropriate Church singing, including the maintenance of perfect ensemble in unison singing, consistent tempi from each side of the choir and using the middle register of the voice, rather than the high register.[62] He equates tempi with the nature of the service, recommending the use of slower tempi for more solemn feast days. He expects strict observance of the appropriate modes and allows no improvisation.

The most important discussion, in terms of aesthetics, is found in Conrad's sixth major topic, 'Singing with Proper Refinement,' which he says he finds many clerics to have overlooked, to the extent of becoming 'a vicious habit.' He begins this discussion with a general definition of proper refinement.

> Singing with proper refinement means avoiding all that reprehensible coarseness (of which we will speak below) which is commonly and frequently practiced in singing even by those with a certain reputation and by those who observe the five marks of good singing discussed previously. This fact we cannot pass over in silence. First of all, let us explain what we mean in this context by 'proper refinement.' *Urbs* is the word for city, and in the cities men are generally more discriminating than they are in the country or in villages, thus in this instance 'refined' means 'discriminating' or 'skillful.' Hence the adverb *urbaniter*. Singing with proper refinement is thus singing with discrimination and without coarseness … There are so many of these crudities that I despair of enumerating all of them. Still I would like to enumerate and explain in sufficient detail the most important, obvious and frequently committed ones, so that if they become better known they can in the future be more easily avoided. An evil unrecognized is avoided only with difficulty.

He begins with basic vocal production such as singing through the nose and adding an 'h' before vowel sounds. The latter he says reminds him of the sounds butchers make in driving sheep to pasture.

---

[62] This discussion is based on Joseph Dyer, trans., 'Singing with Proper Refinement,' *Early Music* 6, no. 2 (April, 1978): 207ff.

> This is not elegant singing, and we can say without fear of contradiction that it is very coarse.

In this regard he stresses the importance of correct Latin, in the syllables and vowels. Some clerics, he has observed, sound as if they had food in their mouths.

> Indeed, from Frankfurt to Koblenz and as far as Trier I have noticed this very often, especially in students. They all distort the chant, inclined as they are to pronounce the vowels *e* and *i* poorly and without sufficient differentiation—a situation which has not infrequently caused me much displeasure. Their masters ought to restrain them from this error forthwith, lest they perpetuate it into old age.

He criticizes inaccurate intonation, especially in ascending and descending pitches. This may have been caused in part by his next objection, forcing the voice.

> Truly I know people better instructed than others in chant who nevertheless render all their singing unworthy of praise by this very defect. Though it appears to them that they are singing well, this is just because no one has suggested to them how offensive this fault really is, and how much to be avoided.

We find his next topic the most interesting of all. Modern clinical research has proven that the brain automatically increases the perception of high tones, beginning at the third space C of the treble clef. The most evident cause of this, now genetic, brain function is undoubtedly due to the need for the species to discern speech clearly, beginning with animal speech (the tiger outside the cave). While most modern choral and ensemble conductors are unfamiliar with the physical reasons many have learned from experience that a more beautiful sound is achieved by creating more volume in the lower pitches, and less in the upper, to accommodate for this automatic brain function. This knowledge of this practical adjustment is not new. It is discussed, for example, by Praetorius in volume three of his *Syntagma Musicum* of 1619. The following discussion by Conrad, on the subject of singing too loud in the upper register, is the earliest we know to offer the correct accommodation for this problem.

> Another fault which is more obvious than the others is singing high notes with an unstintingly full and powerful voice. This is even more careless than what we have cited above, as will soon become evident. When this shouting is done by individuals with resonant and trumpet-like voices it disturbs and confuses the singing of the entire choir, just as if the voices of cattle were heard among the singers. In a certain eminent collegiate establishment I once heard singers with these trumpet-like voices singing with all their strength in the highest register as if they wished to break the windows of the choir, or at least to shake them. As I marveled not a little at their coarseness, I was moved to make up this rhyme:
>
>> In choir you bellow
>> Like cows in the meadow!
>
> I use this jingle in an informal fashion in my efforts and teaching regarding the art of good singing in order to ridicule all those presuming to sing loudly in the high register, to the end that they might recognize their careless crudeness and, after recognizing, zealously desist from it.
>
> In order to recognize this error completely it must be realized that whoever wishes to sing well and clearly must employ his voice in three ways: resonantly and trumpet-like for low notes, moderately in the middle range and more delicately for the high notes—the more so the higher the chant ascends …
>
> Therefore, let him who wishes to sing flawlessly never again presume to sing with a full and strong voice in the upper register, for this disfigures the chant, pointlessly weighs down and fatigues the singer, makes him hoarse and consequently useless for singing. The human throat is delicate and easily injured when it is abused, as it is by loud singing in the upper register. The harm having been done, hoarseness soon ensues. Everyone has experienced this personally.

Conrad carefully explains that connected portions of chant must correspond in their tonal relationships. He has been so disturbed by this as to think, or even say: 'What clods these monks are!'

His next objection is purely aesthetic in nature. He demands enthusiastic singing from the heart.

> Another error is singing sleepily and lifelessly and without affection, like a poor old woman on the brink of the grave. This deprives the chant of the joy appropriate to it, and as it is less well heard it seems to be more of a moan than a chant … Behold how animatedly, affectively and with what great joy singing should be done, lest we fall into

yet another extreme: some shouting loudly, while others can scarcely be heard. The old proverb rings true: 'Either too little or too much runs the game.' Happy those who hew to the golden mean!

If his concern above was that the singer inspire, his final concern is that he not detract.

The last error to be mentioned at this time is singing with inappropriate deportment: not standing straight but moving back and forth, holding the head up too high or noticeably to one side, resting the head on the hand and either distorting the mouth or opening it too widely. It would be tedious to enumerate all the other kinds of inappropriate behavior which are to be avoided for the simple reason that they provoke laughter in the beholder, who ought rather to be moved to devotion by the chant.

Brant, in his tale, 'Noise in Church,' presents a more humorous view of Church music. He portrays an atmosphere during the Church service which makes one wonder how effective the music could have been in such an environment.

> One must not ask who they may be
> Whose dogs in church bark furiously
> While people pray at mass or sing,
> Who bring a hawk that flaps its wing
> And rings its bell with tinkling gay,
> That one can neither sing nor pray.
> The hood is lowered o'er the hawk,
> There's pattering and many a squawk,
> Affairs are aired and tongues are loose,
> There's clattering with wooden shoes,
> That brings disturbance, great ado;
> He peers to Lady Kriemhild's pew
> To mark if she will turn and gape
> And make the cuckoo-bird an ape.
> If men would leave their dogs at home
> To watch for thieves that prowl and roam,
> While men would worship there in church,
> If birds were left upon the perch,
> And wooden shoes were worn for street
> To pick up dirt or mud or peat,
> And other people's ears be spared—
> But when have fools for others cared?[63]

63 Brant, *Ship of Fools*, 44.

In his tale, 'Of Prattling in Church' Brant makes reference to a curious figure attached to the organ pipes of the Strassburg Cathedral, which expanded and contracted its features and raised its arms comically while the organ was being played.

> Of those men hardly dare I speak
> Who into church do merely peek,
> They scarcely show themselves before
> They've made their exit through the door.
> What good and reverential prayers
> Are prayed by men of such affairs!
> They're paid rich prebends while they gape
> Upon the bearded organ ape.[64]

64 Ibid., 91.

ART MUSIC

As with other countries, there is much growth in the German civic band movement during the Renaissance. Keith Polk, in his wonderful study of German civic music of this period,[65] dates the period of growth from about 1350. He points out that improvement in the manufacture of the shawm at about this time may have been influential, thus a comment in the *Limburger Chronik* of 1360,

65 Keith Polk, 'Instrumental Music in the Urban Centers of Renaissance Germany,' 159–186.

> The manner of shawm playing, which was previously not so good, has been changed and improved. Thus, one who was considered a good player in this area just five or six years ago doesn't amount to a hill of beans now.[66]

66 Quoted in ibid., 164.
… der endauc itzunt net eine flige.

With many towns averaging four players by the end of the fourteenth century, during the fifteenth century we begin to find larger civic ensembles, as seven to ten players in Bremen, six players in Halle in 1482 and nine in Lübeck in 1454.[67] By the fifteenth century, string players and string ensembles appear in civic records, although they appear somewhat earlier in court records.[68]

67 Walter Salmen, *Der Fahrende Musiker im Europäischen Mittelalter* (Kassel: Hinnenthal, 1960), 89, and Edmund Bowles, *Musikleben im 15. Jahrhundert* (Leipzig: Deutscher Verlag für Musik, 1977), 13.

68 Polk, 'Instrumental Music in the Urban Centers of Renaissance Germany,' 180.

While most accounts of the activity of these civic bands are concerned with functional and entertainment duties, there are some clues to performances to which people listened to as art music. Principally, the tradition of playing spiritual music from towers, called *Abblasen*, begins during this century. For example, a civic statute for Weissenfels in 1483 mentions the tower performances of what is purely surrogate clock signals, but then mentions separately *Abblasen*, which were performed in the morning, at noon and once in the evening.[69]

But there is also some evidence of the typical Sunday concerts found in other countries at this time. One statue from Basel requires the civic band not only to play for the banquets given in the city hall, but also every Sunday after the sermon and in the evening on the Rheinbrücke bridge.[70] We should also mention, in this regard, that the manuscript known as the 'Lochamer Liederbuch,' of ca. 1490, is evidently repertoire of the Nürnberg civic band and much of this music seems to us to be non-functional in character.

Beginning with Frederick III (reigning 1440–1493) and his son, Maximilian I, we have the first period in which the practice of court music can be documented in pictures. The *Weisskunig*, a book containing two hundred and fifty-one woodcuts, of which more than one hundred are by Hans Burgkmair, is a biography of Frederick III. A number of these woodcuts picture his musicians, although entirely in functional duties, such as playing for jousts and with the military.

Much better known is the extraordinarily beautiful one hundred and thirty-seven woodcuts, by the foremost artists of the fifteenth century, known as *The Triumph of Maximilian I*. This is a book of pictures, in which all members of Maximilian's court, and more, are pictured in a vast parade. Each woodcut includes a fancy blank scroll intended to include text to accompany the picture in question. While these were left incomplete, the text, which was written by Maximilian himself, survives separately and the two together give us a vivid picture of his personal musical establishment. These are especially valuable for us today, for not only was Maximilian an unusually cultured man, having been reared in the court of Philip the Good, but because it was Maximilian who began the long musical history of Vienna.

In plates 19 and 20 we see Maximilian's basic indoor wind band of two shawms, two crumhorns and the trombonist Neyschl, who was the leader of this ensemble. The instructions and information associated with these plates[71] tell us their purpose was to perform for the joy of the emperor, that they performed frequently and includes an aesthetic assessment of their instrumentation.

[69] Arno Werner, *Vier Jahrhunderte im Dienste der Kirchenmusik* (Leipzig: Mersseburger, 1933), 275.

[70] K. Nef, 'Die Stadtpfeiferei und die Instrumentalmusiker in Basel,' in *Sammelbande der Internationalen Musikgesellschaft* (1908), 396.

[71] The quoted texts are those which Maximilian dictated to his secretary, Treitzsaurwein. Following, in parentheses, are additional materials which were found after his death. See Stanley Appelbaum, *The Triumph of Maximilian I* (New York: Dover, 1964).

And Neyschl shall direct them, and his verse, borne by a boy, shall read: How to the Emperor's joy and by his command he combined such diverse instruments in the merriest way.

> (The trombone and the shawm adorn
> The joyous sound of curving horn,
> Each to the others well adjusted.
> Since musical command to me
> I have performed quite frequently.)

Plates 25 and 26 show Maximilian's church musicians, seven adult singers and six boys, together with a trombonist and a cornettist. The text material for these plates again suggest that this ensemble was listened to with care by Maximilian.

Stewdl shall be leader of the trombonists, Augustin of the cornet players, and their verse, borne by a boy on the car, shall read thus: How by the Emperor's instructions they attuned the trombones and cornets in most joyous manner.

> (The cornets and trombones we placed
> So that the choral song they graced,
> For His Imperial Majesty
> Has often in such harmony
> Taken great pleasure, and rightly so,
> As we have had good cause to know.)

The great tradition of aristocratic love songs, which flourished from the twelfth to fourteenth centuries, are no longer described in this literature. We do see this tradition, now at the peasant level, in Brant's, *The Ship of Fools*. He includes a poem called, 'Of Serenading at Night,' which is very critical of the tradition of singing evening serenades to one's lover, primarily, it appears, because the singer usually had a wife at home.

> The dance of fools would now be o'er,
> Though there'd be something still in store,
> For we've not mentioned those gallants
> Who walk the streets and would entrance
> The girls, to whom they're very sweet,
> And wend their way from street to street,
> While playing lutes for all to hear
> At doors from which a girl may peer,
> And do not from the street go dashing

Until a night-pot's dregs come splashing,
Or till a rock has struck their pate.
The pleasure's never very great,
Since wintry blasts may nip his nose
Who late at night a-courting goes
With lute, song, piping, boisterous thumping,
In lumber yards o'er timber jumping,
Priests, students, laity hell-bent,
They hum a fool's accompaniment.
One screams, shouts, bleats with might and main
As though he feared he's being slain,
One fool will tell the motley crew
Where they've arranged their rendezvous,
And there the music is begun.
'In secrecy' the thing is done,
So everyone may well agree,
E'en fishers noise it publicly.
One leaves his wife alone in bed
Who'd rather play with him instead,
If he goes duncing none the less
And all ends well, I miss my guess.[72]

[72] Brant, *Ship of Fools*, 62.

EDUCATIONAL MUSIC

Nan Cooke Carpenter finds the study of music in the German universities during the fourteenth century firmly in the hands of the Scholastics, with music still being associated with mathematics.[73] The books and content seem clearly tied to Paris.

The students, however, were equally interested in performance, for various edicts warn them about wandering about at night playing instruments and singing.[74]

During the fifteenth century university statutes in Vienna and Heidelberg clearly specify the study of music as part of the lectures of the arts faculty.[75] In addition, the University of Vienna began to present plays with musical chorus and solos, written by humanists such as Celtes and Wimpheling.

[73] Carpenter, *Music in the Medieval and Renaissance Universities*, 100ff. A music school in Köln was one of the institutions from which the university itself was formed.

[74] Ibid., 103.

[75] Ibid., 224, 230.

FUNCTIONAL MUSIC

Much of the information in the civic statutes of fifteenth-century Germany deals with the usual requirements for functional music, especially the ancient watch duties and welcoming ceremonies for visiting nobles. With respect to this last duty, Marix, in her chronicle of Philip the Good's journey through Germany, Switzerland and Austria in 1454, documents such performances by civic wind bands in dozens of towns of all sizes.[76]

It is evident from the many statutes of German towns regulating the performance of their civic musicians in private weddings that this was a primary source of extra income for the civic musicians. There seems to have been a desire for lots of music, for as early as 1303 a statute of Bremen limits the number of players to eight and a regulation in Munich of 1322 permits eight for wealthy citizens, four for the less affluent and only two for poor townsfolk.[77]

A civic statute of Köln for 1439 limits private weddings to four civic musicians, establishes their pay and also warns the musicians not to accept more than one wedding per day.[78] The punishment for civic musicians who broke such regulations may have been rather severe. In the torture tower [*Folter-tor*] in Rothenburg-on-the-Tauber, one can see today a special torture device for musicians. It has a heavy iron collar which was fixed to the poor wretch's neck and to this collar was attached an iron imitation of a musical instrument, with a mouthpiece which fits just under the chin. The guilty musician's fingers were held down over six finger holes by means of a metal bar and he and his instrument were no doubt chained to a post in the public square.

In the *Triumph of Maximilian I*, mentioned above, we have an unusually detailed picture of fifteenth-century military music under the emperor. The initial plates of this collection picture four fife players and five drummers on horseback, in identical uniforms and wearing swords. Three fife players appear to be playing two-part music, while the third holds the blank sign intended to have included the following information. Most interesting here, is the aesthetic description of military music, 'gay and stern.'

> I, Anthony of Dornstätt, have played my fife
> For Maximilian, great in strife,
> In many lands on countless journeys,
> In battles fierce and knightly tourneys,

---

76 Marix, *Histoire de la Musique*, 66–73.

77 *The New Grove Dictionary* (1980), VII, 204ff.

78 Hans Moser, 'Zur Mittelalterlichen Musikgeschichte der Stadt Köln,' in *Archiv für Musikwissenschaft* (Hildesheim, 1964), 156.

At grave times or in holiday,
And so in this Triumph with honor I play.
(Gladly and oft my fife I blew
In proper style, with honor true,
Serving the Imperial arms
In knightly joust and war's alarms.
Always prepared, the fifer blows
Tunes gay and stern, as this Triumph shows.)

A similar picture of the young Maximilian at war is found in the *Weisskunig*, the pictorial biography of his father. Here we read of the style of the music and its aesthetic purpose.

> The young *Weisskunig* [Maximilian] brought the manly and cheerful fife and drum. When he went to battle, the fife and drum not only gladdened the hearts of men, but filled the air with the sound that proclaimed that the young king conquered many lands, and always defeated his enemies.[79]

One set of plates requested by Maximilian for his *Triumph* were never made. They were to have been entitled, 'The Emperor's Journey to His Burgundian Wedding,' and would have pictured fifteen trumpeters and three drummers in Austrian uniforms. We have something similar, in plates 115–117, the 'Imperial Trumpeters,' which show no fewer than twenty-five trumpet players and five timpani players (two timpani per player, also on horse).

A musically more interesting outdoor ensemble, seen in plates 77–79, is called the 'Burgundian Fifers.' All we know of this ensemble is what Maximilian wrote before the plate was completed:

> After them shall come on horseback Burgundian fifers in the Burgundian colors with bombardons, shawms and rauschpfeiffen. And they shall all be wearing laurel wreaths.

We have a final interesting view of the functional music surrounding Maximilian I in the reports of the 'journalists' who covered his Congress of Vienna in 1515. For the opening of this Congress he had prepared a fanfare by forty-five trumpets, forty-five trombones and six timpanists.[80] These writers were particularly interested in the military bands of the East, which were to their ears quite foreign. They describe the tones of the horns as 'unclean,' the crumhorns as 'torrid' and the shawms as 'coarse.' The Eastern trum-

79 Plate 33, in this book, with text quoted in Christine Mather, 'Maximilian I and his Instruments,' in *Early Music* 3, no. 1 (Jan. 1975): 44.

80 J. F. Huguenin, *Les chroniques de la ville de Metz* (Metz, 1838), 586.

pets they thought created a buzz, not unlike that of 'wasps and horseflies.'[81] In so far as the ensemble itself, it was described as 'in confusion,'[82] a frequently used adjective by Western listeners describing the music of the East.

There are also numerous accounts of large ensembles of wind instruments, mostly shawms and trumpets, attending the weddings and coronations of lesser nobles throughout the German-speaking lands. An interesting example is the wedding of Albrecht of Brandenburg (1440–1486) with Anna von Sachsen in 1472, for which five shawms and six trumpets participated.[83] The court records for this occasion says 'The musicians filled each day with their harmony.'[84]

The accounts of a royal Danish wedding in 1404 include an early reference to trombones playing with shawms.[85] We should also mention that the manuscript known as the 'Glogauer Liederbuch' (ca. 1477–1488), one of the earliest collections contained in partbooks, represents the repertoire of the ensemble belonging to the Duke of Glogau in Silesia.

Like their brothers the secular nobles, the Church bishops of fifteenth-century Germany also employed personal wind bands. These can be documented in numerous towns beginning about 1430.[86] When gathering for a church conference, these bishops brought their musicians with them. The most extensively documented such event in the fifteenth century was the great Council of Constance, 1414–1418. Here assembled no fewer than three popes (John XXIII of Rome, Gregory XII, the Avignon pretender, and Benedict XIII, who was a creation of Ludwig of Bavaria), five patriarchs, thirty-three cardinals, forty-seven archbishops, fifty-three hundred priests, three hundred noblemen and fifteen hundred knights in an attempt to deal with the problem of the three popes and also with the growing Hussite movement in Bohemia.

In all, during the course of the four years, some sixty-three thousand visitors came to this town of seven thousand! One report said that it was so crowded that five hundred accidental drownings occurred in the lake.[87] And apparently everyone brought his personal musicians, for one account speaks of three hundred and forty-six 'pfifer, prussuner und spillut,'[88] another four hundred and twenty-six minstrels, actors and wind players and still another five hundred winds and singers.[89] One official reported one thousand seven hundred musicians, which must have included the entire period of the Council.[90]

81 Salmen, *Der Fahrende Musiker*, 151.

82 Huguenin, *Les chroniques de la ville de Metz*, 586.

83 G. Schmidt, *Die Musik am Hofe des Markgrafen von Brandenburg-Ansbach vom ausgehenden Mittelalter bis 1806* (München, 1953), 4.

84 Quoted in Karl Heinrich Ritter von Lang, *Neuere Geschichte des Fürstentums Biruth* (Göttingen, 1798), I, 12.

Musikanten erfüllten solche Tage mit ihren harmonien.

85 'Chronicle of Rhthm. Majus,' in E. M. Fant, *Scriptores Rerum medii Aevi* (Upsala, 1818), I, ii, 61. Here the trombones are called 'bassooners,' a Danish corruption of the old German 'Pusuner,' or trombone.

86 Walter Salmen, *Der Fahrende Musiker*, 163, 176; H. Federhofer, 'Beitrage zur altern Musikgeschichte Karntens,' in *Carinthia* (1955), CXLV, 377; and J. H. Wylie, *History of England under Henry the Fourth* (London, 1884), IV, 236.

87 Ernest Henderson, *A Short History of Germany* (New York: Macmillan, 1916), I, 208.

88 M. Schuler, 'Die Musik in Konstanz während des Konzils 1414-1418,' in *Acta Musicologica* (1966), 163 and J. Riegel, *Die Teilnuhmerlisten Konstanzer Konzils* (Freiburg, 1916), 74ff.

89 R. Fester, 'Die Fortsetzung der Flores temporum von Reinbold Slecht,' in *Zeitschrift für die Geschichte des Oberrheins* (1894), 132; A. Henne, *Die Klingenberger Chronik* (Gotha, 1861), 193 and O. Nedden, *Quellen und Studien zur oberrheinischen Musikgeschichte im 15. und 16 Jahrhundert* (Kassel: Bärenreiter, 1931), 53.

90 M. R. Buck, ed., *Ulrichs von Richental Chronik des Constanzer Conzils* (Tüblingen, 1882), 215.

Among the individual ensembles mentioned was one with the pope from Rome, consisting of shawms and trombones, but they may have been hired for the occasion as one observer who heard them said they played in 'wild discord.'

> … prosuner und pfiffer, die ymer me dar prosonten und pfiffen zu wilderstrit.[91]

One who certainly had to hire temporary musicians for the occasion was the Emperor Sigismund, who was not well supported financially by the other German princes and constantly complained of needing money. A miniature published by one of the eyewitness to this gathering shows the ensemble of Sigismund, consisting for four trumpets and three shawms. As they appear not being in identical dress, it is assumed they were not permanent employees.[92]

Musically, the most interesting reference is to the arrival of the ensemble of the English prelates.

> The trombonists played together in three parts as one is otherwise accustomed to sing.[93]

ENTERTAINMENT MUSIC

For both wind and string musicians, playing entertainment music for banquets must have been a common experience. We have two rather unusual reports of this duty, the first relative to a trick planned by King Matthias Corvinus of Hungary. During his war with Poland, in 1473, he found himself and his troops trapped in the city of Wratislavia, surrounded by the Polish troops. Corvinus, to give the impression he had sufficient supplies for a long siege, set up tables on the wall, had his officers appear luxuriously dining to the music of his wind band joined by dancing girls. After a couple of days watching, while themselves subsisting on field rations, the Polish troops became disheartened and submitted favorable terms for a peace.[94]

The second unusual portrait we have of banquet music at this time is an eyewitness account by a visiting French journalist of Maximilian I dining alone in 1492!

---

91 Ulrichs von Richental, *Das Konzil zu Konstanz* (Konstanz: Starnberg Keller, 1964), 252.

92 Copies in Prag, Universitní knihova (Ms. XVI A 17, fol. 70) and the New York Public Library (Spencer Collection, Ms. 32, fol. 86).

93 Gerald Hayes, 'Musical Instruments,' in *New Oxford History of Music* (London, 1960), III, 425ff.

> Die pusauner pusaunoten über einnander mit dreyen stymmen, als man sunst gerwonlichen singet.

94 Kastner, *Manuel Général de Musique Militaire*, 103.

His Majesty sits in a hall covered with tapestry, without another person except his court [jongleurs]. At every meal, mid-day or evening, there were 10 trumpeters and 10 other kinds. There were two large timpani of fine copper covered with ass skins and standing in two baskets. In the middle sat a man with a thick stick which he let loose in beats on [the timpani] so that the tone was in unison with the other instruments, as is used in Hungary or Turkey, it was amazing and humorous to hear.[95]

[95] Quoted in Huguenin, *Les chroniques de la ville de Metz*, 586.

Aside from our curiosity about Maximilian's digestion, with ten trumpets playing in what must have been a relatively small hall, we should like to call the reader's attention to this early account of the traditional timpani role in the aristocratic trumpet ensemble. The timpani functioned not as a rhythmic instrument, but as the harmonic bass to the trumpets.

In Brant we get a glimpse of entertainment music among the lower classes. In his tale, 'Of Coarse Fools,' he complains that sense and prudence are both dead and grossness lives in every house. This leads him to the following characterization of peasant singing and general condemnation of lower entertainment.

> The sow the *matins* does recite,
> The donkey sings the *prime* all right,
> St. Ruffian sings the *tierce* with might,
> Hatmakers' boys recite the *sext*,
> Coarse felters do compose the text.
> Rude rabble doth recite the *none*,
> And gluttoners the words intone,
> The *vespers* from a sow's voice sing.
> And lastly the *compline* is done,
> When *all is full* at length is sung.
>
> ......
>
> The one who's quite the foulest swine
> Is given a brimming glass of wine.
> Applause is his with vim and zest,
> He's asked to tell another jest.
> They say: 'A great success you've scored!
> You keep us thus from being bored!'
> 'Be sociable, gay, debonair!
> [Eat, drink and be merry]
> Let's all be cheerful while we're here,
> Good fellow should rejoice, not pout,
> Let's laugh and sing, carouse and shout!'
>
> ......

> To have a good time's not a sin!
> The priests can say whate'er they may,
> Let them forbid this, that for aye!
> If this were sinful, as they claim,
> Then why, why do they do the same?[96]

96 Brant, *Ship of Fools*, 72.

The severely serious Brant sounds almost like a medieval Church father when he condemns the evils of dancing.

> I'd take all those for fools almost
> Who skill and joy in dancing boast,
> Cavorting, prancing as they must,
> With weary feet in dirt and dust,
> But later then I called to mind
> That dance and sin are one in kind,
> That very easily 'tis scented:
> The dance by Satan was invented
> When he devised the golden calf
> And taught some men at God to laugh,
> And Satan dancing still doth use
> To hatch out evil, to abuse.
> It stirs up pride, immodesty,
> And prompts men ever lewd to be.
> The pagan Venus gives her hand
> And purity is rudely banned.
> Could viciousness to joy give birth?
> There's naught more evil here on earth
> Than giddy dancing gayly done
> At kermess, first mass, where the fun
> Is shared by priests and laity,
> Where cowls can flap in zephyrs free.
> They swing their partners in the breeze
> Till girls' bare legs high up one sees,
> Their other sins I will not treat.
> They'd rather swing their girls than eat;
> When Jack and Maggy swirl and sway
> They never wait a single day,
> They strike a bargain willy nilly
> And trade a she-goat for a billy.
> If some class that as recreation
> I call it base abomination;
> some crave for dances many a tide
> Whom dances never satisfied.[97]

97 Ibid., 61.

13 FOURTEENTH- AND FIFTEENTH-CENTURY SPAIN

The Iberian peninsula, occupied by Rome from 206 BC and by Moslems after the eighth century AD, did not begin to become Spanish until the latter Middle Ages. The strong Church influence there resulted in little important literature until John I of Aragon asked troubadours from Toulouse to come to Barcelona and organize a school for their poetry in 1388. Influence from the humanist movement only arrived with Italians, such as Pietro d'Anghiera toward the end of the fifteenth century. Thus in this chapter we see Spanish literature in its first stage of development. We find, therefore, a certain tentative quality in the major fourteenth-century work, *The Book of True Love* (1330), where the author, Juan Ruiz, invites anyone who knows the art of poetry to change it or add to it as he sees fit.

> Whoever hears it, if he knows the art of poetry,
> May add more to it, change, improve it, if he wishes to.[1]

[1] Juan Ruiz, *The Book of True Love*, trans. Saralyn Daly (University Park: Pennsylvania State University Press, 1978), 1629.

ON THE PHYSIOLOGY OF AESTHETICS

The earliest philosophical view on the organization of the mind in this literature is found in this same book by Ruiz, of whom almost nothing certain is known, except that he was called the archpriest of Hita, a village north of Guadalajara. In this lengthy book of lyric poetry, Ruiz writes,

> [There are] three things which some schooled in philosophy say are intrinsic in the soul and particularly belong to it. They are: understanding, will, and memory. These, I say, if they are good, bring comfort to the soul and prolong the life of the body and bring to it honor and profit and good reputation. For through true understanding man understands the good and from this, knows the bad.[2]

[2] Ibid., 10ff.

He follows this by observing that the fear of God is both the beginning of all wisdom and 'true understanding.'

The soul, Ruiz says, stores 'true understanding and good will' in memory and compels the body to do good works by which man is saved. Poor memory, therefore, is partly responsible for sin and Ruiz adds that 'human nature is more ready for and inclined toward evil than good.' His most interesting observation here is that painting, writing and sculpture were invented for the purpose of keeping things in the memory.

We find in this literature as well a few observations on the nature of experience, as related to knowledge. Ruiz maintains that from long life itself comes knowledge and experience.[3] A similar thought occurs in the play *Celestina* (1496) by Fernando de Rojas:

> I may be young, but I've seen many things in my time; and seeing many things is what you call experience.[4]

Another character in this play, Celestina, also says 'experience only comes with age.'[5]

Finally, it is interesting that Ruiz makes a strong argument in favor of astrology, which he suggests provides truths which one can find neither in years of study nor in the Bible. Astrology, he says, cannot be called 'mere accident' and his argument for its validity follows the logic that since God made Nature 'and all happenings therein,' this must presumably include the movements of the stars and planets. He concludes, therefore, that 'believing the laws of nature shape our fates is not a sin.'[6] He also adds that men born under the sign of Venus are consumed with a desire for Love which they can never suppress.[7]

ON THE PSYCHOLOGY OF AESTHETICS

On the general subject of the emotions, we find a rather extraordinary insight by Ruiz on the universality of emotions.

> Examine, then, your inner self, inspect your feelings well,
> And by your heart you'll judge how others' passions surely go.[8]

Rojas refers to the capacity of the emotions to interfere with Reason (which arrives through the senses), when the character

---

3   Ibid., 886.

4   Fernando de Rojas, *La Celestina*, trans. J. M. Cohen (New York: New York University Press, 1966), act 1. Rojas was born in 1477, died in 1541, and was apparently an attorney in Talavera.

5   Ibid.

6   Ruiz, *The Book of True Love*, 123.

7   Ibid., 152.

8   Ibid., 565.

Parmeno says 'don't let passion dull your ears, or hope of pleasure blind your eyes.'[9] Later in this play, Melibea makes a similar observation.

9   Rojas, *La Celestina*, act 1.

> For when the heart is heavy with grief, the ears are closed to counsel, and at such times good advice rather inflames than allays the passions.[10]

10 Ibid., act 20.

In Renaissance literature, the emotion most discussed by writers was Love. Ruiz begins his discussion with an almost Darwinian observation regarding Love and human nature.

> Wise Aristotle says, and what he says of course is true,
> That all men struggle most for two things: first, what he must do
> To feed himself and keep alive, and second, in this view,
> To have sex with a pleasing woman who is compliant, too.
>
> If I myself had said it, I'd be heaped with slurs and shame,
> But this philosopher said it, and I can't be held to blame.
> No need to have much doubt of what the wise man has proposed,
> His words are proven by our acts, no matter what we claim.[11]

11 Ruiz, *The Book of True Love*, 71ff.

Speaking in its favor, Ruiz finds that Love affects some important positive changes in the character of men.

> Love makes now subtly smooth the fellow who was rough and rude;
> It makes the gallant, mute before, soon murmur soft sweet words,
> It makes the coward fearless with a daring attitude;
> It makes the slothful idler brisk, alert and unsubdued.
>
> Young bachelors it keeps in vigor hard and masculine,
> It makes a graybeard shed his age much as a snake its skin;
> And him who's black as pitch it makes a fair and handsome man.
> Love can bestow high value on a man not worth a pin.[12]

12 Ibid., 156ff.

But then later, Ruiz dramatically changes course and attacks Love for the evil it causes.

> You're false, a cheat, a liar, who tricks mankind against his will.
> You can't save one lone person, although millions you can kill.
>
> With ruses, wiles and flattery, and subtle lies to boot,
> You poison people's tongues—you dip your darts in poison, too.
> Whoever serves you most, you wound, and hurt most when you shoot.

> You part sweetheart and swain, by anger that is born in you.
>
> You drive a lot of people mad with bad arts you know well,
> You take away their sleep, their appetite and wish to drink,
> Many you cause to dare so much with you, they're on the brink
> Of losing both their body and their soul, unless they think …
>
> You trap people, and from then on you give them no relief,
> You drag them day by day into a worried, troubled life.
> Him who had trusted you, you chain into your gang of grief,
> And make him slave through endless days for just a toy too brief.[13]

13 Ibid., 182ff.

Regarding the emotions, Rojas points out, as we have seen above, that the emotions can interfere with Reason. Later he adds the thought that unexpected Pleasure can do the same.

> Unexpected and sudden pleasures cause confusion, and great confusion prevents clear thinking.[14]

14 Rojas, *La Celestina*, act 5.

In this same play, the character Parmeno provides an observation frequently found in early literature, that Pleasure is always accompanied by Pain.

> Pleasure never comes in this life without worries to match. It's a saying I've often heard, and now I know from experience that it's true. Clear and cheerful sunshine is followed by dark clouds and rain, and pleasures give place to pain and death. Laughter and delight are succeeded by tears, wailing, and mortal grief, and ease and comfort by great sorrows and sadness.[15]

15 Ibid., act 8.

ON THE PHILOSOPHY OF AESTHETICS

Of the traditional subjects discussed by early writers concerned with aesthetics in general, the only one considered in the Spanish literature of this period is the traditional question of Art imitating Nature. A passage in Rojas suggests that in his fifteenth-century view Art was regarded as rather distantly related to its model in Nature. His servant having sung a song about Nero burning Rome, Calisto, an unhappy lover, is thinking of the fire within himself, when he says,

There's as much difference between the fire you sing of and the one that burns me as between appearance and reality, or a painting and a living thing.[16]

Later in his play, Calisto doubts that any painter 'could portray such features, such a model of all beauty' as he finds in his lady.[17]

On Poetry

Ruiz, in the introduction to his *The Book of True Love* says that 'words serve the intention and not intention the words,' and then gives indication of his thorough understanding of the rules of poetry.

> And I composed this book also to give people a lesson and example in counting verses and rhyming and composing poetry, for the songs and rhymes and lyrics and ballads and poems, which I have made here, are completely according to the rules this art requires.[18]

He explains that one purpose of his poetry and song is to give pleasure, for sorrow invites sin. It is also interesting that Ruiz mentions here aesthetic criteria pertaining to how the verse 'strikes the ear.'

> This is the saying of a sage, which Cato said again:
> A man, among the sufferings which on his heart are laid,
> Must mingle pleasures and enjoy glad words, not to be too staid,
> Because great sorrow always draws great sinning in its train.
>
> Since men at sober sense can't laugh or find in life much cheer,
> So I must try to introduce some jesting stories here:
> Each time you hear them, you need not consider seriously,
> Except about my style in verse and how it strikes your ear.[19]

The talented Juan del Encina wrote what we may believe is the earliest treatise on poetry in the Spanish language, *Arte de poesia castellana* (The Art of Castilian Poetry), for in the Preface he states that he knows of no previous such work, except for his teacher's Grammar of 1492.[20] In his introduction, Encina also points to the powers of poetry to move and mollify the heart or inflame courage, as was known by the ancients. He refers to the ancient Greek philosophers again in mentioning their belief that poetry should be an integral part of public life.[21]

16 Ibid., act 1.

17 Ibid., act 6.

18 Ruiz, *The Book of True Love*, 10ff.

19 Ibid., 44ff.

20 Henry Sullivan, *Juan del Encina* (Boston: Twayne, 1976), 107. His teacher was the Spanish humanist, Antonio de Nebrija.

21 The discussion on poetry is taken from ibid., 108ff.

For success, Encina says, the poet must have a natural wit, but without polishing his wit by the rules of the art he will remain as 'a fertile but untilled land.' He adds that this discipline, as is the case in oratory, is necessary not only to persuade but to *sooth the ear*.

In the third chapter of his treatise, Encina provides us with a valuable insight through his perspective regarding the distinction between a poet and a troubadour, a difference he finds as great as between a musician and a stone-cutter! The poet, says Encina, is the more knowledgeable, requiring an understanding of the proportion and metrical distinctions between strophes, stanzas, lines and syllables. The troubadour, or minstrel, is merely one who performs a preexistent work. His lack of appreciation of the troubadour is evident when he writes,

> Oh how many do we see in this Spain of ours who enjoy the reputation of troubadours and who care not whether they toss in a syllable or two too many or too few, nor bother whether the rhyme be perfect or imperfect!

As an example of his poetry, there is a poem both humorous and painful, '*Juan del enzina a una dama que le pidió una cartilla para aprender a leer*,'[22] written to his lady love.

> You ask me for a letter
> To teach you to read;
> Here it is so marvelously done
> I cannot believe it myself:
> Because I believe you must be jesting
> And it is right for me not to believe,
> Since there is nothing good in existence
> Which you do not already know.
> ......
> And if you will be pleased to look
> Upon these letters set down here,
> They will themselves convey to you
> Your gracefulness and my grieving:
> The letter A stands for my ardor
> The letter B for your beauty
> The letter C for cruelty
> And D stands for my dolor …

22 'Juan del Encina to a Lady who Begged of him a Letter to Teach her to Read,' quoted in ibid., 118.

Fourteenth- and Fifteenth-Century Spain

Encina's villancicos were intended to have musical accompaniment. One of these poems, 'Levanta, Pascual, levanta,' includes lines describing the music of a festive civic occasion.

> Soon, soon shall all be there
> Within the ramparts of the city
> With very great solemnity,
> With sweet songs and gracious air.[23]

On Drama

Encina is also considered the Father of Spanish drama, his works dating from about 1495. Many of these short plays are rural in character, inspired perhaps by the lyric poetry of the Greeks. In one of these, known as VIII, 'Egloga representada por las mesmas personas,' we find the city man dreaming of the peace of the country in a tribute to Nature worthy of Rousseau.

> And he that knows what 'tis to rest
> Amidst his flock the livelong night,
> Sure he can never find delight
> In courts, by courtly ways oppressed.
> O, what a pleasure 'tis to hear
> The cricket's cheerful, piercing cry!
> And who can tell the melody
> His pipe affords the shepherd's ear?[24]

Encina combines his abilities as a composer and playwright by including songs in his plays, often at the beginning or the end of the play. Many of these are songs requiring four singers, such as the song, 'Today let us feast and drink,' from the play known as *Eclogue VI*.[25] In his *Auto del Repelón*, which has only three characters, he hastily adds a character at the end in order to make possible such a four-voice composition.[26]

One of the followers of the example of Encina was Gil Vicente, who introduced choral songs in his plays.[27]

---

23 'Arise, Pascual, arise,' quoted in ibid., 123ff.

24 Quoted in ibid., 61ff.

25 Encina was also a gifted singer and was a member of the papal choir in Rome, where he journeyed in anger over his failure to achieve the post of choirmaster of the Salamanca Cathedral.

26 Reese, *Music in the Renaissance*, 583.

27 Ibid., 586.

ON THE AESTHETICS OF MUSIC

We might begin by mentioning Ruiz's recognition that music reflects the experience of life, which he expresses by quoting an old proverb, 'A bird will neither sing nor weep, if kept in isolation.'[28]

Regarding the purposes of music, Rojas in his *Celestina* gives a typical instance of the use of music to provide solace. Melibea, says,

> But I pray you, Father, have some stringed instrument brought to me so that I can wile away my grief by singing and playing. For though my sufferings torment me, sweet sounds and harmonies will much abate it.

Ruiz, however, suggests the solace brought by music is not permanent, in observing 'Although the jongleurs comfort, they don't heal our agonies.'[29] And similarly, when in the woes of Love, he mentions 'singing girls can't bring relief.'[30]

In another place, Ruiz offers delight as a primary purpose of music.

> That I, with little songs, may rhyme a book of poetry
> So that those who can hear can find delight and modest glee.[31]

Rojas in his play *Celestina* gives the same purpose. Melibea requests a song from Lucrecia and when it is finished she exclaims 'Oh how sweet it is to hear you! It makes me melt with delight.'[32] After a second song, another character, Calisto, cries 'the sweetness of your singing overwhelms me.'

Still another purpose of music which Ruiz offers, is to sing of joy.

> So I may in adoration
> All your joys in song portray.[33]

Finally, Ruiz offers a more practical purpose of music, which is to aid in courting the young lady.

> If you can play upon some instrument of music, do;
> If you have talent and are trained in singing sweetly, sing,
> But not too long or often—merely where it's proper to:
> Wherever she can listen, just put your skills on view.[34]

---

28 Ruiz, *The Book of True Love*, 111.

29 Ruiz, *The Book of True Love*, 649.
30 Ibid., 841.

31 Ibid., 12.

32 Rojas, *La Celestina*, act 19. Requesting another song, Melibea offers to improvise a vocal accompaniment.

33 Ruiz, *The Book of True Love*, 21.

34 Ibid., 515.

A final observation may have some relationship with performance practice. Ruiz offers some advice about tempi with regard to speaking, which might be taken as good advice for musical communication as well.

> No one can understand a man who speaks too fast, you know,
> And one who speaks too slow annoys whoever wants to hear.[35]

35 Ibid., 551.

ART MUSIC

Among the Aragon kings, the first to establish an important musical body within his court was Jaime II (1291–1327). Both he and Juan I (1350–1396) went to considerable effort to attract foreign artists to their courts and as early as 1391, Aragonese court musicians were traveling to Germany to buy instruments and recruit German musicians to take back.[36] Juan was also a composer.[37]

Alfonso V (1416–1458) had an ensemble of fifteen, including both strings and winds. In 1423, when visiting Paris, he heard a wind ensemble apparently belonging to Philip the Good and the latter made him a gift of the entire ensemble!

Fernando V (1474–1516) and Isabella (1474–1504), patrons of Columbus, maintained separate musical establishments, reflecting their Aragonese and Castilian backgrounds even though they successfully united these kingdoms. After the death of Isabella, in 1504, Ferdinand united the musical organizations. Although Reese mentions only the sacred music of Ferdinand and Isabella, which he maintains they 'particularly favored,'[38] the scope of their musical establishments suggest a much wider appreciation of music. Isabella employed a wind band (*Menestriles Altos*) together with some seventy singers,[39] strings and several organists. Indications are that Isabella was no indifferent listener to her musicians.

36 H. Anglès, 'Musikalische Beziehungen zwischen Deutschland und Spanien in der Zeit vom 5. bis 14. Jahrhunderts,' in *Archiv für Musikwissenschaft* (1959), XVI, 5.

37 Reese, *Music in the Renaissance*, 575.

38 Ibid., 578.

39 Sullivan, *Juan del Encina*, 129.

> If anyone of those who were saying or singing the psalms, or other things of the church, made any slip in diction or in the placing of a syllable, she heard and noted it, and afterwards—as teacher to pupil—she emended and corrected it for them.[40]

40 L. Marineus Siculus, *De las cosas memorables de España* (1539), 182v.

For her leisure, as well, Isabella enjoyed music, especially private 'concerts' while she and her ladies worked at needlepoint.[41] She gave

41 Sullivan, *Juan del Encina*, 129.

a high priority to the musical education of her children, influenced by a book *Vergel de Príncipes* by Ruy Sánchez de Arévalo, which argued for the ability of music to foster moral virtue, including the preparation for political leadership. One of her children, Juan, who died in 1497, was an active performer, as we see in an account by a contemporary, Gonzalo de Oviedo.

> My Lord prince Juan was naturally inclined to music and he understood it well, although his voice was not as good as he was persistent in singing; but it would pass with other voices. And for this purpose during siesta time, especially in summer, Juan de Anchieta, his chapel master, and four or five boys, chapel boys with fine voices, who went to the palace, and the prince sang with them for two hours, or however long he pleased to, and he took the tenor, and was very skilled in the art.[42]

This same source reveals that Juan owned a number of instruments, which he also played.

Fernando had six minstrels in 1491, eight in 1500 and in 1505 seven trumpets, four percussion and nine minstrels, one of whom is identified as a player of the trombone [*sacabuche*]. By 1511 he had an eleven-member wind band.[43] After his noon meal, his secretary reports, there was string music.

> This morning his highness attended Mass in the church, as usual, after eating there was vihuela music, after which he went to Vespers.[44]

The strong troubadour influence in Spain can be seen especially in its preference for love songs. Of the important composer, Juan del Encina, Reese writes, without further comment, that 'The majority of his compositions, however, are love songs.'[45] Thus, sharing the narrow interest in sacred music of his musicological colleagues, he is not troubled to simply omit the greater part of this eminent composers's repertoire.

The central character, a priest, in Ruiz's, *The Book of True Love*, speaks of writing numerous love songs[46] and it is interesting that he sends them to his lover by messenger, in the manner of the thirteenth-century troubadours.

> I sent this brief song to her, which I'll put in by and by,
> Through a go-between of mine whom I had trained as my ally.[47]

42 Gonzalo Fernández de Oviedo, *Libro de la cámara real del príncipe don Juan* (Madrid, 1870), 182ff.

43 H. Anglès, 'La música en la corte del rey Don Alfonso V de Aragon,' in *Gesammelte Aufsätze zur Kulturgeschichte Spaniens* (1940), 155.

44 Tess Knighton, 'The Spanish Court of Ferdinand and Isabella,' in *The Renaissance* (Englewood Cliffs: Prentice Hall, 1989), 343.

45 Reese, *Music in the Renaissance*, 583.

46 Ruiz, *The Book of True Love*, 170.

47 Ibid., 80.

In one place, however, the priest complains that instead of taking the song to the lady, the messenger went singing it loudly through the market![48]

In the course of his book, he provides us with an extensive catalog of types of songs familiar to fourteenth-century Spain. First, he mentions writing a love song which is 'deeply sad.'

> By writing her a sad song that with practice she could learn
> And sing in sadness by herself, since I could not have her.
>
> To satisfy the wishes of my lady, as she bade,
> I made a song so deeply sad, because this love was sad.[49]

Another song he composes he calls 'somber, bitter—in fact, lovesick.'[50] Next, 'in sadness and disgust' he wrote a 'vulgar song.'[51] Still another song he calls 'average, its not exactly pretty but, I think, not low and cheap.'[52]

In another place he says he wrote a simple mountain song, but he does not describe the music, although he includes the lyrics.[53] In this song to a mountain girl, the priest reveals that he can play the guitar and dance to any song[54] (in another place it is reported that he 'plays instruments of music, knows the arts of troubadours').[55] Later, for this same girl, the priest wrote three songs, two carols and a dancing song, but none seemed to inspire the girl to love.[56]

For a saint, Maria Del Vado, the priest writes 'poor praise-songs' in deep humility.[57] Later he mentions writing dance songs, street songs, songs for blind men and for 'scholars who are always on the prowl at night.'[58] Here also Ruiz provides an interesting discussion of the instruments which accompany song.

> In order that the instruments be suited and attuned
> To fit the songs and make the tune and melody rebound,
> I've noted here such instruments, of all of those I've tried,
> As best accompany the songs, according to their sound.
>
> Arabian songs do not go well with *viuela* played with bows,
> Nor is the *çinfonia* or guitar fit for those songs;
> The citola and bagpipes do not suit an Arab man;
> They suit the taverns best for low-class dance.
>
> The shepherd's flute, bandora, *caramillo* and *çanpoña*, some claim,
> Do not like Arab songs, and scholars are to them averse,
> Although, through others' pressure, they may speak it to their shame;
> Whoever makes them sing in it, he should be fined, or worse.

48 Ibid., 1625.

49 Ibid., 91ff.

50 Ibid., 103.
51 Ibid., 114.
52 Ibid., 986.
53 Ibid., 996.

54 Ibid., 1000ff.
55 Ibid., 1489.

56 Ibid., 1021.

57 Ibid., 1045ff. Ruiz gives the lyrics for this song.

58 Ibid., 1513. A similar contemporary list of instruments is found in Juan del Encina's poem 'Triunfo de Amor.'

In these books we have contended that one hallmark of art music is the presence of the contemplative listener. Ruiz seems to have intuited this idea, for in the following passage he draws a relationship, between the psychological state of the reader and the nature of what he absorbs from a book, in an analogy with music.

> A relative am I, the book, to instruments, you'll find.
> How so you tune me, well or badly, I'll resound in kind,
> Strike notes and hold them, gay or sad, just as your heart's inclined:
> If you know how to play, you'll always have me in your mind.[59]

Rojas refers to the importance of the listener when Celestina describes a singer for whom even the birds stop to listen.

> His only relief is to take up his lute and sing. He sings the most mournful songs all about the departure of the soul and having courage in the face of death, just like those that great musician the Emperor Hadrian sang, I suppose, when he knew he was going to die. I don't know much about music, but he seems to make that lute speak. When he sings, the very birds stop to listen with more pleasure than when they listened to the singer of old [Orpheus] who moved the trees and the stones, as they say, with his song.[60]

Closely related to this is a striking passage by Rojas, who poses the question: Can a musician play in tune, if he himself is 'out of tune?' In this passage, the love sick Calisto decides to sing a song of love.

> CALISTO: Sempronio!
> SEMPRONIO: Sir?
> CALISTO: Bring me my lute.
> SEMPRONIO: Here it is, sir.
> CALISTO (sings):
> > *Can any grief compare*
> > *With what I bear?*
> SEMPRONIO: The lute's out of tune.
> CALISTO: How can a man tune it who is himself out of tune? What sense of harmony can he have who is himself full of discords? A man whose will refuses to obey his reason, who has barbs in his breast, in whom peace and war, love and hate, injury, guilt, and suspicions battle together? Here, take the lute and sing me the saddest song you know.[61]

[59] Ibid., 70.

[60] Ibid., act 4.

[61] Rojas, *La Celestina*, act 1.

EDUCATIONAL MUSIC

The university at Salamanca. along with Paris, Bologna and Oxford, was one of the important centers for the study of music and the first in Europe to have an endowed chair in music (1254), although the associated records reveal that the music professor received the lowest pay of the faculty.[62]

The treatises on music produced in this university tended to remain in the old Scholastic mold, in which music was firmly rooted in the larger field of mathematics. The *Musica practica* (1482) by Ramos de Pareja was one of the few to put forward original ideas, although this treatise is also heavily grounded in mathematics. One of his innovations was the replacement of the solmisation syllables based on Guido with a new set of his invention based on the octave. This brought upon him great controversy, which was due in part, according to Reese, by the establishment of a chair in music at the University of Bologna in 1450—the mathematical faculty demanding the music belonged to its field.[63]

The treatise *Lux bella* (1492) by Domingo Durán is also heavily weighted with mathematics (based on Boethius), but also includes a section on the uses and effects of music.[64]

[62] Enrique Esperabé y Arteaga, *Historia pragmática é interna de la Universidad de Salamanca* (Salamanca, 1914–1917), I, 22.

[63] Reese, *Music in the Renaissance*, 587.

[64] Carpenter, *Music in the Medieval and Renaissance Universities*, 218.

FUNCTIONAL MUSIC

Ruiz, in his *The Book of True Love*, describes an Easter procession in a fourteenth-century town, in which we see jongleurs and members of Religious Orders. Long lists of musical instruments are common in early poetry, but of particular interest here is the aesthetic description of the sounds of the various instruments.

> And then the drums came forth with many other instruments.
> Then came out, with a strident sound, the two-stringed Moor's guitar,
> High-pitched as to its range, so to its tone both harsh and bold;
> Big-bellied lute which marks the time for merry, rustic dance,
> And Spanish guitar which with the rest was herded in the fold.
>
> The noisy, shrill rebec, with note so high it seems a squeak,
> Was joining in the tunes the Moor was twanging on his harp.
> And with them all, the *salterio* much higher than a peak;
> The picking *viyuela* among these others gaily skipped and hopped.

> The smaller zither [caño] and the harp and Moorish rebec played;
> Along with them the French recorder hummed a gay gavotte;
> The flute stood out above them higher than a lofty crag;
> Without the side drum's taps it is not worth an apricot.
>
> The bowing of the *vihuela de arco* produces sweet dance songs,
> At times quite soft and lulling, and at others very loud,
> Sweet sounds, delicious, bright and clear and always in good tune,
> Which make the people merry and delight the swarming crowd.
>
> The sweet *caño* came out with the little tambourine,
> Its jambles made of brass made sounds that are so sweet and clean;
> Portable organs there were playing country jigs and songs,
> And the poor comic minstrel girl played choruses between.
>
> The bagpipes and the Moorish flute, the *çinfonia*,
> The *baldosa*, with their tight strings,
> And with all these the French *odreçillo* were playing well in tune,
> The silly bass bandora threw in its notes without delay.
>
> The horns and trumpets now came out with the timpani.
> It was a long time since there'd been such entertainment here,
> Such great rejoicing as the people mingled,
> The hillsides and the fields were full of jongleurs far and near.[65]

Ruiz indicates that the Sunday after Easter was a popular date for weddings and on this day he reported joyous song, banquets and priests and jongleurs running from wedding to wedding.[66]

A well-known ballad, 'The Loss of Alhambra,' describes military music from the time of Fernando and Isabella.

> When the Alhambra's walls be gained,
> On the moment he ordained
> That the trumpet straight should sound
> With the silver clarion round.
>   Woe is me, Alhambra!
> When the hollow drums of war
> Beat the loud alarm afar,
> That the Moors of town and plain
> Might answer to the martial strain,
>   Woe is me, Alhambra![67]

---

65   Ruiz, *The Book of True Love*, 1225ff.

66   Ibid., 1315.

67   Quoted in Mary Purcell, *The Great Captain* (New York: Doubleday, 1962), 57.

ENTERTAINMENT MUSIC

Rojas, in his play *Celestina*, offers somewhat of a philosophical justification for entertainment. The character Celestina observes,

> You can't enjoy anything alone. Don't be sour and unsociable, for Nature detests gloom and strives for pleasure. It's pleasant to share your delights with your friends … Let's have some music. Let's make up rhymes. Let's sing catches, tell riddles, play at competitions.[68]

68 Rojas, *La Celestina*, act 1.

Ruiz's only reference to entertainment music is of the girl who sings in a house of entertainment.

> Once the ballad-singing girl begins her song at night,
> Feet start to beat and drown the babblers in the joy and fuss.
>
> For weavers and dancing girls are never seen with idle feet,
> At the loom, at playing castanets their fingers always beat.[69]

69 Ruiz, *The Book of True Love*, 470ff.

Among the aristocratic entertainments of this period, perhaps the most documented were those surrounding the marriage of the king of Castile, Enrique IV, in 1440. Most notable, the host, the count of Haro, had constructed in a large field near his palace a kind of fifteenth-century Disneyland. An entire forest was transplanted, together with puzzled deer, boars and bears and a nearby man-made lake was stocked with fish. Behind the lake a huge temporary building of twenty levels was built, with each level carpeted with green sod. The guests took their places on the various levels and enjoyed a great banquet, while watching hunters kill the helpless game in the artificial forest and anglers pull fish from the lake. After the meal, the party danced until breakfast, when each lady found a gold ring set with jewels by her plate. We are happy to report the count also distributed two great sacks of coins to the exhausted musicians.[70]

70 Townsend Miller, *Henry IV of Castile* (New York: Lippincott, 1972), 22.

After the wedding party continued on to Valladolid, a great tournament was scheduled. This tournament got out of hand, as was sometimes the case, and turned into a bloodbath. This, plus the necessity for a public beheading and the occurrence of a number of (natural) aristocratic deaths, ruined the festive mood and caused the remainder of the entertainments to be canceled.

Enrique's royal trumpeters also played a role in the final event of this great wedding celebration. It was their duty to announce to the court, by way of a fanfare, the moment the royal bride ceased to be a virgin. They were placed by the door of the bridal chamber and three notaries were required by law to stand by the bed (beyond curtains, we presume!), ready to pass the word on to the trumpeters. Regretfully we report that on this occasion the trumpets never played, and thus history has awarded Henry the sobriquet, 'the Impotent.'

14 FIFTEENTH-CENTURY ENGLAND

GENERAL MUSIC HISTORY TEXTS often find a certain lull in fifteenth-century England, after Dunstable, with no significant new composers. For example, Reese characterizes the period as one of 'insular conservatism,' and quotes Tinctoris as commenting that the English 'continue to use one and the same style of composition, which shows a wretched poverty of invention.'[1]

While modern music history texts tend to see the fifteenth century primarily from the perspective of Church music, the references to conservatism are not only true, but may well reflect a broader philosophical climate. Here, as in France, there seems to have been a momentary philosophic swing of the pendulum away from the gains of the humanists and back to the old dogma of the Church. Indeed, the debates, given below, between Reason and Sensuality, may well be taken as metaphors for the struggle between the Church and the humanists.

One of the new characteristics of the Renaissance, found among both writers and musicians, was a certain new awareness of posterity. It is a small, but significant, change in focus from thinking of the next life to thinking of future life on earth. John Lydgate (1370–1450), for example, reminds his readers that the deeds of the dead would be forgotten, if it were not for writers.[2] And in a kind of ode to literature, he also contends that the wisdom of literature remains always fresh, is not diminished by time and its longevity is achieved so long as men continue to read it.

> Frut of writyng set in cronicles olde,
> Most delectable of fresshness in tastyng,
> And most goodli & glorious to beholde,
> In cold and heete lengest abidyng,
> Chaung of cesouns may doon it non hyndryng;
> And wher-so be that men dyne or faste,
> The mor men taste, the lenger it wil laste.[3]

1 Reese, *Music in the Renaissance*, 763.

2 John Lydgate, *Fall of Princes*, ed. Henry Bergen (London: Oxford University Press, 1967), VIII, 127ff. This work is ostensibly a translation of Giovanni Boccaccio's *De Casibus Virorum Illustrium*, although Lydgate freely engages in his own commentary and philosophy.

3 Ibid., IV, 1ff.

ON THE PHYSIOLOGY OF AESTHETICS

If there were a regression to a more conservative philosophy in fifteenth-century England, we notice it especially in those philosophers who emphasize the principle that man must be governed only by Reason. Of course, the very fact that philosophers keep reminding the faithful of this, century after century, only points to their recognition of the obvious fact that there are in man other important competing faculties. Thus, the poet Hoccleve (1368–1426) seems frustrated that he could not understand why rebellious youth could not see that Reason leads to the happy life!

> As for the more part youthe is rebel
> Unto reson and hatith hir doctryne:
> Regnynge which, it may nat stande wel
> With yowthe, as fer as wit can ymagyne.
> O yowthe, allas! Why wilt thow nat enclyne
> And unto reuled resoun bowe thee,
> Syn resoun is the verray streighte lyne
> That ledith folk unto felicitee?[4]

4 'La Male Regle de T. Hoccleue,' in M.C. Seymour, *Selections from Hoccleve* (Oxford: Clarendon Press, 1981), lines 65ff.

Lydgate, in addressing the nobles among his readers, goes further and suggests that even Fortune itself can not harm them if only they would act according to Reason.

> That Fortune hath no domynacioun
> Wher noble pryncis be gouerned be resoun.[5]

5 Lydgate, *Fall of Princes*, II, 55.

The most interesting discussions of man's submission to Reason, in this literature, are found in two lengthy passages which are essentially debates between Reason and Sensuality, with the latter term meaning the broader context of the senses.

'Reson and Sensuallyte'

In the first of these, found in John Lydgate's 'Reson and Sensuallyte,'[6] early in the fifteenth century, Dame Nature begins by stating that man has essentially two choices, two paths, he can follow. We take this as another illustration of early deduction, long before the confirmation of modern clinical research, of the fundamentally different forms of understanding in the twin hemispheres of the brain.

6 The discussion begins with line 644.

This is made more evident when Dame Nature explains that these two paths are the Eastern, the way of Reason, and the Western, the way of Sensuality. This conforms perfectly with the nature of the twin hemispheres of the brain, of course, as 'the Eastern,' that is the direction of the right hand, represents the left hemisphere, which includes all of Reason, and the Western direction, referring to the left hand, is similarly an association with the right hemisphere, which includes music, spatial perception and the emotions. It is particularly interesting here, that Dame Reason associates with the right hemisphere (the Western) those things of a passing and transitory nature, characteristics for which music was often criticized in medieval literature.

> The wey of sensualyte,
> which set his entente in al
> To thinges that be temporal,
> Passynge and transytorie,
> And fulfylled of veyn glorie.[7]

Dame Nature now explains that man has been given two Virtues, the Sensitive, by which he perceives things, and Understanding. In contrast to most philosophers by this time, who had agreed that the basis of our understanding comes from information obtained by the senses, Lydgate diminishes the value of sensory information by comparing it with the bark of a tree, which has only doubtful and outward understanding of that which is within. The purpose of intelligence in man, he says, is that he may understand the divine.

Man should be governed only by Reason, 'lest he suffer the great shame of losing his reputation.'[8] Dame Nature acknowledges that man's feelings often conflict with Reason, since sensuality desires only bodily delight. She advises man to set his mind on Heavenly things and hold fast to Reason, whose road leads to Heaven.[9] Interestingly enough, Lydgate now states that 'Genius' is the high priest of Nature, who curses all who act against her laws.[10] He quickly adds that Reason, as Nature's sister, does the same.

Dame Nature now introduces man to three goddesses, Minerva, Juno and Venus, accompanied by Mercury. Minerva, known here also as Lady Pallas, is called the 'chief goddess of wisdom.'[11] Juno is described principally as the goddess of Fortune. Venus is, of course, the goddess of Love. Here Lydgate concentrates on the power of this emotion; no one, he notices, can disobey Venus. It follows that she can turn peace

---

7 John Lydgate, *Lydgate's Reson and Sensuallyte*, ed. Ernst Sieper (London: Oxford University Press, 1901), lines 678ff. Lydgate mentions this traditional left hemisphere prejudice again in his *Fall of Princes*, VI, 18ff, where 'a marvelous woman' appears before him covered with summer flowers on the right side of her body and with the left side 'beaten by winter storms.'

8 Ibid., lines 760ff.

9 Ibid., lines 768, 778, 831 and 844.

10 Ibid., line 863.

11 Ibid., lines 1044. Lydgate also mentions her beautiful face, but not the ancient Greek mythical story of her discovery of the aulos, in which, upon observing how playing it distorted her face, she threw it away. Here Lydgate departs from his subject in a brief reference to the tradition of the swan singing, 'with werbles ful of melodye,' just before it dies and recommends that man too should sing of truth on his fatal day. [Ibid., lines 1247ff]

to war, make people misers or generous, humble the proud, soothe the angry, make cowards manful and the brave coward.[12]

Mercury, Lydgate first describes as a kind of god of the left hemisphere of the brain. He is the god of words, the messenger of celestial secrets, the protector of merchants, is skilled in calculation and gives knowledge to philosophers.[13] But Mercury, in ancient Greek mythology, was sometimes associated with music and so Lydgate also pictures him here holding a flute. In another interesting, and subconscious, reference to the twin hemispheres of the brain (music, of course, being in the right hemisphere), Lydgate describes Mercury as holding the flute in his *left* hand. We are told he plays to comfort his heart and creates such 'sugared harmony' and soothing melodies that no listener could prevent himself from falling asleep.

> In his lifte honde A flowte he helde,
> When so him list the longe day,
> Ther with to pipe and make play,
> Oonly him self for to disporte,
> And his hert to comforte
> Wyth the sugred armonye,
> Which gaf so soote a melodye
> That no man koude him selfe so kepe,
> But hyt wolde make him slepe.[14]

Even the singing of the famous Syrens, Lydgate says, cannot be compared in 'sootheness and in excellent sweetness of this melodious flute.'

'Nature'

The second lengthy discussion of Reason and Sensuality is found in the play, *Nature*, by Henry Medwall (b. 1461). The play opens with Nature stating that there is nothing on earth which is not a partner to her influence. Among the examples she offers, are two musical ones,

> Who taught the cock his watch hours to observe,
> And sing with courage, with shrill throat on high? ...
> Who taught the nightingale to record so well
> Her strange tunes, in silence of the night?

---

12 Ibid., lines 1480ff.

13 Ibid., lines 1663ff.

14 Ibid., lines 1760ff.

Nature introduces the principal discussion with another interesting subconscious deduction of the twin hemispheres of the brain. She tells man that Reason will govern him on his way, but that Sensuality is on *the other side*!

> Address thyself now towards your journey,
> For as of now, you shall no longer here abide.
> Lo, here, Reason, to govern you in your way,
> And Sensuality, upon your other side.
> But Reason I appoint to be your chief guide,
> With Innocence, that is your tender nurse,
> Evermore to win you from the appetite of vice.[15]

15 Henry Medwall, *Nature*, I, 99ff.

Man observes that he has in common with all things in the world, including herbs and trees, the need for continual nourishment sufficient to natural living. Like the sensual beasts, he says, he has the means of knowing the good things he should delight in and to flee the opposite. Then he says to Nature,

> And above all this, you have given me a virtue
> Surmounting all others in high perfection:
> That is understanding, whereby I may anew
> And well discern what is to be done.[16]

16 Ibid., I, 127ff.

Nature responds by warning man once again to 'Let Reason govern you in every situation.'[17]

17 Ibid., I, 159.

Now Sensuality enters and protests to Nature that she should have equal status with Reason and Innocence.[18] She contends, 'I am the chief perfection of his nature!' Without me, man would have no feeling, he might as well be made of wood or stone.

18 Ibid., I, 169ff.

> And now you have put me out of his service,
> And have assigned Reason to be his guide
> With Innocence his nurse; thus am I set aside!

> You made him lord of all beasts living,
> And nothing worthy, as far as I can see;
> For if there be in him no manner of feeling
> No lively quickness, what kind of lord is he?
> A lord made of rags! or carved from a tree!
> And fares as an image carved from stone
> That can do nothing but stand alone!

Allow me to have influence with him, Sensuality pleas with Nature, and I will make him governor of the world. But if 'Reason tickles him in the ear,' he will never be able to do earthly good.

No, says Nature, Reason must be preferred, reminding Sensuality, 'You have brought many men to a wretched end.'[19]

Sensuality now becomes agitated,

> By Christ! yet will I not hide my face,
> For as soon as we shall to the world resort
> I have no doubt he will me support.[20]

The character Reason appears and answers on behalf of Nature.

> Sober yourself, I advise you strongly!
> Be not so passionate, not so furious …
>
> For sensuality, in very deed,
> Is but a means which causes man to fall
> Into much folly and makes him beast-like,
> So that there is no difference, in that at least,
> Between Man and an unreasonable beast.[21]

You should obey me, Reason says to Sensuality, wherever I go. Sensuality answers, 'No, that I shall never do!'[22]

Sensuality now proposes to Reason a bargain, which once again subconsciously reflects the completely separate natures of the twin hemispheres of the brain. It is as if we can hear the right hemisphere speaking to the left,

> Meddle in no point that belongs to me,
> And I promise never to meddle with thee.[23]

And if this is not acceptable, Sensuality proposes that they let man choose for himself.

> For trust me, the very truth is this:
> This man is put in his own liberty,
> And certainly the free choice is his
> Whether he will be governed by thee or me.
> Let us therefore put it to his own jeopardy.[24]

'No sir,' says Reason, 'I know his frailty, his body is disposed to fall.'

---

19 Ibid., I, 211ff.

20 Ibid., I, 241ff.

21 Ibid., I, 246 and 290ff.

22 Ibid., I, 314.

23 Ibid., I, 321.

24 Ibid., I, 330.

Now the character Innocence enters and testifies that he has reared man to be a virgin, 'both in deed and even consent of sin.'[25]

25 Ibid., I, 351ff.

> And I will no longer be of his acquaintance
> If he is not virtuous and of good living;
> For fleshly lust and worldly pleasure
> Has nothing in accord with Innocence.
> But if his behavior and daily demeanor
> Be of such as Reason will allow,
> I shall favor and love him as I do now.

'Well spoken,' says Sensuality, 'now are you two done?' 'No,' says Reason, but Sensuality stops him before he can continue.

> Peace! no more of this disputation!
>   [*to the audience*]
> Here are many fantasies to drive forth the day—
> One chatters like a magpie, the other like a jay!
> And yet, when they both have done what they can,
> I shall rule the man![26]

26 Ibid., I, 365ff.

Man now interrupts this debate, declaring,

> O blessed Lord! what manner of strife is this,
> Between my Reason and Sensuality?[27]

27 Ibid., I, 372.

At length Man decides to subjugate his Sensuality to Reason.

> Reason, Sir, my chief counselor.
> And this, Innocence, my previous nurse,
> And Sensuality, that other, by whom I have power
> To do as all sensuous beasts do.
> But Reason and Innocence, chiefly these two,
> Have the whole rule and governance of me,
> To whom is subdued my Sensuality.[28]

28 Ibid., I, 533.

Soon a new character, The World, enters and speaks on behalf of Sensuality.

> And for Sensuality—I pray you with all my heart
> To accept him to your favor and consideration.
> He has long been of my acquaintance.[29]

29 Ibid., I, 605.

Later another character, Pride, suggests that a 'wild worm' has come into man's head if he thinks he will always be led only be Reason. He doubts that Reason will always endure with man, pointing out that, 'Sensuality ... is chief ruler, when Reason is away.'[30]

Lydgate, in another poem, makes this same point, observing 'When reason fails, sensuality holds the bridle of lecherous insolence.'[31] In this same poem he thinks of an early time in history when, he imagines, sensuality was in fact 'servant to Reason.' The result, he maintains, was a world in which the clergy led lives of perfection, merchants did not cheat, knights supported truth, women did not paint their faces and wise men and scholars were not looked down upon![32]

In the writings of William Caxton (1422–1491), one finds numerous references to the importance of learning in general. In the Prologue to his *Book of Good Manners* (1487) he finds that the common people, without information and learning, are rude and not mannered, 'like unto the beestis brute.'[33] In the Prologue to his *Knight of the Tower* (1484) he states that the purpose of all 'doctrine and teaching' by earlier writers was to inform us through 'science, wisdom and understanding of knowledge' how we should conduct ourselves in the present life.[34] Thus, in another place, he urges nobles, when they have free time on their hands, to read books and to 'suffre nothyng to passe but that he understonde it right well.'[35]

History, especially, Caxton finds to be an indispensable form of knowledge.[36] He defines History as follows,

> Whiche worde *historye* may be descryved thus. Historye is a perpetuel conservatryce of thoos thyngs that have be doone before this presente tyme and also a cotydyan wytnesse of bienfayttes, of malefaytes, grete actes, and tryumphal vyctoryes of all maner peple.

Unlike the 'feyned fables of poetes,' History asserts the truth and is the mother of all philosophy. History should be read by young and old, including nobles and government leaders. The very threat that History will be written, he says, is enough to move 'noble knyghtes to deserve eternal laude' and to check 'cruel tyrauntys for drede of infamye.'

Even his book on *Vocabulary* (1480), Caxton promises,

> Wylle enlyghte the hertes
> Of them that shall lerne it.[37]

30 Ibid., II, 308ff.

31 Lydgate, *Fall of Princes*, II, 2535.

32 Ibid., III, 3146ff.

33 Quoted in N. Blake, *Caxton's Own Prose* (London: Andre Deutsch, 1973), 60.

34 Ibid., 111.

35 'Mirror of the World,' lines 16–20, 73, quoted in Ibid., 114ff.

36 Prologue to 'Polychronicon,' lines 40ff, quoted in Ibid., 129ff.

37 Ibid., 143.

ON THE PSYCHOLOGY OF AESTHETICS

Lydgate, in his poem 'Reson and Sensuallyte,' addresses the subject of Pleasure in the course of his description of the goddess Venus, whom he says always agrees with Nature.[38] Venus has two sons, the first of which is Pleasure. Her son, Pleasure, knows everything of 'mirth and games,' especially music and dance.

[38] Lydgate, 'Reson and Sensuallyte,' lines 2258ff.

> Touche he crafte, and nat be rote,
> Harpe and lute, fythel and Rote,
> And synge songes of pleaunce,
> Maisterly revel and Daunce,
> Pipe and floyte lustely.
> And also eke ful konyngly
> In al the crafte and melody
> of musyke and of Armony,
> What tyme that het hal be do,
> He ys expert.[39]

[39] Ibid., lines 2393ff.

But, he is also expert in what we might call 'left hemisphere games,' dice, chess and games of arthimetic.

The second son of Venus is Cupid. Pleasure and Cupid serve Venus, as Venus serves Nature.[40] Love and Pleasure dwell together and Love could not last without Pleasure. Love is found in Pleasure's garden, where there is no strife or sorrow.[41] The chief gatekeeper of the Garden of Pleasure is Idleness.

[40] Ibid., lines 2488ff.
[41] Ibid., lines 2580ff.

Lydgate now argues against Love as an emotion (right hemisphere). He has man take a *right-hand path*[42] to the (left hemisphere) *non-feeling* huntress, the goddess Diana. Diana warns man that the world is going to the bad, with Virtue, Faith and Trust the victims of Lust.[43] She accuses man of being thoughtless, in choosing the worst of the three goddesses.[44]

[42] Ibid., lines 2724.
[43] Ibid., lines 3116ff.
[44] Ibid., lines 3315ff.

Diana cautions man not to enter the Garden of Pleasure, a place full of sorrowing people. No man who enters, she warns, ever returns from it.[45] In this garden, she says, are monsters, worse than scorpions, with red, blue and green scales, wings and poison in their tails. These are Syrens, with the painted heads of women and with sharp nails, who play the harp and psaltery, making angel-like melody and soothing harmony.

[45] Ibid., lines 3588ff.

> Eche hath an hede of a woman
> And everych hath a mayde face

> Of syghte lusty to enbrace,
> Her nayles kene and wonder sharpe.
> The [first] playeth on an harpe
> Myd of the see, fer from the londe,
> The seconde toucheth with her honde
> On a sawtre delytable,
> The thirdde also, most agreable,
> Aungelyke of melodye,
> Ful of soote armonye,
> Syngeth songes Amerouse,
> Wonderly delyciouse.[46]

46 Ibid., lines 3628ff.

Diana recommends to man instead her Forest of Chastity, where there are no Syrens' songs.[47] Man, however, having a choice and observing 'That's my fate,' decides to explore the Garden of Pleasure.[48] On the wall outside the Garden of Pleasure, he sees pictures of Hate, Felony, Villainy, Covetousness, Avarice, Envy, Sadness, Age, Hypocrisy, and Poverty. This does not alarm him, on the contrary looking at them 'dyde me gret good.'[49] He is welcomed into the garden by Courtesy, who explains the Garden is meant only for amusement.[50]

47 Ibid., lines 4356ff.

48 Ibid., lines 7453ff.

49 Ibid., lines 4940ff.

50 Ibid., lines 5001ff.

Within the Garden he finds, among other things, music. First, he hears a nightingale singing heavenly clear notes, with no discord. He doubts that anyone could describe such ravishing sound, the sugared melody or the soothing harmony.[51] Pleasure too was singing, as fresh as any nightingale, with clear lusty music like the Syrens, of joy, mirth and lustiness.[52]

51 Ibid., lines 5202ff.

52 Ibid., lines 5254ff.

Man next meets Cupid, with the five arrows of Beauty, Simplicity, Truth and Freedom, Company and Good Looks in his bow.[53] But in a second bow, 'black and foul' were the arrows Pride, Felony, Shame, Despair, and Change of Mind. Their wounds, he says, are almost deadly. Following behind Cupid and Dame Beauty were Riches, Freedom, Largess, Courtesy, Idleness and Youth, hand in hand.

53 Ibid., lines 5448ff.

Now man encounters an ensemble of gods playing music in honor of Cupid. Here, after man is told to be still, Lydgate lists all the instruments of the minstrels, indeed, he says, more than any man could name. There are string instruments from Germany, Arragon and Spain and for dancing trumpets, loud shawms and flutes. These were exceptional performances, with no discords, in tune, with good ensemble and no errors in rhythm. No one, Lydgate observes, could be so sorrowful or oppressed with heaviness that he would not have been comforted by this music.

And yt syt nat me to be stille
But tel, how they wer provyded
Of Instrumentys of Musyke,
For they koude the practyke
Of al manner Mynstralcye
That any man kan specifye;
For ther wer rotys of Almanye
And eke of Arragon and spayne,
Songes, stampes, and eke dounces,
Dyuers plente of pleaunces,
And many vnkouth notys newe
Of swiche folkys as lovde trewe,
And Instrumentys that dyde excelle,
Many moo than I kan telle:
Harpys, fythels, and eke rotys,
Wel accordyng with her notys,
Lutys, Rubibis, and geterns,
More for estatys than taverns,
Orgnys, cytolys, monacordys.
And ther wer founde noo discordys,
Nor variance in ther sovns,
Nor lak of noo proporsiouns,
Ther was so noble accordaunce;
And for folkys that lyst daunce
Ther wer trumpes and trumpetes,
Lowde shally and docetes,
Passyng of gret melodye,
And floutys ful of armonye,
Eke Instrumentys high and lowe
Wel mo than I koude knowe,
That I suppose, ther is no man
That aryght reherse kan
The melodye that they made:
They wer so lusty and so glade …
Ther melodye was in all
So heuenly and celestiall
That ther nys hert, I dar expresse,
Oppressed so with hevynesse,
Nor in sorrow so y-bounde,
That he sholde ther ha founde
Comfort hys sorrowe to apese
To a-settle his hert at ese.[54]

54 Ibid., lines 5564ff.

ON THE PHILOSOPHY OF AESTHETICS

Lydgate, in his poem 'Reson and Sensuallyte,' clearly sets the standard for Beauty as being that which 'Dame Nature' has created. Indeed, he has Nature challenge man to look around and see if he can find anything lacking in beauty.

> But that you go and visit
> Around the world, in length and breadth,
> And consider, and take good heed,
> If there fails in my workings
> In fairness of anything,
> Or in beauty anything wanting.[55]

Indeed, when man accepts this challenge, he discovers his 'cunning too feeble and faint' to praise the beauties of Nature as they deserve.[56]

Aside from the numerous mystery plays, we find during the fifteenth century the first harbingers of the more traditional theater which will climax so gloriously during the following century. At the beginning of his play, *Fulgens and Lucres*, Henry Medwall identifies the purpose of his play as bringing pleasure to the observer, as well as truth and reason. Then he sadly reflects that at this time one cannot always tell the truth, rather one must lie and flatter.

> PUBLIUS CORNELIUS. This play ... I am sure,
>   Is made for the same intent and purpose:
>   To do every man both mirth and pleasure;
>   Wherefore I can not think or suppose
>   That they will one word therein disclose
>   But such as shall stand with truth and reason,
>   In good manner according to the season.
> GAIUS FLAMINIUS. Yes, but truth may not be said always,
>   For sometimes it causes grudge and spite.
> CORNELIUS. Yes, so goes the world, nowadays,
>   That a man must say the crow is white!
> FLAMINIUS. Yes, that he must, by God almighty!
>   He must both lie and flatter now and then
>   That causes him to dwell among worldly men;
>   In some courts such men shall most win.[57]

There is very little discussion of poetry as an art form during this century in England, but we do find an interesting description of the

---

55 Ibid., lines 518ff.

56 Ibid., lines 980ff.

57 Henry Medwall, *Fulgens and Lucres*, I, 155ff.

poet by John Lydgate. He says of poets that they must live in solitude, they should walk by crystal springs and climb high mountains at sunrise and they should study hard and be content with moderate food. They should be secluded from the tumult of the world and live according to their means and by the support of their princely patrons. Their chief duty is to labor to reprove vices, not to be rudely offensive or to injure men, but always to conclude with virtue.[58]

58 Lydgate, *Fall of Princes*, III, 3807ff.

ON THE AESTHETICS OF MUSIC

It is curious that by the fifteenth century one not only still finds reference to the 'music of the spheres,' but, as in Lydgate, that this celestial music represents the source, the 'root and growth' of the music of earth.[59] In another poem, he recalls that the ancient authors had determined that the planets are, 'the mother of music.'

59 Lydgate, 'Reson and Sensuallyte,' lines 276ff.

> How the seuene planetes in ther cours hem dresse,
> Meuyng of sterris, sparklyng in ther brihtnesse,
> With reuolociouns of the speeris nyne,
> Moodres of musik, as auctours determyne.[60]

60 Lydgate, *Fall of Princes*, IV, 1166ff.

We do not find in England much discussion of the influence of music on character, although Lydgate, in his history, the *Fall of Princes*, contends that the ancients civilized the common people through music and the resultant concord made possible both philosophy and the building of cities. Music, he suggests, contributes to peace and prudent policies.

> Philisophres of the goldene ages
> And poetes that [found] out fressh [songs],
> As kyng Amphioun with his fair langages
> And with his harpyng made folk of [low] degrees,
> As laborers, tenhabite first cities;—
> And so bi musik and philosophie
> Gan first of comouns noble policie.

> The cheeff of musik is mellodie & accord;
> Welle of philosophie sprang out of prudence,
> Bi which too menys gan unite & concord
> With politik vertu to have ther assistence:
> Wise men to regne, subiectis do reuerence.

> And bi this ground, in stories men may see,
> Wer bilt the wallis of Thebes the cite.
>
> Accord in musik causith the mellodie;
> Wher is discord, ther is dyuersite,
> And wher is [peace] is prudent policie
> In ech kyngdam and euery gret [country].[61]

He also adds that Achilles, when in a mood of wrath, could only be stilled by the sound of a harp.

> Which instrument bi his gret suet[e]nesse
> Put al rancour out of his remembraunce …[62]

In all early literature, from the ancient societies through the Middle Ages, some form of the word 'sweet' was always associated with the most beautiful music. What was 'honeyed' music in ancient Greek literature is in fifteenth-century English literature often 'sugared' music, as in one of Lydgate poems.

> Herd of angelis, with sugrid notis cleer,
> Celestial song in ther melodie …[63]

Regarding the purposes of music, we find here, as was the case in earlier literature, reference to the ability of music to soothe the listener. We have seen above, in Lydgate's 'Reson and Sensuallyte,' the concert by the gods which we were told would comfort even the most sorrowful of men. In another poem by Lydgate a lover suffering the pains of love specifically leaves his room to go 'into the woods to hear the birds sing' in order to 'find succor' and 'some release' from his pain.

> As he, alas, that nygh for sorow deyde,
> My sekenes sat ay so nygh myn hert.
> But for to fynde socour of my smert,
> Or attelest sum relesse of [my] peyn
> That me so sore halt in euery veyn,
> I rose anon and thoght I wol[de] goon
> Vnto the wode to her the briddes sing …[64]

And similarly, in Medwall's *Fulgen and Lucres*, we find,

---

61 Ibid., VI, 337ff.

62 Ibid., VI, 417ff.

63 John Lydgate, *The Life of Saint Alban and Saint Amphibal*, ed. J.E. Van Der Westhuizen (Leiden: Brill, 1974), 4127.

64 'A Complaynt of a Loveres Lyfe,' 15ff, in John Lydgate, *John Lydgate Poems* (Oxford: Clarendon Press, 1966).

And if in hunting you have no delight,
Then you may dance a while for your disport;
You shall have at your pleasure, both day and night,
All manner of minstrels to bring you comfort.[65]

65 *Fulgens and Lucres*, II, 555ff.

A closely related purpose of music which we find emphasized in this literature is to bring joy to the listener. Thus, the character David appears with his harp in *The Procession of the Prophets*, one of the Wakefield mystery plays, and sings,

Mirth I make for all men,
With my harp and fingers ten,
And make them not dismayed …[66]

66 Quoted in Martial Rose, *The Wakefield Mystery Plays* (London: Evans Brothers, 1961), 122.

A particularly interesting reference to this purpose of music is found in William Caxton's *The Game of Chess* (1474), the first book ever printed in England. In this book, which uses chess as a metaphor for the various levels of society, under 'the pawn,' Caxton discusses the physician. The physician, he says, must know the basic Liberal Arts: grammar, logic, geometry, arithmetic, music and astronomy. Caxton now briefly discusses the value of these arts for the physician, saying, for example, that the value of astronomy is to be able to determine the time of day. Regarding music, he merely recommends to the physician without further explanation, 'the Joyous songes of musyque.'[67]

Lydgate also mentions that one purpose of music is to please the audience. He presents this idea as an analogy, in a discussion of Rhetoric and Oratory, when he wishes to suggest that the speaker should please the audience just as musicians do with their melodious songs.

67 William Axon, *Caxton's Game and Playe of the Chesse* (London, 1883), 119.

So the langage of rethoriciens
Is a glad obiect to mannys audience,
With song mellodious of musiciens …[68]

68 Lydgate, *Fall of Princes*, VI, 3487ff. Earlier, beginning with line 3288, he places Rhetoric within the rational branch of philosophy and suggests the orator must have natural wit, broad knowledge, affability and lead a virtuous life. The orator must clothe himself with five skills: invention, disposition, elocution, pronunciation and memory.

In another work, 'The Daunce of Machabree,' Lydgate refers once again to the ability of musicians to bring pleasure to people. He also makes the observation that the musician who is a master will, at the same time, demonstrate the 'science' of his art to the listener. In this poem, in which Death speaks to the individual members and professions of society, the following lines are entitled, 'Death speaketh to the Minstrel.'

> O THOU Minstrall, that can so note and pipe
> Unto folkes for to done pleasaunce,
> By thy ryght [hand] annone I shall the gripe,
> With these other to gone upon my daunce;
> There is no scape nother auoydaunce,
> On so syde to contraire my sentence:
> For in musike by craft and accordanunce
> Who maister is shewen his science.

In the 'Minstrel's answer to Death,' the musician protests that he finds the rhythms and meters of the 'Dance of Death' very confusing. He argues that if Death does not permit him to remain on earth, people will continue to dance, but will feel nothing in their heart.

> THIS new daunce is to me so straunge,
> Wonder divers and passingly contrarye;
> The dredefull footyng doth so oft chaunge
> And the measures so oft tymes varye,
> Which now to me is nothyng necessarye.
> If it wer so that I might asterte!
> But many a man, if I shal nought tary,
> Oft daunseth, but nothyng of hert.[69]

69 John Lydgate, 'The Daunce of Machabree,' contained at the end of Part III, *Fall of Princes*, 1040.

ART MUSIC

We have frequently mentioned in these books the importance of evidence of the contemplative listener as a hallmark of Art Music. In John Lydgate's poem 'Reson and Sensuallyte,' the narrator, in describing his reaction to listening to the singing of birds, employs language often used to describe persons moved by human music. He is listening to the birds of Spring, who, interestingly enough, both sing and *chant*.[70]

70 Lydgate, 'Reson and Sensuallyte,' line 196.

> I was so intent to hear
> Her warbles and her notes clear
> That my imagination
> So strong was in conclusion
> I was ravished …[71]

71 Ibid.,' line 199ff.

Much fifteenth-century English poetry was still thought of as a form of music, as we can see in a dedicatory note at the head of a poem called 'Three Roundels,' in which the poet refers to them as 'three chansons.'[72] Similarly, at the beginning of Part Two of Lydgate's 'The Temple of Glass,' we find,

> Icy commence le secund parti *de la songe*.

In another work, Lydgate, writing of his teacher, Chaucer, calls him a 'poet,' but immediately speaks of his poetry as songs [*dite*], listing familiar musical forms.

> This said poete, my maistir in his daies,
> Maad and compiled ful many a freesh dite,
> Compleyntis, baladis, roundelis, virelaies
> Ful delectable to heryn and to see ...[73]

The fifteenth century is the period which saw a tremendous growth in the establishment of civic wind bands in England. They appear in fine uniforms and with silver medallions. These musicians were not always paid in keeping with their appearance, but one contemporary noted,

> Observe that in those dayes they payd there mynstrells better than thyre preistes.[74]

The duties of these civic musicians were no doubt still primarily functional in nature, but there are indications of services which are more of a 'concert' nature than before. A document regarding the London civic wind band of 1454 requires them to play 'for the recreation of the people'[75] and another of 1484 mentions their serenading the citizens with carols on Christmas Day.[76] There is also evidence that the civic wind bands were paid at this time to supply the music needed for drama productions in the theater.[77]

The English and Scottish kings also began to be much more active in their support of music during the fifteenth century. Henry IV (1399–1413) was himself a flute player and there are many extant documents relative to the care of his six permanent minstrels. Henry V (1413–1422) increased the number of his household musicians to eighteen and there is an eyewitness account of his wind band giving an hour-long concert twice a day (before and after

72 'Three Roundels,' in Seymour, *Selections from Hoccleve*, 29.

73 Lydgate, *Fall of Princes*, I, 351ff.

74 Edmonstoune Duncan, *The Story of Minstrelsy* (Detroit, 1968), 99.

75 Walter Woodfill, *Musicians in English Society* (Princeton: Princeton University Press, 1953), 45.

76 Paul Kendall, *Richard the Third* (New York: Norton, 1955), 365.

77 Joseph Bridge, 'Town Waits and their Tunes,' in *Proceedings of the Musical Association* 54 (1928): 81.

battle) during his siege of Melun in 1420. Several chroniclers mention the occasion of his marriage to Catherine, daughter to Charles VI of France, in 1420. On this occasion Henry issued the promise that any minstrel who came to help celebrate his wedding would be given a newly minted gold coin. According to one eyewitness, thousands took him up on the offer!

> ... and in front of the chariot lead a great melody of trumpets, clarions, minstrels, and many other instruments by the hundreds and thousands, and one knows that many players appeared this day because it was ordered that each of them would receive this day a salut d'or which the king had recently begun to forge.[78]

Henry VI (1422–1461 and 1470–1471) seems to have had some problem keeping his compliment of musicians stable, for an order of 1456 empowers his staff to force into his service any 'young men of comely appearance, trained in the art of minstrelsy.'[79] Henry seems to have recruited his singers by the same process, for in one order he commands an official,

> to take throughout England such and so many boys as he or his deputies shall see to be fit and able to serve God and the King in the Chapel Royal.[80]

There is also evidence that by this time the various English dukes were also beginning to maintain, on average, four or more musicians.[81]

Under the first of the kings of the House of York, Edward IV (1461–1470 and 1471–1483), the household music grew considerably and now included singers and string players [*strengemen*]. Richard III (1483–1485), although he represents one of the darker chapters of English history, was educated in 'musicke, and other cuninge exercises of humanity.'[82] Another source relates that he finished each day by 'rehearsing the polite arts of harping, singing, piping, and dancing.'[83]

Henry VII (1485–1509) again increased the number of royal musicians and for his funeral in addition to singers and ceremonial instruments we find an ensemble of shawms and trombones and three separate ensembles called simply 'minstrels.'

During the fifteenth century all four Scottish kings, James I, II, III, and IV were musicians. James I (1424–1437) was also a composer and it was reported that the was singing and performing on several instruments on the very eve of his assassination.[84]

---

78 Marix, *Histoire de la Musique et des Musiciens de la Cour de Bourgogne sous le règne de Philippe le Bon*, 24.

79 John Stevens, *Music & Poetry in the Early Tudor Court* (London: Methuen, 1961), 307.

80 Quoted in Reese, *Music in the Renaissance*, 767.

81 Ibid., 300.

82 Gerald Hayes, *King's Music* (London: Oxford University Press, 1937), 42.

83 Paul Kendall, *Richard the Third*, 52.

84 Henry Farmer, 'Music in Mediaeval Scotland,' in *Proceedings of the Musical Association* 54 (1930): 76.

FUNCTIONAL MUSIC

Among the functional duties of the English civic bands, the most frequently documented is their appearances in the annual Lord Mayor's Procession in London. For this event even the various trade guilds hired their own wind bands, as we can see in a document of the Grocers' Company of 1435, which authorized payment to,

> the handys of John Dodyn for mynstrelles … amending of Baneris and hire of barges for … goyng be watir to Westminster.[85]

The keen competition among the guild bands on such occasions can be judged by a dispute in 1483 when two rival guilds fought over the precedence of their barges in the procession, resulting in 'bloodshed and loss of life.'[86]

A great water pageant in 1501, celebrating the marriage of prince Arthur and Katherine of Aragon, featured the entire court traveling down the Thames to Greenwich. An eyewitness reported hearing,

> the moost goodly and plesaunt mirthe of trumpetts, clarions, shalmewes, tabers, recorders and other dyvyrs instruments, to whoes noyse upon the water hathe not been hard the like.[87]

Roger Bowers mentions an expansion in church choirs which took place in the latter part of the fifteenth century in the major English churches as well as the fact that the composers of church music were not full-time composers, but generally singers composing as a sideline.[88] Thus, not being hired to satisfy a patron, they were able to enjoy artistic freedom in composing their polyphony.

ENTERTAINMENT MUSIC

In Medwell's *Fulgens and Lucres* we read of an example of rather enthusiastic entertainment music associated with weddings,

> At the least, it is merry being
> With men in time of wedding;
> For all that while they do no thing
> But dance and make revel,
> Sing and laugh with great shouting …[89]

---

85 Alan Warwick, *A Noise of Music* (London: Queen Anne Press), 21.

86 Ibid., 22.

87 Stevens, *Music & Poetry*, 237.

88 Roger Bowers, 'Obligation, Agency, and Laissez-Faire: The Promotion of Polyphonic Composition for the Church in Fifteenth-Century England,' in Iain Fenlon, ed., Music in *Medieval and Early Modern Europe* (Cambridge: Cambridge University Press, 1981), 9ff.

89 *Fulgens and Lucres*, I, 406ff.

Finally, in the literature of fifteenth-century England we find for the first time since before the Christian era, music and musicians associated with humorous scenes. In Medwell's play, *Fulgens and Lucres*, for example, when some characters are in need of entertainment, one proposes a basse danse in the Spanish style and calls for the minstrels. Another character answers that one of the shawm players has a sore lip and is so sick he cannot play.[90]

In the anonymous *The Shepherds*, one of the Chester mystery plays, there is a scene in which the illiterate [English] shepherds who heard the angel sing, announcing to them the birth of Jesus, argue at length trying to decide what the [Latin!] words were which they heard in this music. 'Gloria' was heard by one as 'grorus glorus.' No, says another, it was 'glorus, glarus, glorius,' etc. Finally, they give up and decide that they should sing something to bring them solace and a passing Trowle teaches them to sing a popular song, 'Trolly, lolly, lolly, lo.'[91]

In another mystery play, in a passage which seems incomplete, there appears to be the humorous suggestion of a trio of devils.

2ND DEMON. Nibble the alto shall ye,
Then the treble falls to me …[92]

In Medwall's *Fulgens and Lucres* there is a challenge to a singing contest, much like those found in ancient Greek lyric poetry. A character declares he can sing as well as any man in Kent and will sing any kind of song his opponent selects. When he begins to sing, he first complains of being in poor voice and then is accused of incorrect rhythm. When he offers to begin again, the lady who is to be the prize of the contest says, no, we will try this by some other manner of mastery than singing![93]

Granted, these are very mild forms of humor associated with music and we should not want to make too much of the point. Nevertheless, we must regard humor as yet another facet of the more complete picture of man made possible by the humanists. And perhaps, in its own way, the presence of humor represents the final break with the grim Christian fathers of the Middle Ages, who said, after all, that the true Christian should never laugh![94]

90 Ibid., II, 375ff.

91 *The Shepherds*, 386ff., quoted in David Mills, *The Chester Mystery Cycle* (East Lansing: Colleagues Press, 1992), 140ff.

92 *The Judgement*, quoted in Rose, *The Wakefield Mystery Plays*, 454.

93 *Fulgens and Lucres*, I, 1110ff.

94 The premise for this belief was because in no case is Jesus described as laughing in the New Testament!

EPILOGUE

IN THE FOLLOWING TWO VOLUMES in this series the reader will discover that sixteenth century art music begins to share many of the characteristics of art music as we know it today. Consider, for example, this description of a group of listeners to a performance by the lute virtuoso, Francesco da Milano, in 1555.

> He made the very strings to swoon beneath his fingers and transported all who listened into such gentle melancholy that one present buried his head in his hands, another let his entire body slump into an ungainly posture with members all awry, while another, his mouth sagged open and his eyes more than half shut, seemed, one would judge, as if transfixed upon the strings, and yet another, with chin sunk upon his chest, hiding the most sadly taciturn visage ever seen, remained abstracted in all his senses save his hearing, as if his soul had fled from all the seats of sensibility to take refuge in his ears where more easefully it could rejoice in such enchanting symphony.[1]

1 Pontus de Tyard, *Solitaire second* (1555).

This description of art music must make startling and puzzling reading to anyone who knows the Renaissance only from general music history texts, which leave the impression that the history of Renaissance music is the history of polyphonic church music, with a chapter or two set aside for some secular vocal forms. But what led to a performance such as the one above? It was certainly not the tradition of polyphonic Church music which prepared an aesthetic experience of this nature. There are no descriptions of fourteenth- and fifteenth-century Church music performances which describe listeners like these. So where did such music come from? Did it just magically appear from nowhere? Are we missing something?

The truth is Renaissance music consisted of a great deal more than Church music. In the present book alone, one will find a great many references to a vast scene of musical performance which is nowhere discussed in today's general music history texts. And it was this 'missing music,' *secular* art music, which prepared the way for performances such as the one above.

The irony is that the very music upon which musicology has constructed its history for this period we call 're-birth,' is music which more than a few persons actually living during the Renaissance considered to be Scholastic and anachronistic. And they were absolutely correct. Renaissance polyphonic Church music was the final development of a philosophy which held music to be a branch of mathematics. The entire concept of proportions and the approach to part-writing, not to mention the theoretical treatises of this period, clearly demonstrate the aesthetic kinship of the Church composers to the older Scholastic mathematics-based theories of music.

In writing the narrow history it has, musicology has in the process obscured our view of many important individuals. Consider, for example, a few men from the fourteenth century. Petrarch was praised by his contemporaries as a musician, but we have abandoned him to the Department of Ancient Literature. Why didn't Gustave Reese tell us that Chaucer was a composer?[2] And poor Machaut. He went to considerable lengths to collect, organize and even index his secular music so it would be remembered by posterity. We are convinced that he would have been utterly astonished and bewildered at the thought that anyone would remember him as a composer of Church music.

For the fifteenth century, let us only mention Leonardo da Vinci. Not only was he also a musician, but one of his contemporaries said he 'surpassed all musicians of his time.' Why is Leonardo *the musician* not mentioned in general music history texts?

Someone needs to write a new general history of music in the Renaissance and it needs to accomplish two things. First, it needs to account for the *entire* broad spectrum of music making in the fourteen, fifteenth and sixteenth centuries, and not just Church music and secular vocal music. Second, there is a great need to clarify the fact that the important story in the Renaissance is not the story of the death of Scholasticism in music, but the story of the birth of Humanism.

2 The single reference to Chaucer in his *Music in the Renaissance* is for the purpose of telling us who his daughter married!

BIBLIOGRAPHY

Aerde, R. van. *Notes pour server à l'histoire de la musique du theatre et de la danse à Malines*. Malines, 1925.
Alberti, Leon Battista. *I Libri dela Famiglia*. Translated by Renée Watkins. Columbia: University of South Carolina Press, 1969.
Anglès, H. 'La musica en la corte del rey Don Alfonso V de Aragon.' *Gesammelte Aufsätze zur Kulturgeschichte Spaniens* (1940).
———. 'Musikalische Beziehungen zwischen Deutschland und Spanien in der Zeit vom 5. bis 14. Jahrhunderts.' *Archiv für Musikwissenschaft* (1959).
Anonymous. *Il Novellino*. Translated by Edward Storer. London: Routledge, 1925.
———. *Journal d'un Bourgeois de Paris*. Paris, 1888.
———. *The Pearl*. Translated by Mary Hillmann. Convent Station, NJ: College of Saint Elizabeth Press, 1959.
———. *Villotta*. Quoted in John Addington Symonds. *Renaissance in Italy*. New York: Capricorn Books, 1964.
Appelbaum, Stanley. *The Triumph of Maximilian I*. New York: Dover Publications, 1964.
Axon, William. *Caxton's Game and Playe of the Chesse*. London, 1883.
Baines, Anthony. 'Fifteenth-century Instruments in Tinctoris's De Inventine et Usu Musicae.' *The Galpin Society Journal* 3 (March 1950): 19–26.
Barbure, L. de. 'La musique à Anvers aux XIVe, XVe, et XVIe Siècles.' *Annales de l'Académie Royale d'Archéologie de Belgique* (1906).
Bazin-Tacchella, Sylvie. *Le Livre du Voir-Dit de Guillaume de Machaut*. Paris: Société des bibliophiles français, 1875.
Bergin, Thomas G. 'An Introduction to Bocaccio.' In *Decameron*. Translated by Mark Musa and Peter Bondanella. New York: Norton, 1977.
Bernard, M. B. 'Recherches sur l'histoire de la Corporation des Ménétriers ou Joueurs d'Instruments de la Ville de Paris.' *Bibliothèque de l'École chantes* (April, 1842).
Blake, N. *Caxton's Own Prose*. London: Andre Deutsch, 1973.
Blunt, Anthony. *Artistic Theory in Italy, 1450–1600*. Oxford: Clarendon Press, 1959.
Boccaccio. 'Medea.' In *Concerning Famous Women*. Translated by Guido Guarino. New Brunswick: Rutgers University Press, 1963.
———. *Amorous Fiammetta*. Translated by Edward Hutton. Westport: Greenwood Press, 1926.
———. *Decameron*. Translated by John Payne. Berkeley: University of California Press, 1982.
———. *Decameron*. Translated by Mark Musa and Peter Bondanella. New York: Norton, 1977.
———. *Filostrato*. Translated by Nathaniel Griffin and Arthur Myrick. New York: Bilbo and Tannen, 1967.
———. *L'Ameto*. Translated by Judith Serafini-Sauli. New York: Garland, 1985.
———. *The Corbaccio*. Translated by Anthony Cassell. Urbana: University of Illinois Press, 1975.
———. *The Fates of Illustrious Men*. Translated by Louis Hall. New York: Ungar, 1965.
———. *Theseus*. Translated by Bernadette McCoy. New York: Medieval Text Association, 1974.
Boehner, Philotheus. *Ockham, Philosophical Writings*. Edinburgh: Thomas Nelson, 1959.
Bowers, Roger, 'Obligation, Agency, and Laissez-Faire: The Promotion of Polyphonic Composition for the Church in Fifteenth-Century England,' in Iain Fenlon, *Music in Medieval and Early Modern Europe*. Cambridge: Cambridge University Press, 1981.

Bowles, Edmund. 'Instruments at the Court of Burgundy.' *The Galpin Society Journal* 6 (July 1953): 41–51.
———. *Musikleben im 15. Jahrhundert*. Leipzig: Deutscher Verlag für Musik, 1977.
Brant, Sebastian. *The Ship of Fools*. Translated by Edwin Zeydel. New York: Columbia University Press, 1944.
Bridge, Joseph, 'Town Waits and their Tunes.' *Proceedings of the Musical Association* 54 (1928): 63–92.
Buchon, Jean Alexandre. *Chroniques de Froissart*. Paris: Verdière, 1824.
Buck, M. R., ed. *Ulrichs von Richental Chronik des Constanzer Conzils*. Tüblingen, 1882.
Byrne, Maurice. 'Instruments for the Goldsmiths Company.' *The Galpin Society Journal* 24 (July 1971): 63–68.
Calmo, Andrea. *Lettere*. Edited by Vittorio Rosso. Turin: Loescher, 1888.
Carpenter, Nan Cooke. *Music in the Medieval and Renaissance Universities*. Norman: University of Oklahoma Press, 1958.
Casteele, D. Van de. 'Préludes historiques dur la Ghilde des ménéstrels de Bruges.' *Annales de la Société d'Emulation* (3e série), III.
Cellesi, L. 'Documenti per la storia musicale di Firenze.' *Rivista Musicale Italiana* (1927).
Champion, Pierre. *La vie de Charles d'Orléans*. Paris: H. Champion, 1911.
Chaucer, Geoffrey. *The Complete Works of Geoffrey Chaucer*. Edited by F. N. Robinson. Boston: Houghton Mifflin, 1933.
Clercq, J. du. *Mémoires*. Paris, 1838.
Closson, E. *La facture des instruments de musique en Belgique*. Brussels: Degrace, 1935.
Commynes, Philippe de. *The Memoirs of Philippe de Commynes*. Translated by Isabelle Cazeau. Columbia: University of South Carolina Press, 1969.
Comper, Frances. *The Life of Richard Rolle*. London: Dent, 1929.
Conrad von Zabern. *De modo bene cantandi*. Translated by Joseph Dyer as 'Singing with Proper Refinement.' *Early Music* 6, no. 2 (April 1978): 207–227.
Cortesi, Paolo. 'De cardinalatu libri tres,' in *Music and Culture in Italy from the Middle Ages to the Baroque*. Cambridge: Harvard University Press, 1984.
D'Amico, John. *Renaissance Humanism in Papal Rome*. Baltimore: Johns Hopkins University Press, 1983.
Deschamps, Eustache. *Oeuvres complètes*. 11 vols. Paris, 1878–1903.
d'Escouchy, Mathieu. *Chronique*. Paris, 1863–1864.
Dahnk, E., 'Musikausubung an den Hofen von Burgund und Orleans wahrend des 15. Jahrhunderts.' *Archiv für Kulturgeschichte* (1934–1936).
Davies, R. T. *Medieval English Lyrics*. Evanston: Northwestern University Press, 1964.
Duncan, Edmonstoune. *The Story of Minstrelsy*. Detroit, 1968.
Durant, Will. *The Reformation*. New York: Simon and Schuster, 1957.
———. *The Renaissance*. New York: Simon and Schuster, 1953.
Dyer, Joseph. 'Singing with Proper Refinement.' *Early Music* 6, no. 2 (April 1978): 207–227.
Esperabé y Arteaga, Enrique. *Historia pragmática é interna de la Universidad de Salamanca*. Salamanca, 1914–1917.
Fant, E. M. *Scriptores Rerum medii Aevi*. Upsala, 1818.
Farmer, Henry. 'Music in Mediaeval Scotland.' *Proceedings of the Musical Association* 54 (1930): 69–90.
Federhofer, H. 'Beitrage zur altern Musikgeschichte Karntens.' *Carinthia* (1955).
Fester, R. 'Die Fortsetzung der Flores temporum von Reinbold Slecht.' *Zeitschrift für die Geschichte des Oberrheins* (1894).
Figg, Kristen. *The Short Lyric Poems of Jean Froissart*. New York: Garland Publishing, 1994.

Fons-Mélicocq, Alexandre de la. 'Les minstrels de Lille,' in *Archives historiques et littéraires du Nord*. Valenciennes: Bureau des archive, 1885.

Froissart, Jean. *Chroniques de Froissart*. Osnabrück: Biblio Verlag, 1967.

———. *The Chroniques de Froissart*. Translated by John Bourchier [1523]. New York: AMS Press, 1967.

Gachard, Louis Prosper. *Collection de documents inédits concernant la Belgique*. Bruxelles, 1833–1835.

Galpin, Francis William. *Old English Instruments of Music*. London: Methuen, 1910.

Ghisi, Federico. 'An Angel Concert in a Trecento Sienese Fresco.' In *Aspects of Medieval and Renaissance Music*. New York: Norton, 1966.

Gilliodts-Van Severen, Louis. 'Les ménestrels de Bruges.' *Essais d'Archéologie Brugeoise*. Bruges, 1912.

Giovio, Paolo. *Leonardi Vencii Vita*. 1528.

Goldron, Romain. *Minstrels and Masters*. [N.p.]: H. S. Stuttman, 1968.

Gower, John. 'Prologue to *Confessio Armantis*,' quoted in *Survey of British Poetry*. New York: Poetry Anthology Press, 1988.

———. 'The Voice of One Crying.' Translated by Eric Stockton, *The Major Latin Works of John Gower*. Seattle: University of Washington Press, 1962.

Grossmann, Walter. *Die einleitenden Kapitel des 'Speculum Musicae'*. Leipzig, 1924.

Grove, George. *The New Grove Dictionary of Music and Musicians*. Edited by Stanley Sadie. London: Macmilan, 1980.

Gundersheimer, Werner. *Ferrara*. Princeton, NJ: Princeton University Press, 1973.

Hayes, Gerald, 'Musical Instruments.' *New Oxford History of Music*. London, 1960.

———. *King's Music*. London: Oxford University Press, 1937.

Henderson, Ernest. *A Short History of Germany*. New York: Macmillan, 1916.

Henne, Anton. *Die Klingenberger Chronik*. Gotha, 1861.

Huguenin, J. F. *Les chroniques de la ville de Metz*. Metz, 1838.

Hunt, Leigh. *Stories from the Italian Poets*. London: Chapman and Hall, 1846.

Jacquot, Albert. *La musique en Lorraine*. Paris: de A. Quantin, 1882.

Jacquot, Jean. *La Musique Instrumental de la Renaissance*. Paris, 1955.

John XXII. *Docta Santorum*, quoted in H. E. Wooldridge. *The Oxford History of Music*, 2nd edition. London: Oxford University Press, 1929.

Kastner, Georges. *Manuel Général de Musique Militaire*. Paris, 1848.

Kendall, Paul. *Richard the Third*. New York: Norton, 1955.

Kinkeldy, Otto. *Orgel und Klavier in der Musik des 16. Jahrhunderts*. Leipzig, Breitkopf & Härtel, 1910.

Knighton, Tess. 'The Spanish Court of Ferdinand and Isabella,' in *The Renaissance*. Englewood Cliffs: Prentice Hall, 1989.

Kristeller, Paul, 'Music and Learning in the Early Italian Renaissance.' *The Journal of Renaissance and Baroque Music* (1947).

La Marche, Olivier de. *Mémoires*. Paris, 1883–1888.

———. *Mémoires*. Paris, 1885.

Laborde, Léon Emmanuel Simon Joseph de. *Les ducs de Bourgogne*. Paris, 1849.

Lang, Karl Heinrich Ritter von. *Neuere Geschichte des Fürstentums Biruth*. Göttingen, 1798.

Langland, William. *Piers Plowman*. Translated by E. Talbot Donaldson. New York: Norton, 1990.

Larner, John. *Culture and Society in Italy, 1290–1420*. New York: Scribner's, 1971.

Lefébre, L. *Histoire du theater de Lille*. Lille, 1907.

Lefèvre, Jean. *Chronique*. Paris, 1876.

Lescurel, Jehan de. 'Amour, voulés vous accorder,' in Nigel Wilkins, *One Hundred Ballades, Rondeaux and Virelais*. Cambridge: University Press, 1969.

Lettenhove, Kervyn de. 'Chroniques relatives à l'histoire de Belgique sous la domination des ducs de Bourgogne,' in *Livre des trahisons de France*. Brussels, 1873.

———. 'Fragment inedit de Froissart.' *Bulletin de l'Académie royale de Belgiques* (1886), XXV.

Lockwood, Lewis. 'Strategies of Music Patronage in the Fifteenth Century: the Cappella of Ercole I d'Este,' in *Music in Medieval and Early Modern Europe*. Edited by Iain Fenton. Cambridge: Cambridge University Press, 1981.

Lomazzo, Giovanni Paolo. *Idea del Tempio della Pittura*. Milan: Per Paolo Gottardo Ponto, 1590.

Longman, William. *The History of the Life and Times of Edward the Third*. London: Longsman, Green & Co., 1869.

Lydgate, John. *Fall of Princes*. Edited by Henry Bergen. London: Oxford University Press, 1967.

———. *John Lydgate Poems*. Oxford: Clarendon Press, 1966.

———. *The Life of Saint Alban and Saint Amphibal*. Edited by J. E. Van Der Westhuizen. Leiden: Brill, 1974.

———. *Lydgate's Reson and Sensuallyte*. Edited by Ernst Sieper. London: Oxford University Press, 1901.

Machaut, Guillaume de. *Oeuvres*. Edited by Ernest Hoepffner. Paris: Firmin-Didot, 1908–1921.

———. *Musikalische Werke*. Edited by Friedrich Ludwig. Leipzig: Breitkopf & Härtel, 1926.

———. *La Prise d'Alexandre*. Edited by L. de Mas Latrie. Geneva, 1877.

———. *Le Judgment du roy de Behaigne*. Translated by James Wimsatt and William Kibler. Athens: The University of Georgia Press, 1988.

———. *Remede de Fortune*. Translated by James Wimsatt and William Kibler. Athens: The University of Georgia Press, 1988.

———. *The Judgment of the King of Navarre*. Translated by Barton Palmer. New York: Garland Publishing, 1988.

———. *The Tale of the Alerion*. Translated by Minnette Gaudet and Constance Hieatt. Toronto: University of Toronto Press, 1994.

Manetti, Giannozzo. *The Life of Giovanni Boccaccio*. Quoted in *The Decameron*. Translated by Mark Musa and Peter Bondanella. New York: Norton, 1977.

Marchetto of Padua. *Lucidarium*. Translated by Jan. W. Herlinger. Chicago: University of Chicago Press, 1985.

Marix, Jeanne. *Histoire de la Musique et des Musiciens de la Cour de Bourgogne sous le règne de Philippe le Bon*. Strasbourg: Heitz, 1953.

———. *Histoire de la Musique et des Musiciens de la Cour de Bourgogne sous le règne de Philippe le Bon*. Strasbourg: Heitz, 1939.

Mather, Christine. 'Maximilian I and his Instruments.' *Early Music* 3, no. 1 (Jan. 1975): 42–46.

Miller, Townsend. *Henry IV of Castile*. New York-Philadelphia: Lippincott, 1972.

Mills, David. *The Chester Mystery Cycle*. East Lansing, MI: Colleagues Press, 1992.

Monstrelet, Euguerrand de. *La Chronique d'Enguerran de Monstrelet*. Paris, 1857–1862.

Moser, Hans. 'Zur Mittelalterlichen Musikgeschichte der Stadt Köln.' *Archiv für Musikwissenschaft* (1964).

Motta, Emilio. *Musici alla Corte degli Sforza: ricerche e documenti milanesi*. Milan, 1887.

Nedden. O. *Quellen und Studien zur oberrheinischen Musikgeschichte im 15 und 16 Jahrhundert*. Kassel: Bärenreiter, 1931.

Nef, K. 'Die Stadtpfeiferei und die Instrumentalmusiker in Basel.' *Sammelbande der Internationalen Musikgesellschaft* (1908).

Nicholas of Cusa. *On God as Not-Other*. Translated by Jasper Hopkins. Minneapolis: University of Minnesota Press, 1979.

———. 'A defense of Learned Ignorance.' Translated by Jasper Hopkins, in *Nicholas of Cusa's Debate with John Wenck*. Minneapolis: Banning Press, 1981.

———. 'Compendium.' Translated by William Wertz, in *Toward a New Council of Florence*. Washington, DC: Schiller Institute, 1993.

———. 'De Sapientia.' Translated by John Dolan, in *Unity and Reform*. Chicago: The University of Notre Dame Press, 1962.

———. 'On 'Actualized-possibility.' Translated by Jasper Hopkins, in *A Concise Introduction to the Philosophy of Nicholas of Cusa*. Minneapolis: Banning Press, 1978.

———. 'On Beryllus.' Translated by William Wertz, in *Toward a New Council of Florence*. Washington, DC: Schiller Institute, 1993.

———. 'On Conjectures.' Translated by William Wertz, in *Toward a New Council of Florence*. Washington, DC: Schiller Institute, 1993.

———. 'The Filation of God.' Translated by William Wertz, in *Toward a New Council of Florence*. Washington, DC: Schiller Institute, 1993.

———. 'Theological Complement.' Translated by William Wertz, in *Toward a New Council of Florence*. Washington, DC: Schiller Institute, 1993.

Osgood, Charles, trans. *Boccaccio on Poetry*. New York: The Liberal Arts Press, 1956.

Oviedo, Gonzalo Fernández de. *Libro de la cámara real del principe don Juan*. Madrid, 1870.

Page, Christopher. 'Early 15th-century instruments in Jean de Gerson's Tactatus de Canticis.' *Early Music* 6, no. 3 (July 1978): 339–349.

———. 'Machaut's "Pupil" Deschamps on the Performance of Music.' *Early Music* 5 (1978).

Palisca, Claude V. 'An Italian Renaissance in Music?' In *Humanism in Italian Renaissance Musical Thought*. New Haven: Yale University Press, 1985.

Parrish, Carl. *Dictionary of Musical Terms*. New York: Free Press of Glencoe, 1963.

Petrarch, Francesco. *Letters from Petrarch*. Edited by Morris Bishop. Bloomington: Indiana University Press, 1966.

———. *Petrarch's Bucolicum Carmen*. Translated by Thomas Bergin. New Haven: Yale University Press, 1974.

———. *Petrarch's Lyric Poems*. Translated by Robert Durling. Cambridge: Harvard University Press, 1976.

———. *Remedies for Fortune Fair and Foul*. Translated by Conrad Rawski. Bloomington: Indiana University Press, 1991.

Pirro, André. *Histoire de la Musique de la fin du XIVe siècle a la fin du XVIe*. Paris: Librarie Renouard, 1940.

Pirrotta Nino and Elena Povoledo. *Music and Theatre from Poliziano to Monteverdi*. Cambridge: Cambridge University Press, 1982.

Pirrotta, Nino. 'Ars Nova and Stil Novo.' In *Music and Culture in Italy from the Middle Ages to the Baroque*. Cambridge: Harvard University Press, 1984.

Pisan, Christine de. *Le Livre des Fais et Bonnes Meurs du Sage Roy Charles V*. Edited by S. Solente. Paris: H. Champion, 1936.

———. 'Le livre du duc des vrais amants,' in *Oeuvres poétiques*. Paris, 1898.

———. *Christine's Vision*. Translated by Glenda McLeod. New York: Garland Publishing, 1993.

———. *Mirror of Honor: the Treasury of the City of Ladies*. Translated by Charity Willard. Tenafly, NH: Bard Hall Press, 1989.
———. *The Book of the Body Politic*. Translated by Kate Forrhan. Cambridge: Cambridge University Press, 1994.
———. *The Book of the Duke of True Lovers*. Translated by Thelma Fenster. New York: Persea Books, 1991.
———. *The Epistle of the Prison of Human Life*. Translated by Josette Wisman. New York: Garland Publishing, 1984.
Poliziano, Angelo. *Orpheus*. Translated by Louis Lord. Oxford: Oxford University Press, 1931.
———. *Stanze*. Translated by David Quint. University Park, PA: Pennsylvania State University Press, 1993.
Polk, Keith. 'Civic Patronage and Instrumental Ensembles in Renaissance Florence.' AD [Xerox], ca. 1982.
———. 'Ensemble Instrumental Music in Flanders: 1450–1550.' AD [Xerox], ca. 1982.
———. 'Instrumental music in the Urban Centres of Renaissance Germany.' *Early Music History*, VII.
Pontus de Tyard. *Solitaire second* (1555).
Prizer, William F. 'North Italian Courts, 1460–1540,' in *The Renaissance*. Edited by Ian Fenlon. Englewood Cliffs: Prentice Hall, 1989.
Prizer, William, 'Music and Ceremonial in the Low Countries.' *Early Music History* 5 (1985): 113–153.
Purcell, Mary. *The Great Captain*. Garden City, NY: Doubleday, 1962.
Purcell, Sally. *The Poems of Charles of Orleans*. Cheshire: Caranet Press, 1973.
Purvis, J. S. *The York Cycle*. London: S.P.C.K., 1957.
Rastall, Richard. 'Some English consort-Groupings of the late Middle Ages.' *Music & Letters* 55, no. 2 (1974): 179–202.
Reese, Gustave. *Music in the Middle Ages*. New York: Norton, 1940.
———. *Music in the Renaissance*. New York: Norton, 1959.
Richter, Jean Paul, ed. *The Literary Works of Leonardo da Vinci*. London: Phaidon, 1970.
Riegel, J. *Die Teilnuhmerlisten Konstanzer Konzils*. Freiburg, 1916.
Robinson, James. *Petrarch, The First Modern Scholar and Man of Letters*. New York: Putnam, 1914.
Rojas, Fernando de. *La Celestina*. Translated by J. M. Cohen. New York: New York University Press, 1966.
Rokseth, Y. *La musique d'orgue au XVe siècle et au début du XVIe*. Paris, 1930.
Rolle, Richard. 'Desyre and Delit.' Edited by Hope Allen, in *English Writings of Richard Rolle*. Oxford: Clarendon Press, 1963.
———. 'Love is Life.' Edited by Celia and Kenneth Sisam. *The Oxford Book of Medieval English Verse*. Oxford: Clarendon Press, 1970.
———. *Sir Gawain and the Green Knight*. Translated by Marie Borroff. New York: Norton, 1967.
———. *The Pricke of Conscience*. Berlin: A. Asher, 1863.
———, 'Of the Vertu,' in *English Prose Treatises of Richard Rolle*. Edited by Humphrey Milford for the English Text Society. London: Oxford University Press, 1866.
Rose, Martial. *The Wakefield Mystery Plays*. London: Evans Brothers, 1961.
Ruiz, Juan. *The Book of True Love*. Translated by Saralyn Daly. University Park, PA: Pennsylvania State University Press, 1978.
Sachs, Curt. *The History of Musical Instruments*. New York: Norton, 1940.
———. *World History of the Dance*. New York, 1937.
Salmen, Walter. *Der Fahrende Musiker im Europäischen Mittelalter*. Kassel: J. P. Hinnenthal-Verlag, 1960.

Sanctis, Francesco de. 'Boccaccio and the Human Comedy.' In *The Decameron*. Translated by Mark Musa and Peter Bondanella. New York: Norton, 1977.
Schmidt, Günther. *Die Musik am Hofe des Markgrafen von Brandenburg-Ansbach vom ausgehenden Mittelalter bis 1806*. München, 1953.
Schuler, M., 'Die Musik in Konstanz während des Konzils 1414–1418.' *Acta Musicologica* (1966).
Seymour, M. C. *Selections from Hoccleve*. Oxford: Clarendon Press, 1981.
Siculus, Marineus L. *De las cosas memorables de España* (1539).
Simons, Eric Norman. *The Reign of Edward IV*. London: F. Muller, 1966.
Slootmans, Korneel, 'De Hoge Lieve Vrouwe van Bergen-op-Zoom.' *Jaerboek van de Oudheidkundige Kring de Ghulden Roos*, XXV.
Smith, Joseph F. 'Ars Nova—A Re-Definition?' *Musica Disciplina* (1964), XVIII.
Smithers, Don L. *The Music and History of the Baroque Trumpet*. London: Dent, 1973.
Steegmann, Mary, trans. *Tales from Sacchetti*. Westport: Hyperion Press, 1978.
Steele, Robert. *The English Poems of Charles of Orleans*. London: Oxford University Press, 1941.
Stevens, John. *Music & Poetry in the Early Tudor Court*. London: Methuen, 1961.
Stinger, Charles. *Humanism and the Church Fathers*. Albany: State University of New York Press, 1977.
———. *The Renaissance in Rome*. Bloomington: Indiana University Press, 1985.
Strunk, Oliver. *Source Readings in Music History*. New York: Norton, 1950.
Subirá, José. *Historia de la Música*. Barcelona: Salvat, 1947.
Sullivan, Henry. *Juan del Encina*. Boston: Twayne, 1976.
Symonds, John Addington. *Renaissance in Italy*. New York: Capricorn Books, 1964.
———. *Renaissance in Italy*. New York: Holt, 1881.
Tagliavini, L. F. 'La Scuola musicale Bolognese.' *Musiciati della scuola emiliana*. Siena, 1956.
Telemachos. 'Odyssey,' quoted in Nino Pirrotta, 'Music and Cultural Tendencies in 15th Century Italy.' *Journal of the American Musicological Society* (1966).
The Norton Anthology of English Literature. Edited by M. H. Abrams, et. al. New York: Norton, 1968.
The Practica musicae of Franchinus Gafurius. Translated by Irwin Young. Madison: University of Wisconsin Press, 1969.
Thibault, G. 'Le concert Instrumental au XVe Siècle,' in Jean Jacquot. *La Musique Instrumental de la Renaissance*. Paris, 1955.
Thompson, James. *Economic and Social History of Europe in the Later Middle Ages*. New York: Century Co., 1931.
Tinctoris, Johannes. *Concerning the Nature and Propriety of Tones*. Translated by Albert Seay. Colorado Springs: Colorado College Music Press, 1976.
———. *Proportionale Musices*. Translated by Albert Seay. *Journal of Music Theory* 1, no. 1 (March 1957): 22–75.
———. *The Art of Counterpoint*. Translated by Albert Seay. American Institute of Musicology, 1961.
Toulmon, B. de. 'Dissertation sur les instruments de musique.' *Memoires de la Société des antiquaries de France* (1844).
Trask, Williard. *Medieval Lyrics of Europe*. New York: World Publishing Company, 1969.
Twici, Guyllaume. *L'art de vénerie*. Translated by A. Dryden. Northhampton, MA, 1908.
Ulrichs von Richental. *Das Konzil zu Konstanz*. Konstanz: Starnberg Keller, 1964.
Valeri, Francesco Malaguzzi. *La Corte di Lodovico il Moro: La vita private e l'arte a Milano nella seconda metà del quattrocento*. Milan: Ulrico Hoepli, 1913

Vaneer Straeten, Edmond. *La Musique aux Pays Bas avante le XIXe Siècle*. New York, 1969.
Vaughan, Richard. *Philip the Good*. New York: Barnes & Noble, 1970.
Vesce, Thomas E., trans. *The Knight of the Parrot*. New York: Garland, 1986.
Vessella, Alessandro. *La Banda*. Milan: Istituto editoriale nazionale, 1935.
Villon, François. 'The Testament.' Edited by William Williams. *The Complete Works of François Villon*. New York: David McKay, 1960.
Vitry, Philippe de. 'Ars Nova.' Translated by Leon Plantinga. *Journal of Music Theory* 5 (1961).
Walsingham, Thomas. *Historia anglicana*. London: Longman, 1863.
Wangermée, Robert. *Flemish Music*. New York, 1968.
Warwick, Alan. *A Noise of Music*. London: Queen Anne Press, 1968.
Werner, Arno. *Vier Jahrhunderte im Dienste der Kirchenmusik*. Leipzig: Mersseburger, 1933.
Wilkins, Nigel. *Two Miracles*. Edinburgh: Scottish Academic Press, 1972.
William of Ockham. 'Epistemological Problems,' in Philotheus Boehner. *Ockham, Philosophical Writings*. Edinburgh: Thomas Nelson, 1959.
Woodfill, Walter. *Musicians in English Society*. Princeton, NJ: Princeton Uniersity Press, 1953.
Wright, Craig. 'Antoine Brumel and Patronage at Paris,' in *Music in Medieval and Early Modern Europe*. Cambridge: Cambridge University Press, 1918.
———. 'Performance Practices at the Cathedral of Cambrai 1475–1550.' *The Musical Quarterly* 64, no. 3 (July 1978): 295–328.
Wylie, James Hamilton. *History of England under Henry the Fourth*. London, 1884.
Young, Irwin, trans. *The Practica musicae of Franchinus Gaffurius*. Madison: University of Wisconsin Press, 1969.

INDEX

A

Adam, first man, 269
Alberti, Leon Battista, b. 1404, Florentine philosopher, 161, 164ff, 167, 169, 172ff
Alberto, Florentine artist, 8
Albrecht of Brandenburg, 1440–1486, 282
Alcibiades, 5th century BC, nephew to Pericles, 36
Alexander the Great, 356–323, 9
Alfonso V, 1416–1458, of Aragon, 295
Ambrosio da Pessano, 15th church singer in Milan, 188
Anthony of Dornstätt, flutist under Maximilian I, 280
Antigonus, teacher of Alexander the Great, 9
Aquilanus, Seraphinus, 15th century singer, 184
Aristotle, 384–322 BC, Greek philosopher, 5, 27, 105, 239, 241, 261, 289
Aristoxenus, 4th Century BC philosopher, 90, 171
Athanasius, 296–373 writer of Alexandria, 35
Augustin, cornettist under Maximilian I, 278
Augustine of Augsburg, 15th century civic musician in Florence, 178

B

Bembo, Pietro, 15th century poet, 181
Binchois, ca. 1400–1460 Franco-Flemish composer, 211, 221, 228, 241
Boccaccio, Giovanni, 1313–1375, Italian writer, 1ff, 8, 18, 28, 32, 45ff, 144
Boethius, 475–524 AD, mathematician, politician, 147, 238ff, 255
Boiardo, Matteo Maria, 1434–1494, Italian philosopher, poet, 165, 168
Boldrani, Pietro, trumpeter in Treviso, 11
Bonandrea, Giovanni, 14th century lecturer in rhetoric at Bologna, 13
Bono, Pietro of Ferrara, Lutanist, 250
Borso d'Este of Ferrara, 1450–1471, 179
Brant, Sebastian, 1457–1521, German writer, 256ff, 260ff, 266, 271, 284ff
Brumel, 162
Burgkmair, Hans, 15th century artist, 277

C

Caligula, 12–41 AD, Roman emperor, 36
Calmeta (Colli), Vincenzo, 1460–1508, Italian writer, 172
Caxton, William, 1422–1491, English writer, 310, 317
Celtes, Conradus, 1459–1508, German Renaissance humanist, 253, 279
Chandos, John, singer under Edward III, 132
Charles IV of France, 14
Charles the Bold of Burgundy, 1433–1477, 214, 216, 223, 229ff, 250
Charles V, 69 footnote 1, 95
Charles VI, 1368–1422, King of France, 212, 320
Charles VII, 1403–1461, King of France, 224
Charles VIII of France, 1483–1498, 213
Charles, Duke d'Orléans, 1394–1465, 213
Chastellain, George, 15th century French chronicler, 228
Chaucer, Geoffrey, 1340–1400, English writer, 137ff, 319, 324
Christine de Pizan, 1364–1430, French writer, 95, 224ff
Cicero, 106 – 43 BC, Roman orator, 18, 26, 36, 56, 171, 245
Ciconia, Johannes, 1335–1411, Italian composer, 11
Colonna, 14th century cardinal, 18
Colonna, Francesco, 1433–1527, Italian monk, writer, 18, 161
Compère, Loyset, 1445–1518, French composer, 162
Confrérie de St. Julien, 14th century, 101
Conrad von Zabern, 1410–1481, writer on church singing, 272ff
Convenevole da Prata, 13th century, teacher of Petrarch, 21
Copernicus, Nicolaus, 1473–1543, 1
Corio, Bernardino, 15th century historian, 180
Cortesi, Paolo, 1465–1510, Italian humanist philolopher, 162 footnote 6, 168, 170, 186

Corvinus, Matthias, 1443–1490, King of Hungary, 283
Cyrus of Persia, 6th century BC, 212

D

Dante, 13th century Roman poet, 12
Demetrius, 2nd century BC, painter, 170
Demoncritus, 460–370 BC, Greek philosopher, 7
Dolcibene, distinguished 14th century performer, 14
Domenico da Prato, 1389–1433, Florentine writer, 10
Domitian, 81–96 AD, Roman emperor, 25, 33
Douglas, Lord James of Scotland, 131
Dufay, Guillaume, 1397–1474, Burgundian composer, 211, 221, 228, 231, 236, 238ff, 244
Dunstable, John, 1390–1453, English composer, 211, 221, 239
Durán, Domingo, 15th century Spanish music treatise, 299

E

Edward II, 1284–1327, King of England, 134
Edward III of England, 1327–1377, 128, 132
Edward IV of England, 1461–1483, 320
Enrique IV, 15th century King of Castile, 301
Ercole I of Ferrara, 1471–1505, 179
Este, Beatrice, 1475–1497, 180
Este, Isabella, 1474–1539, 1805ff
Eustache Deschamps, ca. 1346–1406, French poet, 69, 83, 93, 102

F

Federigo da Montefeltro, 1444–1482, of Urbino, 182
Feltre, Vittorino da, leader of humanist school in Mantua, 185
Ferdinand I of Naples, 237
Fernando V, 1474–1516, of Aragon, 295ff
Ficino, Marsilio, 1433–1499, humanist philosopher, 164, 173
Francesco da Milano, 16th century lutanist, 323
Frederick III, 1440–1493, emperor, Holy Roman Empire, 229, 249, 277
Froissart, 1337–1405, chronicler, 131ff, 227

G

Gaffurio, Franchino, 1451–1522, Italian theorist, 161 fn. 1, 165, 171ff, 187
Galileo, 1564–1642, Italian physicist, 1
Gian Galeazzo, Visconti of Milan, 14th century, 15
Giorgio Vasari, 1511–1574, Italian biographer of artists, 191, 206
Giovio, Paolo, contemporary biographer of Leonardo, 191
Giustiniani, Leonardo, 1388–1446, solo singer, 163, 188
Godefridus, famous 15th century shawm player, 249
Gonzalo de Ovedo, 15th century Spanish writer, 296
Gower, John, 1330–1408, English philosopher, 111, 115
Greban, Arnoul, author of a 15th century mystery play, 221
Gregory the Great, pope, 540–604, 6
Guido d'Arezzo, 241, 299
Gutenberg, Johannes, 1398–1468, German printer, 1

H

Heinrich, German lutanist under Charles the Bold, 250
Henry IV of England, 1399–1413, 319
Henry V of England, 1413–1422, 319
Henry VI of England, 1422–1471, 320
Henry VII of England, 1485–1509, 320
Hoccleve, 1368–1426, English poet, 304
Homer, 8th – 9th century BC, Greek poet, 18
Horace, 65–27 BC, Roman philosopher, 27, 34, 248

I

Isaac, Heinrich, composer, 162, 183
Isabel of Portugal, 1503–1539, wife to Philip the Good, 232
Isabella of Urbino, 182
Isabella, 1474–1504, of Castile, 295ff

J

Jacopo da Bologna, 1340–1386, composer, 10
Jacques de Lièges, 1260–1330, music theorist, 70, 87ff
Jaime II, 1291–1327 of Aragon, 295
James I of Scotland, 1424–1437, 320
Jean de Gerson, 1363–1429, Chancellor of the University of Paris, 218ff, 226
Jean de Muris, ca. 1290–1350, music theorist, 92ff
Jean Froissart, 1337–1405, French poet, chronicler, 80, 86, 97, 99
Jehan de Lescurel, d. 1304, poet, 79

John II of France, 1350–1364, 97, 227
John the Fearless, 1404–1419 of Burgundy, 227ff
John XXII, pope, 1324–1325, 90ff
John XXIII, pope, 282
Juan del Encina, 1468–1529, Spanish philosopher, 291ff, 293 fn. 25
Juan I of Aragon, 1350–1396, 287, 295

K

King of Cyprus, 97

L

Lala of Cyzicus, 1st century BC female ancient painter, 53
Landini, Francesco, Italian composer, 1335–1397, 10
Langland, William, 1332–1386, English writer, 105, 120ff, 127, 130ff, 135
Laudsingers of Santa Maria Novella, 66
Leonardo da Vinci, 1452–1519, Italian artist, inventor, 1, 161, 170, 180, 191ff, 324
Lido, Antonio, 14th century professor of medicine and music at Padua, 13
Lomazzo, 16th century writer on Leonardo as a musician, 191
Loqueille, Richard de, 15th century French poet, 225
Lorenzo da Pavia, 15th century Italian keyboard maker, 181
Lorenzo the Magnificent, 1449–1492, Florentine, 182ff, 185
Louis IX, 1214–1270, King of France, 224
Lovato de Lovati, 14th century Italian poet, 14

Luther, 253
Lydgate, John, 1370–1450, English writer, 303ff

M

Machaut, Guillaume de, 1300–1377, French composer, 4, 69ff, 324
Marchetto of Padua, 1274–1319, music theorist, 5ff, 8ff, 13
Marcus Brutus, 85–42 BC Roman politician, 19
Margaret of England, wife to Charles the bold of Burgundy, 233
Maria d'Aquino, daughter to Robert, King of Naples, 45
Martin le Franc, 1410–1461, French poet, 211
Matteo of Perugia, 15th century church singer in Milan, 188
Maximilian I, 1459–1519, emperor, Holy Roman Empire, 178, 229, 277ff, 283
Medwall, Henry, b. 1461, English playwright, 306ff
Meister Eckhart, 1260–1327, German philosopher, 255
Michelet, Jules, 19th century writer, 1
Monteverdi, 66
Mozart, 26
Müller, Johann, German Renaissance humanist, 253

N

Nero, 37–68, Roman emperor, 36
Newton, Isaac, 1642–1727, 1
Neyschl, 15th century trombonist, Burgundian court, 277ff
Niccolò III of Ferrara, 1393–1441, 179
Nicholas of Cusa, 1401–1464, German philosopher, 254ff

Nicholas V, pope, 1447–1455, 161

O

Obrecht, Jacob, 1457–1505, Flemish composer, 231, 242
Ockeghem, Johannes, 1420–1496, Flemish composer, 211, 221, 238ff, 244
Odington, Walter, 14th century English theorist, 110
Orbus, Charles & Jean, Flemish brothers, artists on the viol, 250

P

Pericles, 495–429 BC Greek General, 36
Peter I, King of Cyprus, 10
Petrarch, Francesco, 1304–1374, 1ff, 8, 10, 12, 18ff, 46, 324
Philip I of Castile, 1478–1506, son of Maximilian I, 230
Philip the Bold of Burgundy, 1363–1404, 227ff
Philip the Good of Burgundy, 1419–1457, 228ff, 280
Philippe de Commynes, 1447–1511, French writer, diplomat, 214ff, 223
Philippe de Vitry, 1291–1361, French composer, music theorist, 32, 92
Pico della Mirandola, Giovanni, 15th century philosopher, 161, footnote 2
Pierre d'Auvergne, 1130–1170 French poet, 31
Pierre de Prost of Bruges, 15th c. instrument maker, 228
Pietro d'Anghiera, Italian musician in Spain, 287
Plato, 429–347 BC, Greek philosopher, 36, 37, 164257, 261
Poliziano, Angelo, 1454–1494, Italian poet, 162ff, 167, 172, 183ff, 185, 187, 189

Porrus, king who fought Alexander the Great, 9
Praetorius, Michael, 16th century composer, conductor, 273
Prosdocimus de Beldemandis, 15th century Italian theorist, 172
Ptolemy, 90
Pucci, Antonio, 14th century singer 12
Pythagoras, 570-490 BC, philosopher, 257, 267

R

Ramos de Pareja, 15th century professor at Salamanca, 299
René of Anjou, 15th century noble, 225
Richard II of England, 1377-1399, 128, 130ff
Richard III of England, 1483-1485, 320
Robert de la Magdelaine, singer under Philip the Good, 228
Rojas, Fernando, 15th century Spanish playwright, 288ff
Rolle, Richard, 14th century English poet, theologian, 110, 113ff, 117ff, 124, 126
Ruiz, Juan, 14th century Spanish poet, 287ff
Ruy Sánchez de Arévalo, 15th century Spanish educator, 296

S

Sacchetti, Franco, 1335-1400, poet & author of 'tales,' 7ff, 10, 12, 14
Salutati, Coluccio, 1331-1406, Church humanist, 6
Sardanapalus, King of, 264
Savonarola, 1452-1498, Florentine friar, politician, 162, 183
Seneca, 4 BC - 65 AD, Roman philosopher, 25, 43
Sforza, Bianca Maria, 1472-1510, 179
Sforza, Francesco, 1401-1466, Milan, 184
Sforza, Galeazzo Maria, 1466-1376, of Milan, 179
Sforza, Giangaleazzo, 1469-1494, Milan, 180
Sforza, Ludovico, 1481-1499, of Milan, 174, 180
Sigismund, 1368-1437, Emperor, Holy Roman Empire, 283
Socrates, 469-399 BC, Greek philosopher, 255, 257, 261
St. Ambrose, 374-397 Bishop of Milan, 6, 35, 66
St. Augustne, 354-430, Church leader, 6, 35, 105
St. Bernard, 12th century church leader, 6
St. Jerome, 347-420, 6, 254
Stewdl, trombonist under Maximilian I, 278

T

Terence, 195-159 Roman playwright, 38
Tinctoris, Johannes, 1435-1511, music theorist, 237ff
Traversari, Ambrogio, 1386-1439, monk, 163, 188
Trithemius, Johannes, abbot of Sponheim, 253
Tunstede, Simon, 14th century English theorist, 110

U

Ugolino of Orvieto, fl. ca. 1430-1435, Italian philosopher, 165

V

Valgulio, Carlo, papal secretary, 1481-1485, 170, 186
Valla, Giorgio, 1447-1500 Italian music theorist and philosopher, 166, 171
Varro, 116 - 27 BC, Roman writer, 38
Vergerio, Pietro, 14th century humanist and professor of logic at Padua, 13
Villon, François, 1431-1463, French poet and thief, 216, 218ff, 225
Virgil, 70-19 BC Roman poet, 6, 18, 38

W

Wenck, John, 15th century German writer, 255
William of Ockham, ca. 1300-1349, English philosopher, 106
Wimpheling, Jakob, 1450-1528, German Renaissance humanist, 253, 279

ABOUT THE AUTHOR

Dr. David Whitwell is a graduate ('with distinction') of the University of Michigan and the Catholic University of America, Washington DC (PhD, Musicology, Distinguished Alumni Award, 2000) and has studied conducting with Eugene Ormandy and at the Akademie fur Musik, Vienna. Prior to coming to Northridge, Dr. Whitwell participated in concerts throughout the United States and Asia as Associate First Horn in the USAF Band and Orchestra in Washington DC, and in recitals throughout South America in cooperation with the United States State Department.

At the California State University, Northridge, which is in Los Angeles, Dr. Whitwell developed the CSUN Wind Ensemble into an ensemble of international reputation, with international tours to Europe in 1981 and 1989 and to Japan in 1984. The CSUN Wind Ensemble has made professional studio recordings for BBC (London), the Koln Westdeutscher Rundfunk (Germany), NOS National Radio (The Netherlands), Zurich Radio (Switzerland), the Television Broadcasting System (Japan) as well as for the United States State Department for broadcast on its 'Voice of America' program. The CSUN Wind Ensemble's recording with the Mirecourt Trio in 1982 was named the 'Record of the Year' by The Village Voice. Composers who have guest conducted Whitwell's ensembles include Aaron Copland, Ernest Krenek, Alan Hovhaness, Morton Gould, Karel Husa, Frank Erickson and Vaclav Nelhybel.

Dr. Whitwell has been a guest professor in 100 different universities and conservatories throughout the United States and in 23 foreign countries (most recently in China, in an elite school housed in the Forbidden City). Guest conducting experiences have included the Philadelphia Orchestra, Seattle Symphony Orchestra, the Czech Radio Orchestras of Brno and Bratislava, The National Youth Orchestra of Israel, as well as resident wind ensembles in Russia, Israel, Austria, Switzerland, Germany, England, Wales, The Netherlands, Portugal, Peru, Korea, Japan, Taiwan, Canada and the United States.

He is a past president of the College Band Directors National Association, a member of the Prasidium of the International Society for the Promotion of Band Music, and was a member of the founding board of directors of the World Association for Symphonic Bands and Ensembles (WASBE). In 1964 he was made an honorary life member of Kappa Kappa Psi, a national professional music fraternity. In September, 2001, he was a delegate to the UNESCO Conference on Global Music in Tokyo. He has been knighted by sovereign organizations in France, Portugal and Scotland and has been awarded the gold medal of Kerkrade, The Netherlands, and the silver medal of Wangen, Germany, the highest honor given wind conductors in the United States, the medal of the Academy of Wind and Percussion Arts (National Band Association) and the highest honor given wind conductors in Austria, the gold medal of the Austrian Band Association. He is a member of the Hall of Fame of the California Music Educators Association.

Dr. Whitwell's publications include more than 127 articles on wind literature including publications in Music and Letters (London), the London Musical Times, the Mozart-Jahrbuch (Salzburg), and 39 books, among which is his 13-volume *History and Literature of the Wind Band and Wind Ensemble* and an 8-volume series on *Aesthetics in Music*. In addition to numerous modern editions of early wind band music his original compositions include 5 symphonies.

David Whitwell was named as one of six men who have determined the course of American bands during the second half of the 20th century, in the definitive history, *The Twentieth Century American Wind Band* (Meredith Music).

A doctoral dissertation by German Gonzales (2007, Arizona State University) is dedicated to the life and conducting career of David Whitwell through the year 1977. David Whitwell is one of nine men described by Paula A. Crider in *The Conductor's Legacy* (Chicago: GIA, 2010) as 'the legendary conductors' of the 20th century.

> 'I can't imagine the 2nd half of the 20th century—without David Whitwell and what he has given to all of the rest of us.' Frederick Fennell (1993)

www.ingramcontent.com/pod-product-compliance
Lightning Source LLC
Chambersburg PA
CBHW080728300426
44114CB00019B/2506